# Microsoft® Office Word 2007

## Brief Edition

# The O'Leary Series

**Computing Concepts**

- *Computing Essentials 2007* Introductory & Complete Editions
- *Computing Essentials 2008* Introductory & Complete Editions

**Microsoft® Office Applications**

- *Microsoft® Office Word 2007* Brief & Introductory Editions
- *Microsoft® Office Excel 2007* Brief & Introductory Editions
- *Microsoft® Office Access 2007* Brief & Introductory Editions
- *Microsoft® Office PowerPoint 2007* Brief Edition

The O'Leary Series

# Microsoft® Office Word 2007

## Brief Edition

**Timothy J. O'Leary**

*Arizona State University*

**Linda I. O'Leary**

Boston   Burr Ridge, IL   Dubuque, IA   New York   San Francisco   St. Louis
Bangkok   Bogotá   Caracas   Kuala Lumpur   Lisbon   London   Madrid   Mexico City
Milan   Montreal   New Delhi   Santiago   Seoul   Singapore   Sydney   Taipei   Toronto

THE O'LEARY SERIES MICROSOFT® OFFICE WORD 2007 BRIEF

Published by McGraw-Hill/Irwin, a business unit of The McGraw-Hill Companies, Inc., 1221 Avenue of the Americas, New York, NY, 10020. Copyright © 2008 by The McGraw-Hill Companies, Inc. All rights reserved. No part of this publication may be reproduced or distributed in any form or by any means, or stored in a database or retrieval system, without the prior written consent of The McGraw-Hill Companies, Inc., including, but not limited to, in any network or other electronic storage or transmission, or broadcast for distance learning.

Some ancillaries, including electronic and print components, may not be available to customers outside the United States.

This book is printed on acid-free paper.

1 2 3 4 5 6 7 8 9 0 QPD/QPD 0 9 8 7

ISBN   978-0-07-329449-0
MHID 0-07-329449-7

Editor in Chief:   *Elizabeth Haefele*
Associate sponsoring editor:   *Janna Martin*
Developmental editor:   *Kelly L. Delso*
Developmental editor I:   *Alaina Grayson*
Marketing manager:   *Sarah Wood*
Lead producer, media technology:   *Ben Curless*
Project manager:   *Marlena Pechan*
Senior production supervisor:   *Jason Huls*
Designer:   *Srdjan Savanovic*
Senior photo research coordinator:   *Jeremy Cheshareck*
Typeface:   *10.5/13 New Aster*
Compositor:   *Laserwords Private Limited*
Printer:   *Quebecor World Dubuque Inc.*

**Library of Congress Cataloging-in-Publication Data**

O'Leary, Timothy J., 1947-
   Microsoft Office Word 2007 / Timothy J. O'Leary, Linda I. O'Leary.—Brief ed.
 p. cm.—(The O'Leary series)
     Includes index.
     ISBN-13: 978-0-07-329449-0 (acid-free paper)
     ISBN-10: 0-07-329449-7 (acid-free paper)
     1. Microsoft Word. 2. Word processing. I. O'Leary, Linda I. II. Title.
  Z52.5.M52O458 2008
  005.52—dc22
                                                    2007003311

# DEDICATION

We dedicate this edition to Nicole and Katie who have brought love and joy to our lives.

# Brief Contents

# Detailed Contents

**Lab 2 Revising and Refining a Document** WD2.1

ix

# Acknowledgments

We would like to extend our thanks to the professors who took time out of their busy schedules to provide us with the feedback necessary to develop the 2007 Edition of this text. The following professors offered valuable suggestions on revising the text:

Adida Awan, Savannah State University

Jacqueline Bakal, Felician College

Chet Barney, Southern Utah University

Bruce W. Bryant, University of Arkansas Community College Morrilton

Kelly D. Carter, Mercer University

Cesar Augusto Casas, St. Thomas Aquinas College

Sally Clements, St. Thomas Aquinas College

Donna N. Dunn, Beaufort County Community College

Donna Ehrhart, Genesee Community College

Saiid Ganjalizadeh, The Catholic University of America

Dr. Jayanta Ghosh, Florida Community College

Carol Grazette, Medgar Evers College/CUNY

Susan Gundy, University of Illinois at Springfield

Greg R. Hodge, Northwestern Michigan College

Christopher M. J. Hopper, Bellevue Community College

Ginny Kansas, Southwestern College

Robert Kemmerer, Los Angeles Mission College

Linda Klisto, Broward Community College North Campus

Nanette Lareau, University of Arkansas Community College Morrilton

Deborah Layton, Eastern Oklahoma State College

Keming Liu, Medgar Evers College/CUNY

J. Gay Mills, Amarillo College

Kim Moorning, Medgar Evers College/CUNY

Dr. Belinda J. Moses, University of Phoenix/Baker College/Wayne County Community College

Lois Ann O'Neal, Rogers State University

Andrew Perry, Springfield College

Michael Philipp, Greenville Technical College

Julie Piper, Bucks County Community College

Brenda Price, Bucks County Community College

Thali N. Rajashekhara, Camden County College

Dr. Marcel Marie Robles, Eastern Kentucky University

Jose (Joe) Sainz, Naugatuck Valley Community College

Pamela J. Silvers, Asheville-Buncombe Technical Community College

Glenna Stites, Johnson County Community College

Joyce Thompson, Lehigh Carbon Community College

Michelle G. Vlaich-Lee, Greenville Technical College

Mary A. Walthall, St. Petersburg College

We would like to thank those who took the time to help us develop the manuscript and ensure accuracy through pain-staking edits: Brenda Nielsen of Mesa Community College–Red Mountain, Rajiv Narayana of SunTech Info-Labs, and Craig Leonard.

Our thanks also go to Linda Mehlinger of Morgan State University for all her work on creating the PowerPoint presentations to accompany the text. We are grateful to Carol Grazette of Medgar Evers College, the author of the Instructor's Manual, for her revision of this valuable resource, and to Harry Knight of Franklin University for his careful revision of the test bank materials and creation of online quizzing materials.

Finally, we would like to thank team members from McGraw-Hill, whose renewed commitment, direction, and support have infused the team with the excitement of a new project. Leading the team from McGraw-Hill are Janna Martin, Associate Editor; Sarah Wood, Marketing Manager; and Developmental Editors Kelly Delso and Alaina Grayson.

The production staff is headed by Marlena Pechan, Project Manager, whose planning and attention to detail have made it possible for us to successfully meet a very challenging schedule; Srdjan Savanovic, Designer; Jason Huls, Production Supervisor; Ben Curless, Media Producer; Jeremy Cheshareck, Photo Researcher; and Betsy Blumenthal, copyeditor—team members whom we can depend on to do a great job.

# Preface

The 20th century brought us the dawn of the digital information age and unprecedented changes in information technology. There is no indication that this rapid rate of change will be slowing—it may even be increasing. As we begin the 21st century, computer literacy is undoubtedly becoming a prerequisite in whatever career you choose.

The goal of the O'Leary Series is to provide you with the necessary skills to efficiently use these applications. Equally important is the goal to provide a foundation for students to readily and easily learn to use future versions of this software. This series does this by providing detailed step-by-step instructions combined with careful selection and presentation of essential concepts.

Times are changing, technology is changing, and this text is changing too. As students of today, you are different from those of yesterday. You put much effort toward the things that interest you and the things that are relevant to you. Your efforts directed at learning application programs and exploring the Web seem, at times, limitless.

On the other hand, students often can be shortsighted, thinking that learning the skills to use the application is the only objective. The mission of the series is to build upon and extend this interest by not only teaching the specific application skills but by introducing the concepts that are common to all applications, providing students with the confidence, knowledge, and ability to easily learn the next generation of applications.

## Instructor's Resource CD-ROM

The **Instructor's Resource CD-ROM** contains a computerized Test Bank, an Instructor's Manual, and PowerPoint Presentation Slides. Features of the Instructor's Resource are described below.

- **Instructor's Manual CD-ROM**   The Instructor's Manual, authored by Carol Grazette of Medgar Evers College, contains lab objectives, concepts, outlines, lecture notes, and command summaries. Also included are answers to all end-of-chapter material, tips for covering difficult materials, additional exercises, and a schedule showing how much time is required to cover text material.

- **Computerized Test Bank**   The test bank, authored by Harry Knight, contains over 1,300 multiple choice, true/false, and discussion questions. Each question will be accompanied by the correct answer, the level of learning difficulty, and corresponding page references. Our flexible Diploma software allows you to easily generate custom exams.

- **PowerPoint Presentation Slides** The presentation slides, authored by Linda Mehlinger of Morgan State University, include lab objectives, concepts, outlines, text figures, and speaker's notes. Also included are bullets to illustrate key terms and FAQs.

## Online Learning Center/Web Site

Found at **www.mhhe.com/oleary,** this site provides additional learning and instructional tools to enhance the comprehension of the text. The OLC/Web Site is divided into these three areas:

- **Information Center** Contains core information about the text, supplements, and the authors.

- **Instructor Center** Offers instructional materials, downloads, and other relevant links for professors.

- **Student Center** Contains data files, chapter competencies, chapter concepts, self-quizzes, flashcards, additional Web links, and more.

## Simnet Assessment for Office Applications

Simnet Assessment for Office Applications provides a way for you to test students' software skills in a simulated environment. Simnet is available for Microsoft Office 2007 and provides flexbility for you in your applications course by offering:

Pre-testing options

Post-testing options

Course placement testing

Diagnostic capabilities to reinforce skills

Web delivery of test

MCAS preparation exams

Learning verification reports

For more information on skills assessment software, please contact your local sales representative, or visit us at **www.mhhe.com**.

## O'Leary Series

The O'Leary Application Series for Microsoft Office is available separately or packaged with *Computing Essentials*. The O'Leary Application Series offers a step-by-step approach to learning computer applications and is available in both brief and introductory versions. The introductory books are MCAS Certified and prepare students for the Microsoft Certified Applications Specialist exam.

# Computing Concepts

*Computing Essentials 2007* offers a unique, visual orientation that gives students a basic understanding of computing concepts. *Computing Essentials* encourages "active" learning with exercises, explorations, visual illustrations, and inclusion of screen shots and numbered steps. While combining the "active" learning style with current topics and technology, this text provides an accurate snapshot of computing trends. When bundled with software application lab manuals, students are given a complete representation of the fundamental issues surrounding the personal computing environment.

# GUIDE TO THE O'LEARY SERIES

The O'Leary Series is full of features designed to make learning productive and hassle free. On the following pages you will see the kind of engaging, helpful pedagogical features that have helped countless students master Microsoft Office Applications.

## EASY-TO-FOLLOW INTRODUCTORY MATERIALS

### INTRODUCTION TO MICROSOFT OFFICE 2007

Each text in the O'Leary Series opens with an Introduction to Office 2007, providing a complete overview of this version of the Microsoft Office Suite.

#### What Is the 2007 Microsoft Office System?

Microsoft's 2007 Microsoft Office System is a comprehensive, integrated system of programs, servers, and services designed to solve a wide array of business needs. Although the programs can be used individually, they are designed to work together seamlessly, making it easy to connect people and organizations to information, business processes, and each other. The applications include tools used to create, discuss, communicate, and manage projects. If you share a lot of documents with other people, these features facilitate access to common documents. This version has an entirely new user interface that is designed to make it easier to perform tasks and help users more quickly take advantage of all the features in the applications. In addition, the communication and collaboration features and integration with the World Wide Web have been expanded and refined.

The 2007 Microsoft Office System is packaged in several different combinations of programs or suites. The major programs and a brief description are provided in the following table.

| Program | Description |
|---|---|
| Word 2007 | Word Processor program used to create text-based documents |
| Excel 2007 | Spreadsheet program used to analyze numerical data |
| Access 2007 | Database manager used to organize, manage, and display a database |
| PowerPoint 2007 | Graphics presentation program used to create presentation materials |
| Outlook 2007 | Desktop information manager and messaging client |
| InfoPath 2007 | Used to create XML forms and documents |
| OneNote 2007 | Note-taking and information organization tools |
| Publisher 2007 | Tools to create and distribute publications for print, Web, and e-mail |
| Visio 2007 | Diagramming and data visualization tools |
| SharePoint Designer 2007 | Web site development and management for SharePoint servers |
| Project 2007 | Project management tools |
| Groove 2007 | Collaboration program that enables teams to work together |

The four main components of Microsoft Office 2007—Word, Excel, Access, and PowerPoint—are the applications you will learn about in this series of labs. They are described in more detail in the following sections.

## Overview of Microsoft Office Word 20[...]

#### What Is Word Processing?

Office Word 2007 is a word processing software application whose p[...] is to help you create any type of written communication. A word pro[...] can be used to manipulate text data to produce a letter, a report, a [...] an e-mail message, or any other type of correspondence. Text data [...] letter, number, or symbol that you can type on a keyboard. The grou[...] the text data to form words, sentences, paragraphs, and pages [...] results in the creation of a document. Through a word processor, y[...] create, modify, store, retrieve, and print part or all of a document.

Word processors are one of the most widely used application software programs. Putting your thoughts in writing, from the simplest note to the most complex book, is a time-consuming process. Even more time-consuming is the task of editing and retyping the document to make it better. Word processors make errors nearly nonexistent—not because they are not made, but because they are easy to correct. Word processors let you throw away the correction fluid, scissors, paste, and erasers. Now, with a few keystrokes, you can easily correct errors, move paragraphs, and reprint your document.

#### Word 2007 Features

Word 2007 excels in its ability to change or edit a document. Editing involves correcting spelling, grammar, and sentence-structure errors. In addition, you can easily revise or update existing text by inserting or deleting text. For example, a document that lists prices can easily be updated to reflect new prices. A document that details procedures can be revised by deleting old procedures and inserting new ones. This is especially helpful when a document is used repeatedly. Rather than recreating the whole document, you change only the parts that need to be revised.

Revision also includes the rearrangement of selected areas of text. For example, while writing a report, you may decide to change the location of a single word or several paragraphs or pages of text. You can do it easily by cutting or removing selected text from one location, then pasting or placing the selected text in another location. The selection also can be copied from one document to another.

To help you produce a perfect document, Word 2007 includes many additional support features. The AutoCorrect feature checks the spelling and grammar in a document as text is entered. Many common errors are corrected automatically for you. Others are identified and a correction suggested. A thesaurus can be used to display alternative words that have a meaning similar or opposite to a word you entered. A Find and Replace feature can be used to quickly locate specified text and replace it with other text throughout a document. In addition, Word 2007 includes a

WD0.1

### INTRODUCTION TO WORD 2007

Each text in the O'Leary Series also provides an overview of the specific application features.

# ENGAGING LAB INTRODUCTIONS

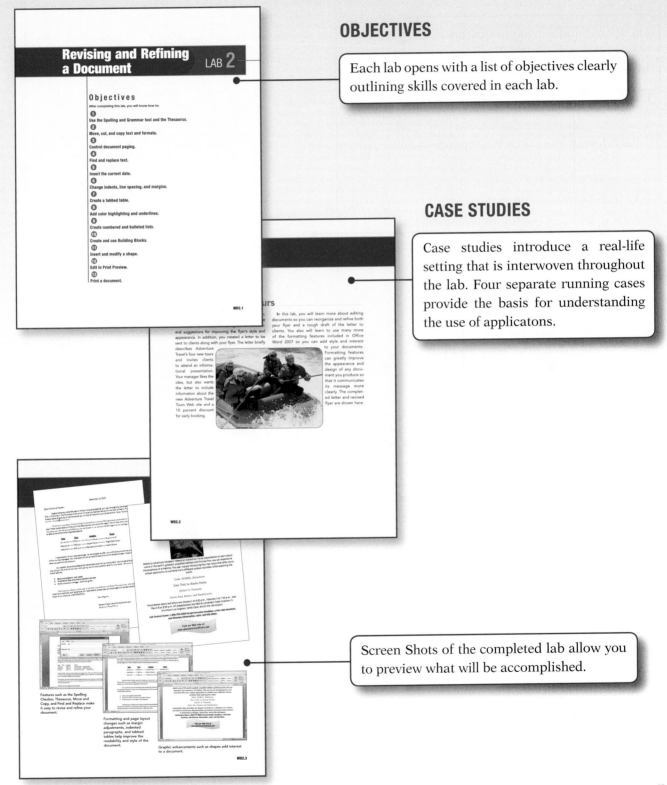

## OBJECTIVES

Each lab opens with a list of objectives clearly outlining skills covered in each lab.

## CASE STUDIES

Case studies introduce a real-life setting that is interwoven throughout the lab. Four separate running cases provide the basis for understanding the use of applicatons.

Screen Shots of the completed lab allow you to preview what will be accomplished.

## NUMBERED AND BULLETED STEPS

Numbered and bulleted steps provide clear step-by-step instructions on how to complete a task, or series of tasks.

All steps and bullets appear in the left-hand margin, making it easy not to miss a step.

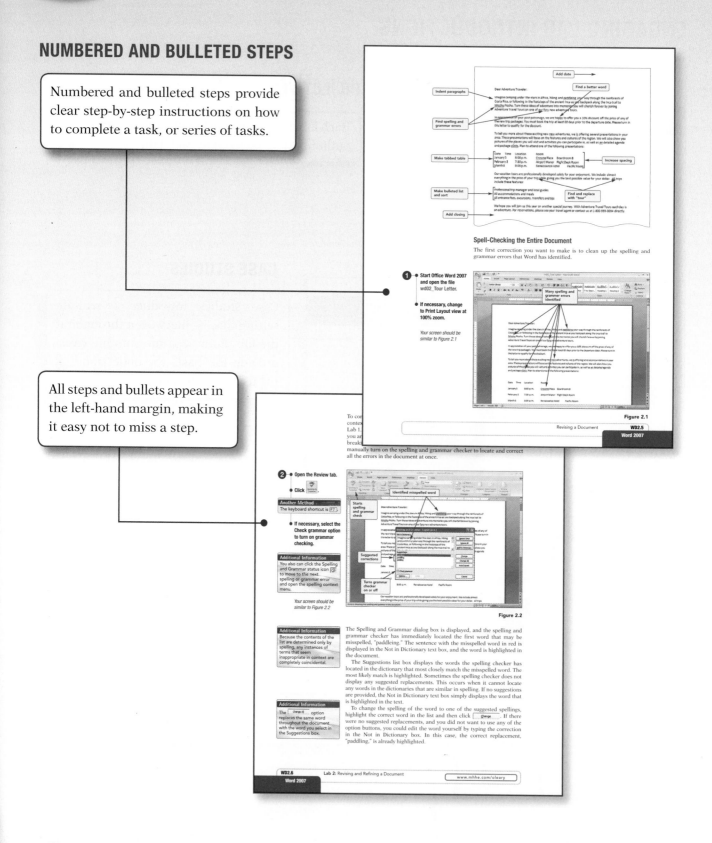

# AND EASY-TO-FOLLOW DESIGN

## TABLES

Tables provide quick summaries of concepts and procedures for specific tasks.

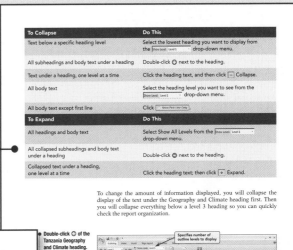

| To Collapse | Do This |
| --- | --- |
| Text below a specific heading level | Select the lowest heading you want to display from the [Show Level: Level 1] drop-down menu. |
| All subheadings and body text under a heading | Double-click ⊖ next to the heading. |
| Text under a heading, one level at a time | Click the heading text, and then click [−] Collapse. |
| All body text | Select the heading level you want to see from the [Show Level: Level 1] drop-down menu. |
| All body text except first line | Click [☑ Show First Line Only]. |

| To Expand | Do This |
| --- | --- |
| All headings and body text | Select Show All Levels from the [Show Level: Level 1] drop-down menu. |
| All collapsed subheadings and body text under a heading | Double-click ⊕ next to the heading. |
| Collapsed text under a heading, one level at a time | Click the heading text; then click [+] Expand. |

To change the amount of information displayed, you will collapse the display of the text under the Geography and Climate heading first. Then you will collapse everything below a level 3 heading so you can quickly check the report organization.

- Double-click ⊖ of the Tanzania Geography and Climate heading.

- Open the [drop-down list].

- Choose Level 3.

*Your screen should be similar to Figure 3.8*

Specifies number of outline levels to display

Three levels displayed

Wavy underlines indicate collapsed heading

**Figure 3.8**

3.12    Lab 3: Creating Reports and Tables    www.mhhe.com/oleary
Word 2007

To correct the misspelled words and grammatical errors, you can use the context menu to correct each individual word or error, as you learned in Lab 1. However, in many cases, you may find it more efficient to wait until you are finished writing before you correct errors. Rather than continually breaking your train of thought to correct errors as you type, you can manually turn on the spelling and grammar checker to locate and correct all the errors in the document at once.

**2** ● Open the Review tab.
● Click [   ].

**Another Method**
The keyboard shortcut is [F7].

● If necessary, select the Check grammar option to turn on grammar checking.

**Additional Information**
You also can click the Spelling and Grammar status icon 📖 to move to the next spelling or grammar error and open the spelling context menu.

*Your screen should be similar to Figure 2.2*

Starts spelling and grammar check

Identified misspelled word

Suggested corrections

Turns grammar checker on or off

**Figure 2.2**

**Additional Information**
Because the contents of the list are determined only by spelling, any instances of terms that seem inappropriate in context are completely coincidental.

**Additional Information**
The [Change All] option replaces the same word throughout the document with the word you select in the Suggestions box.

The Spelling and Grammar dialog box is displayed, and the spelling and grammar checker has immediately located the first word that may be misspelled, "paddleing." The sentence with the misspelled word in red is displayed in the Not in Dictionary text box, and the word is highlighted in the document.

The Suggestions list box displays the words the spelling checker has located in the dictionary that most closely match the misspelled word. The most likely match is highlighted. Sometimes the spelling checker does not display any suggested replacements. This occurs when it cannot locate any words in the dictionaries that are similar in spelling. If no suggestions are provided, the Not in Dictionary text box simply displays the word that is highlighted in the text.

To change the spelling of the word to one of the suggested spellings, highlight the correct word in the list and then click [Change]. If there were no suggested replacements, and you did not want to use any of the option buttons, you could edit the word yourself by typing the correction in the Not in Dictionary box. In this case, the correct replacement, "paddling," is already highlighted.

**WD2.6**    Lab 2: Revising and Refining a Document    www.mhhe.com/oleary
Word 2007

## FIGURES

Large screen figures make it easy to identify elements and read screen content.

## SCREEN CALLOUTS

Meaningful screen callouts identify the results of the steps as well as reinforce the associated concept.

# SUPPORTIVE MARGIN NOTES

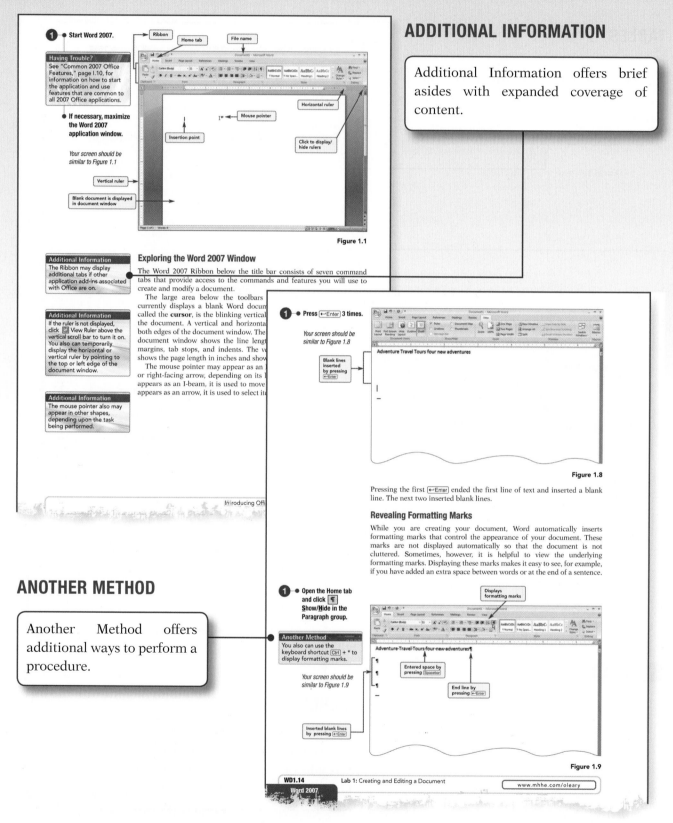

## ADDITIONAL INFORMATION

Additional Information offers brief asides with expanded coverage of content.

## ANOTHER METHOD

Another Method offers additional ways to perform a procedure.

The document now displays the formatting marks. The ¶ character on the line above the insertion point represents the pressing of ⏎Enter that created the blank line. The ¶ character at the end of the text represents the pressing of ⏎Enter that ended the line and moved the insertion point to the beginning of the next line. Between each word, a dot shows where the Spacebar was pressed. Formatting marks do not appear when the document is printed. You can continue to work on the document while the formatting marks are displayed, just as you did when they were hidden.

You have decided you want the flyer heading to be on two lines, with the words "four new adventures" on the second line. To do this, you will insert a blank line after the word Tours. You will move the insertion point to the location in the text where you want to insert the blank line.

**2** • Click on the right side of the "s" in "Tours" before the dot for a space.

• Press ⏎Enter 2 times.

• Press Delete to remove the space at the beginning of the line.

• Press ↓.

*Your screen should be similar to Figure 1.10*

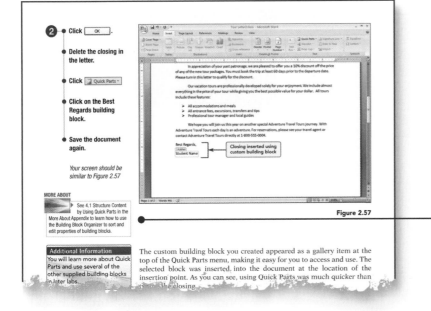

**Figure 1.10**

As you continue to create a document, the formatting marks are automatically adjusted.

### Identifying and Correcting Errors Automatically

**Having Trouble?**
If the green underline is not displayed, click Office Button, click 🔘 Word Options, Proofing, and select the "Check spelling as you type", "Mark grammar errors as you type", and "Check grammar with spelling" options.

Notice that a green wavy underline appears under the word "four." This indicates an error has been detected.

As you enter text, Word is constantly checking the document for spelling and grammar errors. The Spelling and Grammar Status icon in the status bar displays an animated pencil icon 🖉 while you are typing, indicating Word is checking for errors as you type. When you stop typing, it displays either a blue checkmark 📘, indicating the program does not detect any errors, or a red X 📕, indicating the document contains an error.

Identifying and Correcting Errors Automatically    **WD1.15**
**Word 2007**

## HAVING TROUBLE

> Having Trouble helps resolve potential problems as you work through each lab.

**2** • Click [ OK ].

• Delete the closing in the letter.

• Click 🔲 Quick Parts ▾

• Click on the Best Regards building block.

• Save the document again.

*Your screen should be similar to Figure 2.57*

**MORE ABOUT**
📼 See 4.1 Structure Content by Using Quick Parts in the More About Appendix to learn how to use the Building Block Organizer to sort and edit properties of building blocks.

**Additional Information**
You will learn more about Quick Parts and use several of the other supplied building blocks in later labs.

**Figure 2.57**

The custom building block you created appeared as a gallery item at the top of the Quick Parts menu, making it easy for you to access and use. The selected block was inserted into the document at the location of the insertion point. As you can see, using Quick Parts was much quicker than typing the closing.

## MORE ABOUT

> New to this edition, the More About icon directs students to the More About appendix found at the end of the book. Without interrupting the flow of the text, this appendix provides additional coverage required to meet MCAS certification.

# REAL-WORLD APPLICATION

The default range setting, All, is the correct setting. In the Copies section, the default setting of one copy of the document is acceptable. You will print using the default print settings.

**2** • If you need to change the selected printer to another printer, open the Name drop-down list box and select the appropriate printer (your instructor will tell you which printer to select).

• Click ⬚ OK ⬚.

Your printer should be printing the document. The printed copy of the flyer should be similar to the document shown in the Case Study at the beginning of the lab.

### Exiting Word

You are finished working on the flyer for now and want to save the last few changes you have made to the document and close the Word application. The ⬚ Exit Word ⬚ command in the File menu is used to quit the Word program. Alternatively, you can click the ⬚×⬚ Close button in the application window title bar. If you attempt to close the application without first saving your document, Word displays a warning asking if you want to save your work. If you do not save your work and you exit the application, any changes you made since last saving it are lost.

> **Another Method**
> The keyboard shortcut for the Exit command is ⬚Alt⬚ + ⬚F4⬚

**1** • Click ⬚×⬚ Close.

• Click ⬚ Yes ⬚ to save the changes you made to the file.

The Windows desktop is visible again.
If multiple Word documents are open, clicking ⬚×⬚ closes the application window containing the document you are viewing only.

## Focus on Careers

**EXPLORE YOUR CAREER OPTIONS**

**Food Service Manager**
Have you noticed flyers around your campus advertising job positions? Many of these jobs are in the food service industry. Food service managers are traditionally responsible for overseeing the kitchen and dining room. However, these positions increasingly involve administrative tasks, including recruiting new employees. As a food service manager, your position would likely include creating newspaper notices and flyers to attract new staff. These flyers should be eye-catching and error-free. The typical salary range of a food service manager is $34,000 to $41,700. Demand for skilled food service managers is expected to increase through 2010.

| Exiting Word | **WD1.71** |
|---|---|
| | **Word 2007** |

## FOCUS ON CAREERS

Focus on Careers provides an example of how the material covered may be applied in the "real world."

Each lab highlights a specific career, ranging from forensic science technician to food services manager, and presents job responsibilities and salary ranges for each.

## Case Study

### Adventure Travel Tours

Adventure Travel Tours provides information on their tours in a variety of forms. Travel brochures, for instance, contain basic tour information in a promotional format and are designed to entice potential clients to sign up for a tour. More detailed regional information packets are given to people who have already signed up for a tour, so they can prepare for their vacation. These packets include facts about each region's climate, geography, and culture. Additional informational formats include pages on Adventure Travel's Web site and scheduled group presentations.

Part of your responsibility as advertising coordinator is to gather the information that Adventure Travel will publicize about each regional tour. Specifically, you have been asked to provide background information for two of the new tours: the Tanzania Safari and the Machu Picchu trail. Because this information is used in a variety of formats, your research needs to be easily adapted. You will therefore present your facts in the form of a general report on Tanzania and Peru.

In this lab, you will learn to use many of the features of Office Word 2007 that make it easy to create an attractive and well-organized report. A portion of the completed report is shown here.

**WD3.2**

## CONTINUING CASE STUDIES

Within each series application, the same Case Study is used to illustrate concepts and procedures.

# AND INTEGRATION

## WORKING TOGETHER LABS

At the completion of the brief and introductory texts, a final lab demonstrates the integration of MS office applications. Each Working Together lab contains a complete set of end-of-chapter materials.

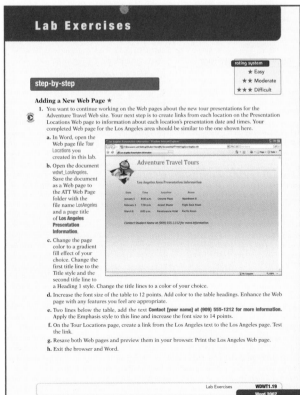

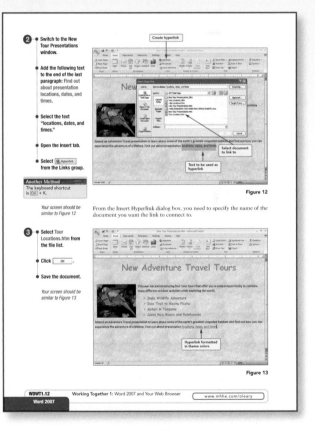

# REINFORCED CONCEPTS

## CONCEPT PREVIEW

Concept Previews provide an overview to the concepts that will be presented throughout the lab.

### Concept Preview

**The following concepts will be introduced in this lab:**

1. **Grammar Checker** The grammar checker advises you of incorrect grammar as you create and edit a document, and proposes possible corrections.
2. **Spelling Checker** The spelling checker advises you of misspelled words as you create and edit a document, and proposes possible corrections.
3. **AutoCorrect** The AutoCorrect feature makes some basic assumptions about the text you are typing and, based on these assumptions, automatically corrects the entry.
4. **Word Wrap** The word wrap feature automatically decides where to end a line and wrap text to the next line based on the margin settings.
5. **Font and Font Size** Font, also commonly referred to as a typeface, is a set of characters with a specific design that has one or more font sizes.
6. **Alignment** Alignment is the positioning of text on a line between the margins or indents. There are four types of paragraph alignment: left, centered, right, and justified.
7. **Graphics** A graphic is a nontext element or object such as a drawing or picture that can be added to a document.

### Introducing Office Word 2007

Adventure Travel Tours has recently upgraded their computer systems at all locations across the country. As part of the upgrade, they have installed the latest version of the Microsoft Office 2007 suite of applications. You are very excited to see how this new and powerful application can help you create professional letters and reports as well as eye-catching flyers and newsletters.

### Starting Office Word 2007

...tion Microsoft Office Word 2007 ...and presentations.

## CONCEPT BOXES

Concept boxes appear throughout the lab providing clear, concise explanations and serving as a valuable study aid.

3 • Click outside the menu to close it.

• Open the spelling context menu for "lern" and choose "learn".

The spelling is corrected, and the spelling indicator in the status bar indicates that the document is free of errors.

### Using Word Wrap

Now you will continue entering more of the paragraph. As you type, when the text gets close to the right margin, do not press ◄Enter to move to the next line. Word will automatically wrap words to the next line as needed.

### Concept 4
**Word Wrap**

4  The word wrap feature automatically decides where to end a line and wrap text to the next line based on the margin settings. This feature saves time when entering text because you do not need to press ◄Enter at the end of a full line to begin a new line. The only time you need to press ◄Enter is to end a paragraph, to insert blank lines, or to create a short line such as a salutation. In addition, if you change the margins or insert or delete text on a line, the program automatically readjusts the text on the line to fit within the new margin settings. Word wrap is common to all word processors.

Enter the following text to complete the sentence.

1 • Press End to move to the end of the line.

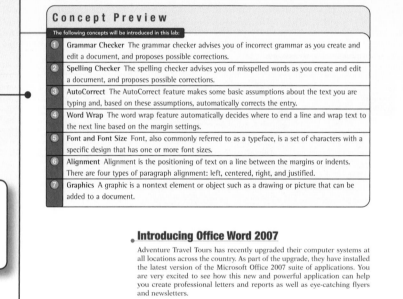

www.mhhe.com/oleary

# REINFORCED CONCEPTS (CONTINUED)

## CONCEPT SUMMARIES

The Concept Summary offers a visual summary of the concepts presented throughout the lab.

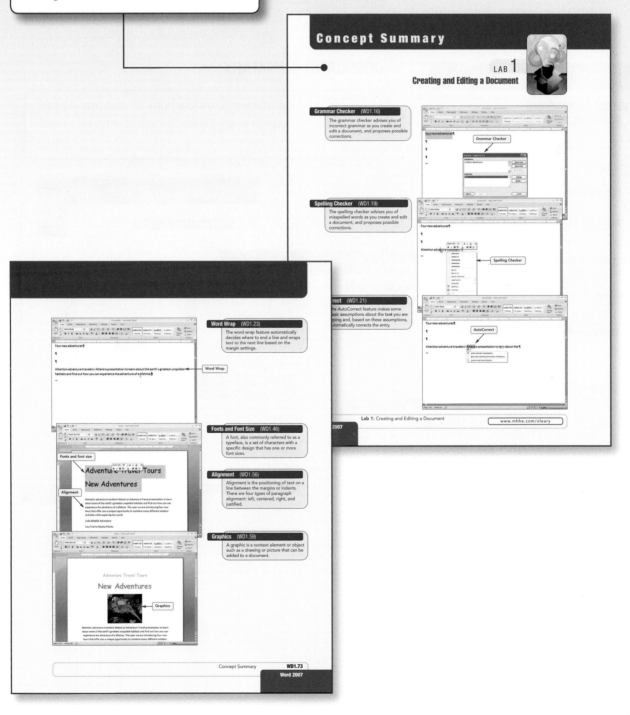

# LAB REVIEW

## KEY TERMS

Includes a list of all bolded terms with page references.

## COMMAND SUMMARY

Command Summaries provide a table of commands and keyboard and toolbar shortcuts for all commands used in the lab.

## END-OF-CHAPTER MATERIALS

Lab Exercises reinforce the terminology and concepts presented in the lab through Screen Identification, Matching, Multiple Choice, True/False, and Fill-In questions.

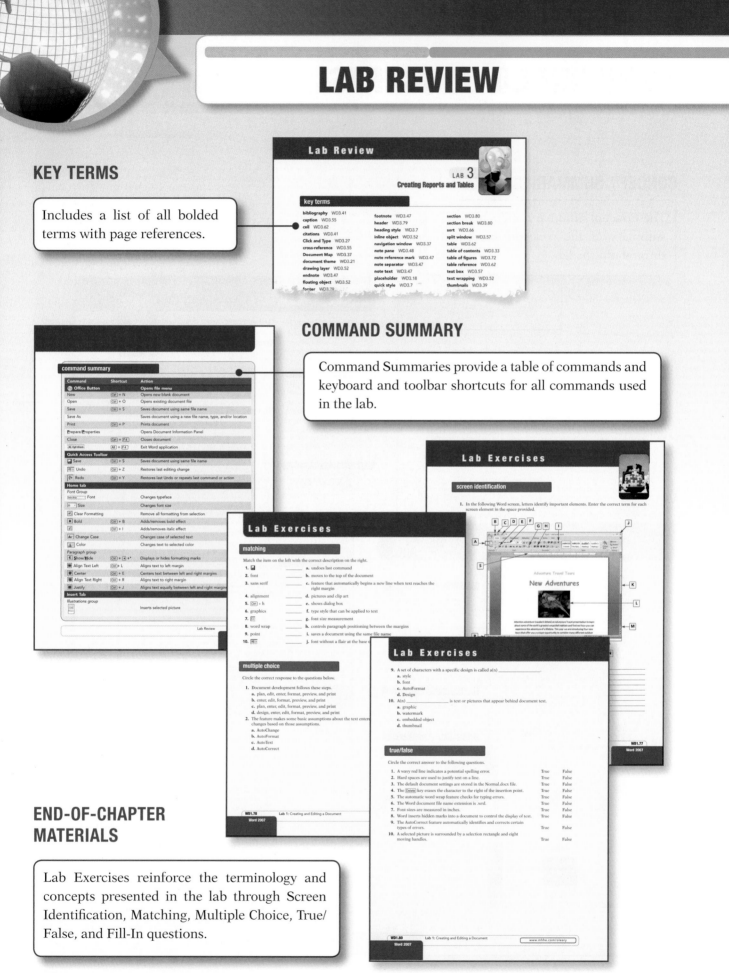

# AND SKILL DEVELOPMENT

## LAB EXERCISES

Lab Exercises provide hands-on practice and develop critical-thinking skills through step-by-step and on-your-own practice exercises. Many cases in the practice exercises tie to a running case used in another application lab. This helps demonstrate the use of the four applications across a common case setting. For example, the Adventure Tours case used in Word is continued in practice exercises in Excel, Access, and PowerPoint.

## ON YOUR OWN

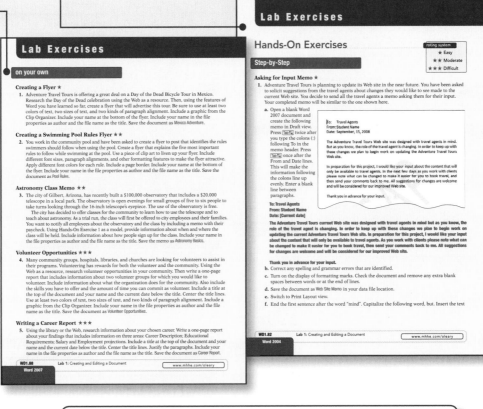

These exercises have a rating system from easy to difficult and test your ability to apply the knowledge you have gained in each lab. Exercises that build off of previous exercises are noted with a Continuing Exercises icon.

# END-OF-BOOK RESOURCES

## COMPREHENSIVE COMMAND SUMMARY

Provides a table of commands and keyboard and toolbar shortcuts for all commands used throughout the entire text.

### 2007 Word Brief Command Summary

| Command | Shortcut | Action |
|---|---|---|
| **Office Button** | | **Opens File menu** |
| New | Ctrl + N | Opens new document |
| Open | Ctrl + O | Opens existing document file |
| Save | Ctrl + S, 💾 | Saves document using same file name |
| Save As | F12 | Saves document using a new file name, type, and/or location |
| Save as/Save As type/ Web Page | | Saves file as a Web page document |
| Print | Ctrl + P | Specify print settings before printing document |
| Print/Print Preview | | Displays document as it will appear when printed |
| Print/Quick Print | | Prints document using default printer settings |
| Prepare/Properties | | Opens Document Information Panel |
| Close | Ctrl + F4 | Closes document |
| Word Options /Proofing | | Changes settings associated with Spelling and Grammar checking |
| Word Options /Advanced/ Mark formatting inconsistencies | | Checks for formatting inconsistencies |
| Exit Word | Alt + F4, ✖ | Closes the Word application |
| **Quick Access Toolbar** | | |
| Save | | Saves document using same file name |
| Undo | Ctrl + Z | Restores last editing change |
| Redo | Ctrl + Y | Restores last Undo or repeats last command or action |
| **Home tab** | | |
| *Clipboard Group* | | |
| Cut | Ctrl + X | Cuts selection to Clipboard |
| Copy | Ctrl + C | Copies selection to Clipboard |
| Paste | Ctrl + V | Pastes item from Clipboard |
| Format Painter | | Copies format to selection |

2007 Word Brief Command Summary    **WDCS.1**    **Word 2007**

| Command | Shortcut | Action |
|---|---|---|
| *Font Group* | | |
| Calibri (Body) ▾ Font | | Changes typeface |
| 11 ▾ Size | | Changes font size |
| Grow Font | | Increases font size |
| Clear Formatting | | Clears all formatting from selected text, leaving plain text |
| Bold | Ctrl + B | Makes selected text bold |
| Italic | Ctrl + I | Applies italic effect to selected text |
| Underline | Ctrl + U | Adds underline below selected text |
| Change Case | | Changes case of selected text |
| Text Highlight Color | | Applies highlight color to selection |
| Font Color | | Changes selected text to selected color |
| *Paragraph group* | | |
| Bullets | | Creates a bulleted list |
| Numbering | | Creates a numbered list |
| Indents and Spacing | | Indents paragraph from left margin |
| Sort | | Rearranges items in a selection into ascending alphabetical/numerical order |
| Show/Hide | Ctrl + ⇧ + * | Displays or hides formatting marks |
| Align Text Left | Ctrl + L | Aligns text to left margin |
| Center | Ctrl + E | Centers text between left and right margins |
| Align Text Right | Ctrl + R | Aligns text to right margin |
| Justify | Ctrl + J | Aligns text equally between left and right margins |
| Line Spacing | Ctrl + # | Changes amount of white space between lines |
| *Styles Group* | | |
| More | | Opens Quick Styles gallery |
| *Editing Group* | | |
| Find ▾ | Ctrl + F | Locates specified text |
| Replace | Ctrl + H | Locates and replaces specified text |
| **Insert tab** | | |
| *Pages group* | | |
| Cover Page | | Inserts a preformatted cover page |
| Blank Page | | Inserts a blank page |
| Page Break | Ctrl + ←Enter | Inserts a hard page break |
| *Tables group* | | |
| Table | | Inserts a table |

**WDCS.2**    **Word 2007**    2007 Word Brief Command Summary    www.mhhe.com/oleary

---

### Glossary of Key Terms

**active window** The window containing the insertion point and that will be affected by any changes you make.

**alignment** How text is positioned on a line between the margins or indents. There are four types of paragraph alignment: left, centered, right, and justified.

**antonym** A word with the opposite meaning.

**author** The process of creating a Web page.

**AutoCorrect** A feature that makes basic assumptions about the text you are typing and automatically corrects the entry.

**bibliography** A listing of source references that appears at the end of the document.

**browser** A program that connects you to remote computers and displays the Web pages you request.

**building blocks** Document fragments that include text and formatting and that can be easily inserted into a document.

**bulleted list** Displays items that logically fall out from a paragraph into a list, with items preceded by bullets.

**caption** A title or explanation for a table, picture, or graph.

**case sensitive** The capability to distinguish between uppercase and lowercase characters.

**cell** The intersection of a column and row where data are entered in a table.

**character formatting** Formatting features such as bold and color that affect the selected characters only.

**citations** Parenthetical source references that give credit for specific information included in a document.

**Click and Type** A feature available in Print Layout and Web Layout views that is used to quickly insert text, graphics, and other items in

a blank area of a document, avoiding the need to enter blank lines.

**clip art** Professionally drawn graphics.

**control** A graphic element that is a container for information or objects.

**cross-reference** A reference in one part of a document related to information in another part.

**cursor** The blinking vertical bar that shows you where the next character you type will appear. Also called the insertion point.

**custom dictionary** A dictionary of terms you have entered that are not in the main dictionary of the spelling checker.

**default** The initial Word document settings that can be changed to customize documents.

**destination** The location to which text is moved or copied.

**Document Map** A feature that displays the headings in the document in the navigation window.

**document properties** Details about a document that describe or identify it and are saved with the document content.

**document theme** A predefined set of formatting choices that can be applied to an entire document in one simple step.

**document window** The area of the application window that displays the contents of the open document.

**drag and drop** A mouse procedure that moves or copies a selection to a new location.

**drawing layer** The layer above or below the text layer where floating objects are inserted.

**drawing object** A simple object consisting of shapes such as lines and boxes.

**edit** The process of changing and correcting existing text in a document.

Glossary of Key Terms    **WDG.1**    **Word 2007**

## GLOSSARY

Bolded terms found throughout the text are defined in the glossary.

## MORE ABOUT APPENDICES

A More About appendix appears at the end of the brief and introductory texts. This appendix offers students additional coverage needed to meet MCAS requirements. Skills pertaining to additional MCAS coverage are denoted by a More About icon in the margins of the text.

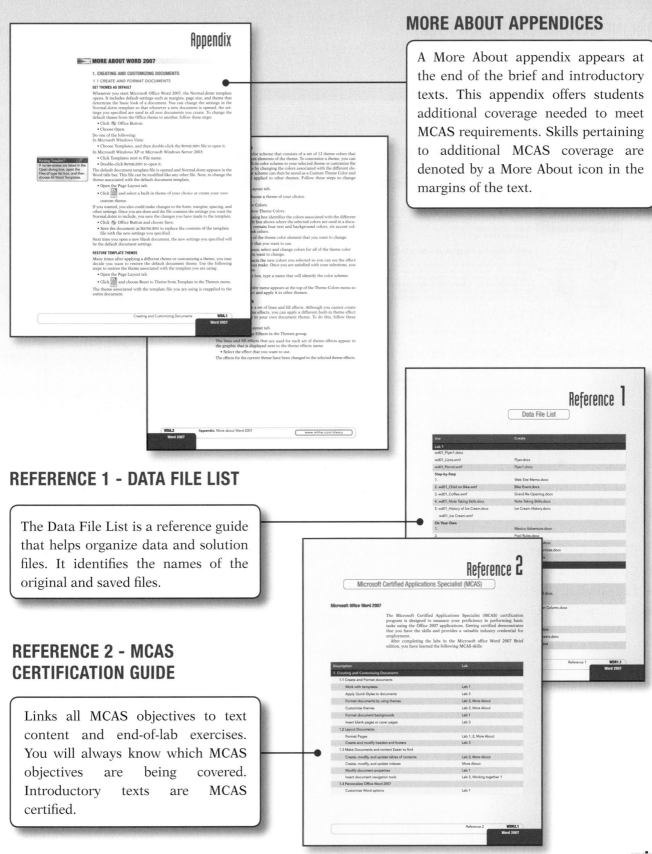

## REFERENCE 1 - DATA FILE LIST

The Data File List is a reference guide that helps organize data and solution files. It identifies the names of the original and saved files.

## REFERENCE 2 - MCAS CERTIFICATION GUIDE

Links all MCAS objectives to text content and end-of-lab exercises. You will always know which MCAS objectives are being covered. Introductory texts are MCAS certified.

# ONLINE LEARNING CENTER (OLC)

**www.mhhe.com/oleary**

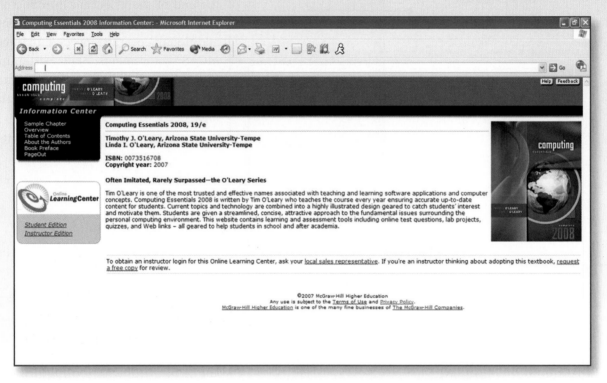

The Online Learning Center follows The O'Leary Series lab by lab, offering all kinds of supplementary help for you. OLC features include:

- Learning Objectives
- Student Data Files
- Chapter Competencies
- Chapter Concepts
- Self-Grading Quizzes
- Additional Web Links

# ABOUT THE AUTHORS

Tim and Linda O'Leary live in the American Southwest and spend much of their time engaging instructors and students in conversation about learning. In fact, they have been talking about learning for over 25 years. Something in those early conversations convinced them to write a book, to bring their interest in the learning process to the printed page. Today, they are as concerned as ever about learning, about technology, and about the challenges of presenting material in new ways, in terms of both content and method of delivery.

A powerful and creative team, Tim combines his 25 years of classroom teaching experience with Linda's background as a consultant and corporate trainer. Tim has taught courses at Stark Technical College in Canton, Ohio, and at Rochester Institute of Technology in upstate New York, and is currently a professor at Arizona State University in Tempe, Arizona. Linda offered her expertise at ASU for several years as an academic advisor. She also presented and developed materials for major corporations such as Motorola, Intel, Honeywell, and AT&T, as well as various community colleges in the Phoenix area.

Tim and Linda have talked to and taught numerous students, all of them with a desire to learn something about computers and applications that make their lives easier, more interesting, and more productive.

Each new edition of an O'Leary text, supplement, or learning aid has benefited from these students and their instructors who daily stand in front of them (or over their shoulders). The O'Leary Series is no exception.

# Introduction to Microsoft Office 2007

## Objectives

After completing the Introduction to Microsoft Office 2007, you should be able to:

**1** Describe the 2007 Microsoft Office System.

**2** Describe the Office 2007 applications.

**3** Start an Office 2007 application.

**4** Recognize the basic application features.

**5** Use menus, context menus, and shortcut keys.

**6** Use the Ribbon, dialog boxes, and task panes.

**7** Use Office Help.

**8** Exit an Office 2007 application.

# What Is the 2007 Microsoft Office System?

Microsoft's 2007 Microsoft Office System is a comprehensive, integrated system of programs, servers, and services designed to solve a wide array of business needs. Although the programs can be used individually, they are designed to work together seamlessly, making it easy to connect people and organizations to information, business processes, and each other. The applications include tools used to create, discuss, communicate, and manage projects. If you share a lot of documents with other people, these features facilitate access to common documents. This version has an entirely new user interface that is designed to make it easier to perform tasks and help users more quickly take advantage of all the features in the applications. In addition, the communication and collaboration features and integration with the World Wide Web have been expanded and refined.

The 2007 Microsoft Office System is packaged in several different combinations of programs or suites. The major programs and a brief description are provided in the following table.

| Program | Description |
| --- | --- |
| Word 2007 | Word Processor program used to create text-based documents |
| Excel 2007 | Spreadsheet program used to analyze numerical data |
| Access 2007 | Database manager used to organize, manage, and display a database |
| PowerPoint 2007 | Graphics presentation program used to create presentation materials |
| Outlook 2007 | Desktop information manager and messaging client |
| InfoPath 2007 | Used to create XML forms and documents |
| OneNote 2007 | Note-taking and information organization tools |
| Publisher 2007 | Tools to create and distribute publications for print, Web, and e-mail |
| Visio 2007 | Diagramming and data visualization tools |
| SharePoint Designer 2007 | Web site development and management for SharePoint servers |
| Project 2007 | Project management tools |
| Groove 2007 | Collaboration program that enables teams to work together |

The four main components of Microsoft Office 2007—Word, Excel, Access, and PowerPoint—are the applications you will learn about in this series of labs. They are described in more detail in the following sections.

# Word 2007

Word 2007 is a word processing software application whose purpose is to help you create text-based documents. Word processors are one of the most flexible and widely used application software programs. A word processor can be used to manipulate text data to produce a letter, a report, a memo, an e-mail message, or any other type of correspondence.

Two documents you will produce in the first two Word 2007 labs, a letter and flyer, are shown here.

A letter containing a tabbed table, indented paragraphs, and text enhancements is quickly created using basic Word features.

September 15, 2008

Dear Adventure Traveler:

Imagine camping under the stars in Africa, hiking and paddling your way through the rainforests of Costa Rica, or following in the footsteps of the ancient Inca as you backpack along the Inca trail to Machu Picchu. Turn these dreams of adventure into memories you will cherish forever by joining Adventure Travel Tours on one of our four new adventure tours.

To tell you more about these exciting new adventures, we are offering several presentations in your area. These presentations will focus on the features and cultures of the region. We will also show you pictures of the places you will visit and activities you can partici to attend one of the following presentations:

| Date | Time |
| --- | --- |
| January 5 | 8:00 p.m. Cro |
| February 3 | 7:30 p.m. Air |
| March 8 | 8:00 p.m. Re |

In appreciation of your past patronage, we of the new tour packages. You must book the trip at letter to qualify for the discount.

Our vacation tours are professionally devel everything in the price of your tour while giving you these features:

➢ All accommodations and meals
➢ All entrance fees, excursions, transfers and
➢ Professional tour manager and local guide

We hope you will join us this year on anoth Travel Tours each day is an adventure. For reservati Travel Tours directly at 1-800-555-0004.

## Adventure Travel Tours
# New Adventures

Attention adventure travelers! Attend an Adventure Travel presentation to learn about some of the earth's greatest unspoiled habitats and find out how you can experience the adventure of a lifetime. This year we are introducing four new tours that offer you a unique opportunity to combine many different outdoor activities while exploring the world.

India Wildlife Adventure

Inca Trail to Machu Picchu

Safari in Tanzania

Costa Rica Rivers and Rainforests

Presentation dates and times are January 5 at 8:00 p.m., February 3 at 7:30 p.m., and March 8 at 8:00 p.m. All presentations are held at convenient hotel locations in downtown Los Angeles, Santa Clara, and at the LAX airport.

Call Student Name 1-800-555-0004 for presentation locations, a full color brochure, and itinerary information, costs, and trip dates.

Visit our Web site at
www.adventuretraveltours.com

A flyer incorporating many visual enhancements such as colored text, varied text styles, and graphic elements is both eye-catching and informative.

The beauty of a word processor is that you can make changes or corrections as you are typing. Want to change a report from single spacing to double spacing? Alter the width of the margins? Delete some paragraphs and add others from yet another document? A word processor allows you to do all these things with ease.

Word 2007 includes many group collaboration features to help streamline how documents are developed and changed by group members. You also can create and send e-mail messages directly from within Word using all its features to create and edit the message. In addition, you can send an entire document as your e-mail message, allowing the recipient to edit the document directly without having to open or save an attachment.

Word 2007 is closely integrated with the World Wide Web, detecting when you type a Web address and automatically converting it to a hyperlink. You also can create your own hyperlinks to locations within documents, or to other documents, including those at external locations such as a Web site or file server. It also includes features that help you quickly create Web pages and blog entries.

## Excel 2007

Excel 2007 is an electronic worksheet that is used to organize, manipulate, and graph numeric data. Once used almost exclusively by accountants, worksheets are now widely used by nearly every profession. Marketing professionals record and evaluate sales trends. Teachers record grades and calculate final grades. Personal trainers record the progress of their clients.

Excel 2007 includes many features that not only help you create a well-designed worksheet, but one that produces accurate results. Formatting features include visual enhancements such as varied text styles, colors, and graphics. Other features help you enter complex formulas and identify and correct formula errors. You also can produce a visual display of data in the form of graphs or charts. As the values in the worksheet change, charts referencing those values automatically adjust to reflect the changes.

Excel 2007 also includes many advanced features and tools that help you perform what-if analysis and create different scenarios. And like all Office 2007 applications, it is easy to incorporate data created in one application into another. Two worksheets you will produce in Labs 2 and 3 of Excel 2007 are shown on the next page.

A worksheet showing the quarterly sales forecast containing a graphic, text enhancements, and a chart of the data is quickly created using basic Excel 2007 features.

A large worksheet incorporating more complex formulas, visual enhancements such as colored text, varied text styles, and graphic elements is both informative and attractive.

What Is the 2007 Microsoft Office System?  I.5

Word 2007

You will see how easy it is to analyze data and make projections using what-if analysis and what-if graphing in Lab 3 and to incorporate Excel data in a Word document as shown in the following figures.

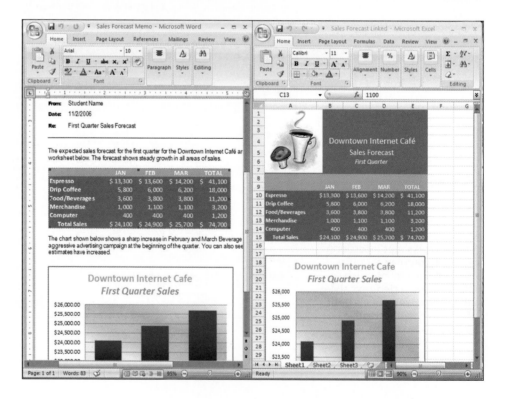

Changes you make in worksheet data while performing what-if analysis are automatically reflected in charts that reference that data.

Worksheet data and charts can be copied and linked to other Office documents such as a Word document.

## Access 2007

Access 2007 is a relational database management application that is used to create and analyze a database. A database is a collection of related data. In a relational database, the most widely used database structure, data is organized in linked tables. Tables consist of columns (called *fields*) and rows (called *records*). The tables are related or linked to one another by a common field. Relational databases allow you to create smaller and more manageable database tables, since you can combine and extract data between tables.

The program provides tools to enter, edit, and retrieve data from the database as well as to analyze the database and produce reports of the output. One of the main advantages of a computerized database is the ability to quickly add, delete, and locate specific records. Records also can be easily rearranged or sorted according to different fields of data, resulting in multiple table arrangements that provide more meaningful information for different purposes. Creation of forms makes it easier to enter and edit data as well. In the Access labs, you will create and organize the database table shown below.

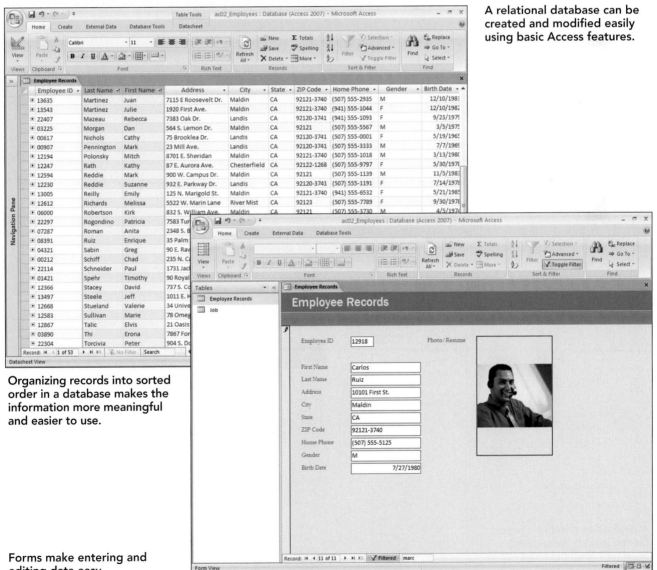

A relational database can be created and modified easily using basic Access features.

Organizing records into sorted order in a database makes the information more meaningful and easier to use.

Forms make entering and editing data easy.

Another feature is the ability to analyze the data in a table and perform calculations on different fields of data. Additionally, you can ask questions or query the table to find only certain records that meet specific conditions to be used in the analysis. Information that was once costly and time-consuming to get is now quickly and readily available. This information can then be quickly printed out in the form of reports ranging from simple listings to complex, professional-looking reports in different layout styles, or with titles, headings, subtotals, or totals.

A database can be queried to locate and display only specified information.

A professional-looking report can be quickly generated from information contained in a database.

## PowerPoint 2007

PowerPoint 2007 is a graphics presentation program designed to help you produce a high-quality presentation that is both interesting to the audience and effective in its ability to convey your message. A presentation can be as simple as overhead transparencies or as sophisticated as an on-screen electronic display. In the first two PowerPoint labs, you will create and organize the presentation shown below.

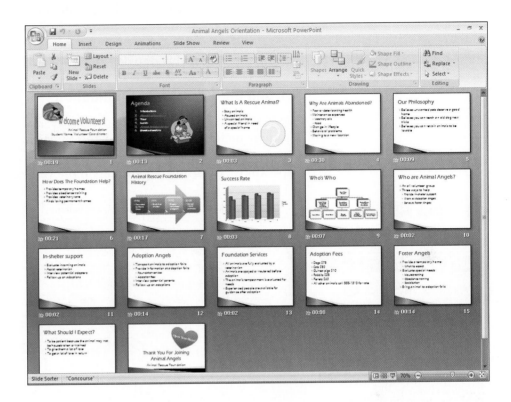

A presentation consists of a series of pages or "slides" presenting the information you want to convey in an organized and attractive manner.

When running an on-screen presentation, each slide of the presentation is displayed full-screen on your computer monitor or projected onto a screen.

What Is the 2007 Microsoft Office System?          I.9

**Word 2007**

# Common Office 2007 Interface Features

**Additional Information**

Please read the Before You Begin and Instructional Conventions sections in the Overview of Microsoft Office Word 2007 (WDO.3) before starting this section.

Now that you know a little about each of the applications in Microsoft Office 2007, we will take a look at some of the interface features that are common to all Office 2007 applications. This is a hands-on section that will introduce you to the features and allow you to get a feel for how Office 2007 works. Although Word 2007 will be used to demonstrate how the features work, only common **user interface** features, a set of graphical images that represent various features, will be addressed. These features include using the File menu, Ribbon, Quick Access Toolbar, task panes, and Office Help, and starting and exiting an application. The features that are specific to each application will be introduced individually in each application text.

## Starting an Office 2007 Application

There are several ways to start a Office 2007 application. The two most common methods are by using the Start menu or by clicking a desktop shortcut for the program if it is available. If you use the Start menu, the steps will vary slightly depending on the version of Windows you are using.

**1** ● Click [start] to display the Start menu.

**Having Trouble?**

In Windows Vista, click 

● **Choose Microsoft Office Word 2007.**

**Having Trouble?**

If you do not see the program name on the Start menu, select All Programs, select Microsoft Office, and then choose Microsoft Office Word 2007.

**OR**

**1** ● **Double-click the shortcut on the desktop.**

**2** ● **If necessary, click Maximize in the title bar to maximize the window.**

*Your screen should be similar to Figure 1*

**Having Trouble?**

Your screen may look slightly different based on your Windows operating system settings.

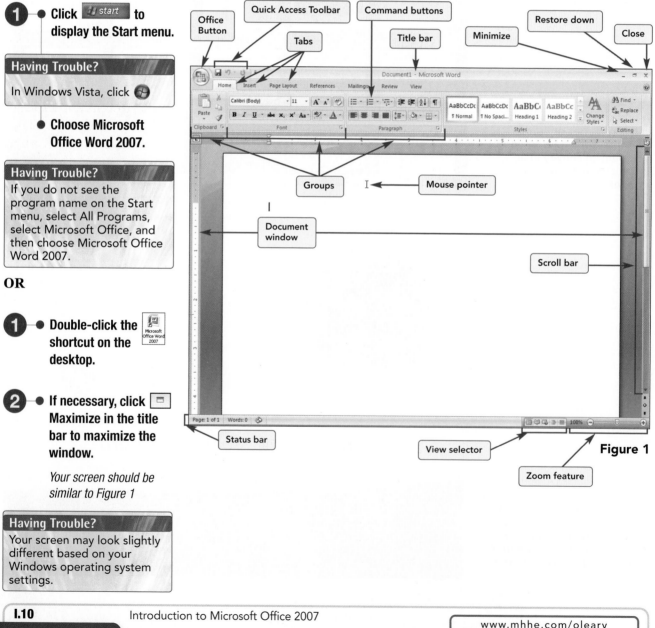

Figure 1

The Word 2007 program is started and displayed in a window on the desktop. The application window title bar displays the file name followed by the program name, Microsoft Word. The right end of the title bar displays the ☐ Minimize, ☐ Restore Down, and ☒ Close buttons. They perform the same functions and operate in the same way as all Windows versions.

Below the title bar is the **Ribbon**, which provides a centralized area that makes it easy to find ways to work in your document. The Ribbon has three basic parts: tabs, groups, and commands. **Tabs** are used to divide the Ribbon into major activity areas. Each tab is then organized into **groups** that contain related items. The related items are commands that consist of command buttons, a box to enter information, or a menu. As you use the Office applications, you will see that the Ribbon contains many of the same groups and commands across the applications. You also will see that many of the groups and commands are specific to an application.

The upper left area of the window's title bar displays the ☐ Office Button and the Quick Access Toolbar. Clicking ☐ Office Button opens the File menu of commands that allows you to work *with* your document, unlike the Ribbon that allows you to work *in* your document. For example, it includes commands to open, save, and print files. The **Quick Access Toolbar** (QAT) provides quick access to frequently used commands. By default, it includes the ☐ Save, ☐ Undo, and ☐ Redo buttons, commands that Microsoft considers to be crucial. It is always available and is a customizable toolbar to which you can add your own favorite buttons.

The large center area of the program window is the **document window** where open application files are displayed. Currently, there is a blank Word document open. In Word, the mouse pointer appears as I when positioned in the document window and as a ☐ when it can be used to select items.

On the right of the document window is a vertical scroll bar. A **scroll bar** is used with a mouse to bring additional lines of information into view in a window. The vertical scroll bar is used to move up or down. A horizontal scroll bar is also displayed when needed and moves side to side in the window. At the bottom of the window is the **status bar**, a view selector, and a document zoom feature. Similar information and features are displayed in this area for different Office applications. You will learn how these features work in each individual application.

## Using the File Menu

Clicking the ☐ Office Button opens the File menu of commands that are used to work with files.

**1** ● **Click** 🔘 **Office Button to open the File menu.**

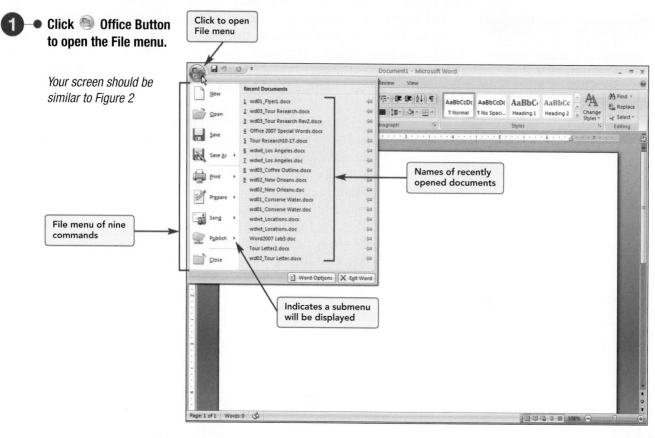

*Your screen should be similar to Figure 2*

File menu of nine commands →

**Click to open File menu**

Names of recently opened documents

Indicates a submenu will be displayed

**Figure 2**

**Additional Information**

Clicking the 📌 next to a file name pins the file and permanently keeps the file name in the recently used list until it is unpinned.

The menu lists nine commands that are used to perform tasks associated with files. Notice that each command displays an underlined letter. This identifies the letter you can type to choose the command. Five commands display a ▶, which indicates the command includes a submenu of options. The right side of the command list currently displays the names of recently opened files (your list will display different file names). The default program setting displays a maximum of 17 file names. Once the maximum number of files is listed, when a new file is opened, the oldest is dropped from the list.

Once the File menu is open, you can select a command from the menu by pointing to it. A colored highlight bar, called the **selection cursor**, appears over the selected command.

**Point to the Open command.**

*Your screen should be similar to Figure 3*

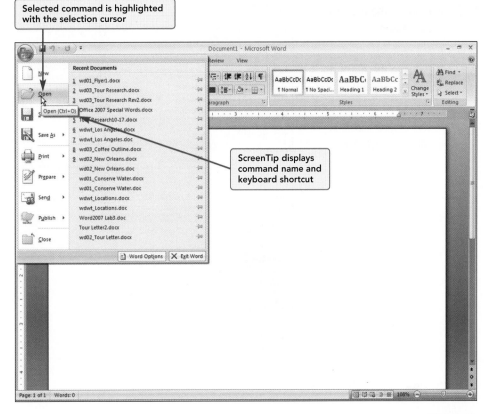

**Figure 3**

A **ScreenTip**, also called a **tooltip**, briefly appears displaying the command name and the keyboard shortcut, Ctrl + O. The keyboard shortcut can be used to execute this command without opening the menu. In this case, if you hold down the Ctrl key while typing the letter O, you will access the Open command without having to open the File menu first. ScreenTips also often include a brief description of the action a command performs.

Next you will select a command that will display a submenu of options.

**3** ● **Point to the Prepare command.**

● **Point to the Mark as Final submenu option.**

*Your screen should be similar to Figure 4*

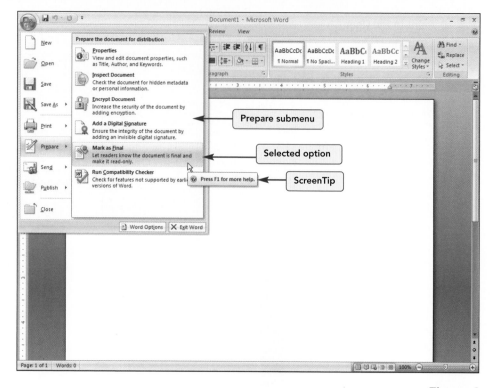

**Figure 4**

The submenu lists the six Prepare command submenu options and the Mark as Final option is selected. A ScreenTip provides information about how to get help on this feature. You will learn about using Help shortly.

**4** ● **Point to the Print command.**

● **Point to the ▸ of the Print command.**

*Your screen should be similar to Figure 5*

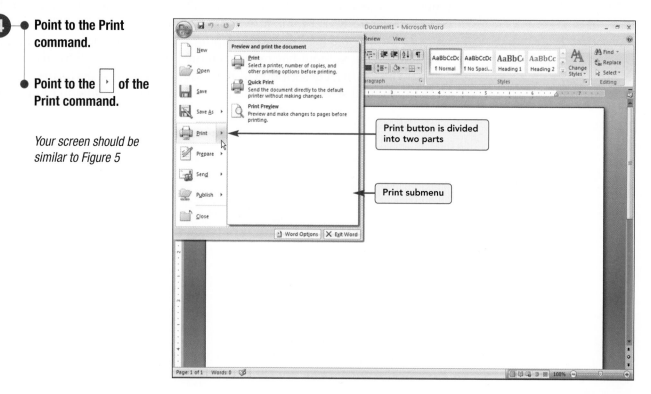

**Figure 5**

So far you have only selected commands; you have not chosen them. To choose a command, you click on it. When the command is chosen, the associated action is performed. Notice the Print command is divided into two parts. Clicking the Print section on the left will choose the command and open the Print dialog box. Clicking · in the right section has no effect.

**5** ● **Click the Print command.**

*Your screen should be similar to Figure 6*

Print dialog box is used to specify print settings

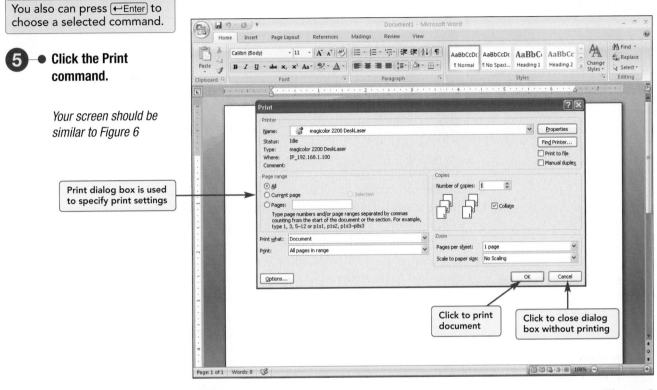

**Figure 6**

In the Print dialog box, you would specify the print settings and click ⬚ OK ⬚ to actually print a document. In this case, you will cancel the action and continue to explore other features of the Office 2007 application.

**6** ● **Click** ⬚ Cancel ⬚ **.**

## Using Context Menus

Another way to access some commands is to use a context menu. A **context menu** is opened by right-clicking on an item on the screen. This menu is context sensitive, meaning it displays only those commands relevant to the item. For example, right-clicking on the Quick Access Toolbar will display the commands associated with using the Quick Access Toolbar only. You will use this method to move the Quick Access Toolbar.

**1** ● Point to the Quick
Access Toolbar and
right-click.

**Another Method**

You also can click ⬚ at the
end of the Quick Access
toolbar to open the menu.

● Click the Show Quick
Access Toolbar below
the Ribbon option.

*Your screen should be
similar to Figure 7*

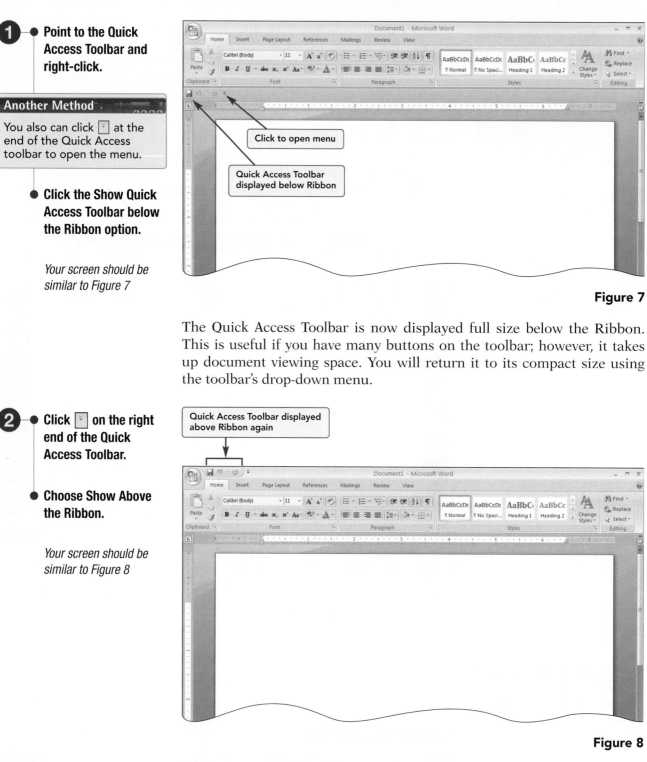

**Click to open menu**

**Quick Access Toolbar
displayed below Ribbon**

**Figure 7**

The Quick Access Toolbar is now displayed full size below the Ribbon.
This is useful if you have many buttons on the toolbar; however, it takes
up document viewing space. You will return it to its compact size using
the toolbar's drop-down menu.

**2** ● Click ⬚ on the right
end of the Quick
Access Toolbar.

● Choose Show Above
the Ribbon.

*Your screen should be
similar to Figure 8*

**Quick Access Toolbar displayed
above Ribbon again**

**Figure 8**

**MORE ABOUT**

▶ See the More About
appendix to learn how to
customize the Quick Access Toolbar.

The Quick Access Toolbar is displayed above the Ribbon again. The
toolbar's drop-down menu contains a list of commands that are often
added to the toolbar. Clicking on the command selects it and adds it to the
toolbar.

## Using the Ribbon

The Ribbon displays tabs that organize similar features into groups. In
Word, there are seven tabs displayed. To save space, some tabs, called
**contextual** or **on-demand tabs**, are displayed only as needed. For example,

when you are working with a picture, the Picture Tools tab appears. The contextual nature of this feature keeps the work area uncluttered when the feature is not needed and provides ready access to it when it is needed.

### Opening Tabs

The Home tab is open when you first start the application or open a file. It consists of five groups: Clipboard, Font, Paragraph, Styles, and Editing. Each group contains command buttons that when clicked on perform their associated action or display a list of additional commands. The commands in the Home tab help you perform actions related to creating the content of your document.

**1** ● **Click on the Insert tab.**

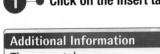
The open tab appears highlighted.

*Your screen should be similar to Figure 9*

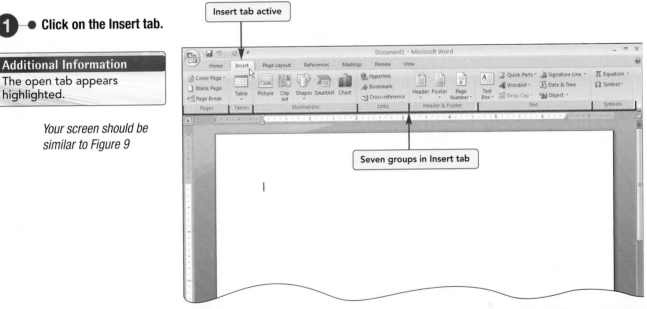

Insert tab active

Seven groups in Insert tab

**Figure 9**

This Insert tab is now the active tab. It contains seven groups whose commands have to do with inserting items into a document.

**2** ● **Click on each of the other tabs, ending with the View tab, to see their groups and commands.**

*Your screen should be similar to Figure 10*

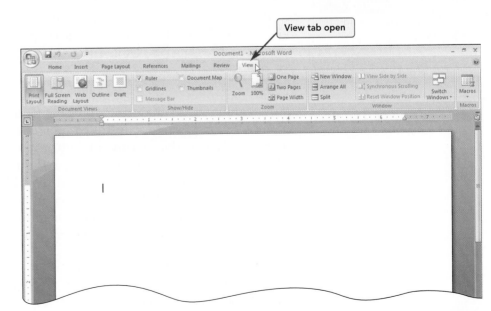

View tab open

**Figure 10**

Each tab relates to a type of activity; for example, the View tab commands perform activities related to viewing the document. Within each tab, similar commands are grouped together to make finding the commands you want to use much easier.

### Displaying Super Tooltips

Many command buttons immediately perform the associated action when you click on them. The buttons are graphic representations of the action they perform. To help you find out what a button does, you can display the button's ScreenTip.

**1** ● **Open the Home tab.**

● **Point to the upper part of the** [Paste] **button in the Clipboard group.**

● **Point to the lower part of the Paste button in the Clipboard group.**

● **Point to** [✓] **Format Painter in the Clipboard group.**

*Your screen should be similar to Figure 11*

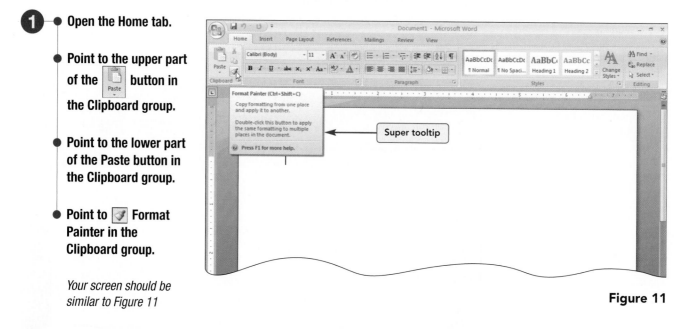

**Figure 11**

Both parts of the Paste button display tooltips containing the button name, the shortcut key combination, [Ctrl] + V, and a brief description of what the button does. Pointing to [✓] Format Painter displays a **super tooltip** that provides more detailed information about the command. Super tooltips may even display information such as procedures or illustrations. You can find out what the feature does without having to look it up in Help. If a feature has a Help article, you can automatically access it by pressing [F1] while the super tooltip is displayed.

### Using Galleries and Lists

Many commands in the groups appear as a **gallery** that displays small graphics that represent the result of applying a command. For example, in the Styles group, the command buttons to apply different formatting styles to text display examples of how the text would look if formatted using that command. These are called **in-Ribbon galleries** because they appear directly in the Ribbon. Other commands include multiple options that appear in **drop-down galleries** or drop-down lists that are accessed by clicking the [▾] button on the right side of the command button. To see an example of a drop-down gallery, you will open the [≡ ▾] Bullets drop-down gallery.

**1** • **Click ☑ in the ☰▾ Bullets button.**

*Your screen should be similar to Figure 12*

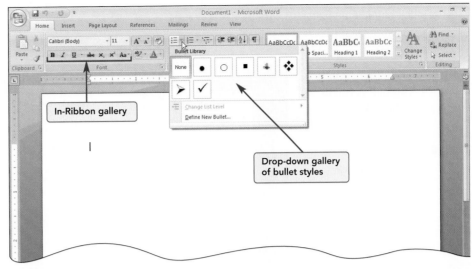

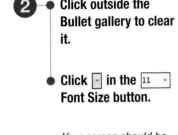

**Figure 12**

A drop-down gallery of different bullets is displayed. The drop-down gallery will disappear when you make a selection or click on any other area of the window. To see an example of a drop-down list, you will open the [11 ▾] Font Size drop-down list.

**2** • **Click outside the Bullet gallery to clear it.**

• **Click ☑ in the [11 ▾] Font Size button.**

*Your screen should be similar to Figure 13*

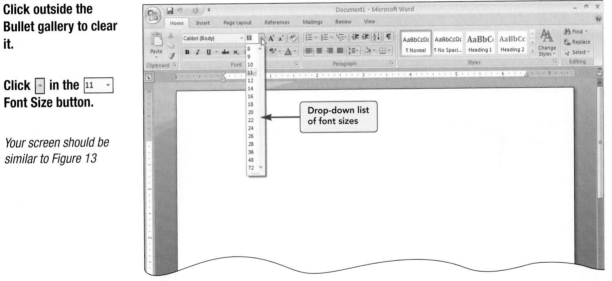

**Figure 13**

If you click on the button itself, not the ☑ section of the button, the associated command is performed.

### Using the Dialog Box Launcher

Because there is not enough space, only the most used commands are displayed in the Ribbon. If there are more commands available, a  button, called the **dialog box launcher**, is displayed in the lower-right corner of the group. Clicking  opens a dialog box or **task pane** of additional options.

**1** ● Click outside the Font size list to clear it.

● Point to the 🔲 of the Paragraph group to see the tooltip.

● Click 🔲 of the Paragraph group.

*Your screen should be similar to Figure 14*

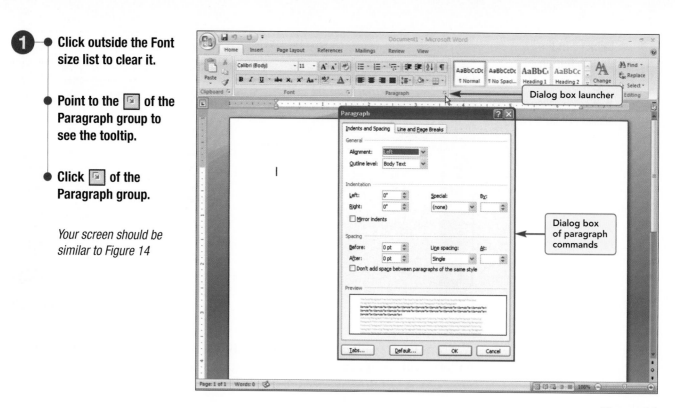

**Figure 14**

The Paragraph dialog box appears. It provides access to the more advanced paragraph settings features. Selecting options from the dialog box and clicking [ OK ] will close the dialog box and apply the settings as specified. To cancel the dialog box, you can click [ Cancel ] or ☒ in the dialog box title bar.

**2** ● Click [ Cancel ] to close the dialog box.

● Click 🔲 in the Clipboard group.

*Your screen should be similar to Figure 15*

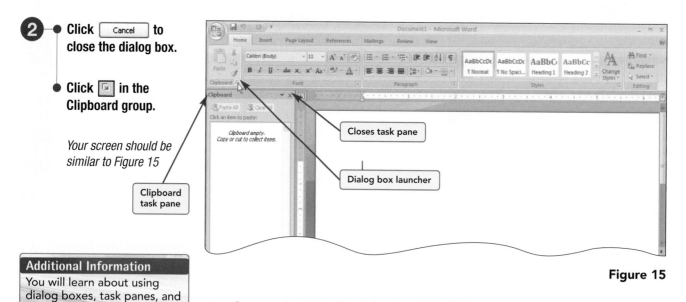

**Figure 15**

A task pane is open that contains features associated with the Clipboard. Unlike dialog boxes, task panes remain open until you close them. This allows you to make multiple selections from the task pane while continuing to work on other areas of your document.

**3** ● Click ☒ in the upper-right corner of the task pane to close it.

## Using Access Key Shortcuts

Another way to use commands on the Ribbon is to display the access key shortcuts by pressing the Alt key and then typing the letter for the feature you want to use. Every Ribbon tab, group, and command has an access key.

**1** ● **Press** Alt.

*Your screen should be similar to Figure 16*

> Access keys appear in KeyTips

**Figure 16**

The letters are displayed in **KeyTips** over each available feature. Now typing a letter will access that feature. Then, depending on which letter you pressed, additional KeyTips may appear. To use a Ribbon command, press the key of the tab first, then the group, and then continue pressing letters until you press the letter of the specific command you want to use. You will use KeyTips to display the Paragraph dialog box again.

**2** ● **Type the letter H to access the Home tab.**

● **Type the letters PG to access the Paragraph group and open the dialog box.**

*Your screen should be similar to Figure 17*

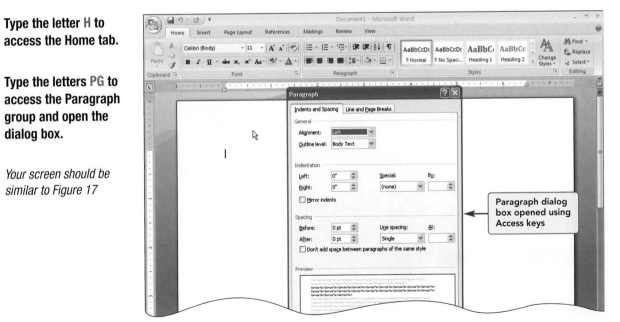

> Paragraph dialog box opened using Access keys

**Figure 17**

Three keystrokes opened the Paragraph dialog box.

Once the Access key feature is on, you can also use the [←] or [→] directional key to move from one tab to another, and the [↓] key to move from a tab to a group and the [↑] key to move from a group to a tab. You can use all four directional keys to move among the commands in a Ribbon. [Tab⇥] and [⇧Shift] + [Tab⇥] also can be used to move right or left. Once a command is selected, you can press [Spacebar] or [←Enter] to activate it.

## Minimizing the Ribbon

Sometimes you may not want to see the entire Ribbon so that more space is available in the document area. You can minimize the Ribbon by double-clicking the active tab.

**1** ● Click [✕] to close the Paragraph dialog box.

● Double-click the Home tab.

*Your screen should be similar to Figure 18*

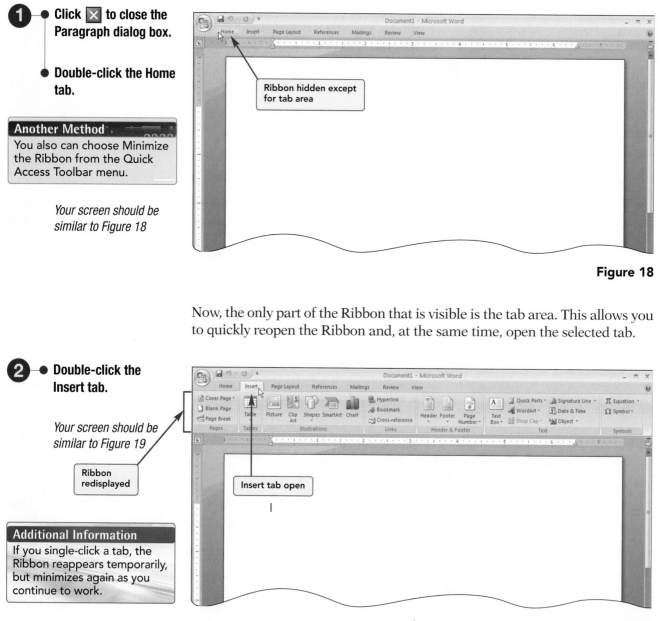

Figure 18

Now, the only part of the Ribbon that is visible is the tab area. This allows you to quickly reopen the Ribbon and, at the same time, open the selected tab.

**2** ● Double-click the Insert tab.

*Your screen should be similar to Figure 19*

Figure 19

The full Ribbon reappears and the Insert tab is open and ready for use.

## Using the Mini Toolbar

Another method of accessing commands is through the Mini toolbar. The **Mini toolbar** appears automatically when you select text in a document and provides commands that are used to format (enhance) text. It also appears along with the context menu when you right-click an item in a document. Both the Mini toolbar and context menus are designed to make it more efficient to execute commands.

You can see what these features look like by right-clicking in a blank area of the document window.

**1** ● **Right-click the blank document window space.**

*Your screen should be similar to Figure 20*

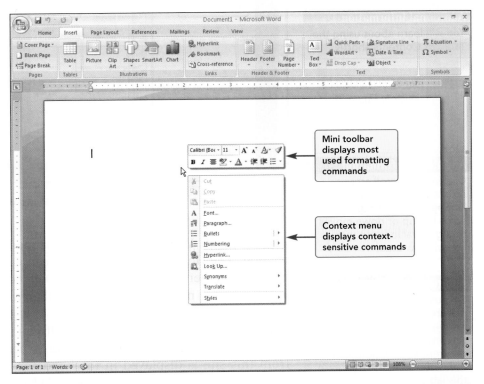

**Figure 20**

The Mini toolbar displays the most frequently used formatting commands. For example, when the Home tab is closed, you can use the commands in the Mini toolbar to quickly change selected text without having to reopen the Home tab to access the command. When the Mini toolbar appears automatically, it is faded so that it does not interfere with what you are doing, but changes to solid (as it is here) when you point at it.

The context menu below the Mini toolbar displays a variety of commands that are quicker to access than locating the command on the Ribbon. The commands that appear on this menu change depending on what you are doing at the time.

## Using Office Help

**Another Method**
You also can press [F1] to access Help.

Notice the ⓘ in the upper-right corner of the Ribbon. This button is used to access the Microsoft Help system. The Help button is always visible even when the Ribbon is hidden. Because you are using the Office Word 2007 application, Office Word Help will be accessed.

The right side of the Help window displays the same Help information about the Ribbon. To close a chapter, click the 🔲 icon.

**3** ● Click 🔲 to close the Using Microsoft Office chapter.

● Click 🔲 Hide Table of Contents in the Help window toolbar to hide the table of contents list again.

### Exiting an Office 2007 Application

Now you are ready to close the Help window and exit the Word program. The ⨯ Close button located on the right end of the window title bar can be used to exit most application windows.

**1** ● Click ⨯ Close in the Help window title bar to close the Help window.

● Click ⨯ Close in the Word window title bar to exit Word.

**Another Method**

You also could choose 🔘 / ⨯ Exit Word or press Alt + F4 to exit an Office application.

The program window is closed and the desktop is visible again.

# Lab Review

## Introduction to Microsoft Office 2007

## key terms

context menu   I.15
contextual tabs   I.16
dialog box launcher   I.19
document window   I.11
drop-down gallery   I.18
gallery   I.18
group   I.11
hyperlink   I.24

in-Ribbon gallery   I.18
KeyTips   I.21
Mini toolbar   I.23
on-demand tab   I.16
Quick Access Toolbar   I.11
Ribbon   I.11
ScreenTip   I.13
scroll bar   I.11

selection cursor   I.12
status bar   I.11
super tooltip   I.18
tab   I.11
task pane   I.19
tooltip   I.13
user interface   I.10

## command summary

| Command/Button | Shortcut | Action |
|---|---|---|
| start | | Opens the Start menu |
| Microsoft Office Word 2007 | | Starts the Word 2007 program |
| Office Button/ ✕ Exit Word | Alt + F4 | Exits Office program |
| ⊚ | F1 | Opens Help window |

# Lab Exercises

## step-by-step

### Using an Office Application ★

1. All Office 2007 applications have a common user interface. You will explore the Excel 2007 application and use many of the same features you learned about while using Word 2007 in this lab.

   **a.** Use the Start menu or a shortcut icon on your desktop to start Office Excel 2007.

   **b.** What shape is the mouse pointer when positioned in the document window area? _____

   **c.** Excel has _____ tabs. Which tabs are not the same as in Word?
   _____

   **d.** Open the Formulas tab. How many groups are in the Formulas tab? _____

   **e.** Which tab contains the group to work with charts? _____

   **f.** From the Home tab, click the Number group dialog box launcher. What is the name of the dialog box that opens? How many number categories are there? _____ Close the dialog box.

   **g.** Display ToolTips for the following buttons located in the Alignment group of the Home tab and identify what action they perform.

   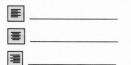

   _____

   _____

   _____

   **h.** Open the Excel Help window. Open the table of contents and locate the topic "What's new in Microsoft Office Excel 2007?" Open this topic and find information on the number of rows and columns in a worksheet. Answer the following questions:

   How many rows are in a worksheet? _____

   How many columns are in a worksheet? _____

   What are the letters of the last column? _____

   **i.** Close the table of contents. Close the Help window. Exit Excel.

## on your own

### Exploring Microsoft Help ★

1. In addition to the Help information you used in this lab, Office 2007 Online Help also includes many interactive tutorials. Selecting a Help topic that starts a tutorial will open the browser program on your computer. Both audio and written instructions are provided. You will use one of these tutorials to learn more about using Word 2007.

   Start Word 2007. Open Help and open the topic "What's New?" Click on the topic "Up to speed with Word 2007." Follow the directions in your browser to run the tutorial. When you are done, close the browser window, close Help, and exit Word 2007.

# Overview of Microsoft Office Word 2007

## What Is Word Processing?

Office Word 2007 is a word processing software application whose purpose is to help you create any type of written communication. A word processor can be used to manipulate text data to produce a letter, a report, a memo, an e-mail message, or any other type of correspondence. Text data is any letter, number, or symbol that you can type on a keyboard. The grouping of the text data to form words, sentences, paragraphs, and pages of text results in the creation of a document. Through a word processor, you can create, modify, store, retrieve, and print part or all of a document.

Word processors are one of the most widely used application software programs. Putting your thoughts in writing, from the simplest note to the most complex book, is a time-consuming process. Even more time-consuming is the task of editing and retyping the document to make it better. Word processors make errors nearly nonexistent—not because they are not made, but because they are easy to correct. Word processors let you throw away the correction fluid, scissors, paste, and erasers. Now, with a few keystrokes, you can easily correct errors, move paragraphs, and reprint your document.

## Word 2007 Features

Word 2007 excels in its ability to change or edit a document. Editing involves correcting spelling, grammar, and sentence-structure errors. In addition, you can easily revise or update existing text by inserting or deleting text. For example, a document that lists prices can easily be updated to reflect new prices. A document that details procedures can be revised by deleting old procedures and inserting new ones. This is especially helpful when a document is used repeatedly. Rather than recreating the whole document, you change only the parts that need to be revised.

Revision also includes the rearrangement of selected areas of text. For example, while writing a report, you may decide to change the location of a single word or several paragraphs or pages of text. You can do it easily by cutting or removing selected text from one location, then pasting or placing the selected text in another location. The selection also can be copied from one document to another.

To help you produce a perfect document, Word 2007 includes many additional support features. The AutoCorrect feature checks the spelling and grammar in a document as text is entered. Many common errors are corrected automatically for you. Others are identified and a correction suggested. A thesaurus can be used to display alternative words that have a meaning similar or opposite to a word you entered. A Find and Replace feature can be used to quickly locate specified text and replace it with other text throughout a document. In addition, Word 2007 includes a variety of tools that automate the process of many common tasks, such as creating tables, form letters, and columns.

You also can easily control the appearance or format of the document. Formatting includes such operations as changing the line spacing and margin widths, adding page numbers, and displaying page headers and footers. You also can quickly change how your text is aligned with the left or right margin. For example, text can be centered between the margins, or justified—evenly aligned on both the left and right margins. Perhaps the most noticeable formatting feature is the ability to apply different fonts (type styles and sizes) and text appearance changes such as bold, italics, and color to all or selected portions of the document. Additionally, you can add color shading behind individual pieces of text or entire paragraphs and pages to add emphasis.

To make formatting even easier, Word 2007 includes Document Themes and Quick Styles. Document Themes apply a consistent font, color, and line effect to an entire document. Quick Styles apply the selected style design to a selection of text. Further, Word 2007 includes a variety of built-in preformatted content that help you quickly produce modern-looking, professional documents. Among these are galleries of cover page designs, pull quotes, and header and footer designs. While selecting many of these design choices, a visual live preview is displayed, making it easy to see how the design would look in your document. In addition, you can select from a wide variety of templates to help you get started on creating many common types of documents such as flyers, calendars, faxes, newsletters, and memos.

To further enhance your documents, you can insert many different types of graphic elements. These include drawing objects, SmartArt, charts, pictures, and clip art. The drawing tools supplied with Word 2007 can be used to create your own drawings, or you can select from over 100 adjustable shapes and modify them to your needs. All drawings can be further enhanced with 3-D effects, shadows, colors, and textures. SmartArt graphics allow you to create a visual representation of your information. They include many different layouts such as a process or cycle that are designed to help you communicate an idea. Once created, you can quickly enhance them using a Quick Style. Charts can be inserted to illustrate and compare data. Complex pictures can be inserted in documents by scanning your own, using supplied or purchased clip art, or downloading images from the World Wide Web. Additionally, you can produce fancy text effects using the WordArt tool.

Word 2007 is closely integrated with the World Wide Web. It detects when you are typing a Web address and converts it to a hyperlink automatically for you. You also can create your own hyperlinks to locations within documents, or to other documents, including those at external locations such as a Web site or file server. Word's many Web-editing features help you quickly create a Web page. Frames can be created to make your Web site easier for users to navigate. Pictures, graphic elements, animated graphics, sound, and movies can all be used to increase the impact of your Web pages.

Group collaboration on projects is common in industry today. Word 2007 includes many features to help streamline how documents are developed and changed by group members. A discussion feature allows multiple people to insert remarks in the same document without having to route the document to each person or reconcile multiple reviewers' comments. You can easily consolidate all changes and comments from different reviewers in one simple step and accept or reject changes as needed.

You also can create and send an entire document by e-mail or Internet Fax service directly from within Word 2007, using all its features to create and edit the message.

# Case Study for Office Word 2007 Labs

As a recent college graduate, you have accepted a job as advertising coordinator for Adventure Travel Tours, a specialty travel company that organizes active adventure vacations. The company is headquartered in Los Angeles and has locations in other major cities throughout the country. Your duties include the creation of brochures, flyers, form letters, news releases, advertisements, and a monthly newsletter, all of which promote Adventure Travel's programs. You are also responsible for working on the company Web site.

## Brief Version

**Lab 1:** Adventure Travel Tours has developed four new tours for the upcoming year and needs to promote them, partly through informative presentations held throughout the country. Your first job as advertising coordinator is to create a flyer advertising the four new tours and the presentations about them.

**Lab 2:** Your next project is to create a letter to be sent to past clients. The letter briefly describes Adventure Travel's four new tours and invites clients to attend an informational presentation.

**Lab 3:** Part of your responsibility as advertising coordinator is to gather background information about the various tour locations. You will write a report that includes a cover page, table of contents list, and footnotes, providing information about Tanzania and Peru for two of the new tours.

**Working Together:** Adventure Travel Tours has a company Web site. You will convert the flyer you developed to promote the new tours and presentations to be used on the Web site.

# Before You Begin

*To the Student*

The following assumptions have been made:

- Microsoft Office Word 2007 has been properly installed on your computer system.

- You have the data files needed to complete the series of Word 2007 labs and practice exercises. These may be supplied by your instructor and are also available at the online learning center Web site found at www.mhhe.com/oleary.

- You are already familiar with how to use Microsoft Windows XP or Vista and a mouse.

*To the Instructor*

A complete installation of Microsoft Office 2007 is required in which all components are available to students while completing the labs. In several labs, an online connection to the Web is needed to fully access a feature.

Please be aware that the following settings are assumed to be in effect for the Office Word 2007 program. These assumptions are necessary so that the screens and directions in the labs are accurate. These settings are made using Office Button/ Word Options in the categories shown below. Features are on when there is a check mark in the check box.

### Popular

- The Mini Toolbar feature is selected.
- Always use ClearType is on.
- The Live Preview feature is enabled.
- The color scheme is set to blue.
- Show feature descriptions in ScreenTips is selected.
- Language is set to English (US).

### Display

- Show white space between pages in Print Layout view is on.
- Show highlighter marks is on.
- Show document tooltips on hover is on.
- Print drawings created in Word is on.

### Proofing

- In the AutoCorrect Options dialog box, all options are on in both the AutoCorrect and AutoFormat tabs. In the AutoFormat as you type tab, all options are on except: Bold and italic with real formatting, Built-in Heading styles, and Define styles based on your formatting.
- Ignore words in Uppercase is on.
- Ignore words that contain numbers is on.
- Ignore Internet and file addresses is on.
- Flag repeated words is on.
- Check spelling as you type is on.
- Check grammar as you type is on.
- Check grammar with spelling is on.

### Advanced/Editing options

- Typing replaces selected text is on.
- When selecting, automatically select entire word is on.
- Allow text to be dragged and dropped is on.
- Use Ctrl+Click to follow hyperlink is on.
- Use smart paragraph selection is on.
- Use smart cursoring is on.
- Keep track of formatting is on.
- Mark Formatting Inconsistencies is off.
- Enable Click and type is on.

### Advanced/Cut, Copy, and Paste

- The four Pasting options are set to their default settings.
- The Insert/paste pictures as option is set to In line with text.
- Keep bullets and numbers when pasting text with Keep Text Only option is on.
- Show Paste Options button is on.
- Use smart cut and paste is on.

**Advanced/Show document content**

- Show drawings and text boxes on screen is on.
- Show text animation is on.
- Show Smart Tags is on.

**Advanced/Display**

- Show 17 Recent Documents.
- Show all windows in the Taskbar is on.
- Show shortcut keys in ScreenTips is on.
- Show horizontal and vertical scroll bars is on.
- Show vertical ruler in Print Layout view is on.

Additionally, the following assumptions are made:

- The feature to access Online Help is on. (From the Help window, open the Connection Status menu and choose Show Content from Office Online.)
- All default settings for the Normal document template are in effect.
- All figures in the text reflect the use of a display monitor set at 1024 by 768 and the Windows XP opearting system. If other monitor settings are used, there may be more or fewer lines of information displayed in the windows than in the figures. If the Windows Vista operating system is used, some features may look slightly different.

# Instructional Conventions

Hands-on instructions you are to perform appear as a sequence of numbered steps. Within each step, a series of bullets identifies the specific actions that must be performed. Step numbering begins over within each topic heading throughout the lab. Four types of marginal notes appear throughout the labs. Another Method notes provide alternate ways of performing the same command. Having Trouble? notes provide advice or cautions for steps that may cause problems. Additional Information notes provide more information about a topic. More About notes refer you to the More About Word 2007 appendix for additional information about related features.

## Commands

Commands that are initiated using a command button and the mouse appear following the word "Click." The icon (and the icon name if the icon does not include text) is displayed following "Click." If there is another way to perform the same action, it appears in an Another Method margin note when the action is first introduced as shown in Example A.

When a feature has already been covered and you are more familiar with using the application, commands will appear as shown in Example B.

**Example A**

**1** ● Select the list of four tours.

● Open the Home tab.

● Click **B** Bold in the Font group.

**Example B**

**1** ● **Select the list of four tours.**

● **Click** B **Bold in the Font group of the Home tab.**

OR

**1** ● **Bold the list of four tours.**

## File Names and Information to Type

Plain blue text identifies file names you need to select or enter. Information you are asked to type appears in blue and bold. (See Example C.)

**Example C**

**1** ● **Open the document** wd01_Flyer.

● **Type** Adventure Travel presents four new trips.

## 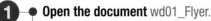 Office Button

Clicking 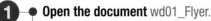 Office Button opens the File menu of commands. File menu commands that you are to use by clicking on the menu option appear following the word "Choose." Items that are to be selected (highlighted) will follow the word "Select" and will appear in black text. You can select items with the mouse or directional keys. Initially these commands will appear as in Example A. As you become more familiar with the application, commands will appear as shown in Example B.

**Example A**

**1** ● **Click**  **Office Button.**

● **Choose Open.**

● **Select My Documents from the Look In drop-down menu.**

● **Select** Flyer1.docx.

● **Click** [ Open ▾ ] .

**Example B**

**1** ● **Choose Open from the File menu.**

● **Choose** Flyer1.docx.

# Creating and Editing a Document

## Objectives

After completing this lab, you will know how to:

**1** Develop a document as well as enter and edit text.

**2** Insert and delete text and blank lines.

**3** Use spelling and grammar checking.

**4** Use AutoCorrect.

**5** Set file properties.

**6** Save, close, and open files.

**7** Select text.

**8** Undo and redo changes.

**9** Change fonts and type sizes.

**10** Bold and color text.

**11** Change alignment.

**12** Insert and size pictures.

**13** Add page borders and watermarks.

**14** Print a document.

## Adventure Travel Tours

As a recent college graduate, you have accepted a job as advertising coordinator for Adventure Travel Tours, a specialty travel company that organizes active adventure vacations. The company is headquartered in Los Angeles and has locations in other major cities throughout the country. You are responsible for coordination of the advertising program for all locations. This includes the creation of many kinds of promotional materials: brochures, flyers, form letters, news releases, advertisements, and a monthly newsletter. You are also responsible for creating Web pages for the company Web site.

Adventure Travel is very excited about four new tours planned for the upcoming year. They want to promote  them through informative presentations held throughout the country. Your first job as advertising coordinator will be to create a flyer advertising the four new tours and the presentations about them. The flyer will be modified according to the location of the presentation.

The software tool you will use to create the flyer is the word processing application Microsoft Office Word 2007. It helps you create documents such as letters, reports, and research papers. In this lab, you will learn how to enter, edit, and print a document while you create the flyer (shown right) to be distributed in a mailing to Adventure Travel Tours clients.

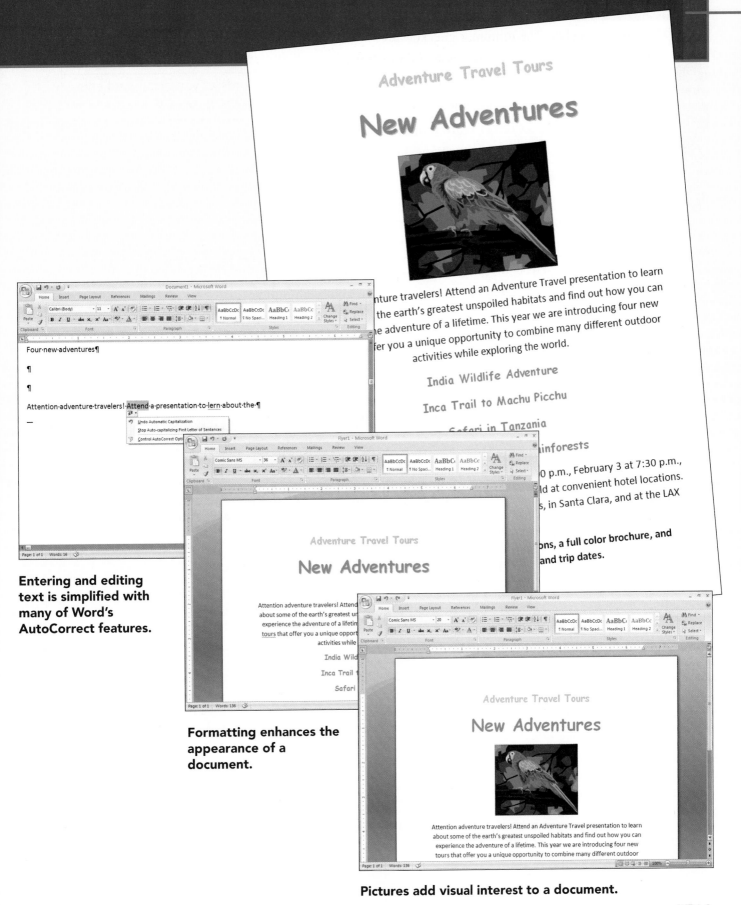

**Entering and editing text is simplified with many of Word's AutoCorrect features.**

**Formatting enhances the appearance of a document.**

**Pictures add visual interest to a document.**

**The following concepts will be introduced in this lab:**

**1** **Grammar Checker** The grammar checker advises you of incorrect grammar as you create and edit a document, and proposes possible corrections.

**2** **Spelling Checker** The spelling checker advises you of misspelled words as you create and edit a document, and proposes possible corrections.

**3** **AutoCorrect** The AutoCorrect feature makes some basic assumptions about the text you are typing and, based on these assumptions, automatically corrects the entry.

**4** **Word Wrap** The word wrap feature automatically decides where to end a line and wrap text to the next line based on the margin settings.

**5** **Font and Font Size** Font, also commonly referred to as a typeface, is a set of characters with a specific design that has one or more font sizes.

**6** **Alignment** Alignment is the positioning of text on a line between the margins or indents. There are four types of paragraph alignment: left, centered, right, and justified.

**7** **Graphics** A graphic is a nontext element or object such as a drawing or picture that can be added to a document.

## Introducing Office Word 2007

Adventure Travel Tours has recently upgraded their computer systems at all locations across the country. As part of the upgrade, they have installed the latest version of the Microsoft Office 2007 suite of applications. You are very excited to see how this new and powerful application can help you create professional letters and reports as well as eye-catching flyers and newsletters.

### Starting Office Word 2007

You will use the word processing application Microsoft Office Word 2007 to create a flyer promoting the new tours and presentations.

**1** ● **Start Word 2007.**

**Having Trouble?**

See "Common 2007 Office Features," page I.10, for information on how to start the application and use features that are common to all Office 2007 applications.

● **If necessary, maximize the Word 2007 application window.**

*Your screen should be similar to Figure 1.1*

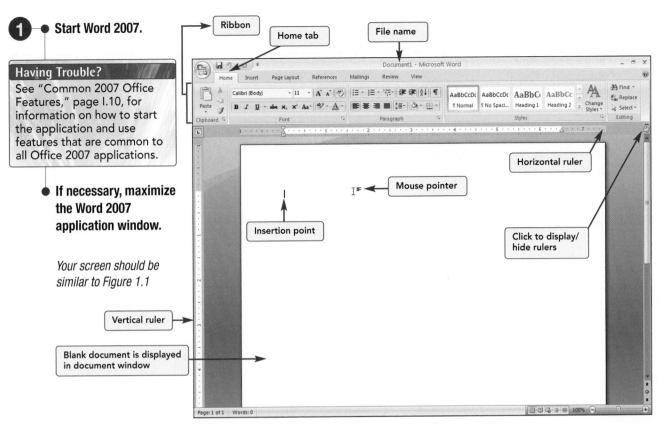

Figure 1.1

**Additional Information**

The Ribbon may display additional tabs if other application add-ins associated with Office are on.

**Additional Information**

If the ruler is not displayed, click [img] View Ruler above the vertical scroll bar to turn it on. You also can temporarily display the horizontal or vertical ruler by pointing to the top or left edge of the document window.

**Additional Information**

The mouse pointer also may appear in other shapes, depending upon the task being performed.

## Exploring the Word 2007 Window

The Word 2007 Ribbon below the title bar consists of seven command tabs that provide access to the commands and features you will use to create and modify a document.

The large area below the toolbars is the **document window**. It currently displays a blank Word document. The **insertion point**, also called the **cursor**, is the blinking vertical bar that marks your location in the document. A vertical and horizontal **ruler** may be displayed along both edges of the document window. The horizontal ruler at the top of the document window shows the line length in inches and is used to set margins, tab stops, and indents. The vertical ruler along the left edge shows the page length in inches and shows your line location on the page.

The mouse pointer may appear as an I-beam (see Figure 1.1) or a left- or right-facing arrow, depending on its location in the window. When it appears as an I-beam, it is used to move the insertion point, and when it appears as an arrow, it is used to select items.

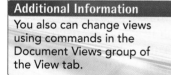

**1** ● **Move the mouse pointer into the left edge of the blank document to see it appear as** ⅄.

● **Move the mouse pointer to the Ribbon to see it appear as** ⅃.

*Your screen should be similar to Figure 1.2*

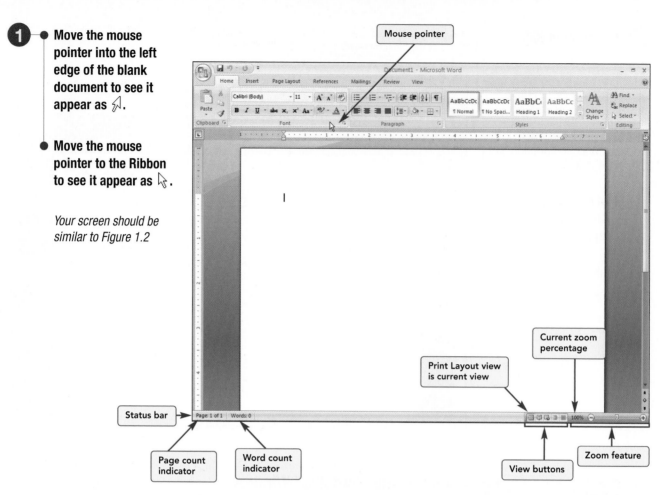

Mouse pointer

Current zoom percentage

Print Layout view is current view

Status bar

Page count indicator

Word count indicator

View buttons

Zoom feature

**Figure 1.2**

# Viewing and Zooming a Document

The status bar at the bottom of the window displays the page and word count indicators. The page indicator identifies the page of text that is displayed onscreen of the total number of pages in the document. The word count indicator displays the number of words in a document. When you first start Word, a new blank document consisting of a single page and zero words is opened.

The right end of the status bar displays five buttons that are used to change the document view and a document zoom feature. Word includes

**Additional Information**

You also can change views using commands in the Document Views group of the View tab.

several views that are used for different purposes. The different document views are described in the table below.

| Document View | Button | Effect on Text |
|---|---|---|
| Print Layout | | Shows how the text and objects will appear on the printed page. This is the view to use when adjusting margins, working in columns, drawing objects, and placing graphics. |
| Full Screen Reading | | Shows the document only, without Ribbon, status bar, or any other features. Useful for viewing and reading large documents. Use to review a document and add comments and highlighting. |
| Web Layout | | Shows the document as it will appear when viewed in a Web browser. Use this view when creating Web pages or documents that will be displayed on the screen only. |
| Outline | | Shows the structure of the document. This is the view to use to plan and reorganize text in a document. |
| Draft | | Shows text formatting and simple layout of the page. This is the best view to use when typing, editing, and formatting text. |

**Additional Information**

Pointing to the items on the status bar displays a ScreenTip that identifies the feature.

**Additional Information**

If you have a mouse with a scroll wheel, you can use it to zoom in or out by holding down Ctrl while turning the wheel forward or backward.

Print Layout view is the view you see when first starting Word or opening a document. You can tell which view is in use by looking at the view buttons. The button for the view that is in use appears highlighted.

The document zoom feature is used to change the amount of information displayed in the document window by "zooming in" to get a close-up view or "zooming out" to see more of the document at a reduced view. The default display, 100 percent, shows the characters the same size they will be when printed. You can increase the onscreen character size up to five times the normal display (500 percent) or reduce the character size to 10 percent. The zoom setting for each view is set independently and remains in effect until changed to another zoom setting.

You will "zoom out" on the document to see the entire page so you can better see the default document settings.

**1** ● **Drag the Zoom Slider to the left to reduce the zoom until the entire page is visible.**

*Your screen should be similar to Figure 1.3*

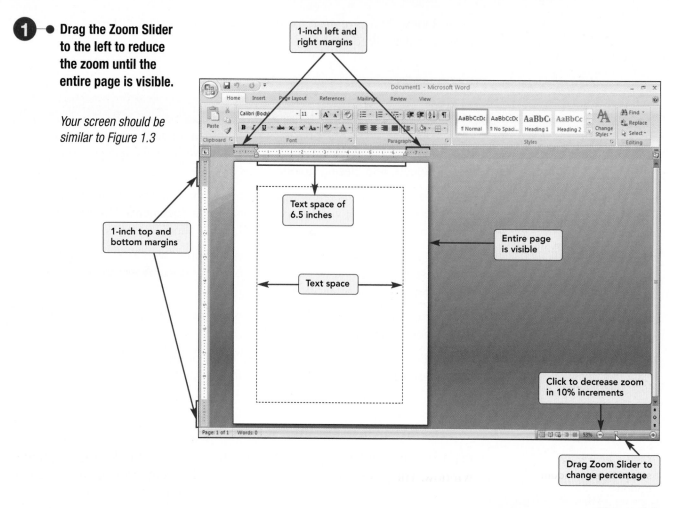

1-inch left and right margins

1-inch top and bottom margins

Text space of 6.5 inches

Text space

Entire page is visible

Click to decrease zoom in 10% increments

Drag Zoom Slider to change percentage

**Figure 1.3**

**Additional Information**

You also can click the ⊖ or ⊕ on the Zoom Slider to increase or decrease the zoom percentage by 10 percent increments.

At this zoom percentage, the entire page is displayed and all four edges of the paper are visible. It is like a blank piece of paper that already has many predefined settings. These settings, called **default** settings, are generally the most commonly used settings. The default document settings are stored in the Normal.dotm template file. A **template** is a document that contains many predefined settings that is used as the basis for the document you are creating. The Normal.dotm file is automatically opened whenever you start Word 2007. The default settings include a standard paper-size setting of 8.5 by 11 inches, 1-inch top and bottom margins, and 1-inch left and right margins.

You can verify many of the default document settings by looking at the information displayed in the rulers. The shaded area of the ruler identifies the margins and the white area identifies the text space. The text space occupies 6.5 inches of the page. Knowing that the default page size is 8.5 inches wide, this leaves 2 inches for margins: 1 inch for equal-sized left and right margins. The vertical ruler shows the entire page length is 11 inches with 1-inch top and bottom margins, leaving 9 inches of text space.

You will use Draft view to create the flyer about this year's new tours. You will use the View tab to change both the view and the Zoom percentage.

**2** • Open the View tab.

• From the Document Views group, click [Draft].

• If necessary, click [ ] to display the ruler.

• From the Zoom group, click [Zoom] to open the Zoom dialog box.

*Your screen should be similar to Figure 1.4*

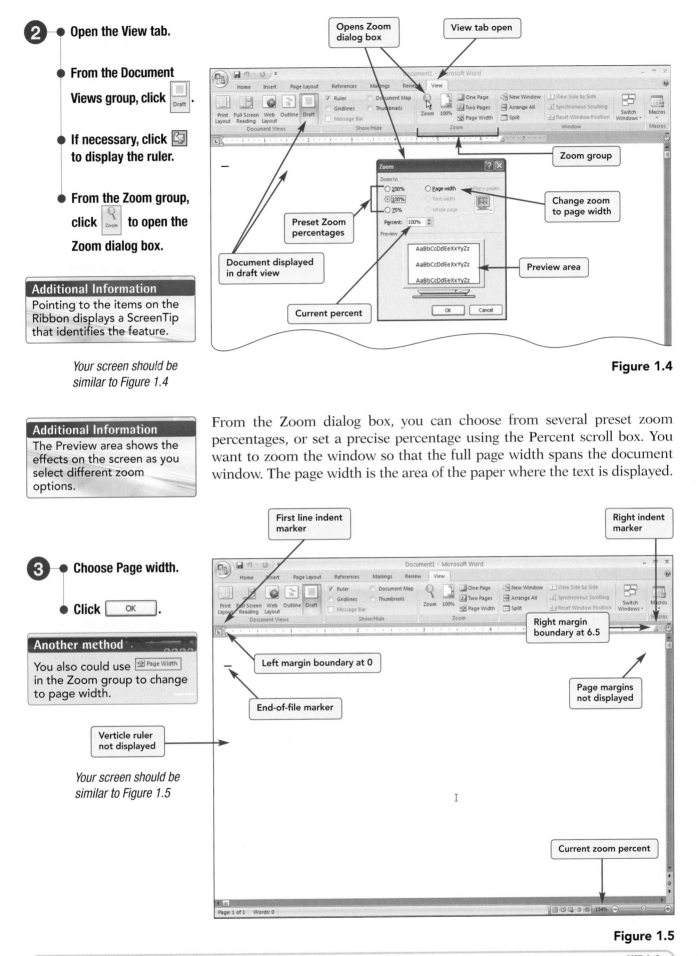

Opens Zoom dialog box

View tab open

Zoom group

Change zoom to page width

Preset Zoom percentages

Document displayed in draft view

Preview area

Current percent

**Figure 1.4**

From the Zoom dialog box, you can choose from several preset zoom percentages, or set a precise percentage using the Percent scroll box. You want to zoom the window so that the full page width spans the document window. The page width is the area of the paper where the text is displayed.

First line indent marker

Right indent marker

**3** • Choose Page width.

• Click [OK].

Right margin boundary at 6.5

Left margin boundary at 0

Page margins not displayed

End-of-file marker

Verticle ruler not displayed

*Your screen should be similar to Figure 1.5*

Current zoom percent

**Figure 1.5**

Viewing and Zooming a Document **WD1.9**

Increasing the zoom to page width increases the magnification to 154% and displays the full text area in the document window. In Draft view, the margins and the edges of the page are not displayed. This allows more space on the screen to display document content. This view also displays the **end-of-file marker**, the solid horizontal line that marks the last-used line in a document.

The ruler also displays other default settings. The symbol ▽ at the zero position is the first-line indent marker and marks the location of the left paragraph indent. The △ symbol on the right end of the ruler line at the 6.5-inch position marks the right paragraph indent. Currently, the indent locations are the same as the left and right margin settings.

# Creating New Documents

Your first project with Adventure Travel Tours is to create a flyer about four new tours. You will use the blank document to create the flyer for Adventure Travel Tours.

## Developing a Document

The development of a document follows several steps: plan, enter, edit, format, and preview and print.

| Step | Description |
|---|---|
| Plan | The first step in the development of a document is to understand the purpose of the document and to plan what your document should say. |
| Enter | After planning the document, you enter the content of the document by typing the text using the keyboard. Text also can be entered using the handwriting feature. |
| Edit | Making changes to your document is called **editing**. While typing, you probably will make typing and spelling errors that need to be corrected. This is one type of editing. Another is to revise the content that you have entered to make it clearer, or to add or delete information. |
| Format | Enhancing the appearance of the document to make it more readable or attractive is called **formatting**. This is usually performed when the document is near completion, after all editing and revising have been done. It includes many features such as boldfaced text, italics, and bulleted lists. |
| Preview and Print | The last step is to preview and print the document. When previewing, you check the document's overall appearance and make any final changes before printing. |

You will find that you will generally follow these steps in the order listed above for your first draft of a document. However, you will probably retrace steps such as editing and formatting as the final document is developed.

During the planning phase, you spoke with your manager regarding the purpose of the flyer and the content in general. The primary purpose of the flyer is to promote the new tours. A secondary purpose is to advertise the company in general.

You plan to include specific information about the new tours in the flyer as well as general information about Adventure Travel Tours. The content also needs to include information about the upcoming new tour presentations. Finally, you want to include information about the Adventure Travel Web site.

## Entering Text

Now that you understand the purpose of the flyer and have a general idea of the content, you are ready to enter the text.

Text is entered using the keyboard. As you type, you will probably make simple typing errors that you want to correct. Word includes many features that make entering text and correcting errors much easier. These features include checking for spelling and grammar errors, auto correction, and word wrap. You will see how these features work while entering the title and first paragraph of the flyer.

### Typing Text

To enter text in a new document, simply begin typing the text. The first line of the flyer will contain the text "Adventure Travel Tours New Adventures." As you begin to enter this line of text, include the intentional error identified in italic.

**1** ● Type Adventure **Traveel** (do not press space after typing the last letter).

*Your screen should be similar to Figure 1.6*

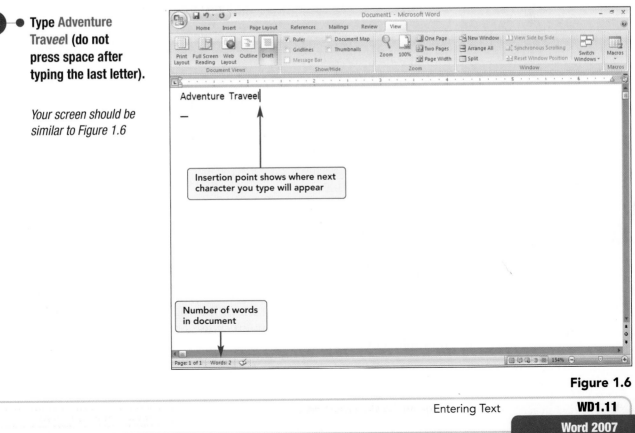

**Figure 1.6**

Notice that, as you type, the insertion point moves to the right and the character appears to the left of the insertion point. The location of the insertion point shows where the next character will appear as you type. Also, the status bar now tells you that there are two words in the document.

# Moving through Text

After text is entered into a document, you need to know how to move around within the text to correct errors or make changes. You see you have made a typing error by typing an extra e in the word travel. To correct this error, you first need to move the insertion point back to the correct position on the line. The keyboard or mouse can be used to move through the text in the document window. Depending on what you are doing, one method may be more efficient than another. For example, if your hands are already on the keyboard as you are entering text, it may be quicker to use the keyboard rather than take your hands off to use the mouse.

You use the mouse to move the insertion point to a specific location in a document simply by clicking on the location. When you can use the mouse to move the insertion point, it is shaped as an I-beam. However, when the mouse pointer is positioned in the unmarked area to the left of a line (the left margin), it changes to an arrow. When the mouse is in this area, it can be used to highlight (select) text.

You use the arrow keys located on the numeric keypad or the directional keypad to move the insertion point in a document. The keyboard directional keys are described in the following table.

| Key | Movement |
|---|---|
| → | One character to right |
| ← | One character to left |
| ↑ | One line up |
| ↓ | One line down |
| Ctrl + → | One word to right |
| Ctrl + ← | One word to left |
| Home | Beginning of line |
| End | End of line |

**1** ● **Press ← or position the I-beam between the e and l and click.**

The insertion point is positioned between the e and l.

Holding down a directional key or key combination moves quickly in the direction indicated, saving multiple presses of the key. Many of the Word insertion point movement keys can be held down to execute multiple moves.

## Using Backspace and Delete

Removing typing entries to change or correct them is one of the basic editing tasks. Corrections may be made in many ways. Two of the most important editing keys are the [Backspace] key and the [Delete] key. The [Backspace] key removes a character or space to the left of the insertion point. It is particularly useful when you are moving from right to left (backward) along a line of text. The [Delete] key removes the character or space to the right of the insertion point and is most useful when moving from left to right along a line.

You will correct the error and continue typing the first line.

**1** ● Press [Backspace] to remove the extra e.

● Press [→] or click at the end of the line.

● Press [Spacebar].

● **Type** Tours four new adventures **and correct any typing errors as you make them using** [Backspace] **or** [Delete]**.**

*Your screen should be similar to Figure 1.7*

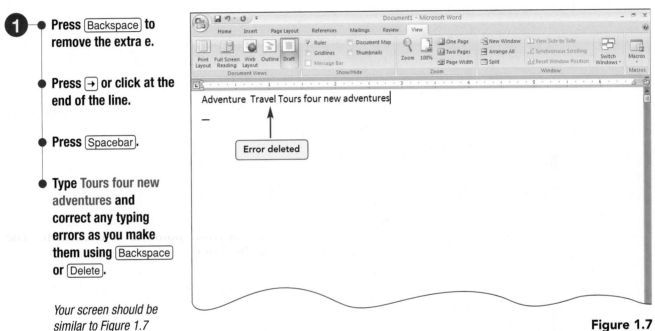

Figure 1.7

## Ending a Line and Inserting Blank Lines

Now you are ready to complete the first line of the announcement. To end a line and begin another line, you simply press [↵Enter]. The insertion point moves to the beginning of the next line. If you press [↵Enter] at the beginning of a line, a blank line is inserted into the document. If the insertion point is in the middle of a line of text and you press [↵Enter], all the text to the right of the insertion point moves to the beginning of the next line.

**1** ● **Press** ⏎Enter **3 times.**

*Your screen should be similar to Figure 1.8*

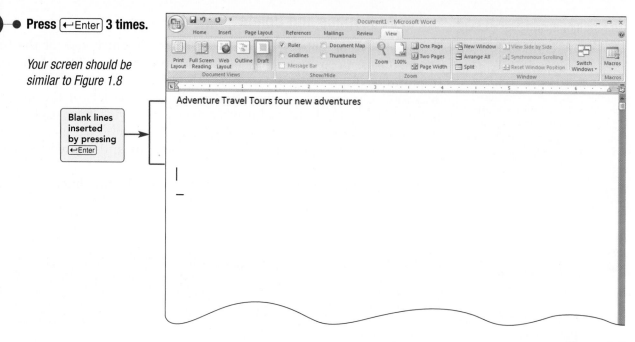

**Blank lines inserted by pressing** ⏎Enter

Adventure Travel Tours four new adventures

**Figure 1.8**

Pressing the first ⏎Enter ended the first line of text and inserted a blank line. The next two inserted blank lines.

## Revealing Formatting Marks

While you are creating your document, Word automatically inserts formatting marks that control the appearance of your document. These marks are not displayed automatically so that the document is not cluttered. Sometimes, however, it is helpful to view the underlying formatting marks. Displaying these marks makes it easy to see, for example, if you have added an extra space between words or at the end of a sentence.

**1** ● **Open the Home tab and click** ¶ **Show/Hide in the Paragraph group.**

**Another Method**

You also can use the keyboard shortcut Ctrl + * to display formatting marks.

*Your screen should be similar to Figure 1.9*

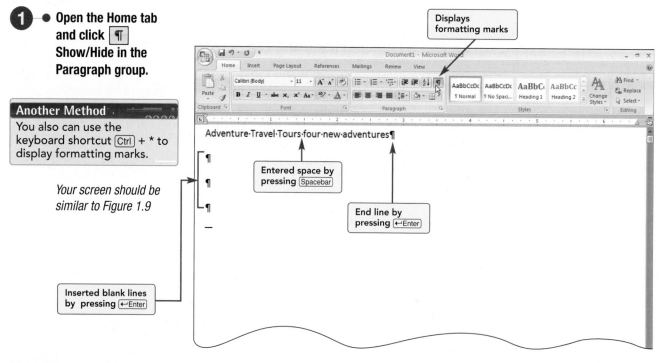

**Displays formatting marks**

Adventure·Travel·Tours·four·new·adventures¶

**Entered space by pressing** Spacebar

**End line by pressing** ⏎Enter

**Inserted blank lines by pressing** ⏎Enter

**Figure 1.9**

The document now displays the formatting marks. The ¶ character on the line above the insertion point represents the pressing of ←Enter that created the blank line. The ¶ character at the end of the text represents the pressing of ←Enter that ended the line and moved the insertion point to the beginning of the next line. Between each word, a dot shows where the Spacebar was pressed. Formatting marks do not appear when the document is printed. You can continue to work on the document while the formatting marks are displayed, just as you did when they were hidden.

You have decided you want the flyer heading to be on two lines, with the words "four new adventures" on the second line. To do this, you will insert a blank line after the word Tours. You will move the insertion point to the location in the text where you want to insert the blank line.

**2** ● Click on the right side of the "s" in "Tours" before the dot for a space.

● Press ←Enter 2 times.

● Press Delete to remove the space at the beginning of the line.

● Press ↓.

*Your screen should be similar to Figure 1.10*

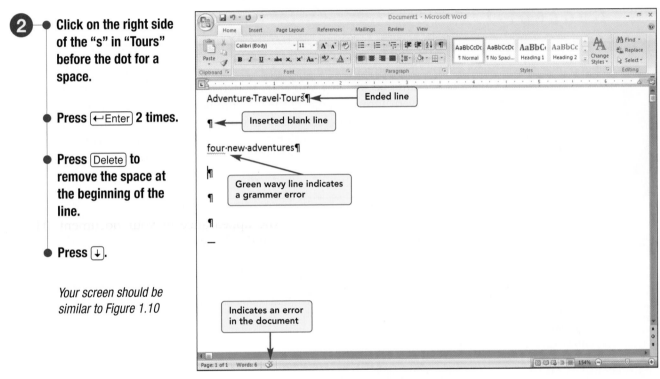

**Figure 1.10**

As you continue to create a document, the formatting marks are automatically adjusted.

## Identifying and Correcting Errors Automatically

Notice that a green wavy underline appears under the word "four." This indicates an error has been detected.

As you enter text, Word is constantly checking the document for spelling and grammar errors. The Spelling and Grammar Status icon in the status bar displays an animated pencil icon ✐ while you are typing, indicating Word is checking for errors as you type. When you stop typing, it displays either a blue checkmark, indicating the program does not detect any errors, or a red X, indicating the document contains an error.

**Having Trouble?**
If the green underline is not displayed, click ⊙ Office Button, click 🗐 Word Options, Proofing, and select the "Check spelling as you type", "Mark grammar errors as you type", and "Check grammar with spelling" options.

In many cases, Word will automatically correct errors for you. In other cases, it identifies the error by underlining it. The different colors and designs of underlines indicate the type of error that has been identified. In addition to identifying the error, Word provides suggestions as to the possible correction needed.

## Checking Grammar

In addition to the green wavy line under "four," the Spelling and Grammar Status icon appears as ⬚ in the status bar. This indicates that a spelling or grammar error has been located. The green wavy underline below the error indicates it is a grammar error.

---

## Concept 1

### Grammar Checker

**1**    The **grammar checker** advises you of incorrect grammar as you create and edit a document, and proposes possible corrections. Grammar checking occurs after you enter punctuation or end a line. If grammatical errors in subject-verb agreements, verb forms, capitalization, or commonly confused words, to name a few, are detected, they are identified with a wavy green line. You can correct the grammatical error by editing it or you can open the context menu for the identified error and display a suggested correction. Because not all identified grammatical errors are actual errors, you need to use discretion when correcting the errors.

---

**1** ● **Right-click the word "four" to open the context menu.**

**Having Trouble?**
Review context menus in the "Common Office 2007 Features" section (page I.15). If the wrong context menu appears, you probably did not have the I-beam positioned on the error with the green wavy line. Press [Esc] or click outside the menu to cancel it and try again.

*Your screen should be similar to Figure 1.11*

**Additional Information**
A dimmed menu option means it is currently unavailable.

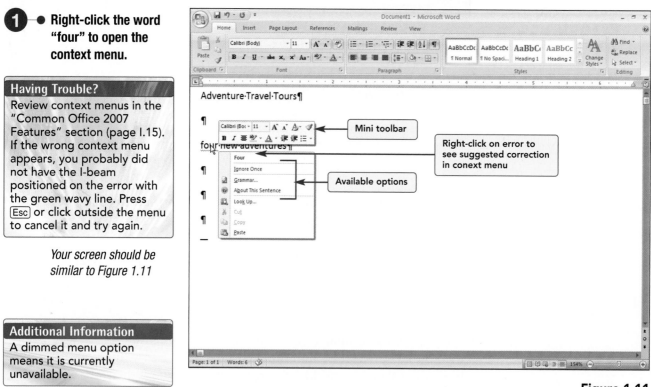

**Figure 1.11**

The Word Mini toolbar and a context menu containing commands related to the grammar error are displayed. The first item on the menu is the suggested correction, "Four." The grammar checker indicates you should capitalize the first letter of the word because it appears to be the beginning of a sentence. It also includes four available commands that are relevant to the item, described below.

| Command | Effect |
| --- | --- |
| Ignore Once | Instructs Word to ignore the grammatical error in this sentence. |
| Grammar | Opens the grammar checker and displays an explanation of the error. |
| About This Sentence | Provides help about the grammatical error. |
| Look up | Looks up word in dictionary. |

To make this correction, you could simply choose the correction from the menu and the correction would be inserted into the document. Although, in this case, you can readily identify the reason for the error, sometimes the reason is not so obvious. In those cases, you can open the grammar checker to find out more information.

**2** ● **Choose Grammar.**

*Your screen should be similar to Figure 1.12*

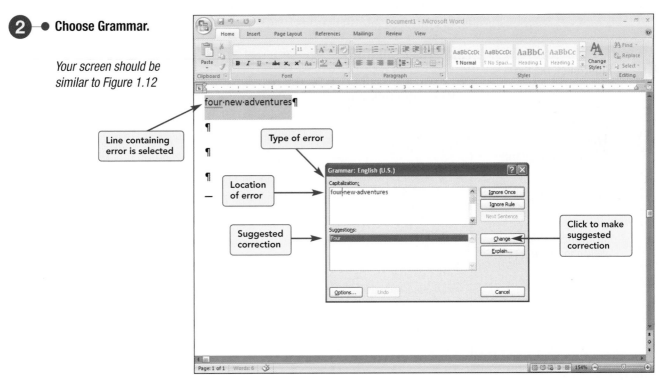

**Figure 1.12**

The Grammar dialog box identifies the type and location of the grammatical error in the upper text box and the suggested correction in the Suggestions box. The line in the document containing the error is also highlighted (selected) to make it easy for you to see the location of the error. You will make the suggested change.

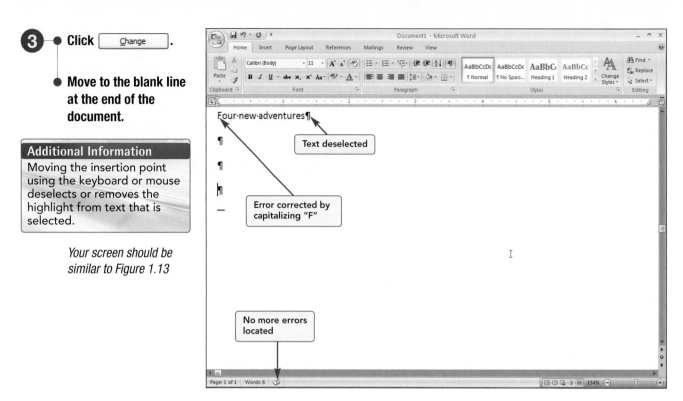

**③** ● Click [ _Change_ ].

● **Move to the blank line at the end of the document.**

**Additional Information**

Moving the insertion point using the keyboard or mouse deselects or removes the highlight from text that is selected.

*Your screen should be similar to Figure 1.13*

**Figure 1.13**

The error is corrected, the wavy green line is removed, and the Spelling and Grammar Status icon returns to .

## Checking Spelling

Now you are ready to type the text for the first paragraph of the flyer.

Enter the following text, including the intentional spelling errors.

**①** ● **Type Attention adventire travellars!**

● **Press** [Spacebar].

*Your screen should be similar to Figure 1.14*

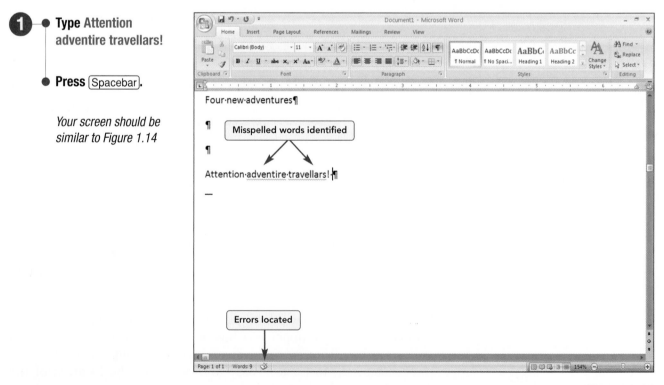

**Figure 1.14**

As soon as you complete a word by entering a space, the program checks the word for spelling accuracy.

## Concept 2

### Spelling Checker

**2** The **spelling checker** advises you of misspelled words as you create and edit a document, and proposes possible corrections. The spelling checker compares each word you type to a **main dictionary** of words supplied with the program. The main dictionary includes most common words. If the word does not appear in the main dictionary, it then checks the **custom dictionary**. The custom dictionary consists of a list of words such as proper names, technical terms, and so on, that are not in the main dictionary and that you want the spelling checker to accept as correct. Adding words to the custom dictionary prevents the flagging as incorrect of specialized words that you commonly use. Word shares custom dictionaries with other Microsoft Office applications such as PowerPoint.

If the word does not appear in either dictionary, the program identifies it as misspelled by displaying a red wavy line below the word. You can then correct the misspelled word by editing it. Alternatively, you can display a list of suggested spelling corrections for that word and select the correct spelling from the list to replace the misspelled word in the document.

Word automatically identified the two words "adventire travellars" as misspelled by underlining them with a wavy red line. The quickest way to correct a misspelled word is to select the correct spelling from a list of suggested spelling corrections displayed on the context menu.

**2** ● **Right-click on "adventire" to display the context menu.**

**Another Method**

You also can position the insertion point on the item you want to display a context menu for and press ⇧Shift + F10 to open the menu.

*Your screen should be similar to Figure 1.15*

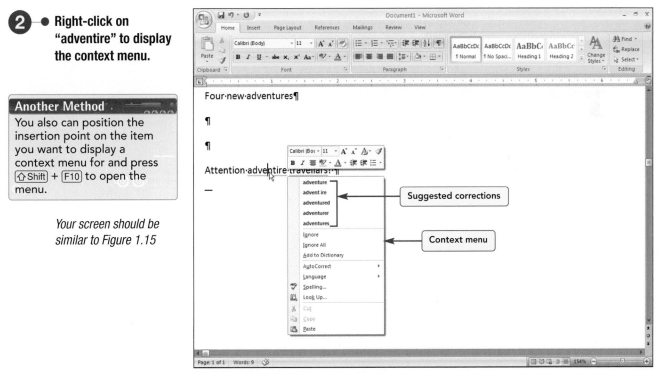

Figure 1.15

A context menu containing suggested correct spellings is displayed. The context menu also includes several related menu options, described in the following table.

| Option | Effect |
| --- | --- |
| Ignore | Instructs word to ignore the misspelling of this word for this occurrence only. |
| Ignore All | Instructs Word to ignore the misspelling of this word throughout the rest of this session. |
| Add to Dictionary | Adds the word to the custom dictionary list. When a word is added to the custom dictionary, Word will always accept that spelling as correct. |
| AutoCorrect | Adds the word to the AutoCorrect list so Word can correct misspellings of it automatically as you type. |
| Language | Sets the language format, such as French, English, or German, to apply to the word. |
| Spelling | Starts the spell-checking program to check the entire document. You will learn about this feature in Lab 2. |
| Look Up | Searches reference tools to locate similar words and definitions. |

Sometimes there are no suggested replacements because Word cannot locate any words in its dictionary that are similar in spelling; or the suggestions are not correct. If this occurs, you need to edit the word manually. In this case, the first suggestion is correct.

**3** ● **Choose "adventure".**

● **Correct the spelling for "travellars".**

*Your screen should be similar to Figure 1.16*

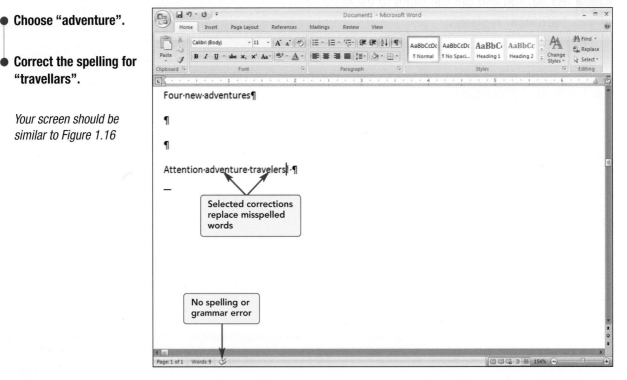

**Figure 1.16**

The spelling corrections you selected replace the misspelled words in the document. The Spelling and Grammar status icon returns to 🗹 , indicating that, as far as Word is able to detect, the document is free from errors.

## Using AutoCorrect

As you have seen, as soon as you complete a word by entering a space or punctuation, the program checks the word for grammar and spelling accuracy. Also, when you complete a sentence and start another, additional checks are made. Many spelling and grammar corrections are made automatically for you as you type. This is part of the AutoCorrect feature of Word.

### Concept 3
#### AutoCorrect

**3** The AutoCorrect feature makes some basic assumptions about the text you are typing and, based on these assumptions, automatically corrects the entry. The AutoCorrect feature automatically inserts proper capitalization at the beginning of sentences and in the names of days of the week. It also will change to lowercase letters any words that were incorrectly capitalized because of the accidental use of the ⇧ Shift key. In addition, it also corrects many common typing and spelling errors automatically.

One way the program automatically makes corrections is by looking for certain types of errors. For example, if two capital letters appear at the beginning of a word, Word changes the second capital letter to a lowercase letter. If a lowercase letter appears at the beginning of a sentence, Word capitalizes the first letter of the first word. If the name of a day begins with a lowercase letter, Word capitalizes the first letter. When Spelling Checker provides a single suggested spelling correction for the word, the program will automatically replace the incorrect spelling with the suggested replacement.

Another way the program makes corrections is by checking all entries against a built-in list of AutoCorrect entries. If it finds the entry on the list, the program automatically replaces the error with the correction. For example, the typing error "withthe" is automatically changed to "with the" because the error is on the AutoCorrect list. You also can add words to the AutoCorrect list that you want to be automatically corrected.

Enter the following text, including the errors (identified in italics).

**1** ● Press End to move to the end of the line.

● Type **attend a presentaation to lern aboutthe**

● Press Spacebar.

*Your screen should be similar to Figure 1.17*

**Having Trouble?**
The "Capitalize first letter of sentences" and "Replace text as you type" AutoCorrect features must be on. Use Office Button/ Word Options / Proofing/ AutoCorrect Options... and select these options if necessary.

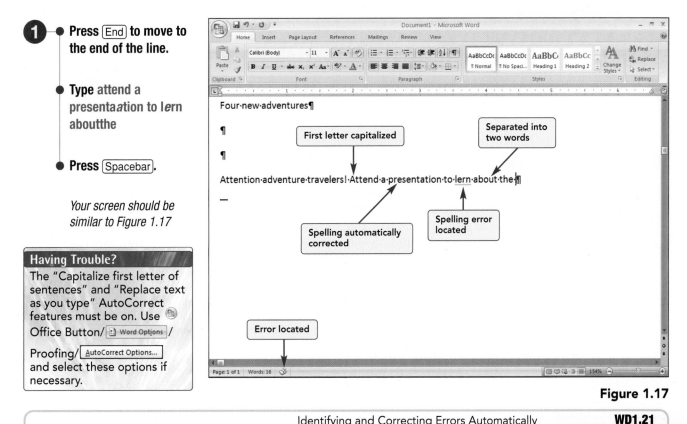

**Figure 1.17**

**MORE ABOUT**

➤ See 1.4 Personalize Office Word 2007, Customize Autocorrect Options in the More About appendix to learn how to customize the AutoCorrect feature.

The first letter of the word "attend" was automatically capitalized because, as you were typing, the program determined that it is the first word in a sentence. In a similar manner, it corrected the spelling of "presentation" and separated the words "about the" with a space. The AutoCorrect feature corrected the spelling of "presentation" because it was the only suggested correction for the word supplied by the Spelling Checker. The word "lern" was not corrected because there are several suggested spelling corrections.

When you rest the mouse pointer near text that has been corrected automatically or move the insertion point onto the word, a small blue box appears under the first character of the word. The blue box changes to the ⚡▾ AutoCorrect Options button when you point directly to it.

**2** ● Point to the word "Attend" to display the blue box.

**Having Trouble?**

If your screen does not display the blue box, click ⊕ Office Button, choose Proofing, AutoCorrect Options, and select the Show AutoCorrect Options buttons check box.

● Point to the blue box.

● Click ⚡▾ AutoCorrect Options.

*Your screen should be similar to Figure 1.18*

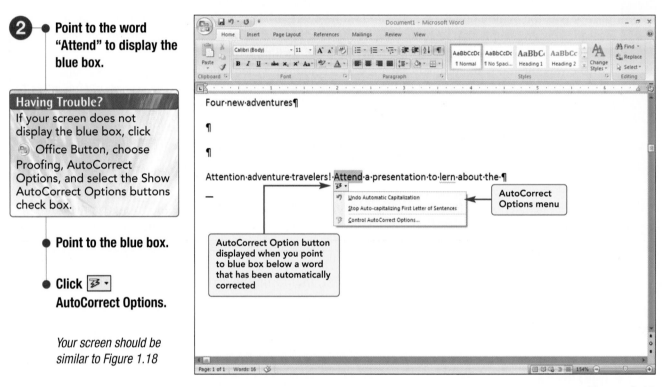

Figure 1.18

**Another Method**

Use ⊕ Office Button/ 📄 Word Options /Proofing/ AutoCorrect Options/ Exceptions to add a word to the exceptions list.

Each time Word uses the AutoCorrect feature, the AutoCorrect Options button is available. The AutoCorrect Options menu allows you to undo the AutoCorrection or to permanently disable the AutoCorrection for the remainder of your document. The Control AutoCorrect Options command is used to change the settings for this feature. In some cases, you may want to exclude a word from automatic correction. You can do this by adding the word to the exceptions list so the feature will be disabled for that word. If you use Backspace to delete an automatic correction and then type it again the way you want it to appear, the word will be automatically added to the exceptions list.

You want to keep all the AutoCorrections that were made and correct the spelling for "lern".

**3** ● Click outside the menu to close it.

● Open the spelling context menu for "lern" and choose "learn".

The spelling is corrected, and the spelling indicator in the status bar indicates that the document is free of errors.

## Using Word Wrap

Now you will continue entering more of the paragraph. As you type, when the text gets close to the right margin, do not press ←Enter to move to the next line. Word will automatically wrap words to the next line as needed.

### Concept 4

**Word Wrap**

**4** The **word wrap** feature automatically decides where to end a line and wrap text to the next line based on the margin settings. This feature saves time when entering text because you do not need to press ←Enter at the end of a full line to begin a new line. The only time you need to press ←Enter is to end a paragraph, to insert blank lines, or to create a short line such as a salutation. In addition, if you change the margins or insert or delete text on a line, the program automatically readjusts the text on the line to fit within the new margin settings. Word wrap is common to all word processors.

Enter the following text to complete the sentence.

**1** ● Press End to move to the end of the line.

● **Type** earth's greatest unspoiled habitats and find out how you can experience the adventure of a lifetime.

● Correct any spelling or grammar errors that are identified.

*Your screen should be similar to Figure 1.19*

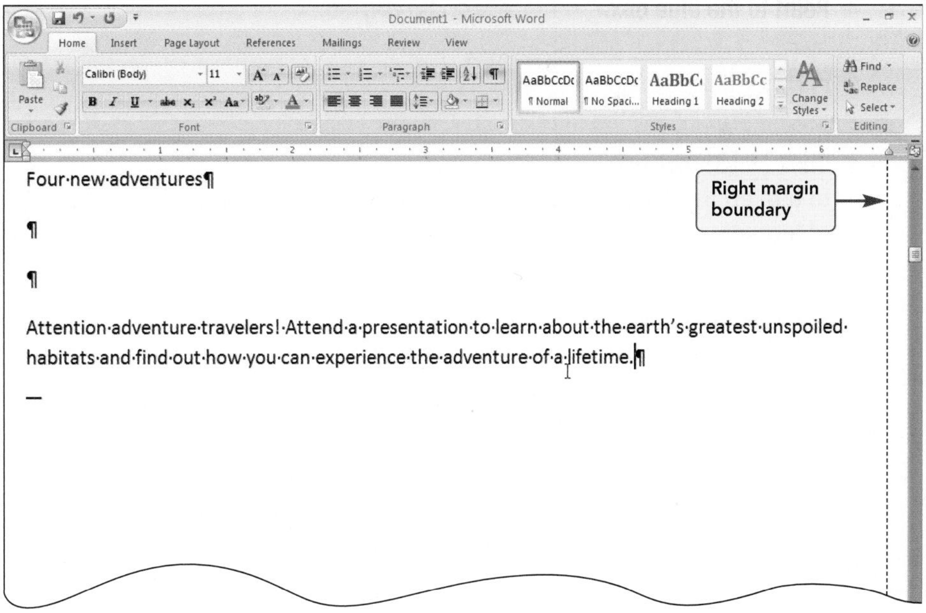

Four·new·adventures¶

¶

¶

Attention·adventure·travelers!·Attend·a·presentation·to·learn·about·the·earth's·greatest·unspoiled· habitats·and·find·out·how·you·can·experience·the·adventure·of·a·lifetime.¶

**Right margin boundary** →

**Figure 1.19**

**Additional Information**

Generally, when using a word processor, separate sentences with one space after a period rather than two spaces, which was common when typewriters were used.

The program has wrapped the text that would overlap the right margin to the beginning of the next line.

You have a meeting you need to attend in a few minutes and want to continue working on the document when you get back. You decide to add your name and the current date to the document. As you type the first four characters of the month, Word will recognize the entry as a month and display a ScreenTip suggesting the remainder of the month. You can insert the suggested month by pressing ←Enter. Then enter a space to continue the date and another ScreenTip will appear with the complete date. Press ←Enter again to insert it.

**Additional Information**

You can continue typing to ignore the date suggestion.

**2**

- **Move to the end of the sentence and press ←Enter twice.**
- **Type your name.**
- **Press ←Enter.**
- **Type the current date beginning with the month and when the ScreenTips appear for the month and the complete date, press ←Enter to insert them.**
- **Press ←Enter twice.**
- **Click ¶ Show/Hide to turn off the display of formatting marks.**

*Your screen should be similar to Figure 1.20*

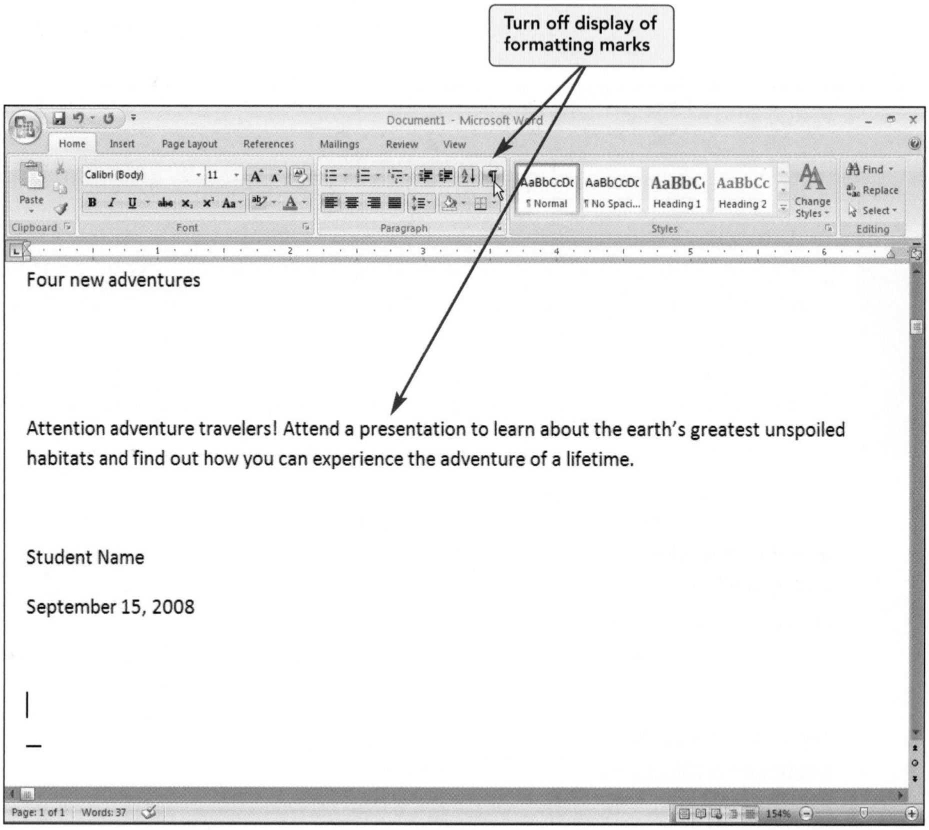


**Figure 1.20**

As you have seen, in many editing situations, it is helpful to display the formatting marks. However, for normal entry of text, you will probably not need the marks displayed. Now that you know how to turn this feature on and off, you can use it whenever you want when entering and editing text.

# Specifying Document Properties

In addition to the content of the document that you create, Word automatically includes details about the document that describe or identify it called **document properties**. Document properties include details such as title, author name, subject, and keywords that identify the document's topic or contents. Some of these properties are automatically generated. These include statistics such as the number of words in the file and general information such as the date the document was created and last modified. Others such as author name and keywords are properties that you can specify. By specifying relevant information as document properties, you can easily organize, identify, and search for your documents later.

## Modifying Document Properties

You will look at the document properties that are automatically included and add documentation to identify you as the author, and specify a document title and keywords to describe the document.

---

**1** ● Click 🗔 Office Button.

● Point to Prepare to select it and click on Properties in the submenu to choose it.

*Your screen should be similar to Figure 1.21*

Document information panel

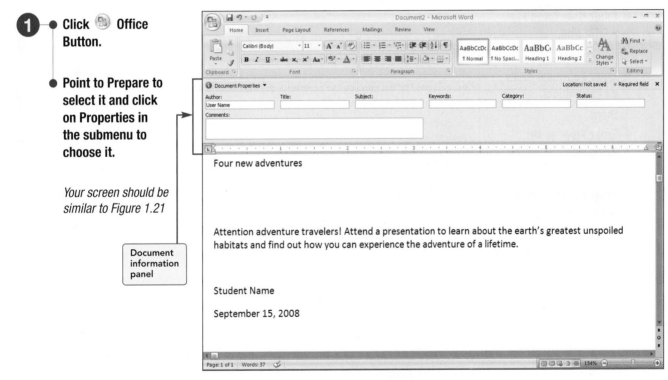

**Figure 1.21**

The Document Information Panel opens and displays the standard properties associated with the document. Most of these properties are blank waiting for you to specify your own information. The Author property may display the user name that is associated with the copy of Word you are using. You will change the author name to your name and add information to fill in the other standard properties.

**2**
- If necessary, select the existing text in the Author text box by triple-clicking on it.

**Additional Information**
You will learn all about selecting text shortly.

- Type **your name** in the Author text box.

- Enter **New Tours Flyer** as the title.

- Enter **Four new tours** as the subject.

- Enter **Flyer** as the keyword.

- Enter **Advertising** as the category.

- Enter **First Draft** as the status.

*Your screen should be similar to Figure 1.22*

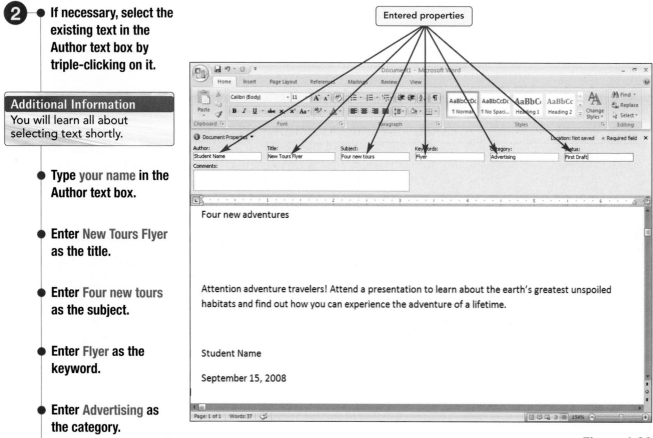

**Figure 1.22**

Next, you will quickly look at the additional information that is stored as document properties.

**Click** [Document Properties ▼] **and choose Advanced Properties from the menu.**

*Your screen should be similar to Figure 1.23*

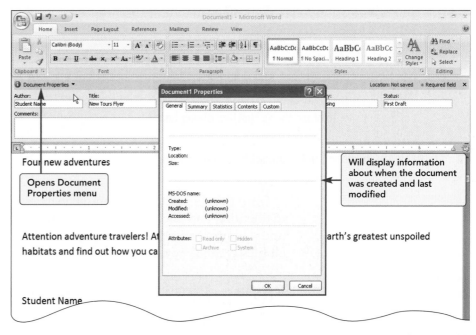

**Figure 1.23**

The General tab displays file system information about the type, location, and size of the document as well as information about when the document was created and modified. This information is automatically generated by the program. Because your document has not been saved yet, this information is blank. Next you will look at the document statistics.

**❹ ● Open the Statistics tab.**

*Your screen should be similar to Figure 1.24*

**Figure 1.24**

This tab includes revision information that identifies who last saved the document, the revision number, and the total editing time in minutes. The Statistics table shows the number of pages, words, lines, paragraphs, and so forth that are in the document. This information also is automatically generated and cannot be changed. The remaining three tabs—Contents, Custom, and Summary—include additional document property information.

You have added all the properties to the document that are needed at this time.

**5** ● Open the Contents, Custom, and Summary tabs to see the content.

● Click [ OK ] to close the Properties dialog box.

● Click [×] to close the Document Information Panel.

Once the standard document properties are specified, you can use them to identify and locate documents. You also can use the automatically updated properties for the same purpose. For example, you can search for all files created by a specified user or on a certain date.

## Saving, Closing, and Opening Files

Before leaving to attend your meeting, you want to save your work to a file. As you enter and edit text to create a new document, the changes you make are immediately displayed onscreen and are stored in your computer's memory. However, they are not permanently stored until you save your work to a file on a disk. After a document has been saved as a file, it can be closed and opened again at a later time to be edited further.

As a backup against the accidental loss of work from power failure or other mishap, Word includes an AutoRecover feature. When this feature is on, as you work you may see a pulsing disk icon briefly appear in the status bar. This icon indicates that the program is saving your work to a temporary recovery file. The time interval between automatic saving can be set to any period you specify; the default is every 10 minutes. After a problem has occurred, when you restart the program, the recovery file is automatically opened containing all changes you made up to the last time it was saved by AutoRecover. You then need to save the recovery file. If you do not save it, it is deleted when closed. AutoRecover is a great feature for recovering lost work but should not be used in place of regularly saving your work.

> **Additional Information**
>
> Use 🗐 Office Button/
> [🔲 Word Options] /Save/
> Save AutoRecover
> Information to set the
> AutoRecovery options.

### Saving a File

You will save the work you have done so far on the flyer. You can use the Save or Save As command on the 🗐 Office Button File menu to save files.

The Save command or the 🖫 Save button on the Quick Access Toolbar will save the active file using the same file name by replacing the contents of the existing disk file with the document as it appears on your screen. The Save As command is used to save a file using a new file name or to a new location. This leaves the original file unchanged. When you create a new document, you can use either of the Save commands to save your work to a file on the disk. It is especially important to save a new document very soon after you create it because the AutoRecover feature does not work until a file name has been specified.

**1** ● Click  Save in the Quick Access Toolbar.

**Another Method**
The keyboard shortcut is Ctrl + S.

*Your screen should be similar to Figure 1.25*

**Having Trouble?**
In Windows Vista, the Save As dialog box layout will be different; however, the same information is displayed.

**Additional Information**
Depending on the dialog box view, the files may be displayed differently and file details such as the size, type, and date modified may be listed.

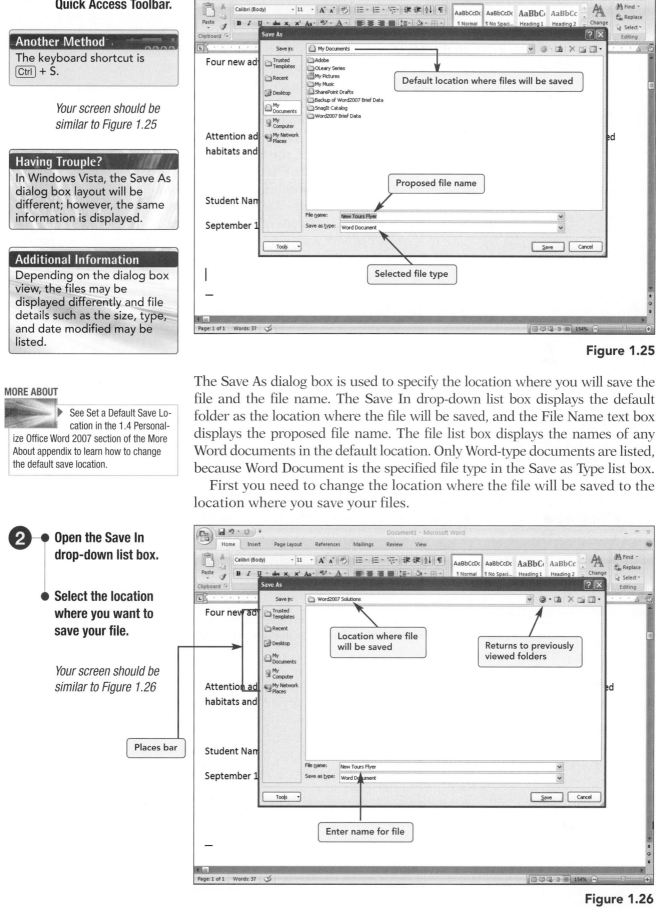

**Figure 1.25**

**MORE ABOUT**

▶ See Set a Default Save Location in the 1.4 Personalize Office Word 2007 section of the More About appendix to learn how to change the default save location.

The Save As dialog box is used to specify the location where you will save the file and the file name. The Save In drop-down list box displays the default folder as the location where the file will be saved, and the File Name text box displays the proposed file name. The file list box displays the names of any Word documents in the default location. Only Word-type documents are listed, because Word Document is the specified file type in the Save as Type list box.

First you need to change the location where the file will be saved to the location where you save your files.

**2** ● Open the Save In drop-down list box.

● Select the location where you want to save your file.

*Your screen should be similar to Figure 1.26*

**Figure 1.26**

Now the large list box displays the names of all Word files, if any, at that location. You also can select the location to save your file from the Places bar along the left side of the dialog box. The icons bring up a list of recently accessed files and folders (My Recent Documents), the contents of the My Documents folder, items on the Windows desktop, and the locations on your computer or on a network. You also can click the ⊕ button in the toolbar to return to folders that were previously opened.

Next, you need to enter a file name and specify the file type. The File Name box displays the default file name, consisting of the first few words from the document. The Save as Type box displays "Word Document" as the default format in which the file will be saved. Word 2007 documents are identified by the file extension .docx. The file type you select determines the file extension that will be automatically added to the file name when the file is saved. The default extension .docx saves the file in XML format. Previous versions of Word used the .doc file extension. If you plan to share a file with someone using Word 2003 or earlier, you can save the document using the .doc file type; however, some features may be lost. Otherwise, if you save it as a .docx file type, the recipient may not be able to view all features.

You will change the file name to Flyer and use the default document type (.docx).

**3** ● Triple-click in the File Name text box to highlight the proposed file name.

● Type **Flyer**.

● Click ⬚ Save ⬚.

*Your screen should be similar to Figure 1.27*

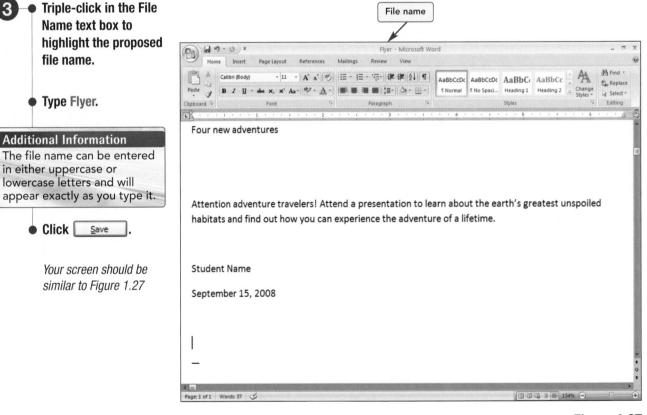

Figure 1.27

The document is saved as Flyer.docx at the location you selected, and the new file name is displayed in the Word title bar.

## Closing a File

Finally, you want to close the document while you attend your meeting.

**1** ● Click  Office Button and choose Close.

*Your screen should be similar to Figure 1.28*

Empty document window

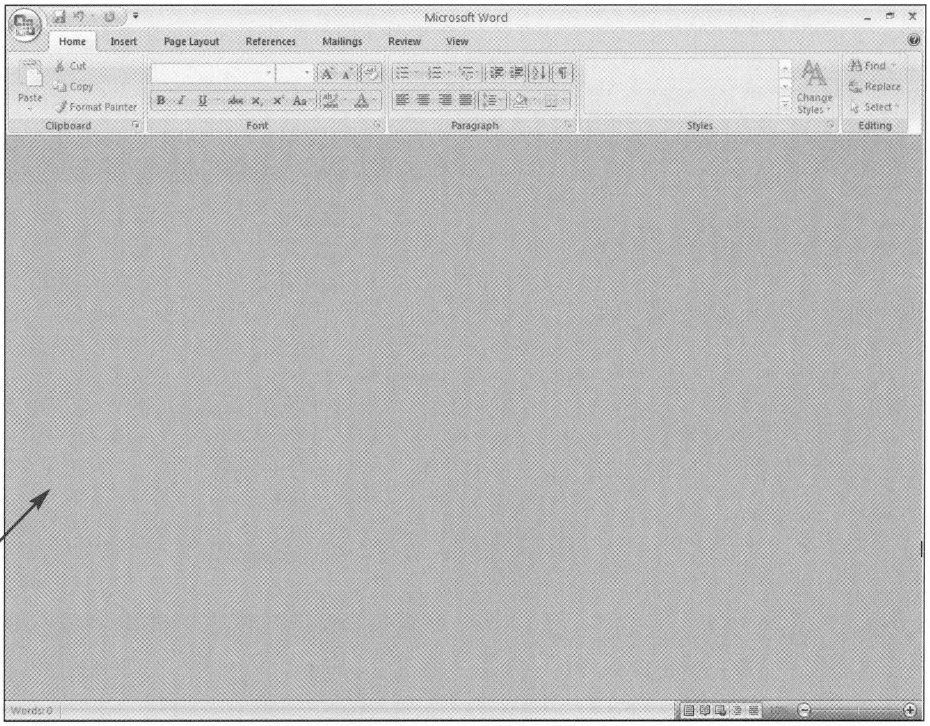

Figure 1.28

Now the Word window displays an empty document window. Because you did not make any changes to the document since saving it, the document window closed immediately. If you had made additional changes, the program would ask whether you wanted to save the file before closing it. This prevents the accidental closing of a file that has not been saved first.

## Opening a File

You asked your assistant to enter the remaining information in the flyer for you while you attended the meeting. Upon your return, you find a note from your assistant on your desk. The note explains that he had a little trouble entering the information and tells you that he saved the revised file as Flyer1. You want to open the file and continue working on the flyer.

**1** ● Click ⊞ **Office Button and choose Open.**

**Another Method**
The keyboard shortcut is
Ctrl + O.

**Having Trouble?**
In Windows Vista, the Open dialog box layout will be different; however, the same information will be displayed.

*Your screen should be similar to Figure 1.29*

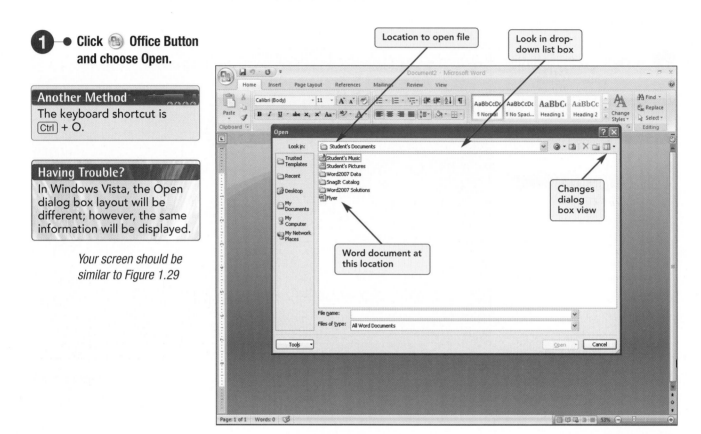

Figure 1.29

**Additional Information**
You can display a preview of the first page of a selected file by choosing Preview from the Views menu.

In the Open dialog box, you specify the location and name of the file you want to open. The current location is the location you last used when you saved the flyer document. As in the Save As dialog box, the Look In drop-down list box displays folders and document files at this location. You will need to change the location to the location containing your data files.

● **Select the location containing your data files from the Look In drop-down list box.**

● **Select** wd01_Flyer1.

● **Open the ▦▾ Views drop-down list.**

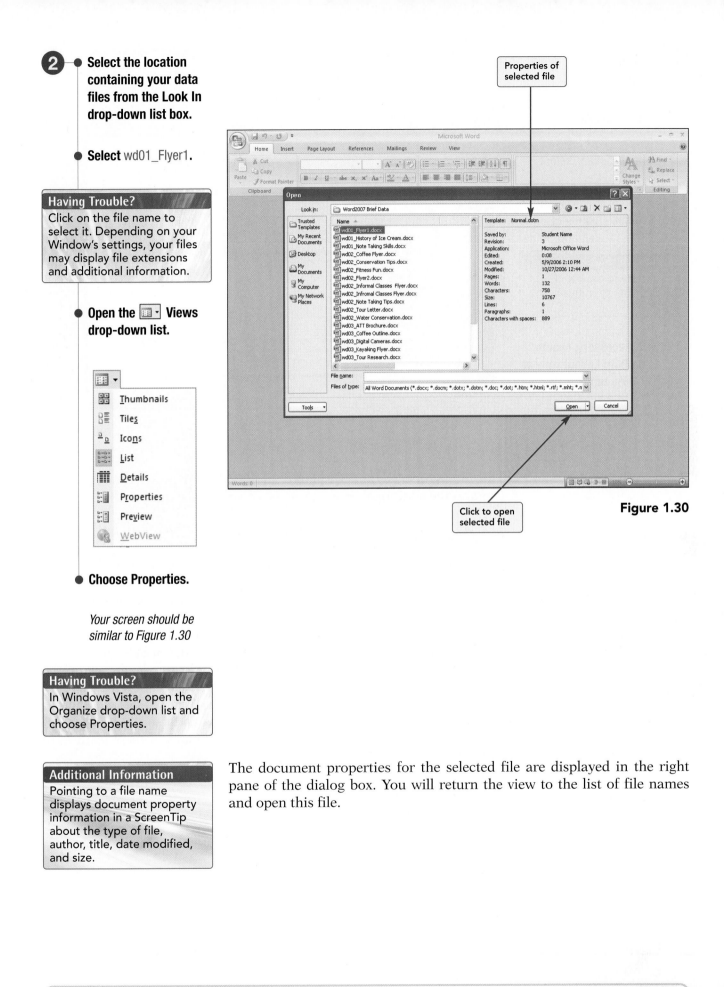

**Figure 1.30**

Properties of selected file

Click to open selected file

● **Choose Properties.**

*Your screen should be similar to Figure 1.30*

The document properties for the selected file are displayed in the right pane of the dialog box. You will return the view to the list of file names and open this file.

**3** ● Open the 🖳 ▾ **Views drop-down list.**

● **Choose List.**

● **If necessary, select** wd01_Flyer1.

● **Click** [ Open ▾ ].

**Another Method**

You also could double-click the file name to both select and open it.

● **If necessary, change to Print Layout view at 100% zoom.**

*Your screen should be similar to Figure 1.31*

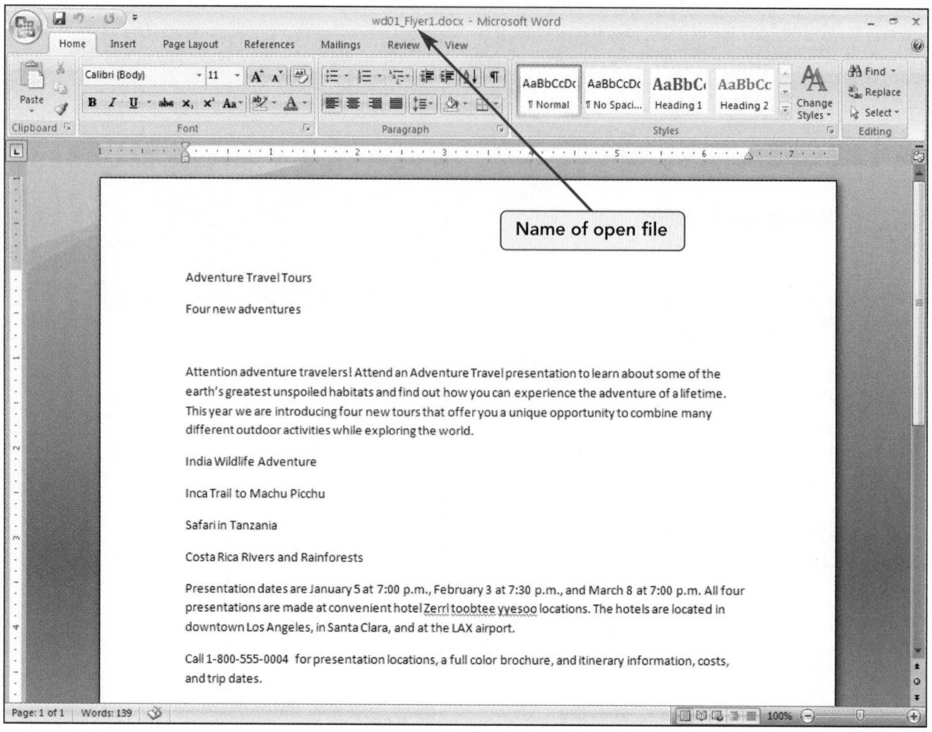

Name of open file

**Figure 1.31**

The file is opened and displayed in the document window. This file contains the additional content you asked your assistant to add to the flyer.

# Navigating a Document

As documents increase in size, they cannot be easily viewed in their entirety in the document window and much time can be spent moving to different locations in the document. Word includes many features that make it easy to move around in a large document. The basic method is to scroll through a document using the scroll bar or keyboard. Another method is to move directly to a page or other identifiable item in the document, such as a table. You also can quickly return to a previous location, or browse through a document to a previous page or item.

Other features that help move through a large document include searching the document to locate specific items and using the Document Map or a table of contents. You will learn about many of these features in later labs.

## Scrolling a Document

Now that more information has been added to the document, the document window is no longer large enough to display the entire document. To bring additional text into view in the window, you can scroll the document using either the scroll bars or the keyboard. Again, both methods are useful, depending on what you are doing. The tables below explain the mouse and keyboard techniques that can be used to scroll a document.

| Mouse | Action |
|---|---|
| Click ▼ | Moves down line by line. |
| Click ▲ | Moves up line by line. |
| Click above/below scroll box | Moves up/down window by window. |
| Drag scroll box | Moves up/down quickly through document. |
| Click ⬆ | Moves to top of previous page. |
| Click ⬇ | Moves to top of next page. |
| Click ⦿ Select Browse Object | Changes how you want the ⬆ and ⬇ buttons to browse through a document, such as by table or graphic. The default setting is by page. |

| Key | Action |
|---|---|
| ↓ | Down line by line |
| ↑ | Up line by line |
| Page Up | Top of window |
| Page Down | Bottom of window |
| Ctrl + Home | Beginning of document |
| Ctrl + End | End of document |

You will use the vertical scroll bar to view the text at the bottom of the flyer. When you use the scroll bar to scroll, the insertion point does not move. To move the insertion point, you must click in a location in the window.

**1**
- Click ⬇ in the vertical scroll bar 12 times.

- Click anywhere in the last line to move the insertion point.

*Your screen should be similar to Figure 1.32*

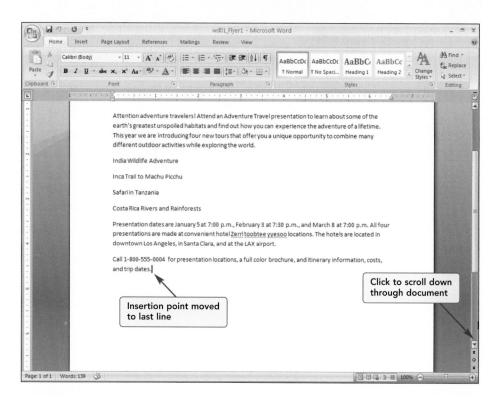

**Click to scroll down through document**

**Insertion point moved to last line**

**Figure 1.32**

**Having Trouble?**
If your screen scrolls differently, this is a function of the type of monitor you are using.

The text at the beginning of the flyer has scrolled off the top of the document window, and the text at the bottom of the flyer is now displayed.

You also can scroll the document using the keyboard. While scrolling using the keyboard, the insertion point also moves. The insertion point attempts to maintain its position in a line as you scroll up and down through the document. In a large document, scrolling line by line can take a while. You will now try out several of the mouse and keyboard scrolling features that move by larger jumps.

**2**
- Hold down ↑ for several seconds until the insertion point is on the first line of the flyer.

- Click below the scroll box in the scroll bar.

- Drag the scroll box to the top of the scroll bar.

- Press Ctrl + End.

*Your screen should be similar to Figure 1.33*

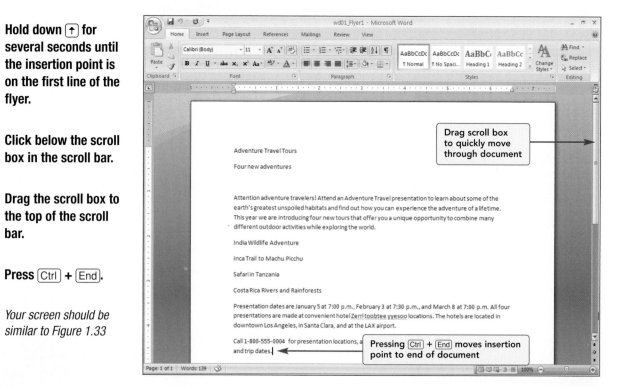

**Drag scroll box to quickly move through document**

**Pressing Ctrl + End moves insertion point to end of document**

**Figure 1.33**

The insertion point is now at the end of the document. Using these features makes scrolling a large document much more efficient. Remember that when scrolling using the mouse, if you want to start working at that location, you must click at the new location to move the insertion point.

# Editing Documents

While entering text and creating a document, you will find that you will want to edit or make changes and corrections to the document. Although many of the errors are identified and corrections are made automatically for you, others must be made manually. You learned how to use the [Backspace] and [Delete] keys earlier to correct errors. But deleting characters one at a time can be time consuming. Now you will learn about several additional editing features that make editing your work more efficient.

After entering the text of a document, you should proofread it for accuracy and completeness and edit the document as needed. After looking over the flyer, you have identified several errors that need to be corrected and changes you want to make to the content. The changes you want to make are shown below.

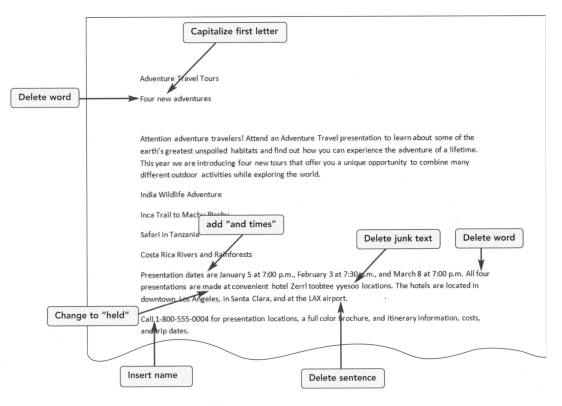

## Inserting Text

As you check the document, you see that the first sentence of the paragraph below the list of trips is incorrect. It should read: "Presentation dates and times are . . . " The sentence is missing the words "and times." In addition, you want to change the word "made" to "held" in the following sentence. These words can easily be entered into the sentence without retyping the entire line. This is because Word uses **Insert mode** to allow new characters to be inserted into the existing text by moving the existing text to the right to make space for the new characters. You will insert the words "and times" after the word "dates" in the first sentence.

- **Press** Ctrl + Home **to move to the top of the document.**

- **Move to "a" in "are" in the first sentence of the paragraph below the list of tours.**

**Additional Information**

Throughout these labs, when instructed to move to a specific letter in the text, this means to move the insertion point to the left side of the character.

- **Type** and times.

- **Press** Spacebar.

*Your screen should be similar to Figure 1.34*

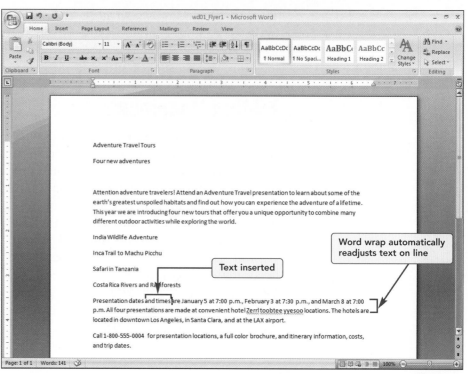

Figure 1.34

The inserted text pushes the existing text on the line to the right, and the word wrap feature automatically readjusts the text on the line to fit within the margin settings.

## Selecting and Replacing Text

In the second sentence, you want to change the word "made" to "held." You could delete this word and type in the new word, or you can select the text and type the new text. Text that is selected is highlighted.

To select text using the mouse, first move the insertion point to the beginning or end of the text to be selected, and then drag to highlight the text you want selected. You can select as little as a single letter or as much as the entire document. You can quickly select a standard block of text. Standard blocks include a sentence, paragraph, page, tabular column, rectangular portion of text, or the entire document. The following tables summarize the mouse and keyboard techniques used to select standard blocks.

**Additional Information**

You can replace existing text using Overtype mode, in which each character you type replaces an existing character. This feature is turned on using  Office Button/ Word Options /Advanced/Use overtype mode.

| To Select | Mouse |
|---|---|
| Word | Double-click in the word. |
| Sentence | Press [Ctrl] and click within the sentence. |
| Line | Click to the left of a line when the mouse pointer is 𝌏. |
| Multiple lines | Drag up or down to the left of a line when the mouse pointer is 𝌏. |
| Paragraph | Triple-click on the paragraph or double-click to the left of the paragraph when the mouse pointer is 𝌏. |
| Multiple paragraphs | Drag to the left of the paragraphs when the mouse pointer is 𝌏. |
| Document | Triple-click or press [Ctrl] and click to the left of the text when the mouse pointer is 𝌏. |

| To Select | Keyboard |
|---|---|
| Next space or character | [⇧Shift] + [→] |
| Previous space or character | [⇧Shift] + [←] |
| Next word | [Ctrl] + [⇧Shift] + [→] |
| Previous word | [Ctrl] + [⇧Shift] + [←] |
| Text going backward to beginning of paragraph | [Ctrl] + [⇧Shift] + [↑] |
| Text going forward to end of paragraph | [Ctrl] + [⇧Shift] + [↓] |
| Entire document | [Ctrl] + A |

To remove highlighting to deselect text, simply click anywhere in the document or press any directional key.

**1** ● **Double click on "made".**

*Your screen should be similar to Figure 1.35*

**Figure 1.35**

Text that is selected can be modified using many different Word features. The Mini toolbar appears automatically when text is selected and the mouse pointer is pointing to the selection. You will learn about using this feature shortly. In this case, you want to replace the selected text with new text.

**2** ● **Type held.**

*Your screen should be similar to Figure 1.36*

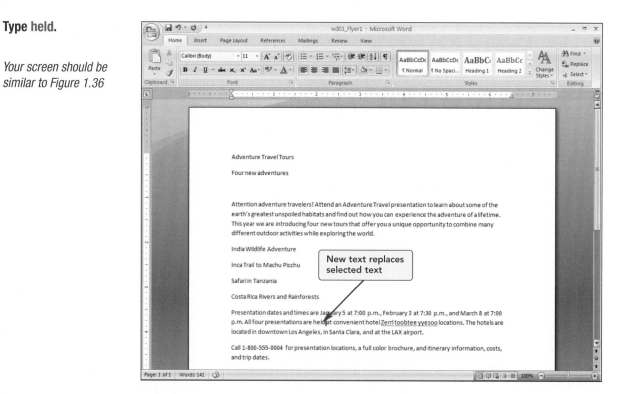

**Figure 1.36**

As soon as you began typing, the selected text was automatically deleted. The new text was inserted in the line just like any other text.

## Deleting a Word

You next want to delete the word "four" from the same sentence. The Ctrl + Delete key combination deletes text to the right of the insertion point to the beginning of the next group of characters. In order to delete an entire word, you must position the insertion point at the beginning of the word.

**1** ● **Move to "f" in "four" in the same sentence.**

● **Press** Ctrl + Delete.

*Your screen should be similar to Figure 1.37*

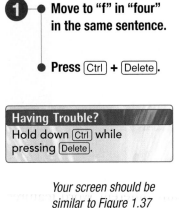

Figure 1.37

The word "four" has been deleted.

## Selecting and Deleting Text

As you continue proofreading the flyer, you see that the end of this sentence contains a section of junk characters. To remove these characters, you could use Delete and Backspace to delete each character individually, or Ctrl + Delete or Ctrl + Backspace to delete each word or group of characters. This is very slow, however. Several characters, words, or lines of text can be deleted at once by first selecting the text and then pressing Delete.

The section of characters you want to remove follows the word "hotel" in the second line of the paragraph below the list of trips. You also decide to delete the entire last sentence of the paragraph.

**1** • Move to "Z" (following the word "hotel").

• Drag to the right until all the text including the space before the word "locations" is highlighted.

• Press [Delete].

• Hold down [Ctrl] and click anywhere in the third sentence of the paragraph below the list of trips.

• Press [Delete].

*Your screen should be similar to Figure 1.38*

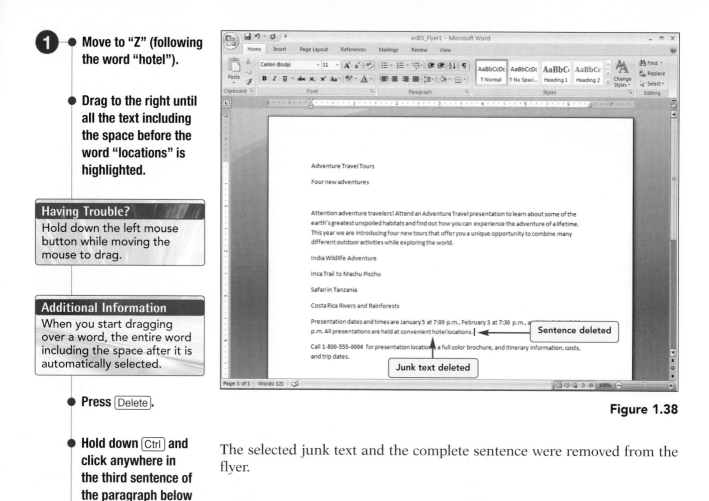

**Figure 1.38**

The selected junk text and the complete sentence were removed from the flyer.

## Undoing Editing Changes

After removing the sentence, you decide it may be necessary after all. To quickly restore this sentence, you can use [↺] Undo to reverse your last action or command.

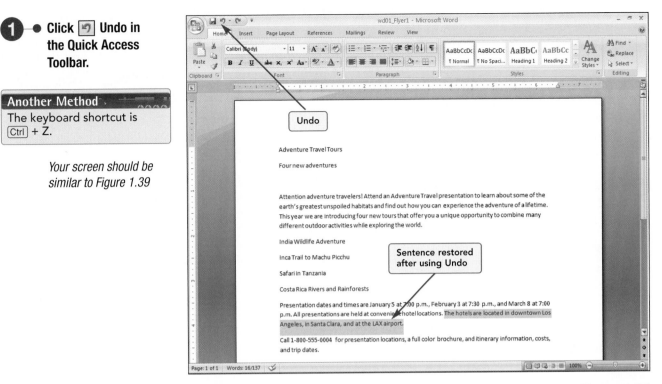

**Figure 1.39**

Undo returns your last deletion and restores it to its original location in
the text, regardless of the current insertion point location. Notice that the
Undo button includes a drop-down list button. Clicking this button
displays a list of the most recent actions that can be reversed, with the
most recent action at the top of the list. When you select an action from
the drop-down list, you also undo all actions above it in the list.

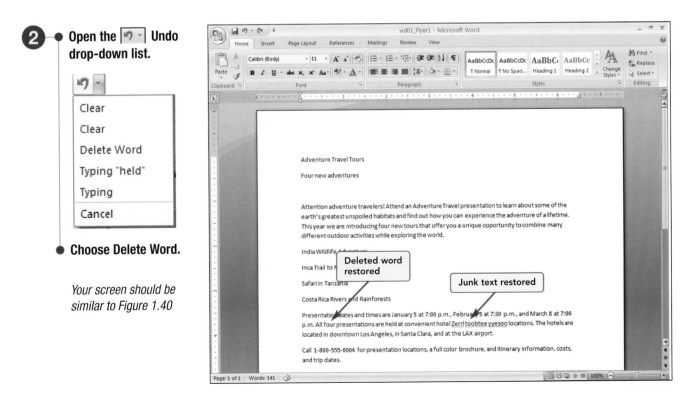

**Figure 1.40**

The junk characters and the word "four" are restored. Immediately after you undo an action, the 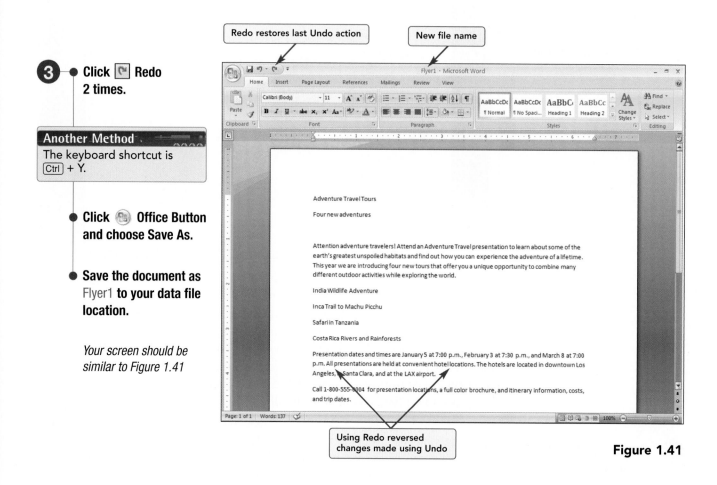 Redo button is available so you can restore the action you just undid. You will restore your corrections and then save the changes you have made to the document to a new file.

**3** ● Click 🔄 Redo 2 times.

**Another Method**
The keyboard shortcut is Ctrl + Y.

● Click 🔘 Office Button and choose Save As.

● Save the document as Flyer1 to your data file location.

*Your screen should be similar to Figure 1.41*

Redo restores last Undo action

New file name

Using Redo reversed changes made using Undo

**Figure 1.41**

Repeatedly using the 🔄 Undo or 🔄 Redo buttons performs the actions in the list one by one. So that you can see what action will be performed, these button's ScreenTips identify the action.

The new file name, Flyer1, is displayed in the window title bar. The original document file, wd01_Flyer 1 is unchanged.

## Changing Case

You also want to delete the word "Four" from the second line of the flyer title and capitalize the first letter of each word. Although you could change the case individually for the words, you can quickly change both using the Change Case command in the Font group.

**1** ● **Move the insertion point to the beginning of the word "Four".**

● **Press** Ctrl + Delete.

● **Click in the left margin to select the entire title line.**

● **From the Font group, click** Aa˅ **Change Case.**

*Your screen should be similar to Figure 1.42*

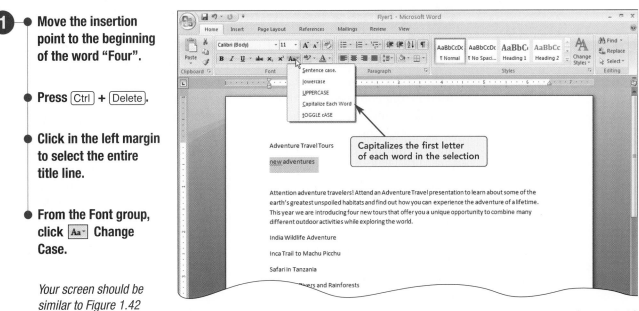

**Figure 1.42**

The Change Case drop-down menu allows you to change the case of selected words and sentences to the desired case without having to make the change manually. You want both words in the title to be capitalized.

**2** ● **Select Capitalize Each Word.**

● **Click anywhere to deselect the title line.**

*Your screen should be similar to Figure 1.43*

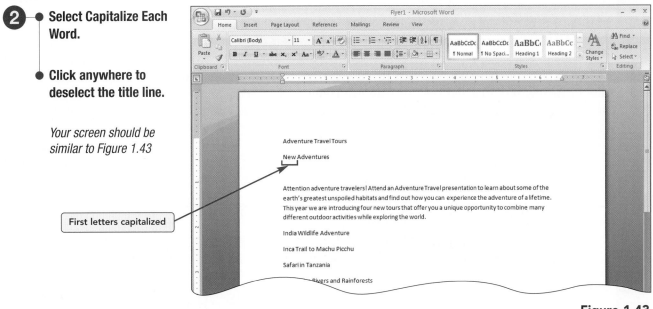

**Figure 1.43**

**Additional Information**
You also can use ⇧Shift + F3 to cycle through and apply the different change case options.

The first letter of each word in the title is now capitalized and the highlight is removed from the text.

# Formatting a Document

Because this document is a flyer, you want it to be easy to read and interesting to look at. Applying different formatting to characters and paragraphs can greatly enhance the appearance of the document. **Character formatting** consists of formatting features that affect the selected characters only. This includes changing the character style and size, applying effects such as bold and italics to characters, changing the character spacing, and adding animated text effects. **Paragraph formatting** features affect an entire paragraph. A paragraph consists of all text up to and including the paragraph mark. Paragraph formatting features include how the paragraph is positioned or aligned between the margins, paragraph indentation, spacing above and below a paragraph, and line spacing within a paragraph.

## Changing Fonts and Font Sizes

The first formatting change you want to make is to use different fonts and font sizes in the flyer.

## Concept 5

### Font and Font Size

5   A **font**, also commonly referred to as a **typeface**, is a set of characters with a specific design. The designs have names such as Times New Roman and Courier. Using fonts as a design element can add interest to your document and give readers visual cues to help them find information quickly.

Two basic types of fonts are serif and sans serif. **Serif fonts** have a flair at the base of each letter that visually leads the reader to the next letter. Two common serif fonts are Roman and Times New Roman. Serif fonts generally are used for text in paragraphs. **Sans serif fonts** do not have a flair at the base of each letter. Arial and Helvetica are two common sans serif fonts. Because sans serif fonts have a clean look, they are often used for headings in documents. A good practice is to use only two types of fonts in a document, one for text and one for headings. Using too many different font styles can make your document look cluttered and unprofessional.

Each font has one or more sizes. **Font size** is the height and width of the character and is commonly measured in points, abbreviated "pt." One point equals about 1/72 inch, and text in most documents is 10 pt or 12 pt.

Several common fonts in different sizes are shown in the table below.

| Font Name | Font Type | Font Size |
|---|---|---|
| Arial | Sans serif | This is 10 pt. <br> This is 16 pt. |
| Courier New | Serif | This is 10 pt. <br> This is 16 pt. |
| Times New Roman | Serif | This is 10 pt. <br> This is 16 pt. |

To change the font before typing the text, use the command and then type. All text will appear in the specified setting until another font setting is selected. To change a font setting for existing text, select the text you want to change and then use the command. If you want to apply font formatting to a word, simply move the insertion point to the word and the formatting is automatically applied to the entire word.

First you want to increase the font size of all the text in the flyer to make it easier to read. Currently, you can see from the Font Size button in the Font group that the font size is 11 points.

● **Triple-click in the left margin when the mouse pointer is ⌐ to select the entire document.**

**Having Trouble?**
The left margin is the white space to the left of the text.

**Another Method**
The keyboard shortcut is Ctrl + A.

● **From the Font group, open the 11 Font Size drop-down list.**

**Another Method**
The keyboard shortcut is Ctrl + ⇧Shift + P.

*Your screen should be similar to Figure 1.44*

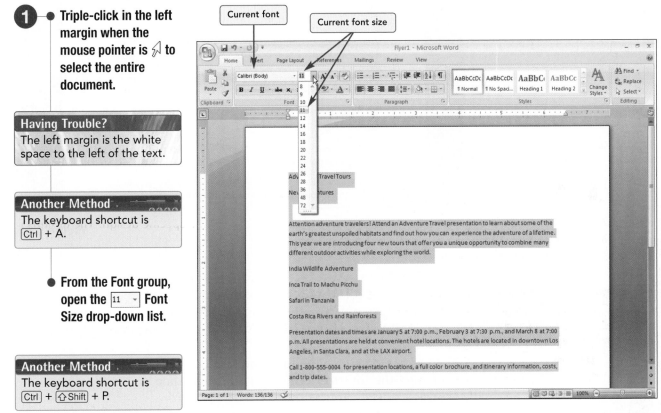

**Figure 1.44**

The current (default) font size of 11 is selected. You will increase the font size to 14 points. As you point to the size options, the selected text in the document displays how it will appear if chosen. This is the **Live Preview** feature of Word.

**2** ● **Point to several different point sizes in the list to see the Live Preview.**

● **Click 14 to choose it.**

*Your screen should be similar to Figure 1.45*

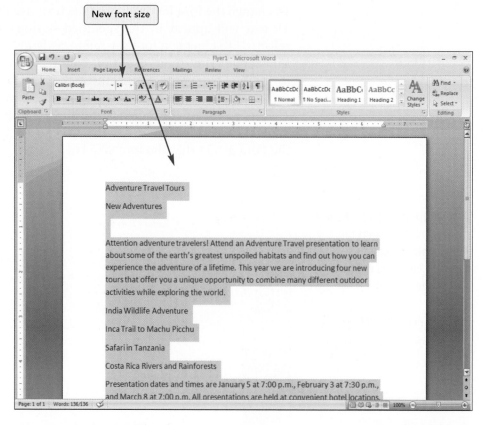

New font size

Figure 1.45

---

The font size of all text in the document has increased to 14 points, making the text much easier to read. The Font Size button displays the new point size setting for the text at the location of the insertion point.

Next you will change the font and size of the two title lines. First you will change the font to Comic Sans MS and then you will increase the font size.

Many of the formatting commands are on the Mini toolbar that appears whenever you select text. The Mini toolbar appears dimmed until you point to it. This is so it is not distracting as you are using features that are not available on the Mini toolbar. To use the Mini toolbar, just point to it to make it solid and choose command buttons just as you would from the Ribbon.

**3** ● Select the two title lines and point to the Mini toolbar.

● Open the Calibri (Boc ▼) Font drop-down menu in the Mini toolbar.

● Choose Comic Sans MS.

*Your screen should be similar to Figure 1.46*

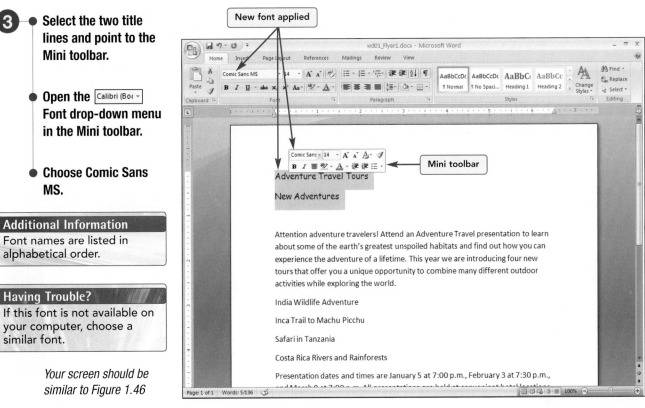

**Figure 1.46**

Using the Mini toolbar to apply the formats is a quick and convenient alternative to using the Ribbon. Next, you will change the font size.

**4** ● Open the 14 ▼ Size drop-down menu in the Mini toolbar.

● Choose 36.

*Your screen should be similar to Figure 1.47*

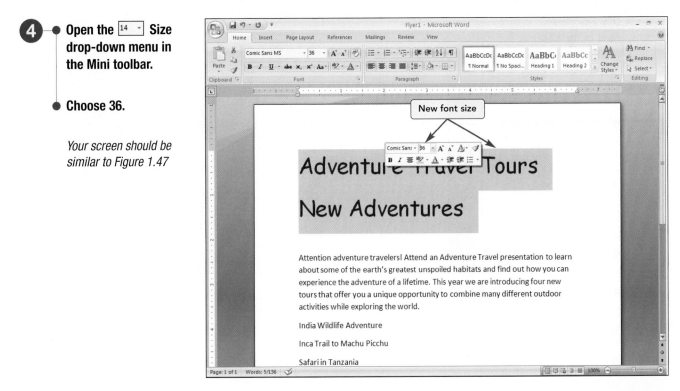

**Figure 1.47**

The selected font and size have been applied to the selection, making the title lines much more interesting and eye-catching. The Font and Font Size buttons reflect the settings in use in the selection. As you look at the title lines, you decide the font size of the first title line is too large. You will reduce it to 20 points.

**5** ● **Select the first title line.**

● **Choose 20 points from the** [36 ▾] **Font Size drop-down menu.**

*Your screen should be similar to Figure 1.48*

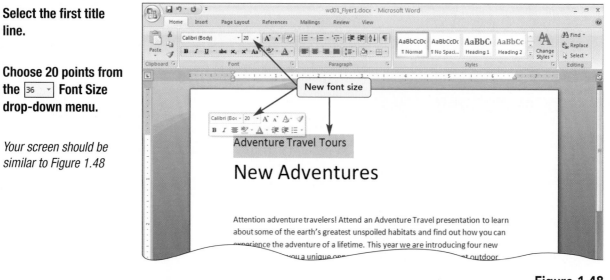

Figure 1.48

Finally, you want to change the font of the list of four tours.

**6** ● **Select the list of four tours.**

● **Use** [Calibri (Body) ▾] **Font in the Mini toolbar to change the font to Comic Sans MS.**

**Additional Information**
Theme fonts and recently used fonts appear at the top of the list. You will learn about themes in Lab 3.

● **Click anywhere on the highlighted text to deselect it.**

● **Reduce the zoom so the entire page is visible.**

*Your screen should be similar to Figure 1.49*

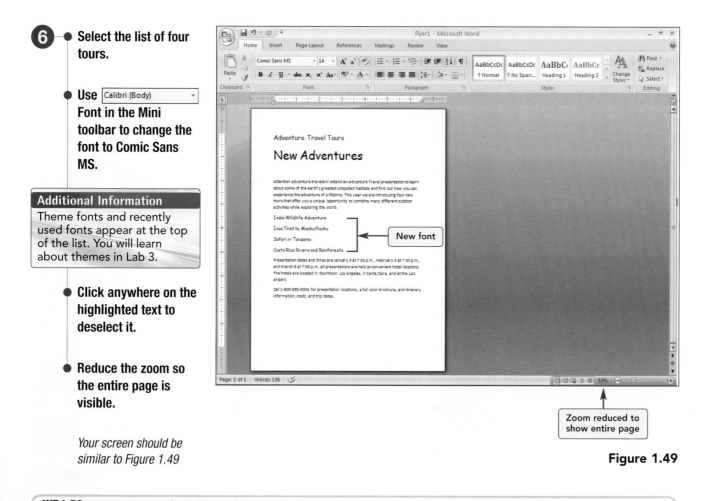

Figure 1.49

The changes you have made to the font and font size have made the flyer somewhat more interesting. However, you want to further enhance the document.

## Applying Character Effects

Next you want to liven up the flyer by adding character effects such as color and bold to selected areas. The table below describes some of the effects and their uses.

| Format | Example | Use |
|---|---|---|
| Bold, italic | **Bold** *Italic* | Adds emphasis. |
| Underline | <u>Underline</u> | Adds emphasis. |
| Strikethrough | ~~Strikethrough~~ | Indicates words to be deleted. |
| Double strikethrough | Double Strikethrough | Indicates words to be deleted. |
| Superscript | "To be or not to be."[1] | Used in footnotes and formulas. |
| Subscript | $H_2O$ | Used in formulas. |
| Shadow | Shadow | Adds distinction to titles and headings. |
| Outline | Outline | Adds distinction to titles and headings. |
| Emboss | Emboss | Adds distinction to titles and headings. |
| Engrave | Engrave | Adds distinction to titles and headings. |
| Small caps | SMALL CAPS | Adds emphasis when case is not important. |
| All caps | ALL CAPS | Adds emphasis when case is not important. |
| Hidden | | Prevents selected text from displaying or printing. Hidden text can be viewed by displaying formatting marks. |
| Color | Color Color **Color** | Adds interest |

**Additional Information**
You will learn about background colors in Lab 2.

First you will add color and bold to the top title line. The default font color setting is Automatic. This setting automatically determines when to use black or white text. Black text is used on a light background and white text on a dark background.

**1**
- Return the zoom to 100%.

- Select the first title line and point to the Mini toolbar.

- Open the 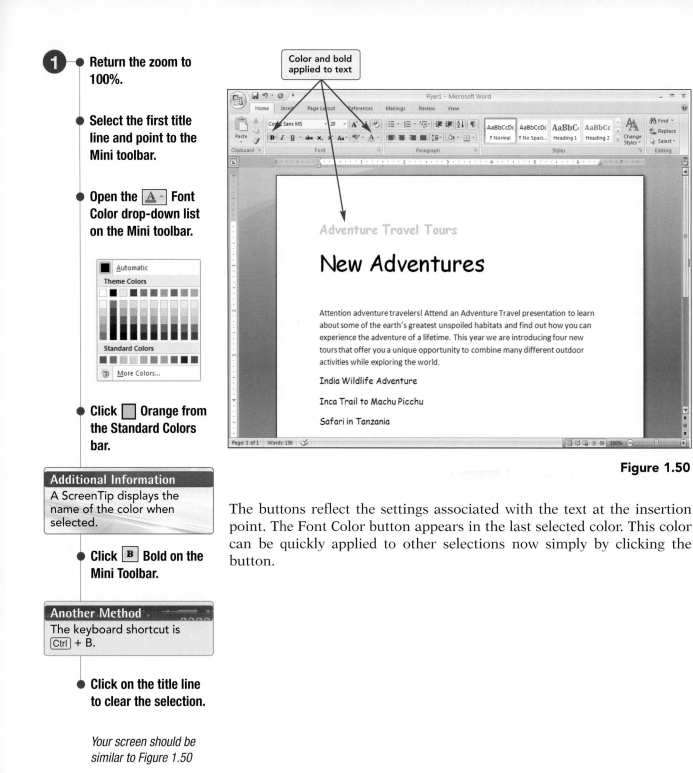 Font Color drop-down list on the Mini toolbar.

- Click ☐ Orange from the Standard Colors bar.

**Additional Information**

A ScreenTip displays the name of the color when selected.

- Click **B** Bold on the Mini Toolbar.

**Another Method**

The keyboard shortcut is Ctrl + B.

- Click on the title line to clear the selection.

*Your screen should be similar to Figure 1.50*

**Figure 1.50**

The buttons reflect the settings associated with the text at the insertion point. The Font Color button appears in the last selected color. This color can be quickly applied to other selections now simply by clicking the button.

Next you will add color and bold to several other areas of the flyer.

**2**
- Select the second title line.

- Using the Mini toolbar, change the font color to green and add bold.

- Select the list of four trips.

- Click 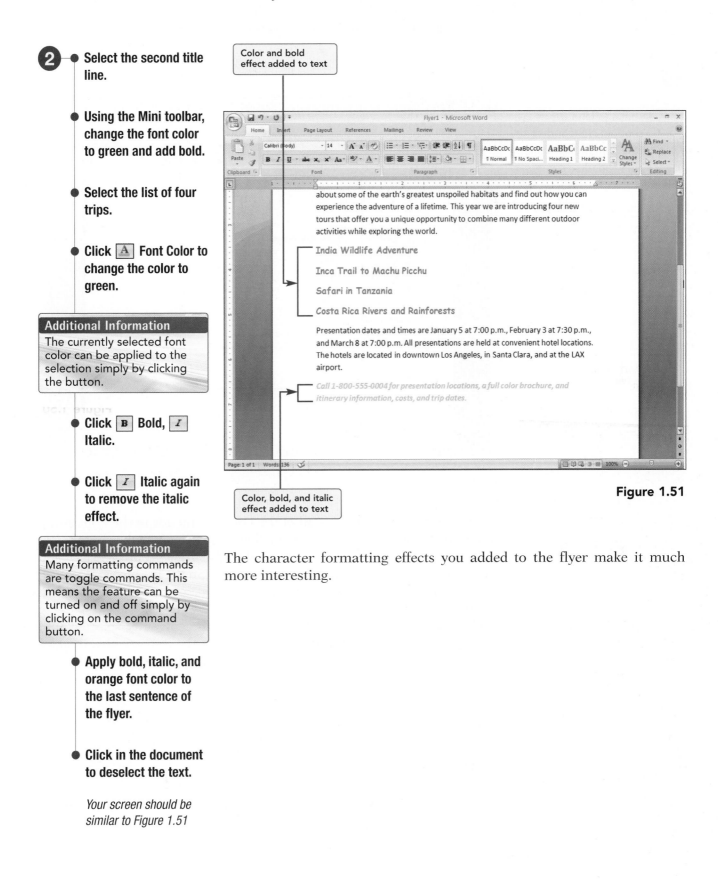 **A** Font Color to change the color to green.

- Click **B** Bold, **I** Italic.

- Click **I** Italic again to remove the italic effect.

- Apply bold, italic, and orange font color to the last sentence of the flyer.

- Click in the document to deselect the text.

*Your screen should be similar to Figure 1.51*

Color and bold effect added to text

about some of the earth's greatest unspoiled habitats and find out how you can experience the adventure of a lifetime. This year we are introducing four new tours that offer you a unique opportunity to combine many different outdoor activities while exploring the world.

India Wildlife Adventure

Inca Trail to Machu Picchu

Safari in Tanzania

Costa Rica Rivers and Rainforests

Presentation dates and times are January 5 at 7:00 p.m., February 3 at 7:30 p.m., and March 8 at 7:00 p.m. All presentations are held at convenient hotel locations. The hotels are located in downtown Los Angeles, in Santa Clara, and at the LAX airport.

*Call 1-800-555-0004 for presentation locations, a full color brochure, and itinerary information, costs, and trip dates.*

Color, bold, and italic effect added to text

**Figure 1.51**

The character formatting effects you added to the flyer make it much more interesting.

The next formatting change you want to make is to add a shadow to the title lines. Since the Ribbon does not display a button for this feature, you need to open the Font dialog box to access this feature.

**3** ● **Select both title lines.**

● **Click** ☐ **in the bottom-right corner of the Font group to open the Font dialog box.**

*Your screen should be similar to Figure 1.52*

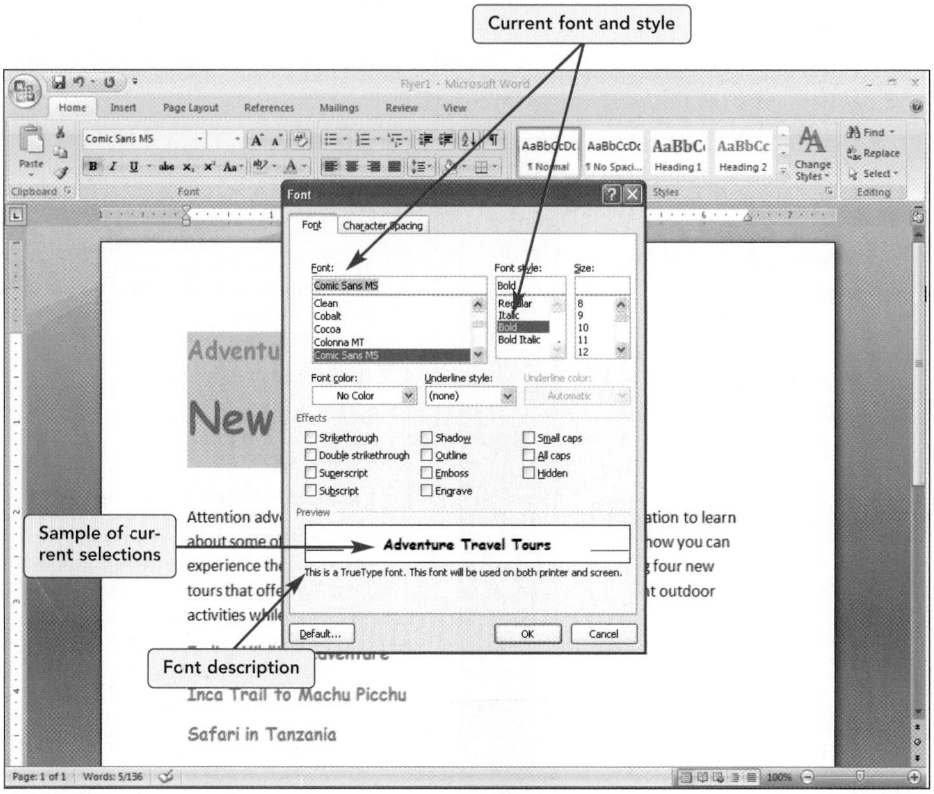

Current font and style

Sample of current selections

Font description

**Figure 1.52**

The Font dialog box contains all of the Font commands in the Font group and more. Using the Dialog Box Launcher to open a dialog box allows you to access the more-advanced or less-used features of a group. The font and font style used in the selected text are identified in the list boxes. However, because the selection includes two different font sizes, the font size is not identified.

The Preview box displays an example of the currently selected font setting. Notice the description of the font below the Preview box. It states that the selected font is a TrueType font. **TrueType** fonts are fonts that are automatically installed when you install Windows. They appear onscreen exactly as they will appear when printed. Some fonts are printer fonts, which are available only on your printer and may look different onscreen than when printed. Courier is an example of a printer font.

You will add a shadow to the selected lines.

**4** • **Choose Shadow.**

• **Click**  **.**

*Your screen should be similar to Figure 1.53*

**Figure 1.53**

A shadow effect has been applied to all text in the selection.

## Setting Paragraph Alignment

The final formatting change you want to make is to change the paragraph alignment.

# Concept 6

## Alignment

6   **Alignment** is the positioning of text on a line between the margins or indents. There are four types of paragraph alignment: left, centered, right, and justified. The alignment settings affect entire paragraphs and are described in the table below.

| Alignment | | Effect on Text Alignment |
|---|---|---|
| | Left | Aligns text against the left margin of the page, leaving the right margin ragged or uneven. This is the most commonly used paragraph alignment type and therefore the default setting in all word processing software packages. |
| | Center | Centers each line of text between the left and right margins. Center alignment is used mostly for headings or centering graphics on a page. |
| | Right | Aligns text against the right margin, leaving the left margin ragged. Use right alignment when you want text to line up on the outside of a page, such as a chapter title or a header. |
| | Justify | Aligns text against the right and left margins and evenly spaces out the words by inserting extra spaces, called soft spaces, that adjust automatically whenever additions or deletions are made to the text. Newspapers commonly use justified alignment so the columns of text are even. |

The commands to change paragraph alignment are available in the Paragraph dialog box. However, it is much faster to use the keyboard shortcuts or command buttons in the Paragraph group shown below.

| Alignment | Keyboard Shortcut | Button |
|---|---|---|
| Left | Ctrl + L | |
| Center | Ctrl + E | |
| Right | Ctrl + R | |
| Justify | Ctrl + J | |

You want to change the alignment of all paragraphs in the flyer from the default of left-aligned to centered.

**1** • **Triple-click in the left margin to select the entire document.**

• **Click ☰ Center in the Mini toolbar.**

**Another Method**

You also can use ☰ in the Paragraph group of the Home tab or in the Paragraph dialog box.

• **Reduce the zoom so the entire page is visible.**

*Your screen should be similar to Figure 1.54*

**Additional Information**

In addition to using the Zoom feature, you can use ⊞ One Page in the Zoom group of the View tab.

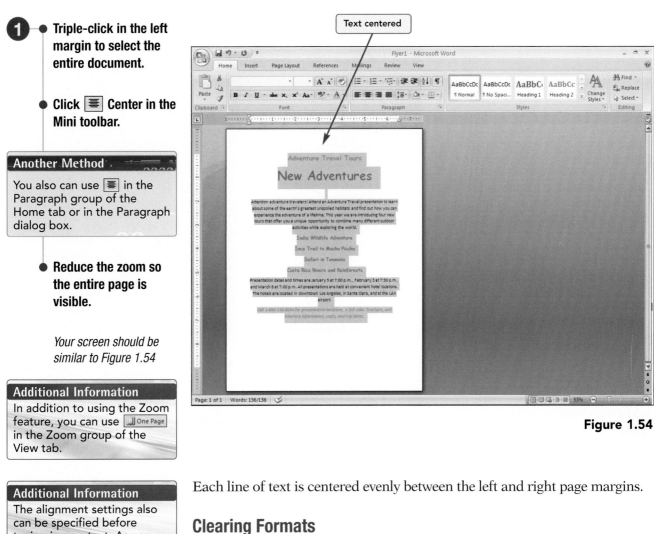

Text centered

**Figure 1.54**

**Additional Information**

The alignment settings also can be specified before typing in new text. As you type, the text is aligned according to your selection until the alignment setting is changed to another setting.

Each line of text is centered evenly between the left and right page margins.

## Clearing Formats

As you look at the entire flyer, you decide the last line is overformatted. You think it would look better if it did not include italics and color. Since it has been a while since you applied these formats, using Undo also would remove many other changes that you want to keep. Instead, you will quickly clear all formatting from the selection and then apply only those you want.

**1**
- **Select the last sentence.**

- **Click** ✏️ **Clear Formatting.**

*Your screen should be similar to Figure 1.55*

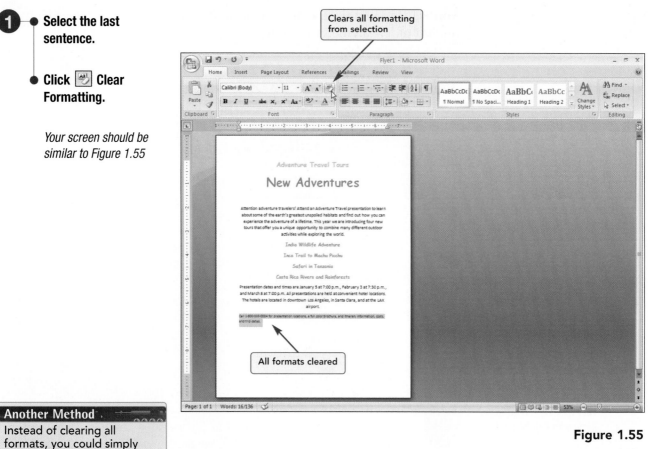

Clears all formatting from selection

All formats cleared

**Figure 1.55**

**Another Method**
Instead of clearing all formats, you could simply reselect the command button to remove the formats that you did not want or select another format to replace it.

All formatting associated with the selection, including text alignment and font size, has been removed and the text appears in the default document font and size.

**2**
- **Format the last sentence to bold, centered, and a font size of 14.**

- **Click** 💾 **Save in the Quick Access Toolbar to save the file using the same file name.**

The formatting of the last sentence looks much better now. As you are working on a document, it is a good idea to save your document frequently to prevent the accidental loss of work from a power outage or other mishap. While AutoRecover is a great feature for recovering lost work, it should not be used in place of regularly saving your work.

**WD1.58**
**Word 2007**
Lab 1: Creating and Editing a Document
www.mhhe.com/oleary

# Working with Graphics

Finally, you want to add a graphic to the flyer to add interest.

## Concept 7

### Graphics

**7** A **graphic** is a nontext element or object such as a drawing or picture that can be added to a document. An **object** is an item that can be sized, moved, and manipulated.

A graphic can be a simple **drawing object** consisting of shapes such as lines and boxes. A drawing object is part of your Word document. A **picture** is an illustration such as a graphic illustration or a scanned photograph. Pictures are graphics that were created using another program and are inserted in your Word document as **embedded objects**. An embedded object becomes part of the Word document and can be opened and edited from within the Word document using the **source program**, the program in which it was created. Any changes made to the embedded object are not made to the original picture file because they are independent. Several examples of drawing objects and pictures are shown below.

**Drawing object**

**Graphic illustration**

**Photograph**

Add graphics to your documents to help the reader understand concepts, to add interest, and to make your document stand out from others.

## Inserting a Picture

Picture files can be obtained from a variety of sources. Many simple drawings called **clip art** are available in the Clip Organizer, a Microsoft Office tool that arranges and catalogs clip art and other media files stored on the computer's hard disk. Additionally, you can access Microsoft's Clip Art and Media Web site for even more graphics.

Digital images created using a digital camera are one of the most common types of graphic files. You also can create picture files using a scanner to convert any printed document, including photographs, to an electronic format. Most images that are scanned and inserted into documents are stored as Windows bitmap files (.bmp). All types of pictures, including clip art, photographs, and other types of images, can be found on the Internet. These files are commonly stored as .jpg or .pcx files. Keep in mind that any images you locate on the Internet may be copyrighted and should only be used with permission. You also can purchase CDs containing graphics for your use.

You want to add a picture to the flyer below the two title lines. You will move to the location in the document where you want to insert a photograph of a lion you recently received from a client. The photograph has been saved as a picture image.

**1** • **Change the zoom to 100%.**

• **Move to the blank line below the second title line.**

• **Open the Insert tab.**

• **From the Illustrations group, click [Picture].**

• **Change the Look In location to the location of your data files.**

• **Select** wd01_Lions.

• **Click [Insert ▾].**

*Your screen should be similar to Figure 1.56*

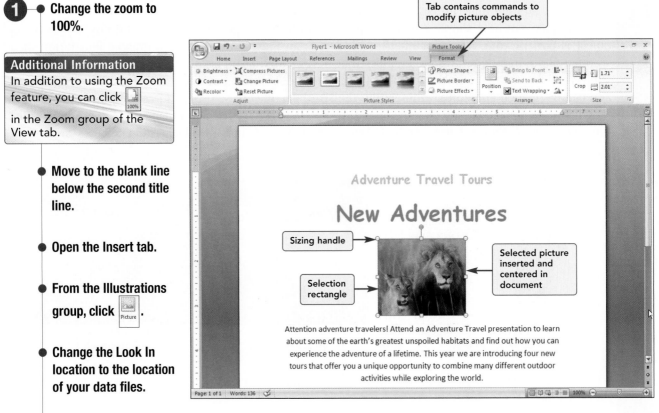

Tab contains commands to modify picture objects

Sizing handle

Selection rectangle

Selected picture inserted and centered in document

**Figure 1.56**

The picture is inserted in the document at the location of the insertion point. It is centered because the paragraph in which it was placed is centered. Notice the picture is surrounded by a **selection rectangle** and four circles and four squares, called **sizing handles**, indicating it is a selected object and can now be deleted, sized, moved, or modified. A Picture Tools tab automatically appears and can be used to modify the selected picture object.

Although you like the picture of the lions that you might see on one of the tours, you want to check the Clip Art Gallery to see if a picture of a tiger or parrot would be better.

**2** • Click to the right side of the graphic to deselect it.

• Open the Insert tab.

• From the Illustrations group, click [Clip Art].

*Your screen should be similar to Figure 1.57*

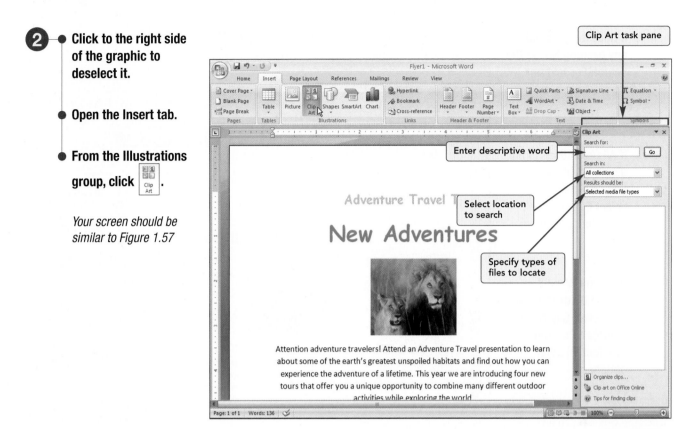

**Figure 1.57**

The Clip Art task pane appears in which you can enter a word or phrase that is representative of the type of picture you want to locate. You also can specify the locations to search and the type of media files, such as clip art, movies, photographs, or sound, to display in the results. You want to find clip art and photographs of animals.

**3** • If necessary, select any existing text in the Search For text box.

• Type **animals**.

• If All Collections is not displayed in the Search In text box, select Everywhere from the drop-down list.

• Open the Results Should Be drop-down list, select Clip Art and Photographs, and deselect all other options.

**Having Trouble?**
Click the box next to an option to select or deselect (clear the checkmark).

• Click [ Go ].

*Your screen should be similar to Figure 1.58*

**Having Trouble?**
Your Clip Art task pane may display different pictures than shown in Figure 1.58.

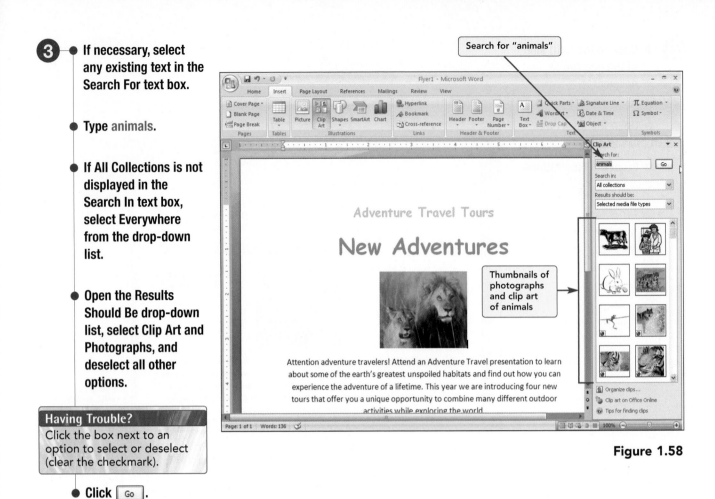

Figure 1.58

The program searches all locations on your computer and, if you have an Internet connection established, Microsoft's Clip Art and Media Web site for clip art and graphics that match your search term. The Results area displays **thumbnails**, miniature representations of pictures, of all located graphics. The pictures stored on your computer in the Microsoft Clip Organizer appear first in the results list, followed by the Office Online clip art.

Pointing to a thumbnail displays a ScreenTip containing the keywords associated with the picture and information about the picture properties. It also displays a drop-down list bar that accesses the item's context menu.

**4** ● **Scroll the list to view additional images.**

● **Point to any thumbnail to see a ScreenTip.**

*Your screen should be similar to Figure 1.59*

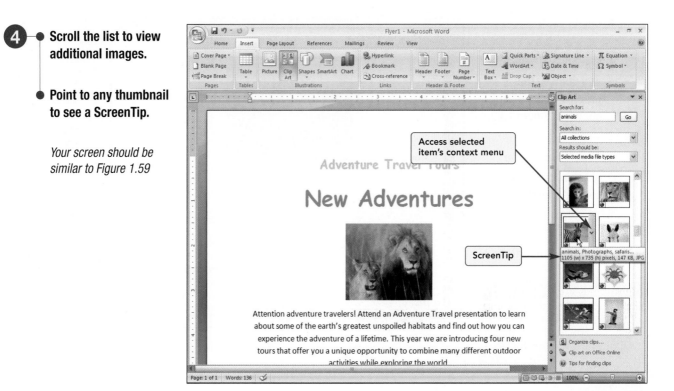

**Figure 1.59**

Each graphic has several keywords associated with it. All the displayed graphics include the keyword "animals." Because so many pictures were located, you decide to narrow your search to display pictures with keywords of "animals" and "parrots" only. Additionally, because it is sometimes difficult to see the graphic, you can preview it in a larger size.

**5** • Add a comma after the word "animals" in the Search For text box and then type parrots.

• Click [ Go ].

• Scroll the results area and point to the graphic of the parrot shown in Figure 1.60.

• Click ˅ next to the graphic to open the context menu.

• Choose Preview/Properties.

*Your screen should be similar to Figure 1.60*

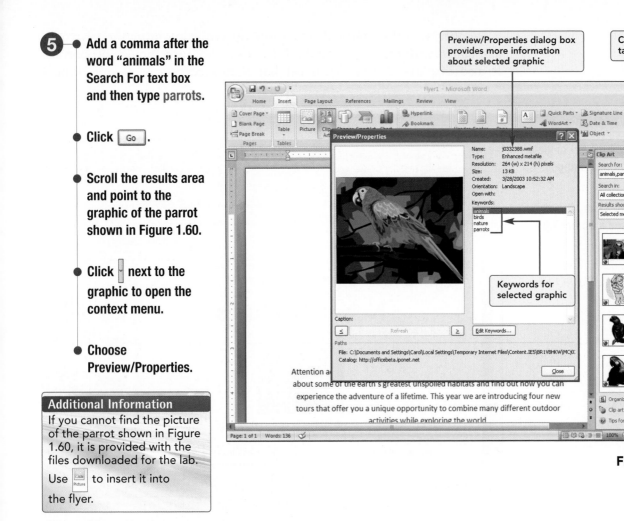

Figure 1.60

Because the search term is more specific, fewer results are displayed. The Preview/Properties dialog box displays the selected graphic larger so it is easier to see. It also displays more information about the properties associated with the graphic, including the keywords used to identify the graphic. You think this looks like a good choice and will insert it into the document.

**6** ● Click [ Close ] to close the dialog box.

● Click on the graphic to insert it in the document.

**Another Method**
You also could choose Insert from the thumbnail's context menu.

● Click ⊠ in the Clip Art task pane title bar to close it.

*Your screen should be similar to Figure 1.61*

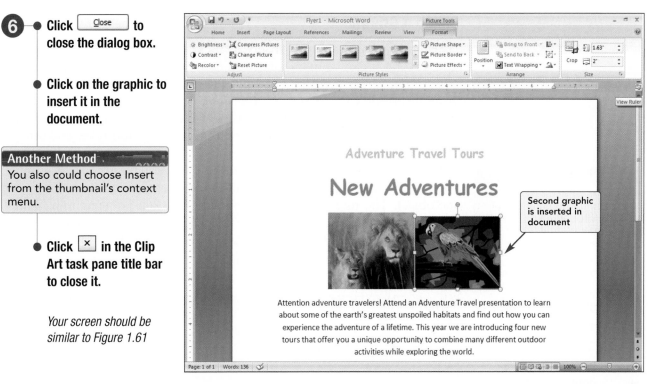

**Figure 1.61**

The clip art graphic is inserted next to the lion picture.

## Deleting a Graphic

There are now two graphics in the flyer. You decide to use the parrot graphic and need to remove the picture of the lion. To do this, you select the graphic and delete it.

**1** ● Click on the lion graphic.

● Press [Delete].

*Your screen should be similar to Figure 1.62*

The lion graphic is removed.

**Figure 1.62**

## Sizing a Graphic

Usually, when a graphic is inserted, its size will need to be adjusted. A graphic object can be manipulated in many ways. You can change its size; add captions, borders, or shading; or move it to another location. A graphic object can be moved anywhere on the page, including in the margins or on top of or below other objects, including text. The only places you cannot place a graphic object are into a footnote, endnote, or caption.

In this case, you want to increase the picture's size. To size a graphic, you select it and drag the sizing handles to increase or decrease the size of the object. The mouse pointer changes to ↖ when pointing to a handle. The direction of the arrow indicates the direction in which you can drag to size the graphic. You want to increase the image to approximately 3 inches wide by 2.5 inches high.

**1** ● **Click on the graphic to select it.**

● **Point to the lower-right corner handle.**

● **With the pointer as a ↖, drag outward from the picture to increase the size to approximately 2.5 inches wide by 2 inches high (use the ruler as a guide and refer to Figure 1.63).**

● **Click anywhere in the document to deselect the graphic.**

● **Click 🖫 Save.**

*Your screen should be similar to Figure 1.63*

Figure 1.63

# Enhancing the Page

The final changes you want to make to the flyer for now are to add a border line around the entire page and to add a watermark in the page background. Borders can add interest and emphasis to various parts of your document, including entire pages, selected text, tables, graphic objects, and pictures. **Watermarks** are text or pictures that appear behind document text. They often add interest or identify the document status, such as marking a document as a Draft. Both page borders and watermarks are features that affect an entire page and are found in the Page Layout tab.

## Adding a Page Border

You want to add a decorative border around the entire page to enclose the text and enhance the appearance of the flyer.

1 ● **Open the Page Layout tab.**

● **Click** [ Page Borders ] **in the Page Background group.**

*Your screen should be similar to Figure 1.64*

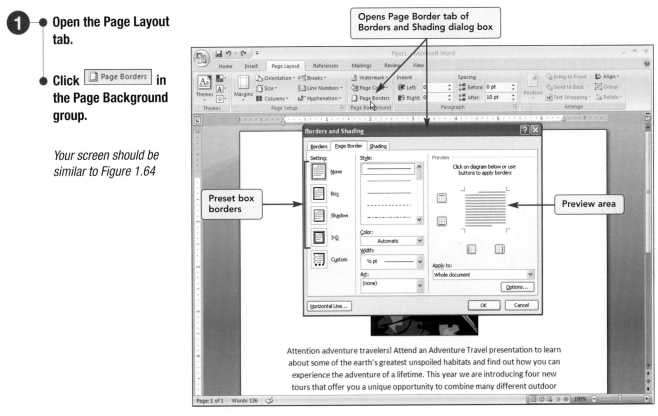

**Figure 1.64**

From the Page Borders tab of the Borders and Shading dialog box, you first select either a preset box border or a custom border. Then you specify the style, color, weight, and location of the border. A page border can be applied to all pages in a document, to pages in selected parts of a document, to the first page only, or to all pages except the first.

You want to create a box border around the entire page of text. As you specify the border settings, the Preview area will reflect your selections.

**2** ● **Choose Box from the Settings area.**

● **Scroll the Style list box and select**

┌─────────────────┐
│ ---·--·-··--··-- │
└─────────────────┘

● **Open the Color palette and select Orange, Accent 6.**

● **From the Width drop-down list box, select 3 pt.**

**Having Trouble?**
Use the None option to remove all border lines, or remove individual lines by selecting the border location again.

*Your screen should be similar to Figure 1.65*

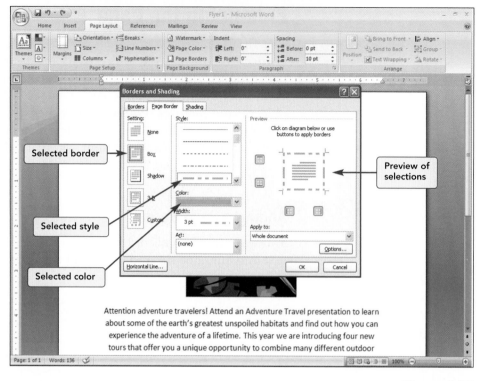

**Figure 1.65**

The Preview area shows how the box page border will appear in the style, color, and point size you selected. The default selection of Document, as to what part of the document to apply the border, is acceptable because the document is only one page long.

**3** ● **Click** [ OK ].

● **Reduce the zoom to display the entire page.**

*Your screen should be similar to Figure 1.66*

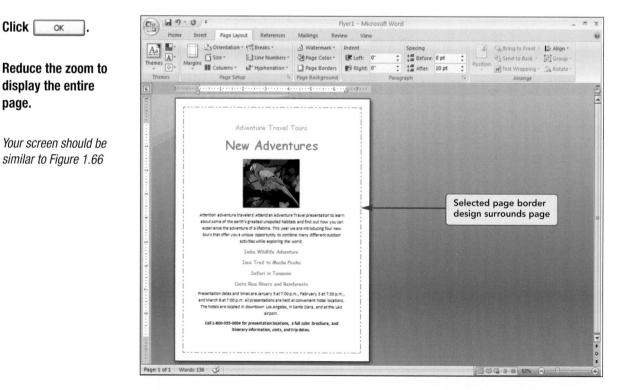

**Figure 1.66**

The specified page border appears in the middle of the margin space around the entire page.

### Adding a Watermark

Finally, you want to add a watermark to the background of the flyer identifying the document as a draft. You can insert a predesigned watermark from a gallery of watermark text, or you can insert a watermark with custom text.

**1** ● **Click** [Watermark ▾] **from the Page Background group.**

● **Scroll the Watermark gallery and choose the Draft1 design from the Disclaimers section.**

**Additional Information**

Choose Remove Watermark from the [Watermark ▾] menu to remove a watermark.

*Your screen should be similar to Figure 1.67*

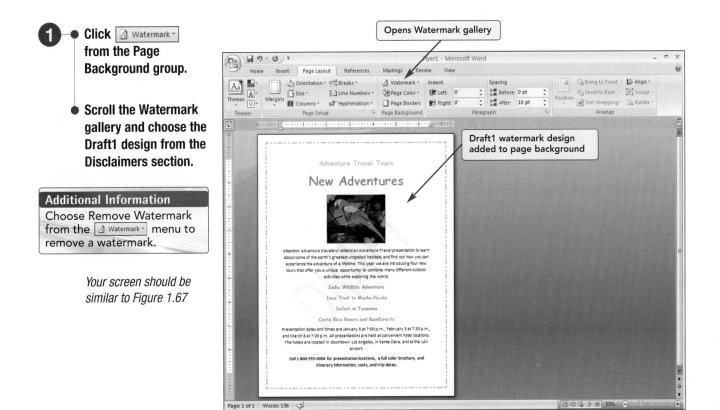

Figure 1.67

**Additional Information**

You can only see watermarks in Print Layout view and Full Screen Reading view or in a printed document.

The DRAFT watermark appears diagonally across the background of the page. The entire page is displayed as it will appear when printed. The flyer looks good and does not appear to need any further modifications immediately.

## Printing a Document

Although you still plan to make several formatting changes to the document, you want to give a copy of the flyer to the manager to get feedback regarding the content and layout.

First you need to add your name to the flyer and to the document properties and check the print settings.

**1** ● Increase the zoom to 100%.

● Scroll to the bottom of the flyer.

● Add your name at before the phone number in the last sentence of the flyer.

● Replace Student Name with your name in the document properties.

● If necessary, make sure your printer is on and ready to print.

● Click 🔵 Office Button and choose Print.

**Figure 1.68**

**Another Method**
The keyboard shortcut for the Print command is Ctrl + P.

**Additional Information**
You also can use Quick Print on the Print submenu to print the active document immediately using the current print settings.

*Your screen should be similar to Figure 1.68*

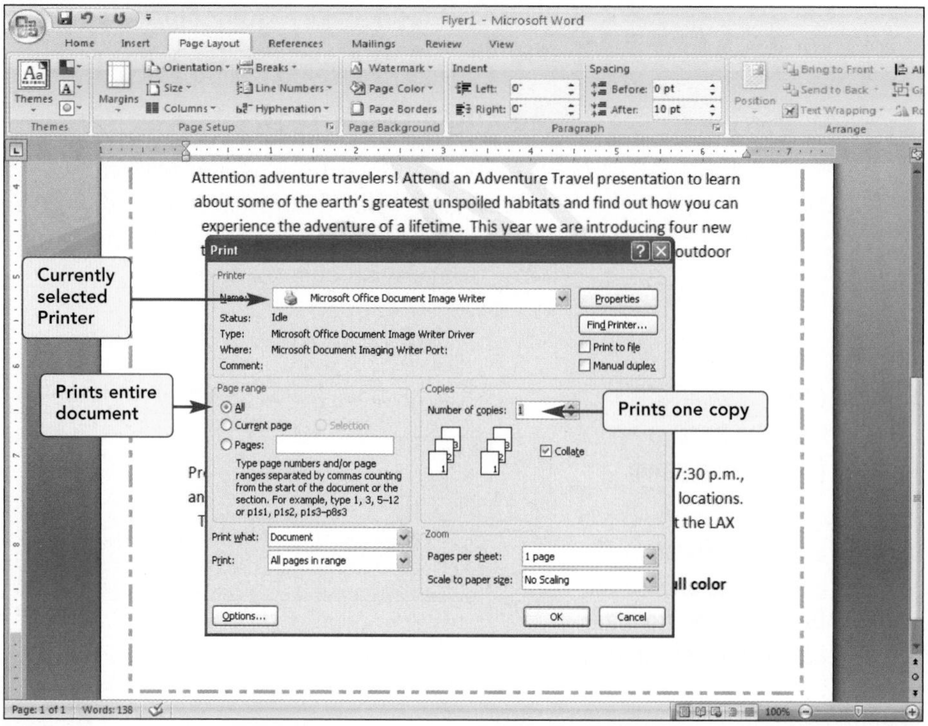

From the Print dialog box, you need to specify the printer you will be using and the document settings. The printer that is currently selected is displayed in the Name drop-down list box in the Printer section of the dialog box.

The Page Range area of the Print dialog box lets you specify how much of the document you want printed. The range options are described in the following table:

| Option | Action |
| --- | --- |
| All | Prints entire document. |
| Current page | Prints selected page or page the insertion point is on. |
| Pages | Prints pages you specify by typing page numbers in the dialog box. |
| Selection | Prints selected text only. |

**Note:** Please consult your instructor for printing procedures that may differ from the following directions.

The default range setting, All, is the correct setting. In the Copies section, the default setting of one copy of the document is acceptable. You will print using the default print settings.

 **If you need to change the selected printer to another printer, open the Name drop-down list box and select the appropriate printer (your instructor will tell you which printer to select).**

● Click [ OK ].

Your printer should be printing the document. The printed copy of the flyer should be similar to the document shown in the Case Study at the beginning of the lab.

## Exiting Word

You are finished working on the flyer for now and want to save the last few changes you have made to the document and close the Word application. The [ ✕ Exit Word ] command in the File menu is used to quit the Word program. Alternatively, you can click the [ ✕ ] Close button in the application window title bar. If you attempt to close the application without first saving your document, Word displays a warning asking if you want to save your work. If you do not save your work and you exit the application, any changes you made since last saving it are lost.

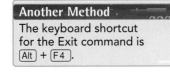

**Another Method**
The keyboard shortcut for the Exit command is [Alt] + [F4].

**1** ● Click [✕] Close.

● Click [ Yes ] to save the changes you made to the file.

The Windows desktop is visible again.

If multiple Word documents are open, clicking [✕] closes the application window containing the document you are viewing only.

# Focus on Careers

**EXPLORE YOUR CAREER OPTIONS**

Food Service Manager
Have you noticed flyers around your campus advertising job positions? Many of these jobs are in the food service industry. Food service managers are traditionally responsible for overseeing the kitchen and dining room. However, these positions increasingly involve administrative tasks, including recruiting new

employees. As a food service manager, your position would likely include creating newspaper notices and flyers to attract new staff. These flyers should be eye-catching and error-free. The typical salary range of a food service manager is $34,000 to $41,700. Demand for skilled food service managers is expected to increase through 2010.

# Concept Summary

## LAB 1
## Creating and Editing a Document

### Grammar Checker (WD1.16)

The grammar checker advises you of incorrect grammar as you create and edit a document, and proposes possible corrections.

four·new·adventures¶

**Grammar Checker**

Grammar: English (U.S.)

Capitalization:
four·new·adventures

Ignore Once
Ignore Rule
Next Sentence

Suggestions:
Four

Change
Explain...

Options...    Undo    Cancel

### Spelling Checker (WD1.19)

The spelling checker advises you of misspelled words as you create and edit a document, and proposes possible corrections.

Four·new·adventures¶

Attention·adventire·travelers!·¶

adventure
advent ire
adventured
adventurer
adventures
Ignore
Ignore All
Add to Dictionary
AutoCorrect
Language
Spelling...
Look Up...
Cut

**Spelling Checker**

### AutoCorrect (WD1.21)

The AutoCorrect feature makes some basic assumptions about the text you are typing and, based on these assumptions, automatically corrects the entry.

Four·new·adventures¶

**AutoCorrect**

Attention·adventure·travelers!·Attend·a·presentation·to·lern·about·the·¶

Undo Automatic Capitalization
Stop Auto-capitalizing First Letter of Sentences
Control AutoCorrect Options...

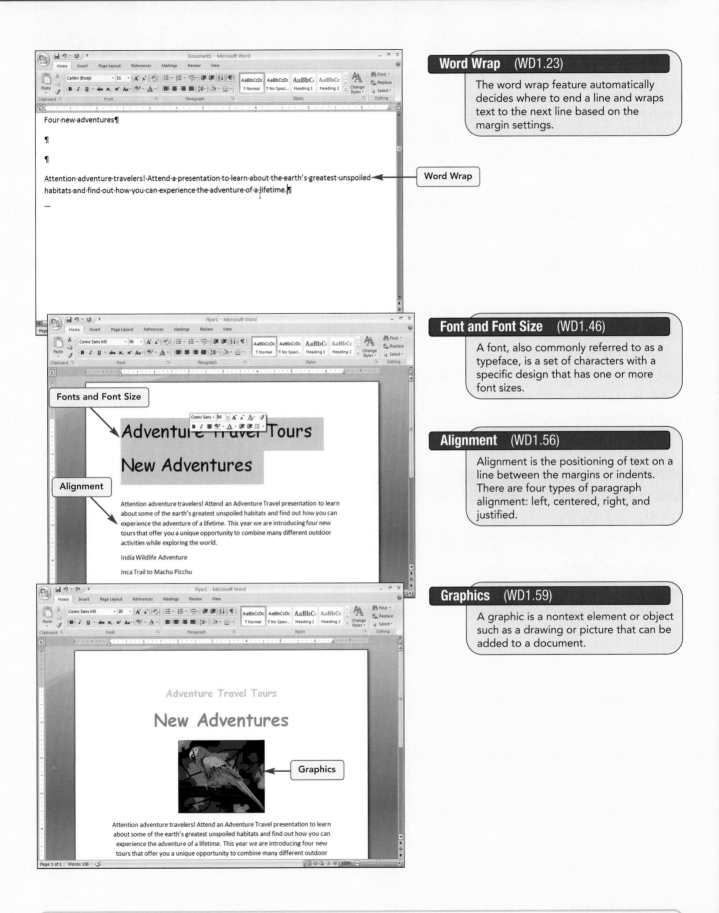

**Word Wrap** (WD1.23)

The word wrap feature automatically decides where to end a line and wraps text to the next line based on the margin settings.

**Font and Font Size** (WD1.46)

A font, also commonly referred to as a typeface, is a set of characters with a specific design that has one or more font sizes.

**Alignment** (WD1.56)

Alignment is the positioning of text on a line between the margins or indents. There are four types of paragraph alignment: left, centered, right, and justified.

**Graphics** (WD1.59)

A graphic is a nontext element or object such as a drawing or picture that can be added to a document.

# Lab Review

LAB **1**

## Creating and Editing a Document

## key terms

alignment WD1.56

AutoCorrect WD1.21

character formatting WD1.46

clip art WD1.59

cursor WD1.5

custom dictionary WD1.19

default WD1.8

document properties WD1.25

document window WD1.5

drawing object WD1.59

edit WD1.10

embedded object WD1.59

end-of-file marker WD1.10

font WD1.46

font size WD1.46

format WD1.10

grammar checker WD1.16

graphic WD1.59

Insert mode WD1.37

insertion point WD1.5

Live Preview WD1.47

main dictionary WD1.19

object WD1.59

paragraph formatting WD1.46

picture WD1.59

ruler WD1.5

sans serif font WD1.46

selection rectangle WD1.60

serif font WD1.46

sizing handles WD1.60

soft space WD1.56

source program WD1.59

spelling checker WD1.19

template WD1.8

thumbnail WD1.62

TrueType WD1.54

typeface WD1.46

watermark WD1.67

word wrap WD1.23

## MCAS skills

The Microsoft Certified Applications Specialist (MCAS) certification program is designed to measure your proficiency in performing basic tasks using the Office 2007 applications. Getting certified demonstrates that you have the skills and provides a valuable industry credential for employment. See Reference 2 MCAS Certification Guide for a complete list of the skills that were covered in Lab 1.

## command summary

| Command | Shortcut | Action |
|---|---|---|
| 🏢 **Office Button** | | **Opens File menu** |
| New | Ctrl + N | Opens new blank document |
| Open | Ctrl + O | Opens existing document file |
| Save | Ctrl + S | Saves document using same file name |
| Save As | F12 | Saves document using a new file name, type, and/or location |
| Print | Ctrl + P | Prints document |
| Prepare/Properties | | Opens Document Information Panel |
| Close | Ctrl + F4 | Closes document |
| ✕ Exit Word | Alt + F4 | Exit Word application |
| **Quick Access Toolbar** | | |
| 💾 Save | Ctrl + S | Saves document using same file name |
| ↺ ▾ Undo | Ctrl + Z | Restores last editing change |
| ↻ Redo | Ctrl + Y | Restores last Undo or repeats last command or action |
| **Home tab** | | |
| *Font Group* | | |
| Calibri (Body) ▾ Font | | Changes typeface |
| 11 ▾ Size | | Changes font size |
| 🅰 Clear Formatting | | Removes all formatting from selection |
| **B** Bold | Ctrl + B | Adds/removes bold effect |
| *I* Italic | Ctrl + I | Adds/removes italic effect |
| Aa▾ Change Case | | Changes case of selected text |
| 🅰 ▾ Color | | Changes text to selected color |
| *Paragraph group* | | |
| ¶ Show/Hide | Ctrl + → +* | Displays or hides formatting marks |
| ☰ Align Text Left | Ctrl + L | Aligns text to left margin |
| ☰ Center | Ctrl + E | Centers text between left and right margins |
| ☰ Align Text Right | Ctrl + R | Aligns text to right margin |
| ☰ Justify | Ctrl + J | Aligns text equally between left and right margins |
| **Insert Tab** | | |
| *Illustrations group* | | |
| 🖼 Picture | | Inserts selected picture |

# Lab Review

command summary (continued)

| Command | Shortcut | Action |
|---------|----------|--------|
| Clip Art | | Accesses Clip Organizer and inserts selected clip |

### Page Layout Tab

*Page Background group*

| Command | Shortcut | Action |
|---------|----------|--------|
| Watermark ▾ | | Inserts ghosted text behind page content |
| Page Borders | | Adds a border around page |

### Review Tab

*Proofing group*

| Command | Shortcut | Action |
|---------|----------|--------|
| ABC Spelling & Grammar | | Opens Spelling and Grammar dialog box |

### View Tab

*Document Views group*

| Command | Shortcut | Action |
|---------|----------|--------|
| Print Layout | 📄 | Shows how text and objects will appear on printed page |
| Full Screen Reading | 📖 | Displays document only, without application features |
| Web Layout | 📄 | Shows document as it will appear when viewed in a Web browser |
| Outline | 📄 | Shows structure of document |
| Draft | 📄 | Shows text formatting and simple layout of page |

*Show/Hide group*

| Command | Shortcut | Action |
|---------|----------|--------|
| ☑ Ruler | 📄 | Displays/hides ruler |

*Zoom group*

| Command | Shortcut | Action |
|---------|----------|--------|
| Zoom | | Opens Zoom dialog box |
| 100% | | Zooms document to 100% of normal size |
| One Page | | Zooms document so an entire page fits in window |
| Page Width | | Zooms document so width of page matches width of window |

# Lab Exercises

## screen identification

1. In the following Word screen, letters identify important elements. Enter the correct term for each screen element in the space provided.

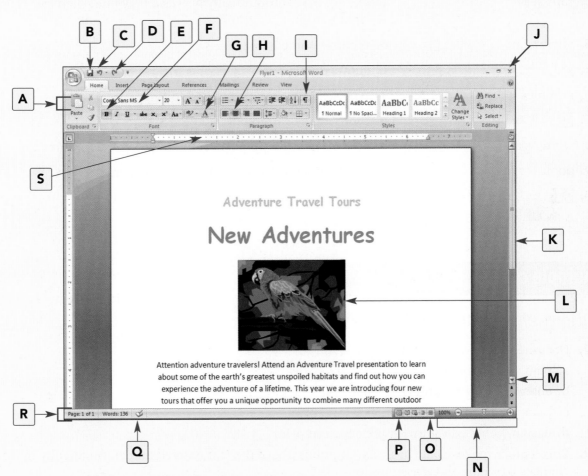

Possible answers for the screen identification are:

| | | | |
|---|---|---|---|
| Scrolls down | Zoom | A. _____ | K. _____ |
| Draft view | Center | B. _____ | L. _____ |
| Tab mark | Spelling and grammar | C. _____ | M. _____ |
| Ribbon |    status icon | D. _____ | N. _____ |
| Save | Redo | E. _____ | O. _____ |
| Print Layout view | Bold | F. _____ | P. _____ |
| Font color | Status bar | G. _____ | Q. _____ |
| Font | Scroll bar | H. _____ | R. _____ |
| Undo | Graphic | I. _____ | S. _____ |
| Show/Hide | Paragraph mark | J. _____ | |
| Close | Ruler | | |

# Lab Exercises

## matching

Match the item on the left with the correct description on the right.

1.  _____   **a.** undoes last command

2. font  _____   **b.** moves to the top of the document

3. sans serif  _____   **c.** feature that automatically begins a new line when text reaches the right margin

4. alignment  _____   **d.** pictures and clip art

5. Ctrl + h  _____   **e.** shows dialog box

6. graphics  _____   **f.** type style that can be applied to text

7.  _____   **g.** font size measurement

8. word wrap  _____   **h.** controls paragraph positioning between the margins

9. point  _____   **i.** saves a document using the same file name

10.  _____   **j.** font without a flair at the base of each letter

## multiple choice

Circle the correct response to the questions below.

1. Document development follows these steps.
   **a.** plan, edit, enter, format, preview, and print
   **b.** enter, edit, format, preview, and print
   **c.** plan, enter, edit, format, preview, and print
   **d.** design, enter, edit, format, preview, and print

2. This feature makes some basic assumptions about the text entered and automatically makes changes based on those assumptions.
   **a.** AutoChange
   **b.** AutoFormat
   **c.** AutoText
   **d.** AutoCorrect

3. Words that are not contained in the main dictionary can be added to the _____ dictionary.

   **a.** custom

   **b.** additional

   **c.** supplemental

   **d.** user defined

4. A(n) _____ is a nontext element or object that can be added to a document.

   **a.** illustration

   **b.** picture

   **c.** drawing

   **d.** all of the above

5. When text is evenly aligned on both margins, it is _____.

   **a.** center aligned

   **b.** justified

   **c.** left aligned

   **d.** right aligned

6. Words that may be spelled incorrectly in a document are indicated by a _____.

   **a.** green wavy line

   **b.** red wavy line

   **c.** blue wavy line

   **d.** purple dotted underline

7. Font sizes are measured in _____.

   **a.** inches

   **b.** points

   **c.** bits

   **d.** pieces

8. The _____ feature shows how various formatting choices would look on selected text.

   **a.** Actual Preview

   **b.** Real Preview

   **c.** Active Preview

   **d.** Live Preview

9. A set of characters with a specific design is called a(n) _____.
   a. style
   b. font
   c. AutoFormat
   d. Design

10. A(n) _____ is text or pictures that appear behind document text.
    a. graphic
    b. watermark
    c. embedded object
    d. thumbnail

## true/false

Circle the correct answer to the following questions.

| | | | |
|---|---|---|---|
| 1. | A wavy red line indicates a potential spelling error. | True | False |
| 2. | Hard spaces are used to justify text on a line. | True | False |
| 3. | The default document settings are stored in the Normal.docx file. | True | False |
| 4. | The Delete key erases the character to the right of the insertion point. | True | False |
| 5. | The automatic word wrap feature checks for typing errors. | True | False |
| 6. | The Word document file name extension is .wrd. | True | False |
| 7. | Font sizes are measured in inches. | True | False |
| 8. | Word inserts hidden marks into a document to control the display of text. | True | False |
| 9. | The AutoCorrect feature automatically identifies and corrects certain types of errors. | True | False |
| 10. | A selected picture is surrounded by a selection rectangle and eight moving handles. | True | False |

## fill-in

Complete the following statements by filling in the blanks with the correct terms.

1. The default document settings are stored in the _____ template file.

2. A small blue box appearing under a word or character indicates that the _____ feature was applied.

3. The _____ feature displays each page of your document in a reduced size so you can see the page layout.

4. To size a graphic evenly, click and drag the _____ in one corner of the graphic.

5. It is good practice to use only _____ types of fonts in a document.

6. Word 2007 documents are identified by the _____ file extension.

7. The _____ at the top of the window contains commands that are organized into related groups.

8. Use _____ when you want to keep your existing document with the original name and make a copy with a new name.

9. A _____ is a miniature representation of all located graphics in the Clip Art task pane.

10. The _____ feature shows how your formatting choices will appear on selected text.

# Hands-On Exercises

## Step-by-Step

### Asking for Input Memo ★

1. Adventure Travel Tours is planning to update its Web site in the near future. You have been asked to solicit suggestions from the travel agents about changes they would like to see made to the current Web site. You decide to send all the travel agents a memo asking them for their input. Your completed memo will be similar to the one shown here.

   a. Open a blank Word 2007 document and create the following memo in Draft view. Press [Tab⇆] twice after you type the colon (:) following To in the memo header. Press [Tab⇆] once after the From and Date lines. This will make the information following the colons line up evenly. Enter a blank line between paragraphs.

   To: Travel Agents
   From: Student Name
   Date: [Current date]

   The Adventure Travel Tours current Web site was designed with travel agents in mind but as you know, the role of the travel agent is changing. In order to keep up with these changes we plan to begin work on updating the current Adventure Travel Tours Web site. In preparation for this project, I would like your input about the content that will only be available to travel agents. As you work with clients please note what can be changed to make it easier for you to book travel, then send your comments back to me. All suggestions for changes are welcome and will be considered for our improved Web site.

   Thank you in advance for your input.

   > To:    Travel Agents
   > From: Student Name
   > Date: September, 15, 2008
   >
   > The Adventure Travel Tours Web site was designed with travel agents in mind. But as you know, the role of the travel agent is changing. In order to keep up with these changes we plan to begin work on updating the Adventure Travel Tours Web site.
   >
   > In preparation for this project, I would like your input about the content that will only be available to travel agents. In the next few days as you work with clients please note what can be changed to make it easier for you to book travel, and then send your comments back to me. All suggestions for changes are welcome and will be considered for our improved Web site.
   >
   > Thank you in advance for your input.

   b. Correct any spelling and grammar errors that are identified.

   c. Turn on the display of formatting marks. Check the document and remove any extra blank spaces between words or at the end of lines.

   d. Save the document as Web Site Memo in your data file location.

   e. Switch to Print Layout view.

**f.** End the first sentence after the word "mind". Capitalize the following word, but. Insert the text "In the next few days" before the word "As," in the fifth sentence. Change the "A" in As to lower case. Delete the word "current" from the first and third sentences.

**g.** Start a new paragraph beginning with the third sentence.

**h.** Change the font size for the entire memo to 14 pt and the alignment of the body of the memo to justified.

**i.** Turn off the display of formatting marks.

**j.** Add an ASAP watermark.

**k.** Include your name in the document properties as author and the file name as the title.

**l.** Save the document again and print the document.

## Promoting Celebrate Bikes Sunday ★★

**2.** You are the program coordinator for the city of Westbrook's Parks and Recreation Department. In next week's newspaper, you plan to run an article to promote bike riding in the community through the Celebrate Bikes Sunday event. Your completed article will be similar to the one shown here.

**a.** Enter the following information in a new Word 2007 document. Leave a blank line between paragraphs.

**Celebrate Bicycling!**

**May is traditionally National Bike Month, so take out your bicycle, tune it up and get a breath of fresh air! And plan to take part in Celebrate Bikes Sunday on 5/8 to learn about the benefits of bike riding.**

**Businesses and organizations participating in the event are all "related to biking in Westbrook and most of them are involved in the development of the trail system" says event director Mary Jo Miller.**

**As part of the activities on this day, the Westbrook Parks and Recreation Department is sponsoring a bike ride from the West Avenue YMCA to the Main Street Park beginning at 11am.**

**At the end of the bike ride, the riders are encouraged to stay for the fun and informative activates in the park. Activities include a bike safety program, entertainment, and food booths. The Safe Route to School program will work with parents and children to find the safest route to either walk or bike to school.**

**Registration is free and available by calling (603) 555-1313, visiting the YMCA during regular business hours or beginning at 10am on Sunday at the YMCA.**

**b.** Correct any spelling or grammar errors. Save the document as Bike Event.

**c.** Turn on the display of formatting marks. Check the document and remove any extra blank spaces between words or at the end of lines.

**d.** In Print Layout view, center the title. Change the title font to Broadway (or a font of your choice), 16 pt, and red font color.

**e.** In the first paragraph, delete the word "traditionally" and change the number 5/8 to "May 8th." Add the text "and bicycle safety" to the end of the second sentence in this paragraph.

**f.** End the first sentence in paragraph 3 after the word "Park". Change the following sentence to "The ride begins at 11 am."

**g.** Delete the phrase "the riders are encouraged to" from the first sentence of the fourth paragraph.

**h.** Add italics, bold, and red font color to the date in the first paragraph, the time in the third paragraph, and the phone number in the last paragraph.

**i.** Justify the paragraphs.

**j.** Increase the font size of the paragraphs to 12 pt.

**k.** Below the title, insert a clip art graphic of your choice of a child riding a bike by searching on the keyword "bike" or use the graphic file wd01_Child on Bike. Center it and adjust the size of the graphic appropriately. Add a blank line above and below the graphic.

**l.** Add your name and the current date on separate lines several lines below the last line. Left-align both lines. Turn off the display of formatting marks.

**m.** Review the document and, if necessary, adjust the size of the graphic to fit the document on a single page.

**n.** Include your name in the file properties as author and the file name as the title.

**o.** Save the document again. Print the document.

## Creating a Grand Opening Flyer ★★

**3.** The Downtown Internet Cafe is planning a grand re-opening celebration. The cafe combines the relaxed atmosphere of a coffee house with the fun of using the Internet. You want to create a flyer about the celebration that you can give to customers and also post in the window of other local businesses about the celebration. Your completed flyer will be similar to the one shown here.

**a.** Open a new Word document and enter the following text, pressing ⏎Enter where indicated.

**Grand Re-Opening Celebration** ⏎Enter (2 times)

**Downtown Internet Cafe** ⏎Enter (2 times)

**Your newly remodeled neighborhood coffee shop** ⏎Enter (2 times)

**Stop on by and enjoy an excellent dark Italian Roast coffee, premium loose teas, blended drinks and quality light fare of sandwiches, pitas and salads.** ⏎Enter (2 times)

**Starting Friday, September 1st and continuing all week through Sunday, September 10th we will take 15 percent off all cappuccino and blended drinks. Plus take $2.00 off any sandwich order.** ⏎Enter (2 times)

So enjoy a drink and use our free wifi service to get online with the fastest connection in the neighborhood! `←Enter` (3 times)

2314 Telegraph Avenue `←Enter`

Cafe Hours: Sunday - Thursday 8:00 a.m. to 9:00 p.m. Friday and Saturday 8:00 a.m. to 12:00 a.m. `←Enter`

**b.** Correct any spelling and grammar errors that are identified.

**c.** Save the document as Grand Re-Opening.

**d.** Type **Join Us for Live Entertainment!** after the location and hours. Use the Undo feature to remove this sentence.

**e.** Turn on the display of formatting marks. Center the entire document.

**f.** Capitalize each word of the third line. Replace the word percent with the % symbol. Change the case of the text "free wifi" to uppercase. Delete the following word, "service."

**g.** Change the first line to a font color of blue, font type of Arial Black or a font of your choice, and size of 24 pt.

**h.** Change the second line to a font color of purple, font type of Arial or a font of your choice, and size of 36 pt.

**i.** Change the third line to a font color of dark red and a font size of 16 pt. Change the last two lines (address and hours) to a font color of dark red.

**j.** Increase the font size of the three paragraphs to 14 points.

**k.** Insert the graphic file wd01_coffee (from your data files) on the middle blank line below the third title line. Size the graphic to be approximately 2 by 2¼ inches using the ruler as a guide.

**l.** Add a page border of your choice to the flyer.

**m.** Add your name and the current date, left-aligned, on one line, below the last line. Turn off the display of formatting marks.

**n.** If necessary, reduce the size of the graphic so the entire flyer fits on one page.

**o.** Include your name in the file properties as author and the file name as the title. Save and print the flyer.

**Grand Re-Opening Celebration**

# Downtown Internet Café

Your Newly Remodeled Neighborhood Coffee Shop

Stop on by and enjoy an excellent dark Italian Roast coffee, premium loose teas, blended drinks and quality light fare of sandwiches, pitas and salads.

Starting Friday, September 1st and continuing all week through Sunday, September 10th we will take 15% off all cappuccino and blended drinks. Plus take $2.00 off any sandwich order.

So enjoy a drink and use our FREE WIFI to get online with the fastest connection in the neighborhood!

2314 Telegraph Avenue

Café Hours: Sunday – Thursday 8:00a.m. to 9:00p.m. Friday and Saturday 8:00a.m. to 12:00a.m.

Student Name-Date

## Preparing a Lecture on Note-Taking Skills ★★★

4.  You teach a college survival skills class and have recently read about the results of a survey conducted by the Pilot Pen Company of America about note-taking skills. The survey of 500 teenagers found that students typically begin taking classroom notes by sixth grade and that only half had been taught how to take classroom notes. It also found that those students trained in note-taking earned better grades. Note-taking becomes increasingly important in high school and is essential in college. Lecture notes are a key component for mastering material. In response to the survey, the pen manufacturer came up with 10 tips for better note-taking. You started a document of these tips that you plan to use to supplement your lecture on this topic. You will continue to revise and format the document. The revised document will be similar to the one shown here.

    a.  Open the Word document wd01_ Note Taking Skills.

    b.  Correct any spelling and grammar errors that are identified. Save the document as Note Taking Skills.

    c.  Switch to Draft view. Turn off the display of formatting marks. Change the font of the title line to a font of your choice, 18 pt. Center and add color of your choice to the title line.

    d.  In the Be Ready tip, delete the word "lots". In the Write Legibly tip, delete the word "cursive" and add the words "an erasable" before the word "pen." Change the tip heading "Margins" to "Use Wide Margins."

    e.  Above the Mark Questionable Material tip, insert the following tip:

    **Fill in Gaps**

    **Check with a classmate or your teacher after class to get any missing names, dates, facts or other information you could not write down.**

    f.  Change the tip heading lines font to Lucida Sans with a font size of 16 pt and a color of your choice.

    g.  Change the alignment of the paragraphs to justified. Use Undo Changes to return the alignment to left. Use Redo Changes to return the paragraphs to justified again.

    h.  Insert a clip art graphic of your choice (search on "pencil") below the title. Size it appropriately and center it.

    i.  Add your name and the current date, centered, on separate lines two lines below the last line.

    j.  Include your name in the file properties as author and the document title as the title. Save the document. Print the document.

## Writing an Article on the History of Ice Cream ★★★

5. Each month the town's free paper prints a fun article on the history of something people are familiar with but might not know anything about. You researched the topic online and found the information you needed about the history of ice cream from the International Dairy Foods Association's Web site at www.idfa.org/facts/icmonth/page7.cfm. You started writing the article a few days ago and just need to continue the article by adding a few more details. Then you need to edit and format the text and include a graphic to enhance the appearance of the article. Your completed article will be similar to the one shown here.

a. Open the file named wd01_History of Ice Cream.

b. Correct any spelling and grammar errors. (Hint: Click [icon] in the status bar to move to each error.) Save the document as Ice Cream History.

c. Enter the following headings at the location shown in parentheses.

**History of Ice Cream** (above first paragraph)

**The Evolution of Ice Cream** (above second paragraph)

**Ice Cream in America** (above third paragraph)

d. Center the article title. Change the font to Impact with a point size of 24. Add a color of your choice to the title.

e. Change the other two headings to bold with a type size of 14 pt. Center the heads. Use the same color as in the title for the heads.

f. Change the alignment of the first paragraph to justified.

g. Add a blank line below the main title of the article and insert the picture wd01_Ice Cream (from your data files) at this location.

h. Size the picture to be 2 inches wide (use the ruler as a guide). Center it below the title.

i. Add a Draft watermark.

j. Add your name and the current date below the last line of the article. View the whole page and, if necessary, reduce the size of the graphic so the entire article fits on one page.

k. Include your name in the file properties as author and the document title as the title. Save the document again. Print the document.

# Lab Exercises

### Creating a Flyer ★

1. Adventure Travel Tours is offering a great deal on a Day of the Dead Bicycle Tour in Mexico. Research the Day of the Dead celebration using the Web as a resource. Then, using the features of Word you have learned so far, create a flyer that will advertise this tour. Be sure to use at least two colors of text, two sizes of text, and two kinds of paragraph alignment. Include a graphic from the Clip Organizer. Include your name at the bottom of the flyer. Include your name in the file properties as author and the file name as the title. Save the document as Mexico Adventure.

### Creating a Swimming Pool Rules Flyer ★★

2. You work in the community pool and have been asked to create a flyer to post that identifies the rules swimmers should follow when using the pool. Create a flyer that explains the five most important rules to follow while swimming at the pool. Use a piece of clip art to liven up your flyer. Include different font sizes, paragraph alignments, and other formatting features to make the flyer attractive. Apply different font colors for each rule. Include a page border. Include your name at the bottom of the flyer. Include your name in the file properties as author and the file name as the title. Save the document as Pool Rules.

### Astronomy Class Memo ★★

3. The city of Gilbert, Arizona, has recently built a $100,000 observatory that includes a $20,000 telescope in a local park. The observatory is open evenings for small groups of five to six people to take turns looking through the 16-inch telescope's eyepiece. The use of the observatory is free.

   The city has decided to offer classes for the community to learn how to use the telescope and to teach about astronomy. As a trial run, the class will first be offered to city employees and their families. You want to notify all employees about the observatory and the class by including a memo with their paycheck. Using Step-by-Step Exercise 1 as a model, provide information about when and where the class will be held. Include information about how people sign up for the class. Include your name in the file properties as author and the file name as the title. Save the memo as Astronomy Basics.

### Volunteer Opportunities ★★★

4. Many community groups, hospitals, libraries, and churches are looking for volunteers to assist in their programs. Volunteering has rewards for both the volunteer and the community. Using the Web as a resource, research volunteer opportunities in your community. Then write a one-page report that includes information about two volunteer groups for which you would like to volunteer. Include information about what the organization does for the community. Also include the skills you have to offer and the amount of time you can commit as volunteer. Include a title at the top of the document and your name and the current date below the title. Center the title lines. Use at least two colors of text, two sizes of text, and two kinds of paragraph alignment. Include a graphic from the Clip Organizer. Include your name in the file properties as author and the file name as the title. Save the document as Volunteer Opportunities.

### Writing a Career Report ★★★

5. Using the library or the Web, research information about your chosen career. Write a one-page report about your findings that includes information on three areas: Career Description; Educational Requirements; Salary and Employment projections. Include a title at the top of the document and your name and the current date below the title. Center the title lines. Justify the paragraphs. Include your name in the file properties as author and the file name as the title. Save the document as Career Report.

# Revising and Refining a Document

## Objectives

After completing this lab, you will know how to:

**1** Use the Spelling and Grammar tool and the Thesaurus.

**2** Move, cut, and copy text and formats.

**3** Control document paging.

**4** Find and replace text.

**5** Insert the current date.

**6** Change indents, line spacing, and margins.

**7** Create a tabbed table.

**8** Add color highlighting and underlines.

**9** Create numbered and bulleted lists.

**10** Create and use Building Blocks.

**11** Insert and modify a shape.

**12** Edit in Print Preview.

**13** Print a document.

# Case Study

## Adventure Travel Tours

After creating the rough draft of the new tours flyer, you showed the printed copy to your manager at Adventure Travel Tours. Your manager then made several suggestions for improving the flyer's style and appearance. In addition, you created a letter to be sent to clients along with your flyer. The letter briefly describes Adventure Travel's four new tours and invites clients to attend an informational presentation. Your manager likes the idea, but also wants the letter to include information about the new Adventure Travel Tours Web site and a 10 percent discount for early booking.

In this lab, you will learn more about editing documents so you can reorganize and refine both your flyer and a rough draft of the letter to clients. You also will learn to use many more of the formatting features included in Office Word 2007 so you can add style and interest to your documents. Formatting features can greatly improve the appearance and design of any document you produce so that it communicates its message more clearly. The completed letter and revised flyer are shown here.

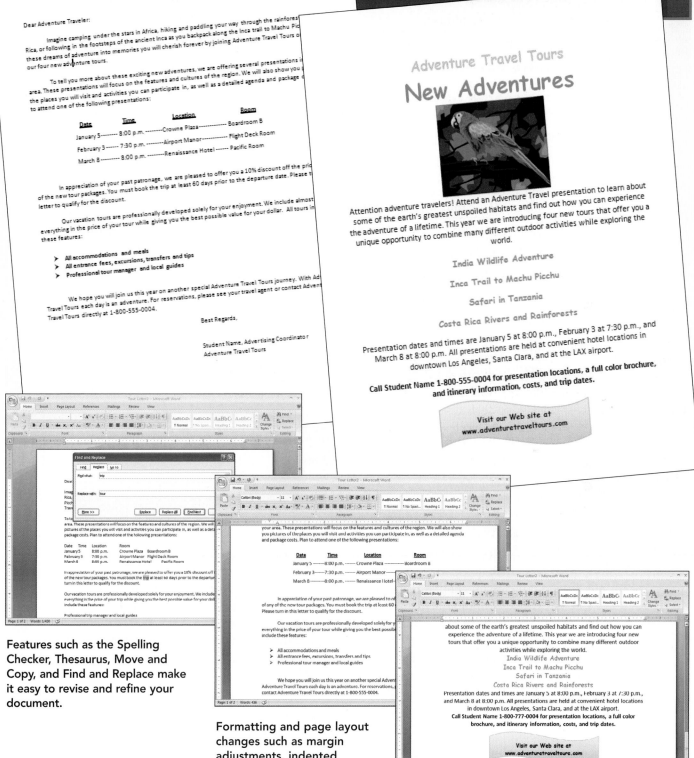

Features such as the Spelling Checker, Thesaurus, Move and Copy, and Find and Replace make it easy to revise and refine your document.

Formatting and page layout changes such as margin adjustments, indented paragraphs, and tabbed tables help improve the readability and style of the document.

Graphic enhancements such as shapes add interest to a document.

# Concept Preview

## Revising a Document

After speaking with the manager about the letter's content, you planned the basic topics that need to be included in the letter: to advertise the new tours, invite clients to the presentations, describe the early-booking discount, and promote the new Web site. You quickly entered the text for the letter, saved it as Tour Letter, and printed out a hard copy. As you are reading the document again, you mark up the printout with the changes and corrections you want to make. The marked-up copy is shown here.

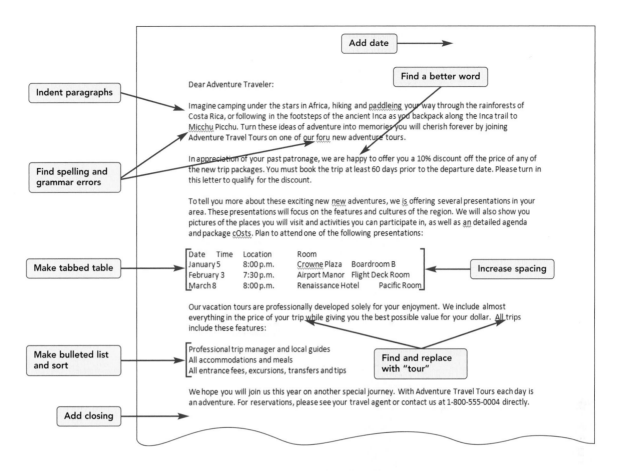

## Spell-Checking the Entire Document

The first correction you want to make is to clean up the spelling and grammar errors that Word has identified.

**1** ● **Start Office Word 2007 and open the file** wd02_Tour Letter.

● **If necessary, change to Print Layout view at 100% zoom.**

*Your screen should be similar to Figure 2.1*

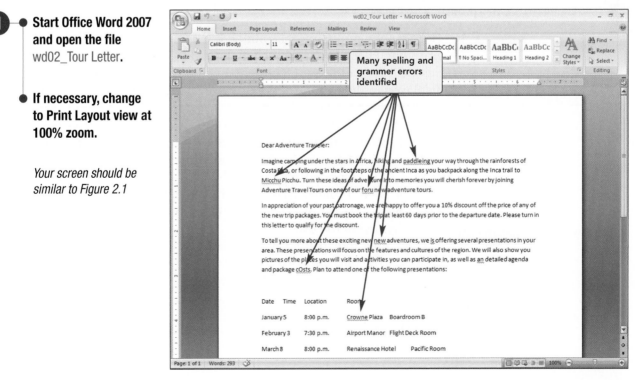

**Figure 2.1**

To correct the misspelled words and grammatical errors, you can use the context menu to correct each individual word or error, as you learned in Lab 1. However, in many cases, you may find it more efficient to wait until you are finished writing before you correct errors. Rather than continually breaking your train of thought to correct errors as you type, you can manually turn on the spelling and grammar checker to locate and correct all the errors in the document at once.

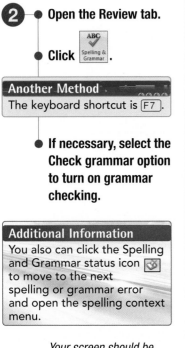

**2** ● **Open the Review tab.**

● **Click** [Spelling & Grammar].

**Another Method**
The keyboard shortcut is F7.

● **If necessary, select the Check grammar option to turn on grammar checking.**

**Additional Information**
You also can click the Spelling and Grammar status icon to move to the next spelling or grammar error and open the spelling context menu.

*Your screen should be similar to Figure 2.2*

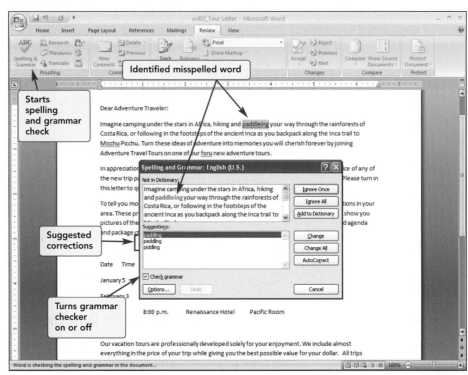

Figure 2.2

**Additional Information**
Because the contents of the list are determined only by spelling, any instances of terms that seem inappropriate in context are completely coincidental.

**Additional Information**
The [Change All] option replaces the same word throughout the document with the word you select in the Suggestions box.

The Spelling and Grammar dialog box is displayed, and the spelling and grammar checker has immediately located the first word that may be misspelled, "paddleing." The sentence with the misspelled word in red is displayed in the Not in Dictionary text box, and the word is highlighted in the document.

The Suggestions list box displays the words the spelling checker has located in the dictionary that most closely match the misspelled word. The most likely match is highlighted. Sometimes the spelling checker does not display any suggested replacements. This occurs when it cannot locate any words in the dictionaries that are similar in spelling. If no suggestions are provided, the Not in Dictionary text box simply displays the word that is highlighted in the text.

To change the spelling of the word to one of the suggested spellings, highlight the correct word in the list and then click . If there were no suggested replacements, and you did not want to use any of the option buttons, you could edit the word yourself by typing the correction in the Not in Dictionary box. In this case, the correct replacement, "paddling," is already highlighted.

**WD2.6**
**Word 2007**
Lab 2: Revising and Refining a Document
www.mhhe.com/oleary

**3** Click [ Change ].

*Your screen should be similar to Figure 2.3*

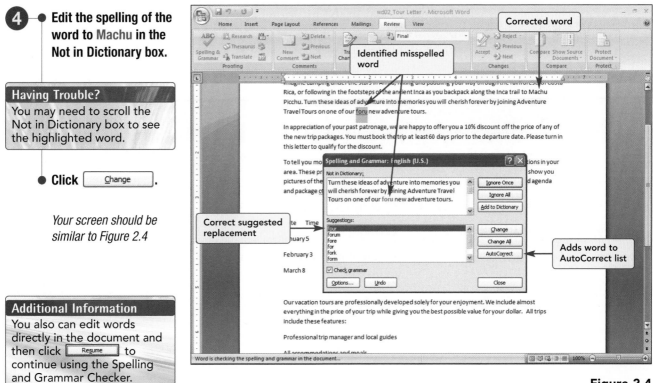

**Figure 2.3**

The spelling checker replaces the misspelled word with the selected suggested replacement and moves on to locate the next error. This time the error is the name of the Inca ruins at Machu Picchu. "Micchu" is the incorrect spelling for this word; there is no correct suggestion, however, because the word is not found in the dictionary. You will correct the spelling of the word by editing it in the Not in Dictionary text box.

**4** Edit the spelling of the word to **Machu** in the Not in Dictionary box.

**Having Trouble?**

You may need to scroll the Not in Dictionary box to see the highlighted word.

Click [ Change ].

*Your screen should be similar to Figure 2.4*

**Additional Information**

You also can edit words directly in the document and then click [ Resume ] to continue using the Spelling and Grammar Checker.

**Figure 2.4**

The next located error, "foru," is a typing error that you make frequently when typing the word four. The correct spelling is selected in the Suggestions list box. You want to change it to the suggested word and add it to the list of words that are automatically corrected.

**5** ● Click AutoCorrect .

**Having Trouble?**
If a dialog box appears telling you an AutoCorrect entry already exists for this word, simply click Yes to continue.

*Your screen should be similar to Figure 2.5*

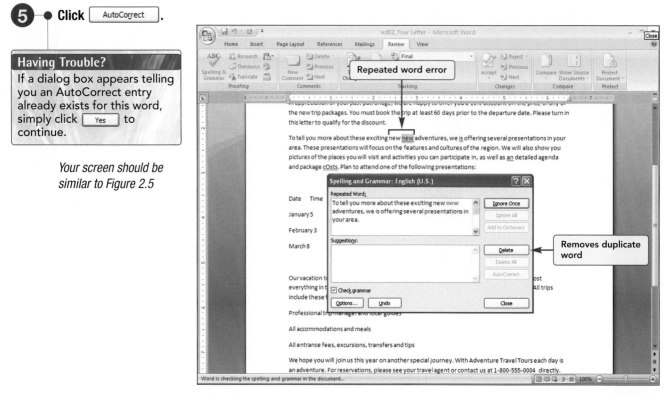

**Figure 2.5**

The word is corrected in the document. Because you also added it to the AutoCorrect list, in the future whenever you type this word incorrectly as "foru," it will automatically be changed to "four." The next five errors that will be identified and their causes are shown in the following table

| Identified Error | Cause | Action | Result |
|---|---|---|---|
| new | Repeated word | Delete | duplicate word "new" is deleted |
| we is | Subject-verb disagreement | Change | we are |
| cOsts | Inconsistent capitalization | Change | costs |
| an detailed | Grammatical error | Change | a |
| Crowne | Spelling error | Ignore Once | accepts the word as correct for this occurrence only |

**6** • **Respond to the spelling and grammar checker by taking the actions in the table above for the five identified errors.**

• **Click [ OK ] in response to the message telling you that the spelling and grammar check is complete.**

• **Move to the top of the document.**

*Your screen should be similar to Figure 2.6*

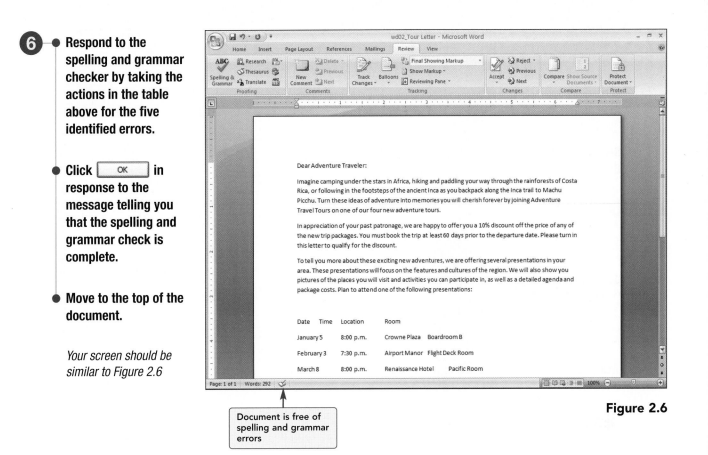

Document is free of spelling and grammar errors

**Figure 2.6**

## Using the Thesaurus

The next text change you want to make is to find a more descriptive word for "ideas" in the first paragraph and "happy" in the second paragraph. To help find a similar word, you will use the thesaurus tool.

---

## Concept 1

### Thesaurus

**1** Word's **thesaurus** is a reference tool that provides synonyms, antonyms, and related words for a selected word or phrase. **Synonyms** are words with a similar meaning, such as "cheerful" and "happy." **Antonyms** are words with an opposite meaning, such as "cheerful" and "sad." Related words are words that are variations of the same word, such as "cheerful" and "cheer." The thesaurus can help to liven up your documents by adding interest and variety to your text.

---

First you need to identify the word you want looked up by moving the insertion point onto the word. Then you use the thesaurus to suggest alternative words. The quickest way to get synonyms is to use the context menu for the word you want to replace.

**1** ● **Right-click on the word "ideas" (first paragraph, second sentence) to display the context menu.**

● **Select Synonyms on the Context menu.**

**Having Trouble?**
Simply point to the menu option to select it.

**Additional Information**
Whenever you right-click an item, both the context menu and Mini toolbar are displayed.

*Your screen should be similar to Figure 2.7*

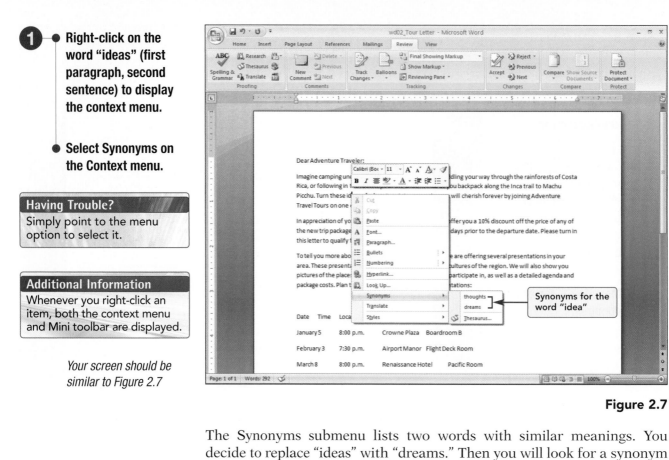

**Figure 2.7**

The Synonyms submenu lists two words with similar meanings. You decide to replace "ideas" with "dreams." Then you will look for a synonym for "happy." You will use the Research pane to locate synonyms this time.

**2** ● **Choose "dreams".**

● **Click on the word "happy" (first sentence, second paragraph).**

● **Click** 🕮 Thesaurus **in the Proofing group.**

**Another Method**
The keyboard equivalent is
⇧Shift + F7 .

*Your screen should be similar to Figure 2.8*

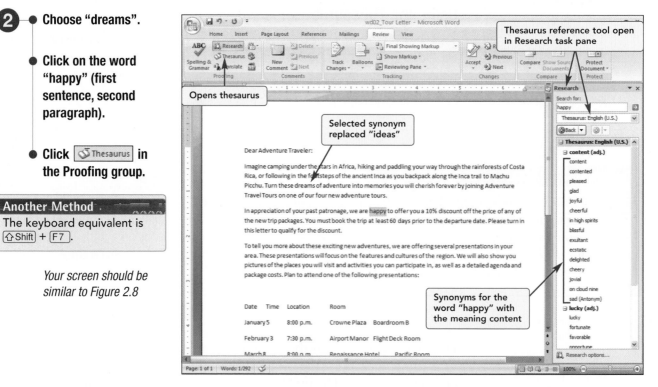

**Figure 2.8**

The thesaurus opens in the Research task pane and the word the insertion point is on is displayed in the Search For text box. The list box displays words that have similar meanings for the word "happy" with a meaning of "content (adj)." The best choice from this list is "pleased." To see whether any other words are closer in meaning, you will look up synonyms for the word "pleased."

**3** • **Choose "pleased".**

**Additional Information**

You also can choose Look Up from the word's drop-down menu to look up synonyms for the word.

*Your screen should be similar to Figure 2.9*

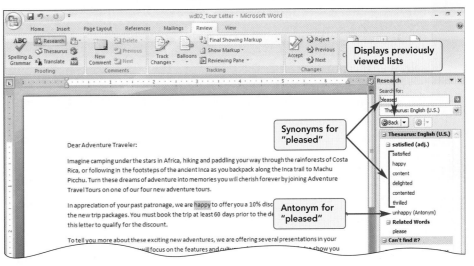

**Figure 2.9**

The word "pleased" is the new search term, and the list displays synonyms, as well as an antonym, for this word. You decide to use "pleased" and will return to the previous list and insert the word into the document.

**4** • **Click Back to display the list for the word "happy."**

• **Open the "pleased" synonym drop-down menu.**

• **Choose Insert.**

• **Close the Research task pane.**

• **Move to the top of the document and save the revised document as** Tour Letter2 **to the appropriate data file location.**

*Your screen should be similar to Figure 2.10*

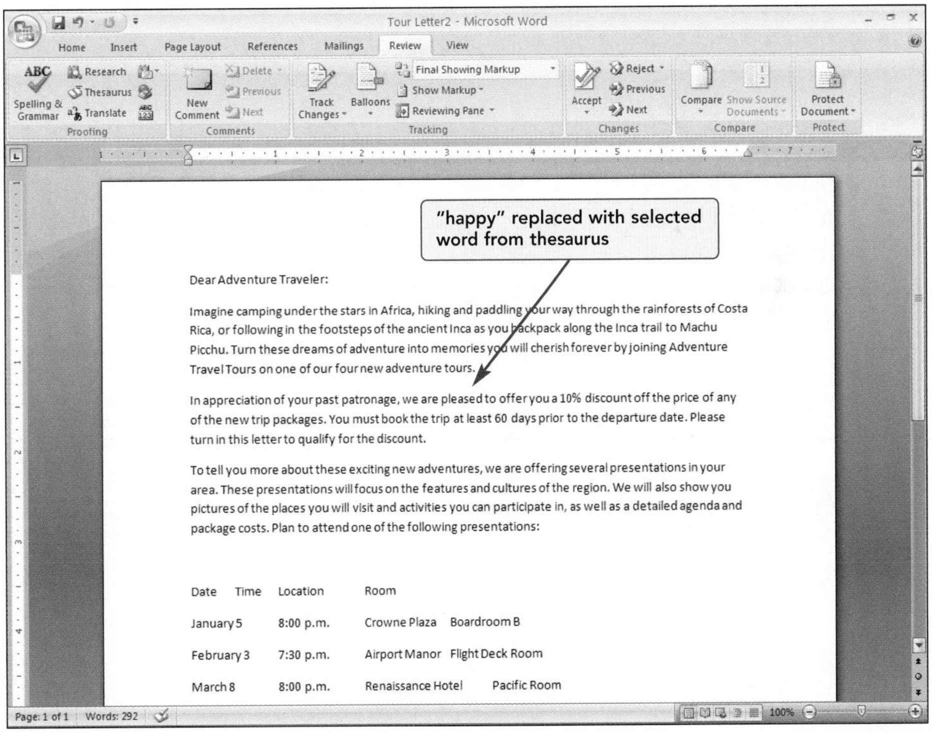

**Figure 2.10**

The word "happy" is replaced with the selected word from the thesaurus.

## Moving and Copying Selections

After looking over the letter, you decide to add the company name in several other locations and to change the order of paragraphs. To make these changes quickly, you can move and copy selections.

## Concept 2

### Move and Copy

**2** Text and graphic selections can be moved or copied to new locations in a document or between documents, saving you time by not having to recreate the same information. A selection that is moved is cut from its original location, called the **source**, and inserted at a new location, called the **destination**. A selection that is copied leaves the original in the source and inserts a duplicate at the destination.

When a selection is cut or copied, the selection is stored in the **system Clipboard**, a temporary Windows storage area in memory. It is also stored in the **Office Clipboard**. The system Clipboard holds only the last cut or copied item, whereas the Office Clipboard can store up to 24 items that have been cut or copied. This feature allows you to insert multiple items from various Office documents and paste all or part of the collection of items into another document.

### Using Copy and Paste

You want to include the company name in the last paragraph of the letter in two places. Because the name has already been entered in the first paragraph, you will copy it instead of typing the name again.

**1** ● Select "Adventure Travel Tours" (first paragraph, last sentence).

● Click 📋 Copy in the Clipboard group of the Home tab.

● Move to the beginning of the word "journey" (last paragraph, first sentence).

● Click [Paste] in the Clipboard group.

**Another Method**

The Copy keyboard shortcut is [Ctrl] + C. The Paste keyboard shortcut is [Ctrl] + V.

*Your screen should be similar to Figure 2.11*

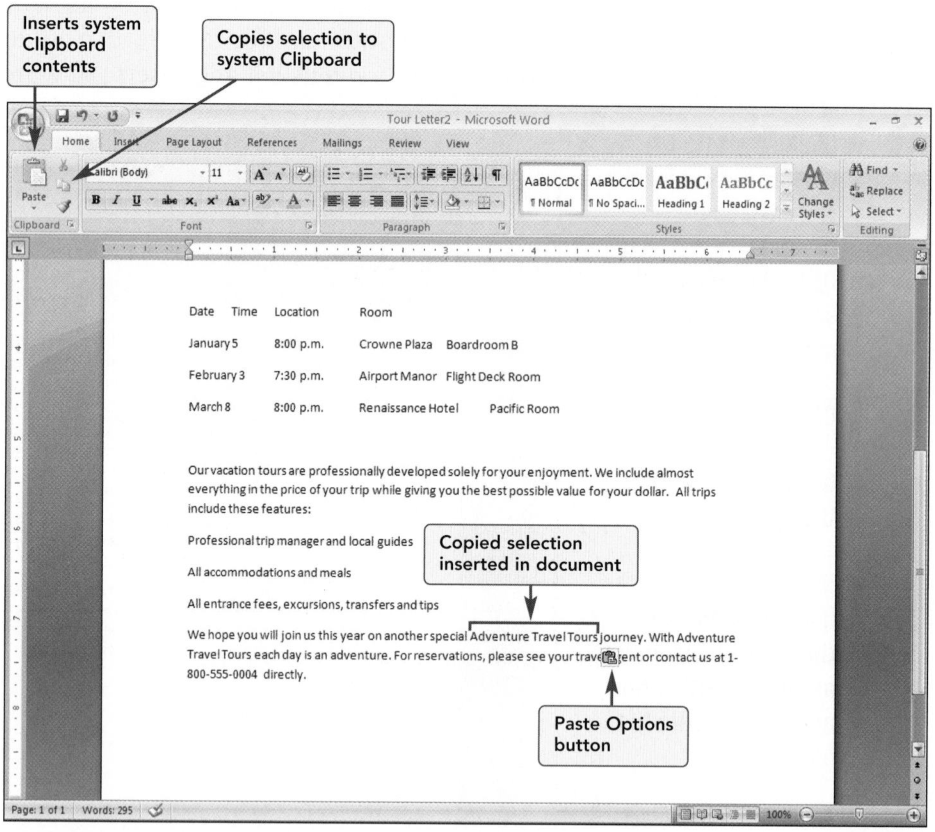

**Additional Information**

Using the [Paste] button or keyboard shortcut inserts the system Clipboard contents, not the Office Clipboard contents. You will learn about using the Office Clipboard in Lab 3.

**Figure 2.11**

The copied selection is inserted at the location you specified. The 📋 Paste Options button appears automatically whenever a selection is pasted. It is used to control the format of the pasted item.

**2** ● **Click the** 🗐 **Paste Options button.**

*Your screen should be similar to Figure 2.12*

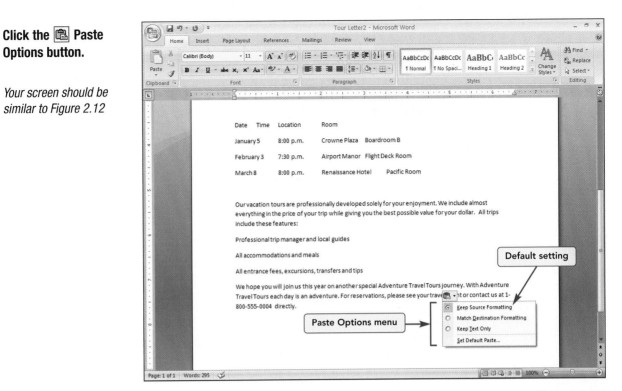

**Figure 2.12**

The Paste options are used to specify whether to insert the item with the same formatting that it had in the source, to change it to the formatting of the surrounding destination text, or to insert text only (from a selection that is a combination of text and graphics). The default, to keep the formatting from the source, is appropriate. The last option is used to change the default paste formatting setting to another.

Next, you want to insert the company name in place of the word "us" in the last sentence of the letter.

**3** ● **Click outside the menu to close it.**

● **Select "us" (last sentence).**

● **Right-click on the selection and choose Paste from the context menu.**

*Your screen should be similar to Figure 2.13*

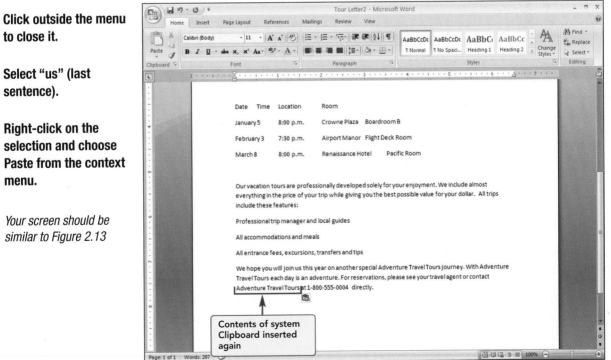

**Figure 2.13**

Moving and Copying Selections

The selected text was deleted and replaced with the contents of the system Clipboard. The system Clipboard contents remain in the Clipboard until another item is copied or cut, allowing you to paste the same item multiple times.

## Using Cut and Paste

You want the paragraph about the 10 percent discount (second paragraph) to follow the list of presentation dates. To do this, you will move the paragraph from its current location to the new location. The Cut and Paste commands in the Clipboard group of the Home tab are used to move selections. You will use the context menu to select the Cut command.

**1** ● **Select the second paragraph.**

**Having Trouble?**
Double-click in the margin space to the left of the paragraph to select it.

● **Click ✄ Cut in the Clipboard group.**

**Another Method**
The Cut keyboard shortcut is Ctrl + X. You also can choose Cut from the context menu.

*Your screen should be similar to Figure 2.14*

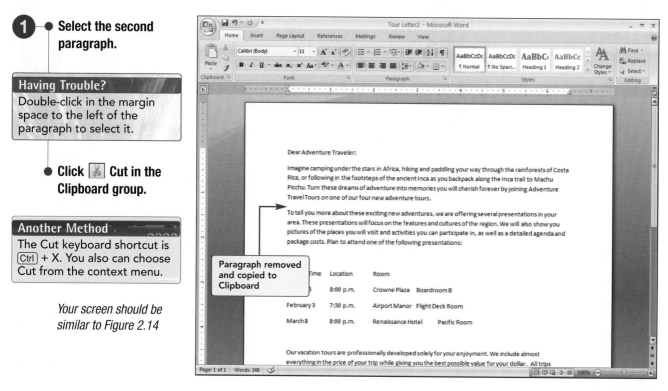

**Figure 2.14**

The selected paragraph is removed from the source and copied to the Clipboard. Next, you need to move the insertion point to the location where the text will be inserted and paste the text into the document from the Clipboard.

**2**
- Move to the beginning of the paragraph below the list of presentation dates.

- Press [Ctrl] + V.

- If necessary, scroll down to view the pasted paragraph.

*Your screen should be similar to Figure 2.15*

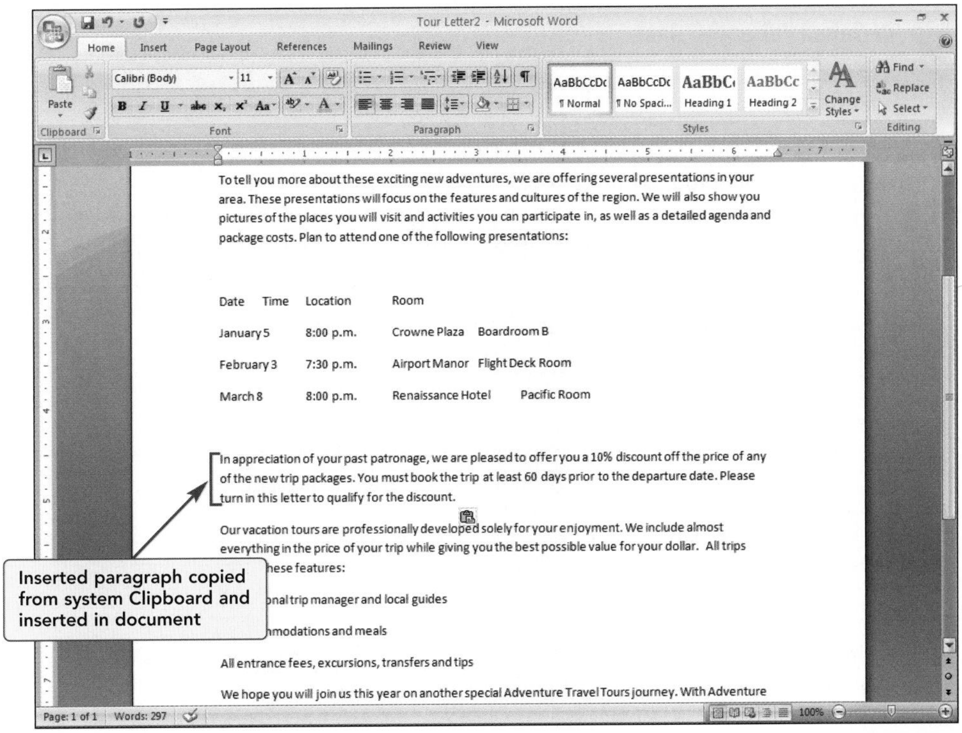

Figure 2.15

The cut paragraph is reentered into the document at the insertion point location. That was much quicker than retyping the whole paragraph!

## Using Drag and Drop

Finally, you also decide to move the word "directly" in the last paragraph so that the sentence reads " . . . contact Adventure Travel Tours directly at 1-800-555-0004." Rather than use Cut and Paste to move this text, you will use the **drag-and-drop** editing feature. This feature is most useful for copying or moving short distances in a document.

To use drag and drop to move a selection, point to the selection and drag it to the location where you want the selection inserted. The mouse pointer appears as as you drag, and a temporary insertion point shows you where the text will be placed when you release the mouse button.

**Additional Information**

You also can use drag and drop to copy a selection by holding down [Ctrl] while dragging. The mouse pointer shape is .

**1**
● Select "directly" (last word in last paragraph).

● Drag the selection to before "at" in the same sentence.

*Your screen should be similar to Figure 2.16*

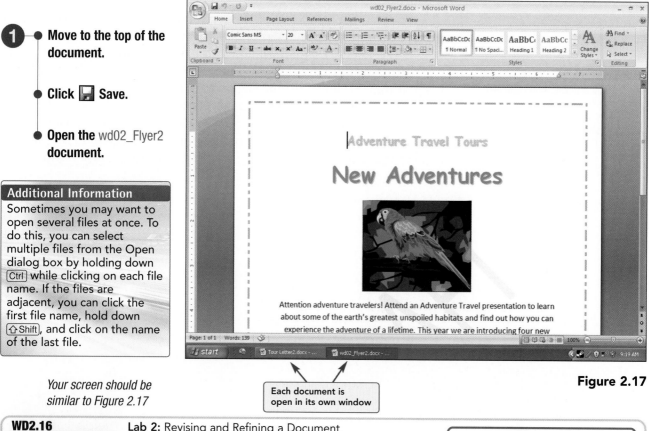

**Figure 2.16**

The selection is moved to the new location.

## Copying between Documents

You plan to include the flyer with the letter to be mailed to clients. To do this, you will open the flyer document and copy it into the letter document file. Because all Office 2007 applications allow you to open and use multiple files at the same time, this is a very simple procedure.

**1**
● Move to the top of the document.

● Click 💾 Save.

● Open the wd02_Flyer2 document.

*Your screen should be similar to Figure 2.17*

**Figure 2.17**

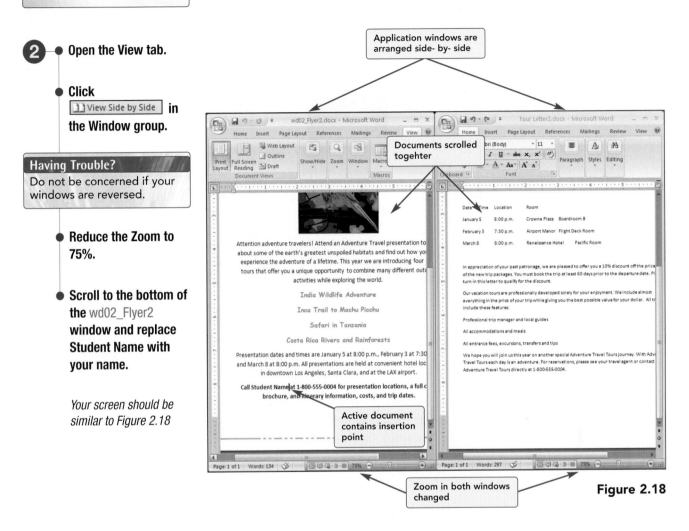
The flyer document is opened and displayed in a separate Word 2007 application window. You made a few changes to the flyer that your supervisor suggested. You would like to see both documents in the window at the same time. This makes it easy to compare documents or to move or copy information between documents.

**2 ● Open the View tab.**

**● Click**
**⎡⎤ View Side by Side** in
the Window group.

**Having Trouble?**

Do not be concerned if your windows are reversed.

**● Reduce the Zoom to 75%.**

**● Scroll to the bottom of the wd02_Flyer2 window and replace Student Name with your name.**

*Your screen should be similar to Figure 2.18*

Application windows are arranged side- by- side

Documents scrolled togehter

Active document contains insertion point

Zoom in both windows changed

**Figure 2.18**

Now, the two Word application windows are arranged side by side on the screen. The flyer contains the insertion point, which indicates that it is the **active window**, or the window in which you can work. Simply clicking on the other document makes it active. Because the windows are side by side and there is less horizontal space in each window, the Ribbon groups are compressed. To access commands in these groups, simply click on the group button and the group commands appear.

Did you notice when you scrolled the document that both documents scrolled together? This is because the windows are **synchronized**, meaning both windows will act the same. When synchronized, the documents in both windows will scroll together so you can compare text easily. If you are not comparing text, this feature can be turned off so that they scroll independently.

**3** ● Click ⬚ to display
the Window group
commands.

● Click
[▤‡ Synchronous Scrolling] to
turn off this feature.

● Scroll to the top of
the wd02_Flyer2
document.

*Your screen should be
similar to Figure 2.19*

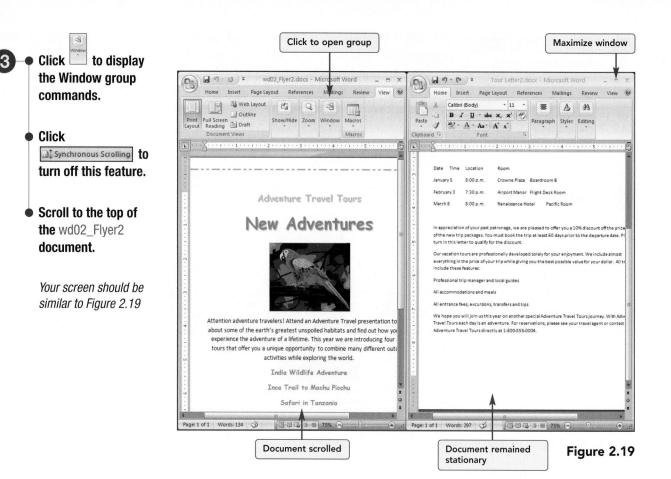

Click to open group

Maximize window

Document scrolled

Document remained
stationary

**Figure 2.19**

The flyer document scrolled while the letter document remained stationary.

Next you will copy the entire flyer to the bottom of the letter document using drag and drop. To copy between documents using drag and drop, hold down the right mouse button while dragging. When you release the button, a context menu appears where you specify the action you want to perform. If you drag using the left mouse button, the selection is moved by default.

**4**

- Click in the Tour Letter2 window to make it active and press Ctrl + End to move to the last (blank) line of the document.

- Click in the Flyer2 window to make it active and drag in the left margin to select the entire flyer.

- Right-drag the selection to the blank line at the end of the letter.

- Release the mouse button and choose Copy Here from the context menu.

- Click ☐ Maximize in the Tour Letter2 title bar to maximize the application window.

- Scroll the window to see the bottom of page one and the top of page two.

*Your screen should be similar to Figure 2.20*

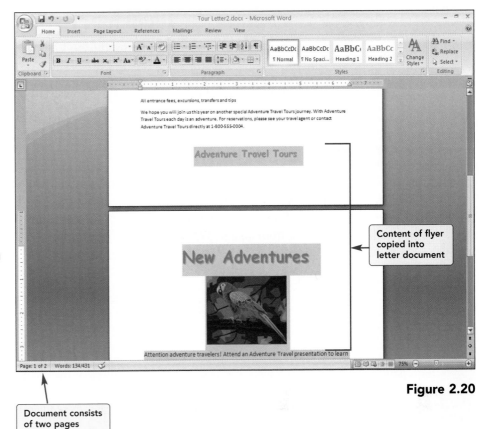

Content of flyer copied into letter document

Document consists of two pages

**Figure 2.20**

**Another Method**

If you did not want to arrange windows, you could just copy the selection in the active window, click on the taskbar button of the other open window to make it active, and then paste the selection in the document.

The letter now consists of two pages. Notice the status bar shows the insertion point location is on page 1 of 2 pages.

# Controlling Document Paging

As text and graphics are added to a document, Word automatically starts a new page when text extends beyond the bottom margin setting. The beginning of a new page is identified by a page break.

## Concept 3

### Page Break

**3** A **page break** marks the point at which one page ends and another begins. Two types of page breaks can be used in a document: soft page breaks and hard page breaks. As you fill a page with text or graphics, Word inserts a **soft page break** automatically when the bottom margin is reached and starts a new page. As you add or remove text from a page, Word automatically readjusts the placement of the soft page break.

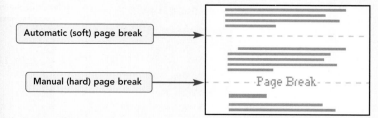

Many times, however, you may want to force a page break to occur at a specific location. To do this you can manually insert a **hard page break**. This action instructs Word to begin a new page regardless of the amount of text on the previous page. When a hard page break is used, its location is never moved regardless of the changes that are made to the amount of text on the preceding page. All soft page breaks that precede or follow a hard page break continue to adjust automatically. Sometimes you may find that you have to remove the hard page break and reenter it at another location as you edit the document.

In Print Layout view, the page break is identified by a space between pages. However you cannot tell if it is a hard or soft page break. You will switch back to Draft view to see the soft page break that was entered in the document. Also notice that images are not shown in Draft view.

**1**
● **Click in the document to deselect the flyer text.**

● **Switch to Draft view at 100% zoom.**

● **If necessary, scroll the document to see the soft page break line.**

*Your screen should be similar to Figure 2.21*

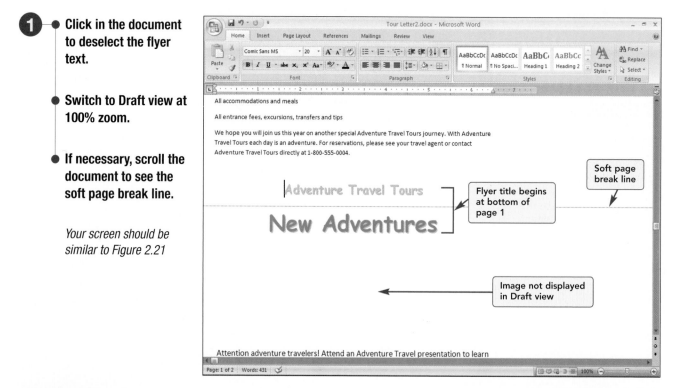

**Figure 2.21**

To show where one page ends and another begins, Word displays a dotted line across the page to mark the soft page break.

### Inserting a Hard Page Break

Many times, the location of the soft page break is not appropriate. In this case, the location of the soft page break displays the flyer title on the bottom of page 1 and the remaining portion of the flyer on page 2. Because you want the entire flyer to print on a page by itself, you will manually insert a hard page break above the flyer title.

**1** ● Move to the beginning of the first line of the flyer.

● Press Ctrl + ↵Enter.

**Another Method**
The Ribbon equivalent is Insert/⟦Page Break⟧ or Page Layout/⟦Breaks ▾⟧/Page.

● Save the document again.

*Your screen should be similar to Figure 2.22*

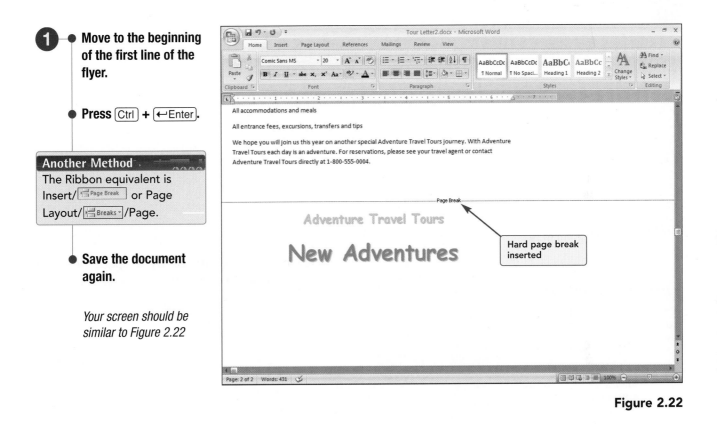

Figure 2.22

**Additional Information**
To remove a hard page break, simply select the hard page break line and press Delete.

A dotted line and the words "Page Break" appear across the page above the flyer title, indicating that a hard page break was entered at that position.

## Finding and Replacing Text

As you continue proofing the letter, you notice that the word "trip" is used frequently. You think that the letter would read better if the word "tour" was used in place of "trip" in some instances. To do this, you will use the Find and Replace feature.

**4**  To make editing easier, you can use the Find and Replace feature to find text in a document and replace it with other text as directed. For example, suppose you created a lengthy document describing the type of clothing and equipment needed to set up a world-class home gym, and then you decided to change "sneakers" to "athletic shoes." Instead of deleting every occurrence of "sneakers" and typing "athletic shoes," you can use the Find and Replace feature to perform the task automatically.

You also can find and replace occurrences of special formatting, such as replacing bold text with italicized text, as well as find and replace formatting marks. Additionally, special characters and symbols, such as an arrow or copyright symbol, can be easily located or replaced. This feature is fast and accurate; however, use care when replacing so that you do not replace unintended matches.

### Finding Text

First, you will use the Find command to locate all occurrences of the word "trip" in the document.

**1** ● **Switch to Print Layout view at 100% zoom.**

● **Move the insertion point to the top of the document.**

**Another Method**
Reminder: Use Ctrl + Home to quickly move to the top of the document.

● **Click** 🔍 Find ▾ **in the Editing group.**

**Another Method**
The keyboard shortcut is Ctrl + F. You also can open the Find and Replace dialog box by clicking the ◉ Select Browse Object button in the vertical scroll bar and selecting Find from the menu.

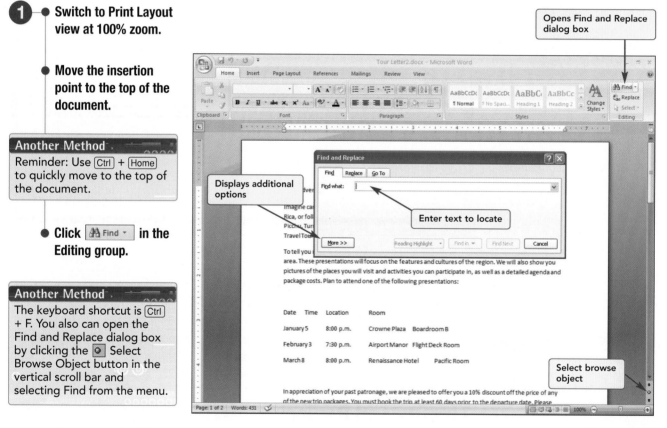

*Your screen should be similar to Figure 2.23*

**Figure 2.23**

The Find tab of the Find and Replace dialog box is used to define the information you want to locate. In the Find What text box, you enter the text you want to locate. In addition, you can use the search options to refine the search.

**2** • Click  .

*Your screen should be similar to Figure 2.24*

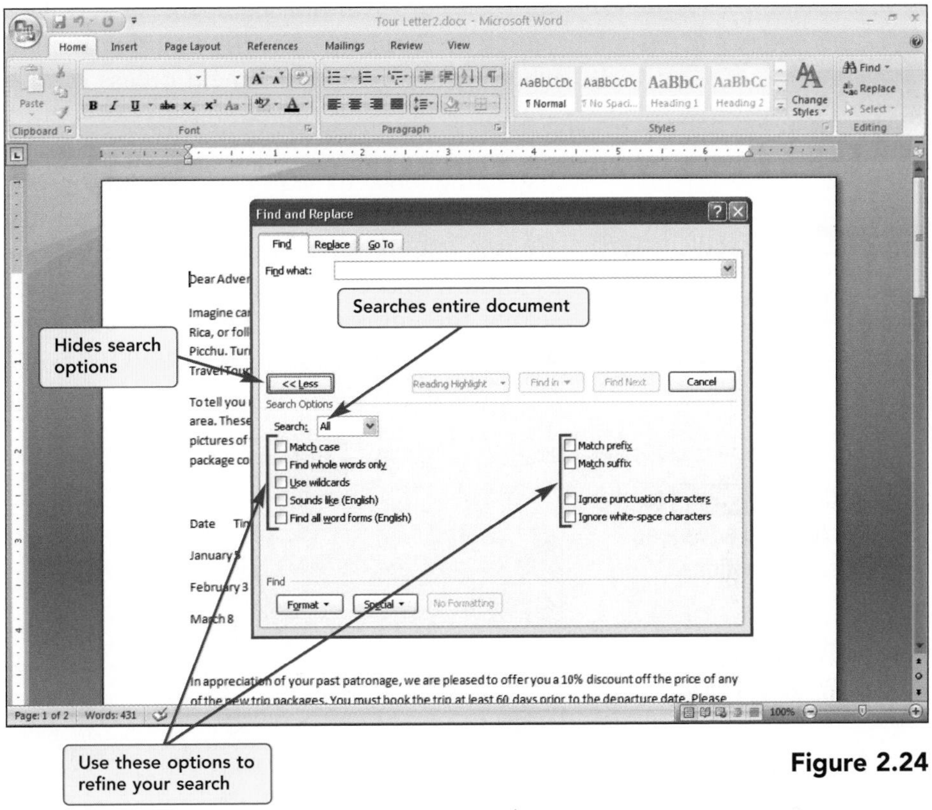

**Additional Information**

Clicking [Format ▾] is used to search for specific formatting such as bold. Clicking [Special ▾] is used to search for special characters and document elements.

**Figure 2.24**

The search options can be combined in many ways to help you find and replace text in documents. They are described in the table below.

| Option | Effect on Text |
| --- | --- |
| Match case | Finds only those words in which the capitalization matches the text you typed. |
| Find whole words only | Finds matches that are whole words and not part of a larger word. For example, finds "cat" only and not "catastrophe" too. |
| Use wildcards | Fine-tunes a search; for example, c?t finds "cat" and "cot" (one-character matches), while c*t finds "cat" and "court" (searches for one or more characters). |
| Sounds like (English) | Finds words that sound like the word you type; very helpful if you do not know the correct spelling of the word you want to find. |
| Find all word forms (English) | Finds and replaces all forms of a word; for example, "buy" will replace "purchase," and "bought" will replace "purchased." |

When you enter the text to find, you can type everything lowercase, because the Match Case option is not selected and the search will not be **case sensitive**. This means that lowercase letters will match both upper- and lowercase letters in the text. To further control the search, you can specify to match prefixes or suffixes. Because these are not selected, a letter or group of letters added at the beginning or end of a word to form another word will not affect the search. For example, the search will find "quick" or "quickly". Finally punctuation and white spaces will be ignored when searching the document unless these options are selected.

Also notice that the Search option default setting is All, which means Word will search the entire document, including headers and footers. You also can choose to search Up to the top of the document or Down to the end of the document from your current location in the document. These options search in the direction specified but exclude the headers, footers, footnotes, and comments from the area to search. Because you want to search the entire document, All is the appropriate setting. You will hide the search options again and begin the search.

**Additional Information**

You will learn about headers, footers, footnotes, and comments in later labs.

**3**

- **Click << Less to close the advanced search options.**
- **Type trip in the Find What text box.**
- **Click Find Next.**

*Your screen should be similar to Figure 2.25*

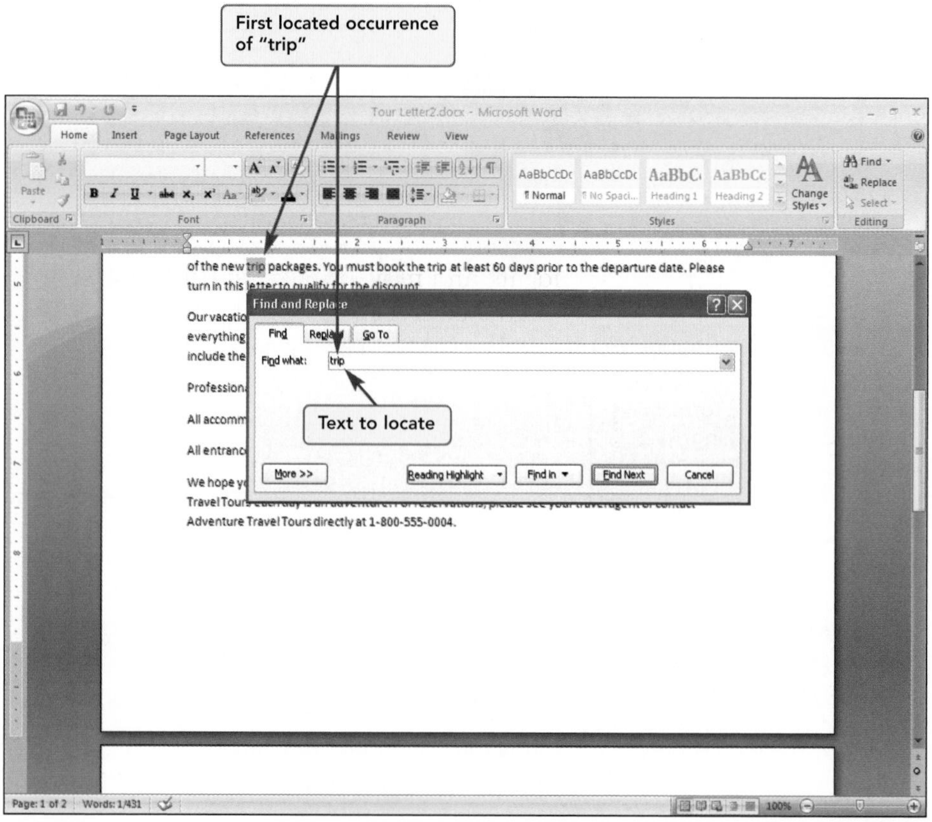


**Figure 2.25**

**Additional Information**

If you use the Up or Down options and the search does not begin at the top of the document, when Word reaches the beginning or end of the document, it asks if you want to continue searching from the end or beginning of the document. You also can highlight text to restrict the search to a selection.

Word searches for all occurrences of the text to find beginning at the insertion point, locates the first occurrence of the word "trip," and highlights it in the document.

**4** ● **Continue to click** **Find Next** **to locate all occurrences of the word.**

**Additional Information**

The Find and Replace dialog box automatically moves out of the way to show the located text.

● **Click** **OK** **when Word indicates the entire document has been searched.**

*Your screen should be similar to Figure 2.26*

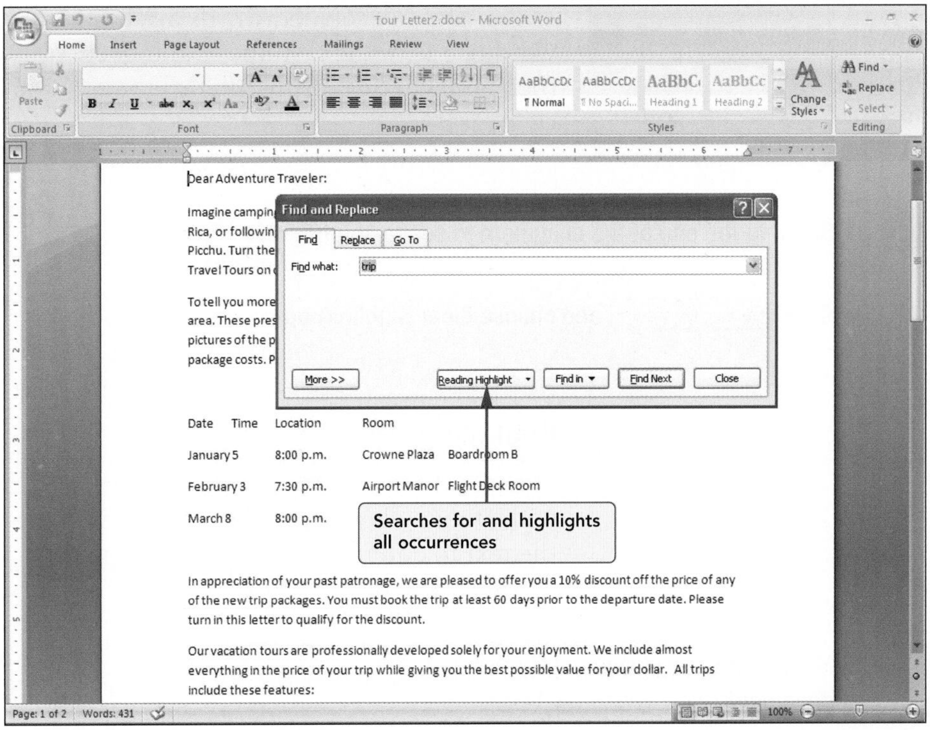

Searches for and highlights all occurrences

**Figure 2.26**

The word "trip" is used six times in the document. Using the Find command is a convenient way to quickly navigate through a document to locate and move to specified information.

To better see all located words, you will highlight them using the Reading Highlight feature.

**5** ● **Click** **Reading Highlight** **.**

● **Choose Highlight All.**

● **If necessary, scroll the document to view the first five highlighted words.**

*Your screen should be similar to Figure 2.27*

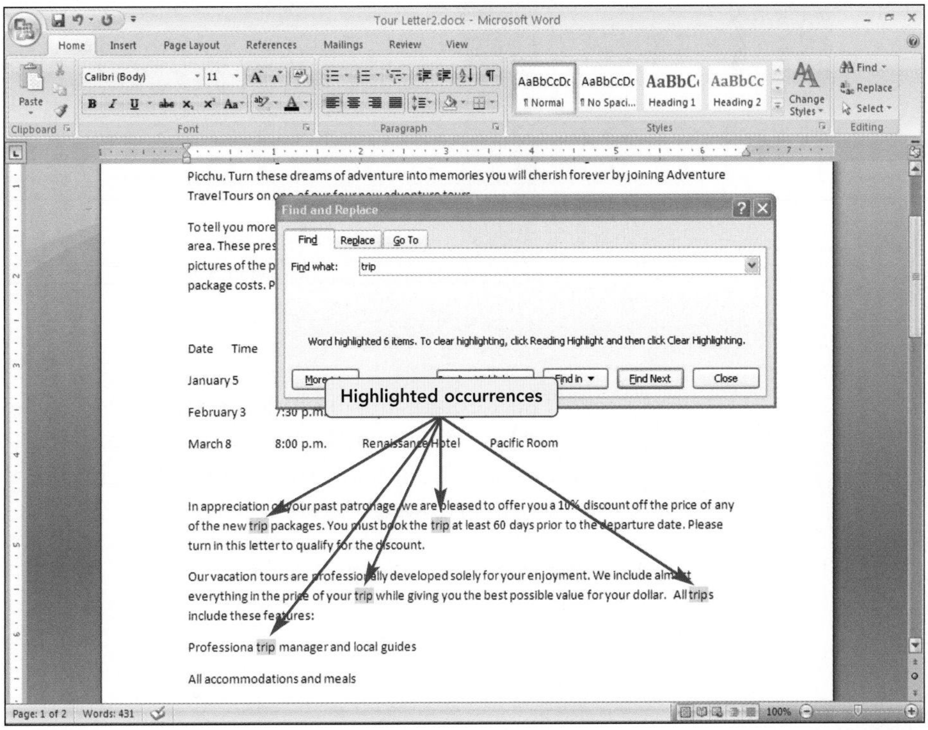

Highlighted occurrences

**Figure 2.27**

Additional Information

The highlight color is determined by the currently selected color in Text Highlight.

The first five located words are highlighted in yellow. The last use of the word trip is in the last line of the flyer. You will move to that location, and then you will turn off highlights.

6
- **Scroll to the end of the document to see the highlighted word.**
- **Click Reading Highlight and choose Clear Highlighting.**

## Replacing Text

You decide to replace several occurrences of the word "trip" in the letter with "tour" where appropriate. You will use the Replace feature to specify the text to enter as the replacement text.

1
- **Move to the top of the document.**
- **Open the Replace tab.**

*Your screen should be similar to Figure 2.28*

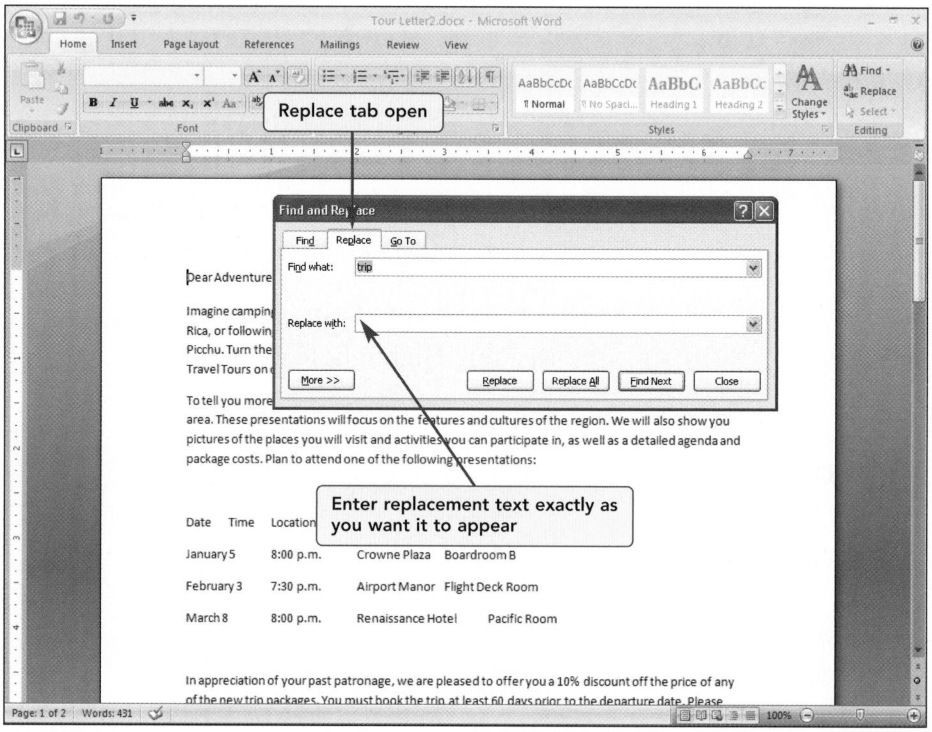


**Figure 2.28**

The Replace tab includes a Replace with text box in which you enter the replacement text. This text must be entered exactly as you want it to appear in your document. You want to find and replace the first occurrence of the word "trip" with "tour."

**2**

- Type **tour** in the Replace with text box.

- Click ⎡Find Next⎤.

- Click ⎡Replace⎤.

*Your screen should be similar to Figure 2.29*

First located word "trip" replaced by "tour"

Second located occurrence of word "trip"

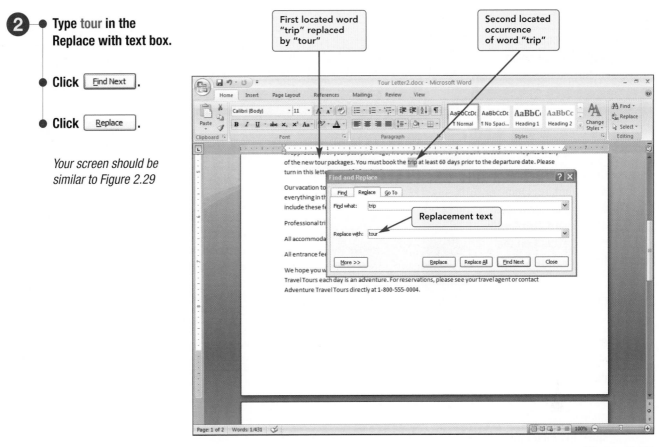

Replacement text

Figure 2.29

Word replaced the first located word with "tour" and has highlighted the second occurrence of the word "trip." You do not want to replace this occurrence of the word. You will continue the search without replacing the highlighted text.

**③** ● Click [Find Next] to skip this occurrence and locate the next occurrence.

● Replace the next located occurrence.

● Continue to review the document, replacing all other occurrences of the word "trip" with "tour," except on the final line of the flyer.

● Click [Find Next].

● Click [OK] to close the information dialog box.

● Click [Close] to close the Find and Replace dialog box.

*Your screen should be similar to Figure 2.30*

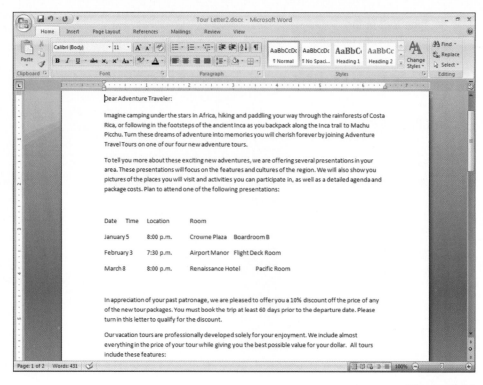

**Figure 2.30**

When using the Find and Replace feature, if you wanted to change all the occurrences of the located text, it is much faster to use  [Replace All]. Exercise care when using this option, however, because the search text you specify might be part of another word and you may accidentally replace text you want to keep. If this happens, you could use Undo to reverse the action.

## Inserting the Current Date

The last text change you need to make is to add the date to the letter. The Date and Time command on the Insert tab inserts the current date as maintained by your computer system into your document at the location of the insertion point. You want to enter the date on the first line of the letter, five lines above the salutation.

**1**
- If necessary, move to the "D" in "Dear" at the top of the letter.

- Press ⌐Enter 2 times to insert two blank lines.

- Move to the first blank line.

- Click  in the Text group of the Insert tab.

*Your screen should be similar to Figure 2.31*

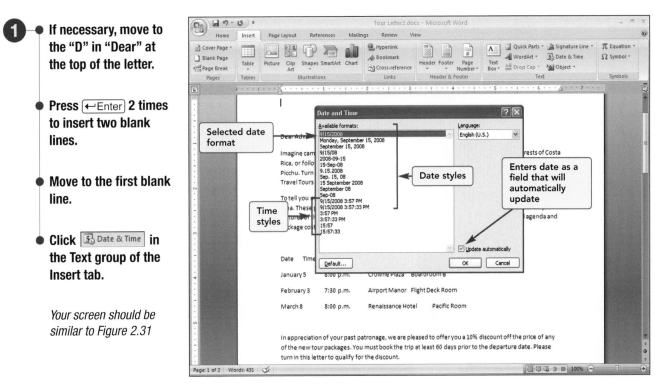

**Figure 2.31**

**Additional Information**

The current time also can be inserted into a document using the same procedure.

From the Date and Time dialog box, you select the style in which you want the date displayed in your document. The Available Formats list box displays the format styles for the current date and time. You want to display the date in the format Month XX, 2XXX, the third format setting in the list.

You also want the date to be updated automatically whenever the letter is opened or printed. You use the Update Automatically option to do this, which enters the date as a field.

## Concept 5

### Field

**5** A **field** is a placeholder that instructs Word to insert information into a document. The **field code** contains the directions as to the type of information to insert or action to perform. Field codes appear between curly brackets {}, also called braces. The information that is displayed as a result of the field code is called the **field result**. Many field codes are automatically inserted when you use certain commands; others you can create and insert yourself. Many fields update automatically when the document changes. Using fields makes it easier and faster to perform many common or repetitive tasks.

**2** • Select the third format setting.

• If necessary, select Update Automatically to display the checkmark.

• Click [ OK ].

• Point to the date.

• Click on the date.

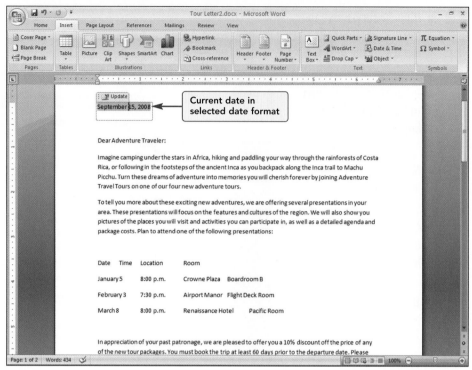

Current date in selected date format

**Figure 2.32**

**Additional Information**
You can use [Alt] + [⇧Shift] + D to insert the current date as a field in the format MM/DD/YY.

*Your screen should be similar to Figure 2.32*

**Having Trouble?**
The date on your screen will reflect the current date on your system. If your date is not shaded, this is because the setting for this feature is off in your program.

**Additional Information**
To show or remove field shading, choose ⊞ Office Button/ [⊞ Word Options]/Advanced and then select Never, Always, or When Selected from the Field Shading box.

The current date is entered in the document in the format you selected. When you point to a field, the entire entry is shaded to identify the entry as a field. When the insertion point is positioned in a field entry, the entire entry is highlighted, indicating it is selected and can be modified.

The date is the field result. You will display the field code to see the underlying instructions.

**3** ● **Right-click on the date and choose Toggle Field Codes from the context menu.**

*Your screen should be similar to Figure 2.33*

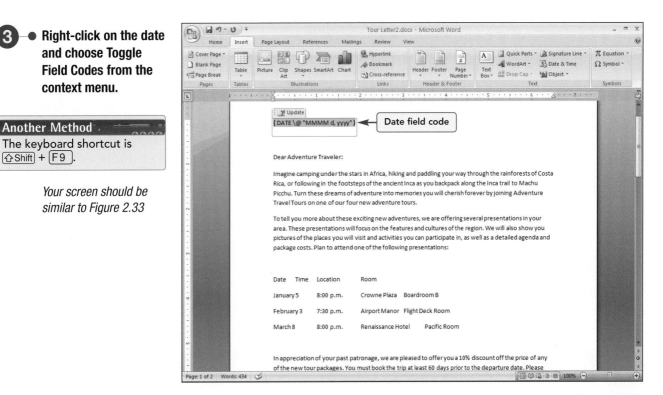

{ DATE \@ "MMMM d, yyyy" } ← Date field code

**Figure 2.33**

The field code includes the field name, DATE, followed by the field properties, in this case the date format instructions. Whenever this document is printed, Word will print the current system date using this format.

**4** ● **Press ⇧Shift + F9 to display the field result again.**

● **Save the document.**

# Modifying Page Layout

Next the manager has suggested that you make several changes to improve the overall appearance of the letter and flyer. Two common page layout features are paragraph settings, such as indents and line spacing, and page margin settings. Other page layout features include page background colors, themes, and vertical alignment and orientation of text on a page.

To give the document more interest, you can indent paragraphs, use tabs to create tabular columns of data, and change the line spacing. These formatting features are all paragraph formats that affect the entire selected paragraph.

## Indenting Paragraphs

Business letters typically use a block layout style or a modified block style with indented paragraphs. In a block style, all parts of the letter, including the date, inside address, all paragraphs in the body, and closing lines, are evenly aligned with the left margin. The block layout style has a very formal appearance. The modified block style, on the other hand, has a more casual appearance. In this style, certain elements such as the date, all paragraphs in the body, and the closing lines are indented from the left margin.

## Concept 6

### Indents

**6** To help your reader find information quickly, you can **indent** paragraphs from the margins. Indenting paragraphs sets them off from the rest of the document. There are four types of indents, and their effects are described below.

| Indent | Effect on Text | Indent | Effect on Text |
|---|---|---|---|
| **Left** | Indents the entire paragraph from the left margin. To "outdent" or extend the paragraph into the left margin, use a negative value for the left indent. | **First Line** | Indents the first line of the paragraph. All following lines are aligned with the left margin. |
| **Right** | Indents the entire paragraph from the right margin. To outdent or extend the paragraph into the right margin, use a negative value for the right indent. | **Hanging** | Indents all lines after the first line of the paragraph. The first line is aligned with the left margin. A hanging indent is typically used for bulleted and numbered lists. |

You want to change the letter style from the block paragraph style to the modified block style. You will begin by indenting the first line of the first paragraph. The quickest way to indent the first line of a paragraph is to press Tab⇥ when the insertion point is positioned at the beginning of the first line. Pressing Tab⇥ indents the first line of the paragraph to the first tab stop from the left margin. A tab stop is a marked location on the horizontal ruler that indicates how far to indent text each time the Tab⇥ key is pressed. The default tab stops are every 0.5 inch.

**1** ● Change the zoom to Page Width.

**Another Method**

Click on the Zoom percentage in the status bar to open the Zoom dialog box.

● **Move to the beginning of the first paragraph.**

● **Press** Tab⇆.

**Another Method**

You can also open the Indents and Spacing tab of the Paragraph dialog box and choose Special/First Line/By 0.5.

*Your screen should be similar to Figure 2.34*

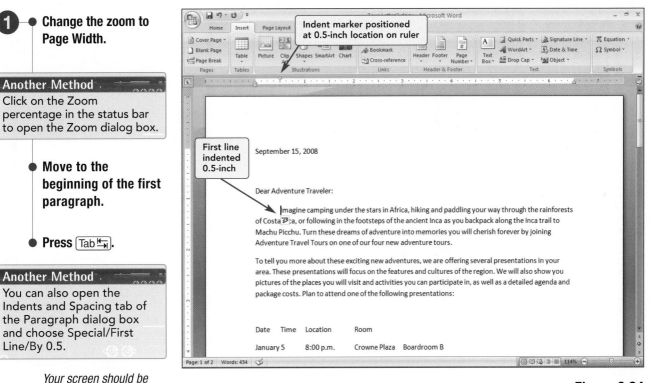

**Figure 2.34**

**Additional Information**

To indent an entire paragraph, click in front of any line except the first line and press Tab⇆.

The first line of the paragraph indents a half inch from the left margin. The text in the paragraph wraps as needed, and the text on the following line begins at the left margin. Notice that the First Line Indent marker on the ruler moved to the 0.5-inch position. This marker controls the location of the first line of text in the paragraph.

If the insertion point was positioned anywhere else within the line of text, pressing Tab⇆ would move the text to the right of the insertion point to the next tab stop and the indent marker would not move.

You can indent the remaining paragraphs individually, or you can select the paragraphs and indent them simultaneously by dragging the upper indent marker on the ruler.

**2** • **Beginning with the second paragraph, select the remaining text on page 1.**

• **Drag the First Line Indent marker on the ruler to the 0.5-inch position.**

*Your screen should be similar to Figure 2.35*

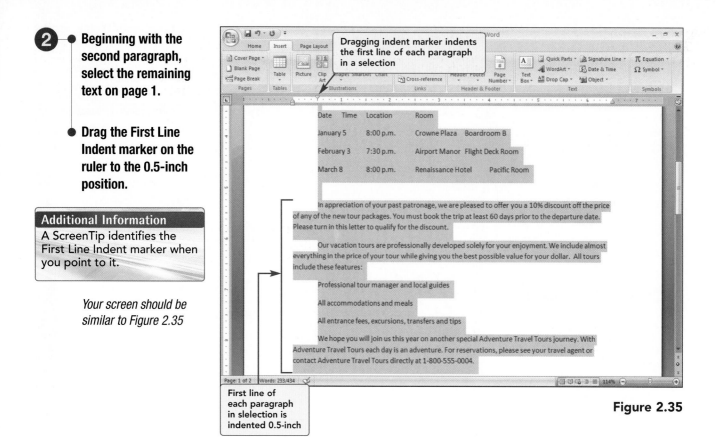

**Figure 2.35**

The first line of each paragraph in the selection is indented. Notice that each line of the presentation date and time information and the list of tour features also are indented. This is because Word considers each line a separate paragraph (each line ends with a paragraph mark.) You decide to further indent the date and time information to the 1-inch position.

**3** • **Select the line of table headings and the three lines of data.**

• **Drag the First Line Indent marker on the ruler to the 1-inch position.**

*Your screen should be similar to Figure 2.36*

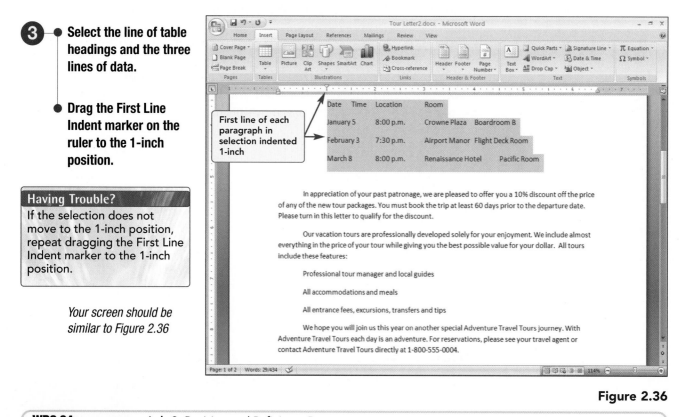

**Figure 2.36**

## Setting Tab Stops

Next you want to improve the appearance of the list of presentation times and dates. The date and time information was entered using the [Tab⇆] key to separate the different columns of information. However, because the default tab stops are set at every 0.5 inch, the columns are not properly aligned. You want to reformat this information to appear as a tabbed table of information so that it is easier to read, as shown below.

| <u>Date</u> | <u>Time</u> | <u>Location</u> | <u>Room</u> |
|---|---|---|---|
| January 5 ----- 7:00 pm -----------Town Center Hotel -------Room 284B |
| February 3 ---- 7:30 pm -----------Airport Manor -------------Conference Room A |
| March 8 ------- 7:00 pm -----------Country Inn----------------Mountainside Room |

To improve the appearance of the information, you will set manual **tab stops** that will align the information in evenly spaced columns. You also can select from five different types of tab stops that control how characters are positioned or aligned with the tab stop. The following table explains the five tab types, the tab marks that appear in the tab alignment selector box (on the left end of the horizontal ruler), and the effects on the text.

To align the information, you will set three left tab stops at the 2-inch, 3-inch, and 4.5-inch positions. You can quickly specify manual tab stop locations and types using the ruler. To select a type of tab stop, click the tab alignment selector box to cycle through the types. Then, to specify where to place the selected tab stop type, click on the location in the ruler. As you specify the new tab stop settings, the table information will align to the new settings.

| Tab Type | Tab Mark | Effects on Text | Example |
|---|---|---|---|
| Left | ⌞ | Extends text to right from tab stop | left |
| Center | ⊥ | Aligns text centered on tab stop | center |
| Right | ⌟ | Extends text to left from tab stop | right |
| Decimal | ⊤ | Aligns text with decimal point | 35.78 |
| Bar | ⊥ | Draws a vertical line through text at tab stop | | |

**1** • If necessary, select the line of table headings and the three lines of information.

• If necessary, click the tab alignment selector box until the left tab icon  appears.

• Click on the 2-inch position on the ruler.

• Click on the 3-inch and the 4.5-inch positions on the ruler.

• Click anywhere in the table to deselect it.

*Your screen should be similar to Figure 2.37*

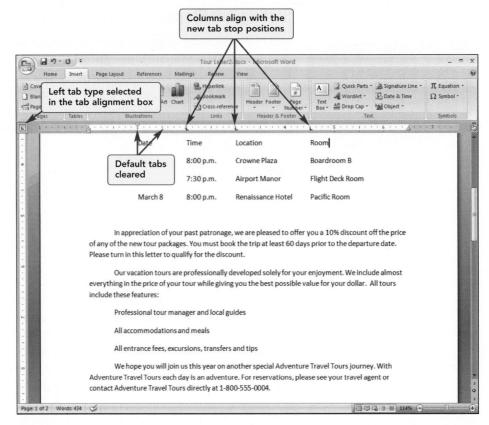

**Figure 2.37**

The three tabbed columns appropriately align with the new tab stops. All default tabs to the left of the manual tab stops are cleared. After looking at the columns, you decide the column headings would look better centered over the columns of information. To make this change, you will remove the three left tab stops for the heading line and then add three center tab stops.

Manual tab stops can be removed by dragging the tab stop up or down off the ruler. They also can be moved by dragging them left or right along the ruler. In addition the Tabs dialog box can be used to make these same changes. You will first drag a tab stop off the ruler to remove it and then you will use the Tabs dialog box to clear the remaining tab stops.

**2**

- Move to anywhere in the table heading line.

- Drag the 2-inch tab stop mark off the ruler.

- Double-click any tab stop to open the Tabs dialog box.

- Click [ Clear All ] to remove the remaining two tab stops.

- Click [ OK ].

- Click the tab alignment selector box until the center tab icon appears.

- Set center tab stops at the 1.25-inch, 2.25-inch, 3.5-inch, and 5-inch positions.

*Your screen should be similar to Figure 2.38*

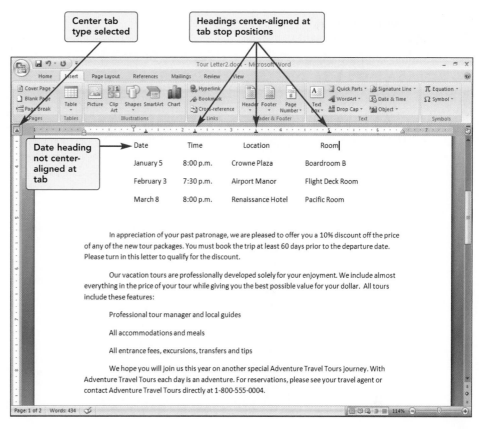

Figure 2.38

The Time, Location, and Room headings are appropriately centered on the tab stops. However, the Date heading still needs to be indented to the 1.25-inch tab stop position by pressing Tab.

**3** **If necessary, move to the "D" in "Date."**

**Press** [Tab⇥].

*Your screen should be similar to Figure 2.39*

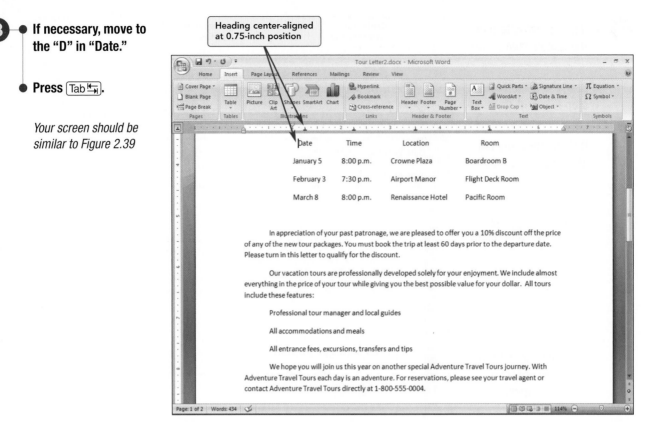

Heading center-aligned at 0.75-inch position

**Figure 2.39**

As you can see, setting different types of tab stops is helpful for aligning text or numeric information vertically in columns. Using tab stops ensures that the text will indent to the same set location. Setting manual tab stops instead of pressing [Tab⇥] or [Spacebar] repeatedly is a more professional way to format a document, as well as faster and more accurate. It also makes editing easier because you can change the tab stop settings for several paragraphs at once.

## Adding Leader Characters

To make the presentation times and location information even easier to read, you will add leader characters before each of the tab stops. **Leader characters** are solid, dotted, or dashed lines that fill the blank space between tab stops. They help the reader's eye move across the blank space between the information aligned at the tab stops. To do this, you use the Tabs dialog box.

- **Select the three lines of presentation information, excluding the heading line.**

- **Double-click any tab stop on the ruler.**

*Your screen should be similar to Figure 2.40*

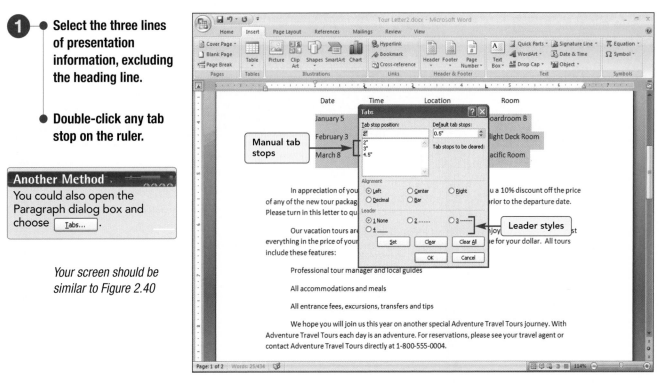

**Figure 2.40**

Notice that the Tabs dialog box displays the manual tabs you set on the ruler. You also can set tab stops using the Tabs dialog box by entering the tab positions in the text box and selecting the tab alignment. You also can clear an individual tab stop by selecting the tab stop position from the list and clicking [ Clear ].

The 2-inch tab stop appears in the Tab stop position text box, indicating it is the tab stop that will be affected by your actions. The Leader setting is None for the 2-inch tab stop. You can select from three styles of leader characters. You will use the third leader style, a series of dashed lines. The leader characters fill the empty space to the left of the tab stop. Each tab stop must have the leader style individually set.

**2**

- Select the `3 -------` leader style.

- Click `Set`.

- Select the 3-inch tab stop setting from the Tab Stop Position list box.

- Select `3 -------`.

- Click `Set`.

- In a similar manner, set the tab leader for the 4.5-inch tab.

- Click `OK`.

- Click in the table to deselect the text.

*Your screen should be similar to Figure 2.41*

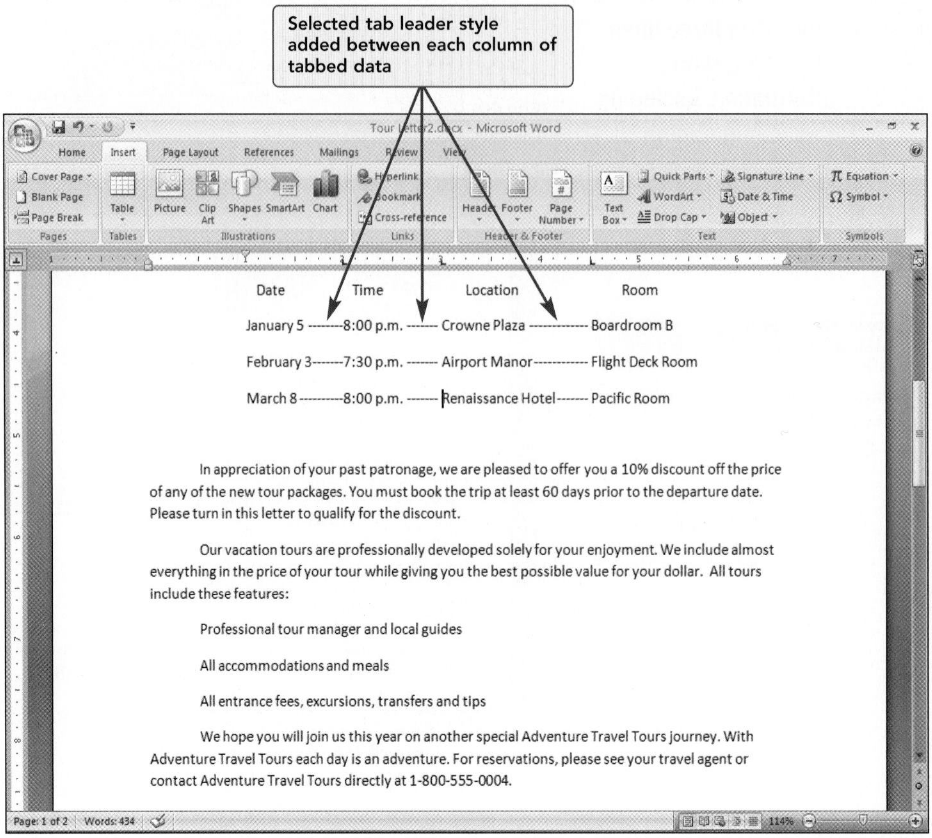

Selected tab leader style added between each column of tabbed data

**Figure 2.41**

The selected leader style has been added to the blank space between each column of tabbed text.

## Changing Line Spacing

You decide you want to adjust the spacing above and below the table as well as between the lines in the table to help make the table stand out from the other text in the letter.

# Concept 7

**7** Adjusting the **line spacing**, or the vertical space between lines of text, helps set off areas of text from others and when increased makes it easier to read and edit text. If a line contains a character or object, such as a graphic, that is larger than the surrounding text, the spacing for that line is automatically adjusted. Additional line spacing settings are described in the table below.

| Spacing | Effect |
| --- | --- |
| Single | Accommodates the largest font in that line, plus a small amount of extra space; the amount of extra space varies with the font that is used. |
| 1.5 lines | Spacing is one and a half times that of single line spacing. |
| Double (2.0) | Spacing is twice that of single line spacing. |
| At least | Uses a value specified in points as the minimum line spacing that is needed to fit the largest font or graphic on the line. |
| Exactly | Uses a value specified in points as a fixed line spacing amount that is not adjusted, making all lines evenly spaced. Graphics or text that is too large will appear clipped. |
| Multiple | Uses a percentage value to increase or decrease the spacing from single spacing. For example, 1.3 will increase the spacing by 33 percent. |

The default line spacing for a Word 2007 document is set to multiple with a 15 percent increase (1.15) over single spacing.

   In addition to changing line spacing within paragraphs, you also can change the spacing before or after paragraphs. The default paragraph spacing adds a small amount of space (10 pt) after a paragraph and no extra space before a paragraph.

The ⬚ command in the Paragraph group of the Home tab can be used to specify standard spacing settings, such as double and triple spacing. It also lets you turn on or off the extra spacing between paragraphs. You want to look at the line spacing settings and make the adjustments from the Paragraph dialog box.

**1**

- **Select the table including the blank lines above and below it.**

- **Open the 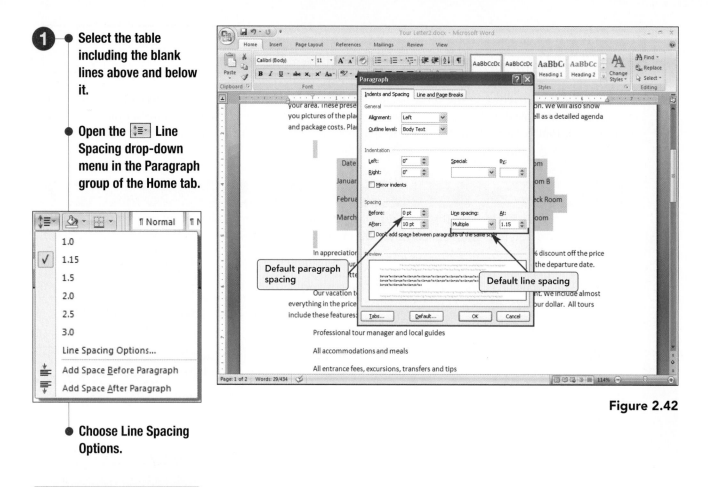 Line Spacing drop-down menu in the Paragraph group of the Home tab.**

- **Choose Line Spacing Options.**

---

**Another Method**

You also could click ⬚ in the Paragraph group to open the Paragraph dialog box to access this feature.

---

**Another Method**

You also can use Ctrl + # to change the line spacing to the number specified.

---

*Your screen should be similar to Figure 2.42*

**Figure 2.42**

The default document line spacing setting, multiple at 1.15, before paragraph spacing of 0 pt, and after paragraph spacing of 10 pt are displayed in the Spacing section of the dialog box. You want to decrease the spacing between each line of the table. Because Word considers each line of the table and the blank lines above and below it as separate paragraphs, you can decrease the space after paragraph setting to achieve this effect. You will also change the line spacing to single to remove the 15 percent spacing increase. As you make these changes, the Preview box will show you a sample of the effect they will have on the text.

- **Select Single from the Line Spacing drop-down menu.**

- **Click the down scroll button of the After box to decrease the spacing to 6 pt.**

- **Click** OK .

*Your screen should be similar to Figure 2.43*

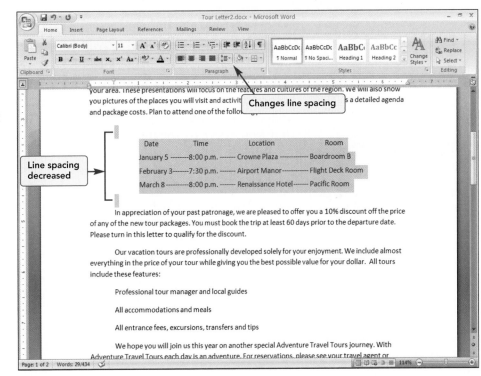

**Figure 2.43**

The change in line and paragraph spacing improves the appearance of the table and makes the information stand out more from the other text in the letter. You think this same change also would be effective in the list of tour features.

- **Select the list of three tour features.**

- **Change the line spacing to Single.**

- **Select the first two items in the feature list and change the space after paragraph to 6 pt.**

**Another Method**

You can also use  in the Paragraph group of the Page Layout tab to adjust paragraph spacing.

*Your screen should be similar to Figure 2.44*

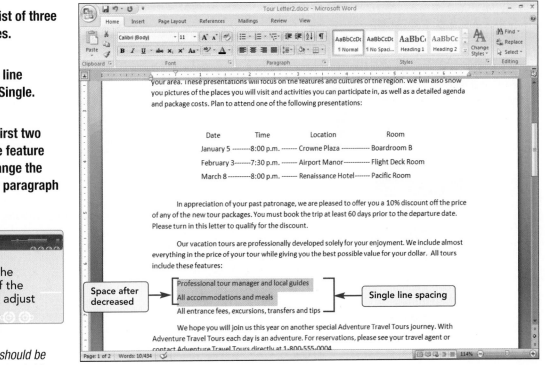

**Figure 2.44**

# More Character Formatting

As you look at the letter, you still feel that the table of presentation dates and times does not stand out enough. You can add emphasis to information in your documents by formatting specific characters or words. Applying color shading or highlighting behind text is commonly used to identify areas of text that you want to stand out. It is frequently used to mark text that you want to locate easily as you are revising a document. Italics, underlines, and bold are other character formats that add emphasis and draw the reader's attention to important items. Word applies character formatting to the entire selection or to the entire word at the insertion point. You can apply formatting to a portion of a word by selecting the area to be formatted first.

**Additional Information**

When you use highlights in a document you plan to print in black and white, select a light color so the text is visible.

## Adding Color Highlighting

First, you want to see how a color highlight behind the tabbed table of presentation times and locations would look.

**1**
● Click anywhere in the table.

● Open the [aby] Text Highlight Color drop-down list in the Font group of the Home tab.

● Select the turquoise color from the color palette.

**Additional Information**

The mouse pointer appears as 🖉 when positioned on text, indicating the highlighting feature is on.

● Select the entire presentation locations table.

**Another Method**

You also can select the area you want to highlight first and then click [aby] to select and apply a color.

● Click [aby] or press [Esc] to turn off the highlighting feature.

*Your screen should be similar to Figure 2.45*

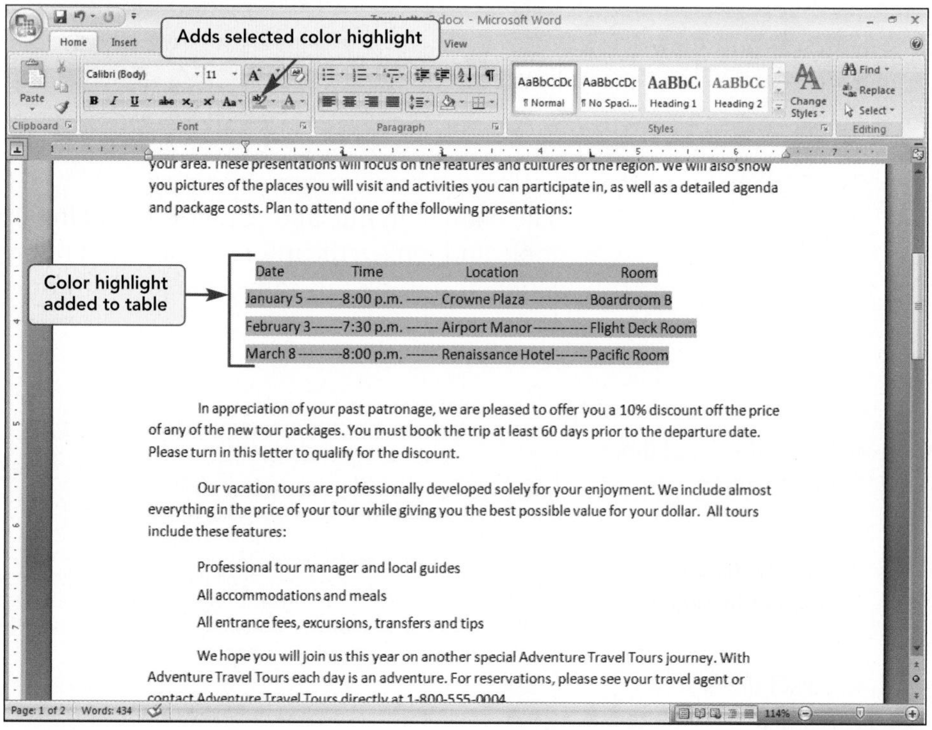

**Figure 2.45**

Although the highlight makes the table stand out, it does not look good.

## Underlining Text

Instead, you decide to bold and underline the headings. The default underline style is a single black line. In addition, Word includes 15 other types of underlines.

**1** ● Click [↩] **Undo.**

● **Select the table heading line.**

● Click [B] **Bold from the Mini toolbar.**

● Click [U ▾] **Underline from the Font group.**

*Your screen should be similar to Figure 2.46*

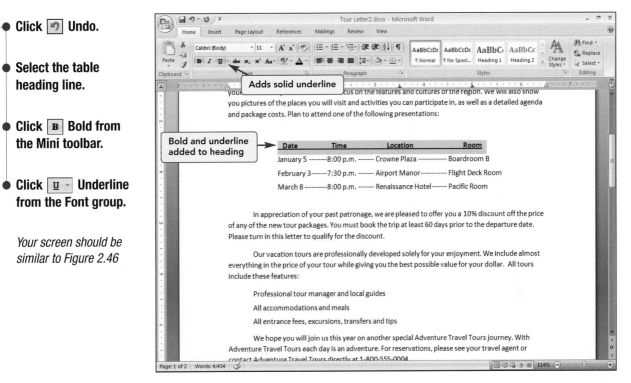

**Figure 2.46**

All the words are bold, and a single black underline has been added below the entire selection. You decide you want the underline to appear under each word only and to stand out more. To do this, you will select another underline style and apply the underline to the word individually. When the insertion point is positioned on a word, the selected underline style is applied to the entire word.

**2**
● Click ↶ Undo to remove the underline.

● Click on the "Room" heading in the table.

● Open the U ▾ Underline drop-down menu.

● Point to the dotted underline style to see the Live Preview.

*Your screen should be similar to Figure 2.47*

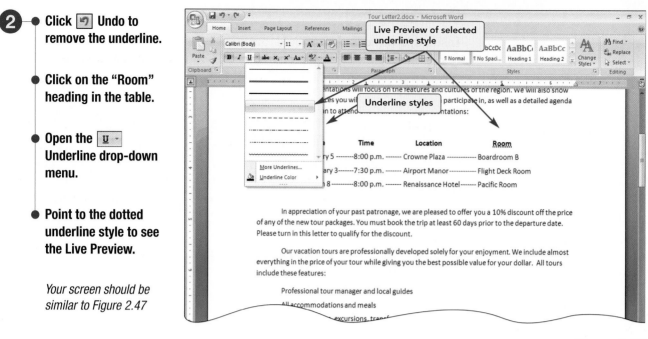

**Figure 2.47**

The eight most popular underline styles are listed in the menu. Using More Underlines will open the Font dialog box, where you can select other styles, clear underlining from a selection using the None option, or select the Words Only option to display a single underline below words in the selection only, not under the spaces between words. Live Preview shows you how the selection will appear in the document.

**3**
● Select several other underline styles and see how they appear in the Live Preview.

● Click the double underline style.

**Additional Information**
Using the keyboard shortcut Ctrl + U adds the default single underline style.

*Your screen should be similar to Figure 2.48*

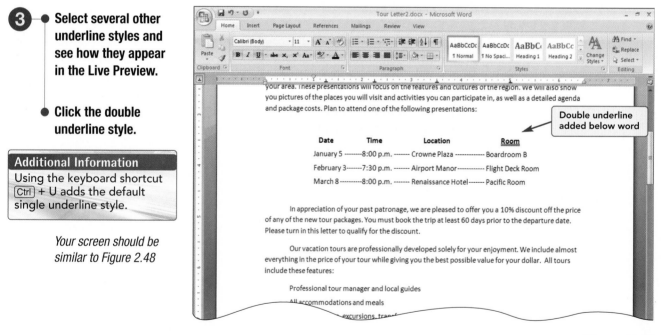

**Figure 2.48**

The selected word is underlined using the double underline style.

## Copying Formats with Format Painter

You want to quickly apply the same formats to the other headings. To do this, you can use the **Format Painter**. This feature applies the formats associated with the current selection to new selections. If the selection is a paragraph (including the paragraph mark), the formatting is applied to the entire paragraph. If the selection is a character, the format is applied to a character, word, or selection you specify.

To use this feature, move the insertion point to the text whose formats you want to copy and click the  Format Painter button. Then select the text to which you want the formats applied. The format is automatically applied to an entire word simply by clicking on the word. To apply the format to more or less text, you must select the area.

**1** ● **If necessary, click on the "Room" heading.**

● **Double-click 🖌 Format Painter in the Clipboard group.**

● **Click on the Date, Time, and Location headings.**

● **Click 🖌 to turn off Format Painter.**

**Another Method**

You can press Esc to turn off Format Painter.

● **Save the document again.**

*Your screen should be similar to Figure 2.49*

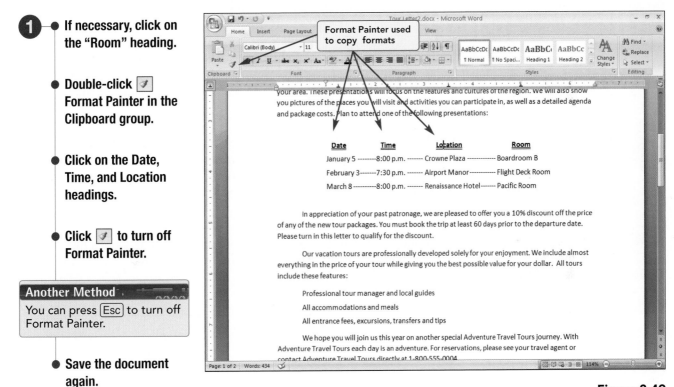

**Figure 2.49**

# Creating Lists

The next change you want to make is to display the three lines of information about tour features as an itemized list so that they stand out better from the surrounding text.

## Concept 8

### Bulleted and Numbered Lists

**8** Whenever possible, add bullets or numbers before items in a list to organize information and to make your writing clear and easy to read. Word includes many basic bullet, a dot or other symbol, and number formats from which you can select. Additionally, there are many picture bullets available. If none of the predesigned bullet or number formats suits your needs, you also can create your own customized designs.

Use a **bulleted list** when you have several items in a paragraph that logically make a list. A bulleted list displays one of several styles of bullets before each item in the list. You can select from several types of symbols to use as bullets and you can change the color, size, and position of the bullet.

Use a **numbered list** when you want to convey a sequence of events, such as a procedure that has to follow in a certain order. A numbered list displays numbers or letters before the text. Word automatically increments the number or letter as you start a new paragraph. You can select from several different numbering schemes to create your numbered lists.

Use an **outline numbered list** to display multiple outline levels that show a hierarchical structure of the items in the list. There can be up to nine levels.

## Numbering a List

Because both bullet and number formats will indent the items automatically when applied, you first need to remove the indent from the three tour features. Then you will try a numbered list format to see how it looks.

**1** ● Select the three tour features.

● Drag the First Line Indent marker on the ruler back to the margin boundary.

● Right-click on the selection and select Numbering from the menu.

**Another Method**

The Ribbon equivalent is  Numbering in the Paragraph group.

*Your screen should be similar to Figure 2.50*

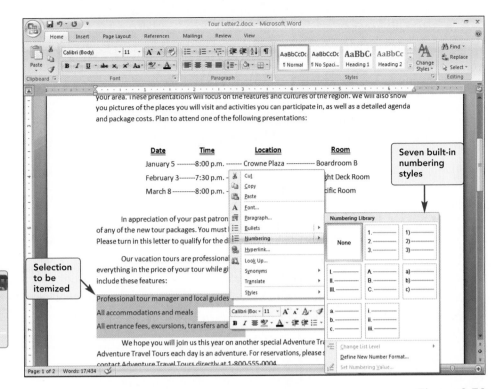

**Figure 2.50**

The Numbering gallery displays examples of seven built-in numbered list formats in the Numbering Library category. The None option is used to remove an existing numbering format. Numbers followed by periods is the default style that is applied when clicking ⬛ Numbering in the Paragraph group. However, if another style has been used since starting Word, the last-used numbering format is inserted.

The numbering gallery also may include a Recently Used category if this feature has already been used since Word 2007 was started. If the document contains another numbered list, the gallery will display the used number style in a Document Number Formats category.

The three options at the bottom of the menu are used to change the indent level of the items, to customize the appearance of the built-in formats, and to set a start number for the list (1 is the default). For example, you could indent the list more, change the color of the numbers, and start numbering with 3 instead of 1.

You will use the second number format that has a number followed by a parenthesis.

**2** ● Select the second (parenthesis style) numbered list format option.

*Your screen should be similar to Figure 2.51*

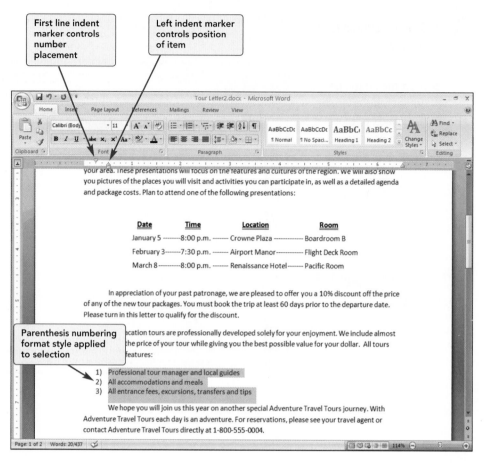

First line indent marker controls number placement

Left indent marker controls position of item

Parenthesis numbering format style applied to selection

**Figure 2.51**

A number is inserted at the 0.25-inch position before each line, and the text following the number is indented to the 0.5-inch position. In an itemized list, the First Line Indent marker on the ruler controls the position of the number or bullet, and the Left Indent marker controls the position of the item following the number or bullet. The Left Indent marker creates a hanging indent. If the text following each bullet were longer than a line, the text on the following lines would also be indented to the 0.5-inch position. Additionally, the extra space between the lines was removed because the feature that adds space between paragraphs of the same style was automatically turned off.

## Bulleting a List

After looking at the list, you decide it really would be more appropriate if it were a bulleted list instead of a numbered list. The solid round bullet format is the default when clicking  Bullets. However, if another style was previously used since starting Word 2007, that style is inserted. The bullet submenu is divided into the same three groups as the Numbering submenu and has similar options.

**1** ● If necessary, select the list of three features.

● Open the ⊟▾ **Bullets** drop-down menu on the Mini toolbar or from the context menu.

**Another Method**

You also can use ⊟▾ **Bullets** in the Paragraph group of the Home tab.

● Choose the ➢ **bullet** format.

*Your screen should be similar to Figure 2.52*

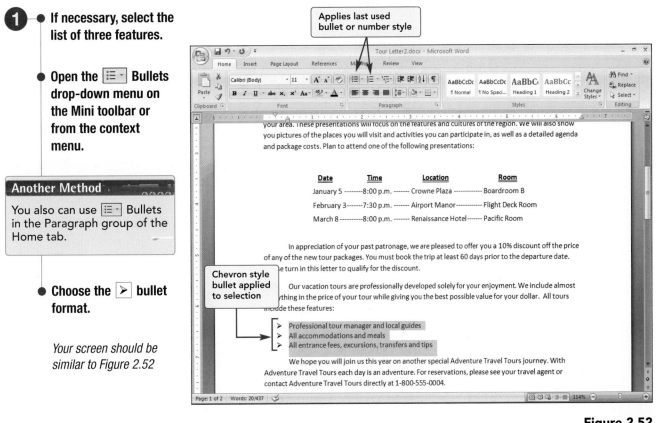

Applies last used bullet or number style

your area. These presentations will focus on the features and cultures of the region. We will also show you pictures of the places you will visit and activities you can participate in, as well as a detailed agenda and package costs. Plan to attend one of the following presentations:

| Date | Time | Location | Room |
| --- | --- | --- | --- |
| January 5 | 8:00 p.m. | Crowne Plaza | Boardroom B |
| February 3 | 7:30 p.m. | Airport Manor | Flight Deck Room |
| March 8 | 8:00 p.m. | Renaissance Hotel | Pacific Room |

In appreciation of your past patronage, we are pleased to offer you a 10% discount off the price of any of the new tour packages. You must book the trip at least 60 days prior to the departure date. Just turn in this letter to qualify for the discount.

Our vacation tours are professionally developed solely for your enjoyment. We include almost everything in the price of your tour while giving you the best possible value for your dollar. All tours include these features:

Chevron style bullet applied to selection

➢ Professional tour manager and local guides
➢ All accommodations and meals
➢ All entrance fees, excursions, transfers and tips

We hope you will join us this year on another special Adventure Travel Tours journey. With Adventure Travel Tours each day is an adventure. For reservations, please see your travel agent or contact Adventure Travel Tours directly at 1-800-555-0004.

**Figure 2.52**

**Additional Information**

To remove bullets or numbers, select the text, open the ⊟▾ drop-down menu, and select None, or click ⊟▾ again.

The selected bullet format is applied to the selection.

## Sorting a List

As you look at the bulleted list, you decide you want the three items to appear in alphabetical order. To make this change quickly, you can sort the list.

# Concept 9

9    Word can quickly arrange or **sort** text, numbers, or data in lists or tables in alphabetical, numeric, or date order based on the first character in each paragraph. The sort order can be ascending (A to Z, 0 to 9, or earliest to latest date) or descending (Z to A, 9 to 0, or latest to earliest date). The following table describes the rules that are used when sorting.

| Sort by | Rules |
|---|---|
| Text | First, items beginning with punctuation marks or symbols (such as !, #, $, %, or &) are sorted. |
| | Second, items beginning with numbers are sorted. Dates are treated as three-digit numbers. |
| | Third, items beginning with letters are sorted. |
| Numbers | All characters except numbers are ignored. The numbers can be in any location in a paragraph. |
| Date | Valid date separators include hyphens, forward slashes (/), commas, and periods. Colons (:) are valid time separators. If unable to recognize a date or time, Word places the item at the beginning or end of the list (depending on whether you are sorting in ascending or descending order). |
| Field results | If an entire field (such as a last name) is the same for two items, Word next evaluates subsequent fields (such as a first name) according to the specified sort options. |

When a tie occurs, Word uses the first nonidentical character in each item to determine which item should come first.

You will use the default Sort settings that will sort by text and paragraphs in ascending order.

**1**

- If necessary, select the entire list.

- Click ⬛↓ in the Paragraph group.

- Click [ OK ] to accept the default settings.

- Click on the document to clear the highlight.

- Increase the space after for the third list item to 12 pt.

*Your screen should be similar to Figure 2.53*

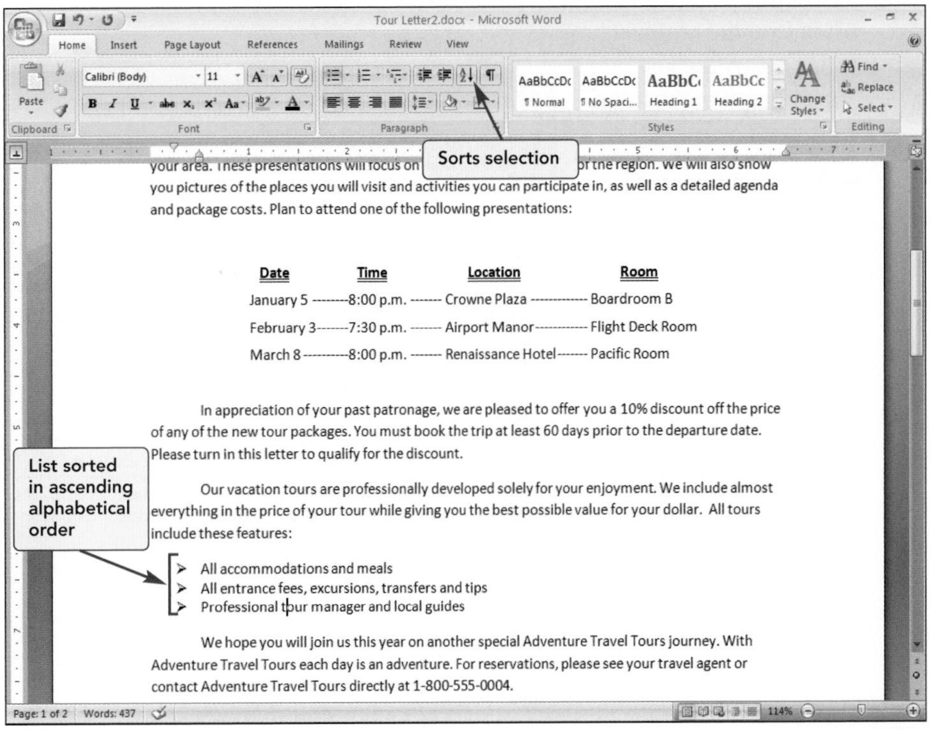

**Figure 2.53**

The three items in the list now appear in ascending sorted order.

## Using Quick Parts

While looking at the letter, you realize that the closing lines have not been added to the document. You can quickly insert text and graphics that you use frequently using the Quick Parts feature. The Quick Parts feature includes reusable pieces of content or document parts, called **building blocks,** that give you a head start in creating content such as page numbers, cover pages, headers and footers, and sidebars. In addition to the supplied building blocks, you also can create your own custom building blocks.

### Using Supplied Building Blocks

You will create the closing for the letter using the Author and Company supplied building blocks that get their information from the file's document properties.

**1** ● Move to the first blank line below the last paragraph of the letter.

● Type Best Regards,.

● Press ←Enter .

● Open the Insert tab and click ▣ Quick Parts ▾ in the Text group.

● Select Document Property and choose Author from the submenu.

*Your screen should be similar to Figure 2.54*

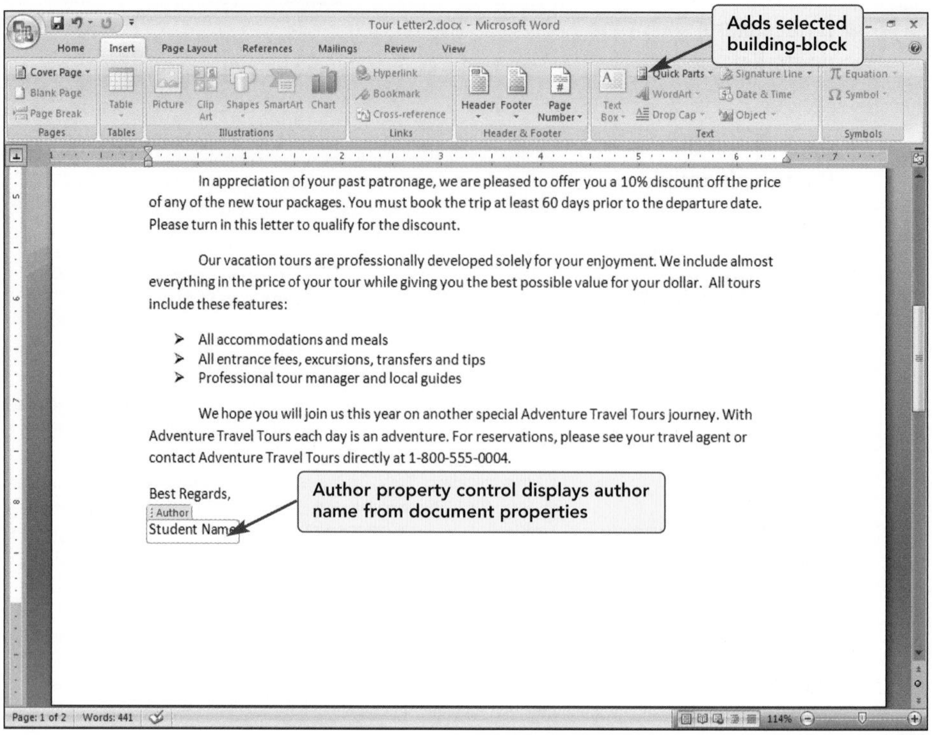

In appreciation of your past patronage, we are pleased to offer you a 10% discount off the price of any of the new tour packages. You must book the trip at least 60 days prior to the departure date. Please turn in this letter to qualify for the discount.

Our vacation tours are professionally developed solely for your enjoyment. We include almost everything in the price of your tour while giving you the best possible value for your dollar. All tours include these features:

➤ All accommodations and meals
➤ All entrance fees, excursions, transfers and tips
➤ Professional tour manager and local guides

We hope you will join us this year on another special Adventure Travel Tours journey. With Adventure Travel Tours each day is an adventure. For reservations, please see your travel agent or contact Adventure Travel Tours directly at 1-800-555-0004.

Best Regards,
Author
Student Name

**Adds selected building-block**

**Author property control displays author name from document properties**

**Figure 2.54**

**Additional Information**

If you change the information stored in the Document Information Panel, any property controls in the document using that information also will be updated.

An Author property control containing the name that is currently stored in the file's Author document property is inserted in the document. A **control** is a graphic element that is a container for information or objects. Controls, like fields, appear shaded when you point to them.

You can update or modify the information displayed in a property control by editing the entry. Any changes you make in the property control are automatically updated in the Document Information Panel. You will change the information in the Author property to your name and then continue to create the closing.

**2**
- Select the text in the Author control and type **your name**.

- Press → to deselect it.

- Type **, Advertising Coordinator** following your name.

- Press ←Enter.

- Insert the Company document property control.

- Select the last two lines and remove the space after the paragraphs.

*Your screen should be similar to Figure 2.55*

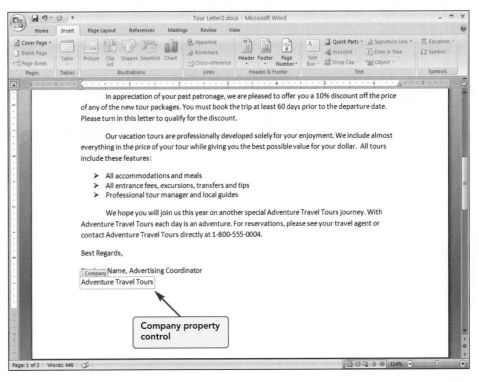

In appreciation of your past patronage, we are pleased to offer you a 10% discount off the price of any of the new tour packages. You must book the trip at least 60 days prior to the departure date. Please turn in this letter to qualify for the discount.

Our vacation tours are professionally developed solely for your enjoyment. We include almost everything in the price of your tour while giving you the best possible value for your dollar. All tours include these features:

➤ All accommodations and meals
➤ All entrance fees, excursions, transfers and tips
➤ Professional tour manager and local guides

We hope you will join us this year on another special Adventure Travel Tours journey. With Adventure Travel Tours each day is an adventure. For reservations, please see your travel agent or contact Adventure Travel Tours directly at 1-800-555-0004.

Best Regards,

Student Name, Advertising Coordinator
Adventure Travel Tours

Company property control

**Figure 2.55**

The closing is now complete and the document properties now include your name as the author. Using document property controls in a document is particularly helpful when the same controls are used multiple times, as in a contract. Then, when one control is updated or edited, all controls of the same type throughout the document are automatically updated.

## Creating a Custom Building Block

In addition to the supplied building blocks, you can create your own. In this case, because you frequently use the same closing when creating correspondence, you will create a building block that you can use to quickly insert this information.

**1** ● **Increase the spacing after of the Best Regards line to 18 pt.**

● **Select the entire closing.**

● **Click**  **.**

● **Choose Save Selection to Quick Part Gallery.**

**Another Method**

The keyboard shortcut is [Alt] + [F3].

*Your screen should be similar to Figure 2.56*

Selection will be used as custom building block

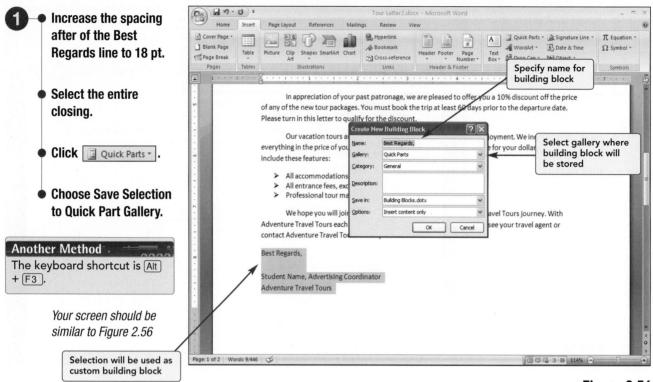

**Figure 2.56**

In the Create New Building Block dialog box, you define the properties for the building block. This includes entering a unique name for the building block, specifying the gallery where you want the building block stored, and other information that is needed to identify and use the building block.

You will use the proposed name, Best Regards, and store it in the Quick Parts Gallery. All the other default settings for this building block are appropriate. After saving the building block, you will erase the closing you typed in the letter and then reinsert it using the stored Quick Part.

**MORE ABOUT**

► See 4.1 Structure Content by Using Quick Parts in the More About appendix to learn more about saving frequently used data as building blocks.

**②** ● Click [ OK ].

● Delete the closing in the letter.

● Click [ Quick Parts ▾ ]

● Click on the Best Regards building block.

● Save the document again.

*Your screen should be similar to Figure 2.57*

**MORE ABOUT**

▶ See 4.1 Structure Content by Using Quick Parts in the More About appendix to learn how to use the Building Block Organizer to sort and edit properties of building blocks.

---

**Additional Information**

You will learn more about Quick Parts and use several of the other supplied building blocks in later labs.

---

In appreciation of your past patronage, we are pleased to offer you a 10% discount off the price of any of the new tour packages. You must book the trip at least 60 days prior to the departure date. Please turn in this letter to qualify for the discount.

Our vacation tours are professionally developed solely for your enjoyment. We include almost everything in the price of your tour while giving you the best possible value for your dollar. All tours include these features:

➢ All accommodations and meals
➢ All entrance fees, excursions, transfers and tips
➢ Professional tour manager and local guides

We hope you will join us this year on another special Adventure Travel Tours journey. With Adventure Travel Tours each day is an adventure. For reservations, please see your travel agent or contact Adventure Travel Tours directly at 1-800-555-0004.

Best Regards,
Author
Student Name

← **Closing inserted using custom building block**

**Figure 2.57**

---

The custom building block you created appeared as a gallery item at the top of the Quick Parts menu, making it easy for you to access and use. The selected block was inserted into the document at the location of the insertion point. As you can see, using Quick Parts was much quicker than typing the closing.

## Adding and Modifying Shapes

You also want to add a special graphic to the flyer containing information about the company Web site to catch the reader's attention. To quickly add a shape, you will use one of the ready-made shapes that are supplied with Word. These include basic shapes such as rectangles and circles, a variety of lines, block arrows, flowchart symbols, stars and banners, and callouts. Additional shapes are available in the Clip Organizer. You also can combine shapes to create more complex designs. To see and create shapes, the view needs to be Print Layout view. In Draft view, shapes are not displayed. If you are using Draft view when you begin to create a shape, the view will change automatically to Print Layout view.

### Inserting a Shape

You want to add a graphic of a banner to the bottom of the flyer.

**1**
- Move to the end of the document.

- Click  in the Illustrations group.

- From the Stars and Banners group, point to the Wave shape.

*Your screen should be similar to Figure 2.58*

Menu of shapes is divided into 7 categories

Wave shape

**Figure 2.58**

The Shapes menu displays seven categories of shapes. Pointing to a shape displays the shape name in a ScreenTip. The recently selected shapes appear at the top of the menu. You will insert the Wave shape at the end of the flyer.

**2**
- Click the Wave shape.

- Click below the last line of the flyer to insert the shape.

- Drag the sizing handles to obtain a shape similar to that shown in Figure 2.59.

**Additional Information**
To maintain the height and width proportions of a shape, hold down ⇧Shift while you drag.

*Your screen should be similar to Figure 2.59*

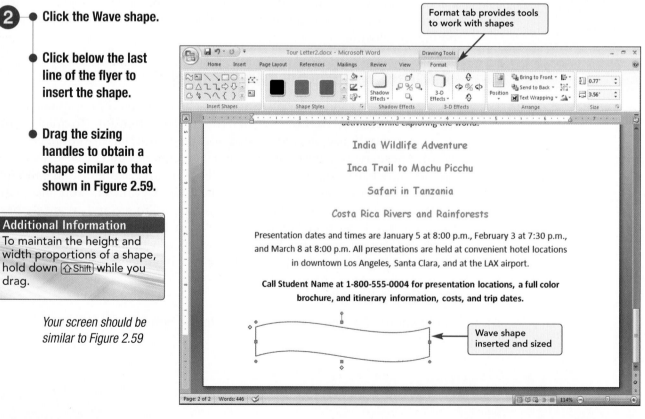

Format tab provides tools to work with shapes

Wave shape inserted and sized

**Figure 2.59**

Notice the Drawing Tools Format tab is displayed and open so you can continue working with the shape.

## Filling the Shape with Color

The shape can be enhanced using many of the features on the Format tab, such as adding a background fill color, gradient, and line color. A **gradient** is a gradual progression of colors and shades, usually from one color to another, or from one shade to another of the same color.

As you make your selections, the Live Preview feature will show how they will look.

**1**

- Open the 🎨 ▾ Shape Fill drop-down menu in the Shape Styles group.

- Choose the orange fill color from the standard colors palette.

- Open the 🎨 ▾ Shape Fill drop-down menu, select Gradient and choose the Linear Up gradient from the Light Variations section (3rd row).

- In the same manner, open the 📝 ▾ Shape Outline menu and choose green.

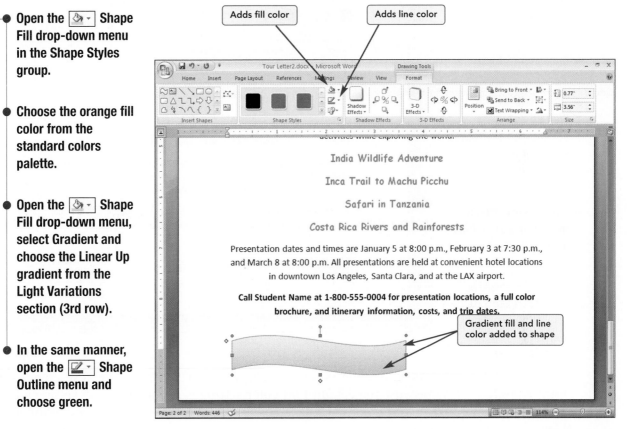

Figure 2.60

**Additional Information**

The color and gradient names appear in a ScreenTip as you point to them.

*Your screen should be similar to Figure 2.60*

## Adding Text to a Shape

Next you will add text to the shape. The manager also has asked you to add information about the company's Web site to the flyer. You will include the Web site's address, called a **URL** (Uniform Resource Locator), in the shape. Word automatically recognizes URLs you enter and creates a hyperlink of the entry. A **hyperlink** is a connection to a location in the current document, another document, or a Web site. It allows the reader to jump to the referenced location by clicking on the hyperlink text when reading the document on the screen.

**1** ● **Right-click on the shape to open the context menu.**

● **Choose Add Text.**

● **Type Visit our Web site at www. adventuretraveltours. com and press** ⟨Spacebar⟩**.**

● **If necessary, adjust the shape size to fully display the text.**

*Your screen should be similar to Figure 2.61*

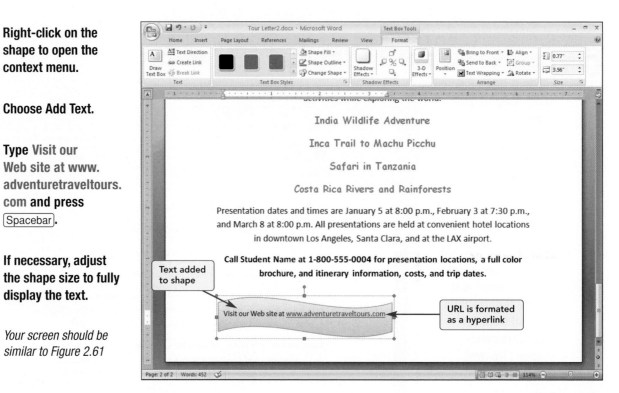

**Figure 2.61**

The text appears in the selected font settings. The text color is black because the default font color setting is Automatic. This setting will make the text color black if the background fill color is light and white if the fill color is dark.

## Removing Hyperlinks

The Web address is automatically formatted in blue and underlined, indicating the entry is a hyperlink. The AutoFormat feature makes certain formatting changes automatically to your document. These formats include formatting a Web address, replacing ordinals (1st) with a superscript (1$^{st}$) and fractions (1/2) with fraction characters (½), and applying a bulleted list format to a list if you type an asterisk (*) followed by a space at the beginning of a paragraph. These AutoFormat features can be turned off if the corrections are not needed in your document.

**Additional Information**

You can turn off the AutoFormat feature so the hyperlinks are not created automatically using Office Button/Word Options/Proofing/AutoCorrectOptions/AutoFormat and clear the Internet and network paths with hyperlinks option.

Because this is a document you plan to print, you do not want the text displayed as a link. Since the hyperlink was created using the AutoFormat feature, you can undo the correction or turn it off using the AutoCorrect Options button.

1. **Right-click on the hyperlink and choose Remove Hyperlink from the context menu.**
   - **Select the text and using the Mini toolbar, change the font to Comic Sans MS, 12 pt, bold, and centered.**
   - **Adjust the shape size as in Figure 2.62.**

**Additional Information**

A ScreenTip appears when you point to a hyperlink with instructions on how to follow a link.

**Another Method**

You also could click Undo to remove the hyperlink AutoFormatting.

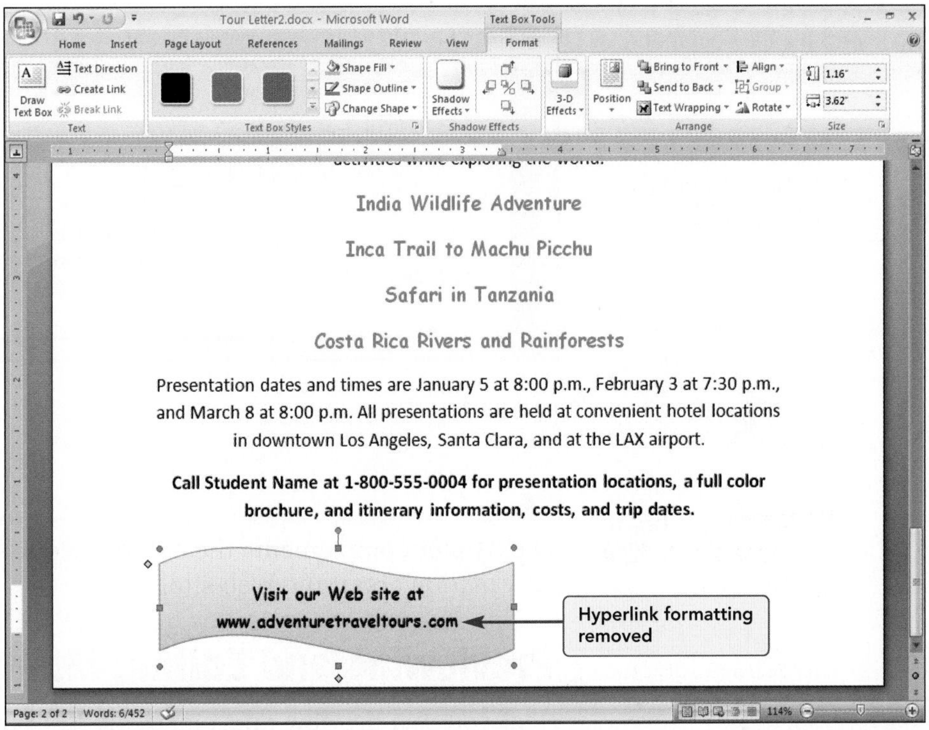


**Figure 2.62**

*Your screen should be similar to Figure 2.62*

The Web address now appears as normal text.

## Moving an Object

Finally, you need to center the shape at the bottom of the flyer. You will do this by dragging the object to the desired location.

**1**

- Point to the shape and when the mouse pointer appears as ⁺⇱, drag the shape to the position shown in Figure 2.63.

- Click outside the shape to deselect it.

- Save the document again.

*Your screen should be similar to Figure 2.63*

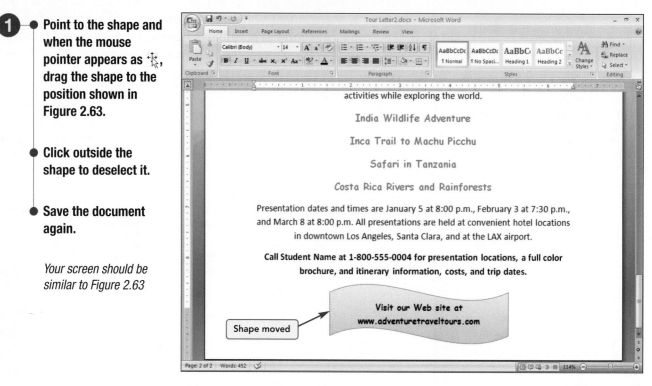

**Figure 2.63**

The banner complements the colors used in the flyer and adds the needed information about the Web site.

## Previewing and Editing Multiple Pages

Next you will preview and make any final changes to the letter and flyer before printing it. When previewing a document, it is often useful to see multiple pages at the same time to check formatting and other items. First, you want to display both pages of your document at the same time in the window.

**1** • Move to the top of the document.

• Use the Zoom slider to reduce the zoom to 50%.

*Your screen should be similar to Figure 2.64*

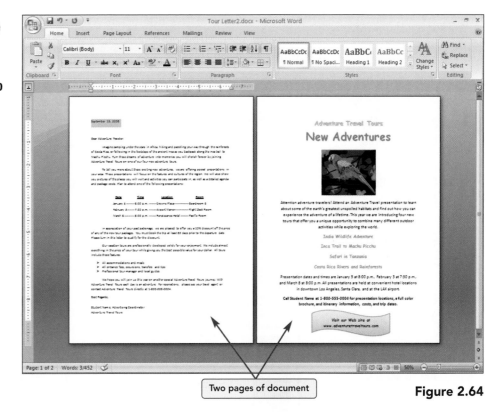

Two pages of document

**Figure 2.64**

Now that you can see the entire letter, you decide to indent the date and closing to the 3.5-inch tab position. You will select both these items at the same time and then change the indent. To select nonadjacent areas in a document, hold down Ctrl while selecting each additional area.

**2** • Select the date.

• Hold down Ctrl and select the closing.

• Drag the upper indent marker to the 3.5-inch position.

*Your screen should be similar to Figure 2.65*

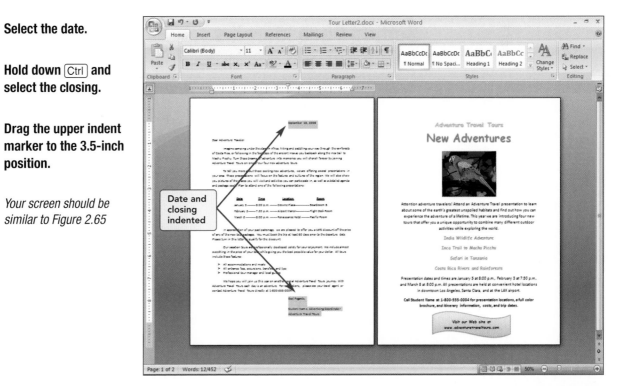

Date and closing indented

**Figure 2.65**

While looking at the document, you decide to emphasize the list of tour features by adding bold. You also want to decrease the space between the tour names in the flyer.

**3** • Select the three bulleted items.

• Click **B** Bold on the Mini toolbar.

• Select the list of four tours in the flyer.

• Decrease the spacing after to 6 pt.

• Click in the list to cear the selection.

*Your screen should be similar to Figure 2.66*

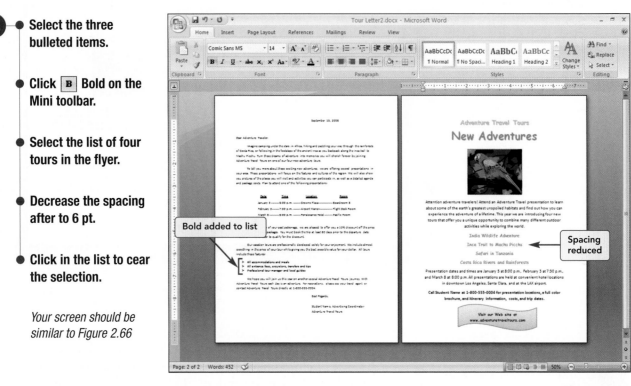

**Figure 2.66**

# Setting Page Margins

Finally, you decide the document may look better if the left and right page margins were narrower.

# Concept 10

## Page Margins

**10** The **page margin** is the blank space around the edge of a page. Generally, the text you enter appears in the printable area inside the margins. However, some items can be positioned in the margin space. You can set different page margin widths to alter the appearance of the document.

Standard single-sided documents have four margins: top, bottom, left, and right. Double-sided documents with facing pages, such as books and magazines, also have four margins: top, bottom, inside, and outside. These documents typically use mirror margins in which the left page is a mirror image of the right page. This means that the inside margins are the same width and the outside margins are the same width. (See the illustrations below.)

You also can set a "gutter" margin that reserves space on the left side of single-sided documents, or on the inside margin of double-sided documents, to accommodate binding. There are also special margin settings for headers and footers. (You will learn about these features in Lab 3.)

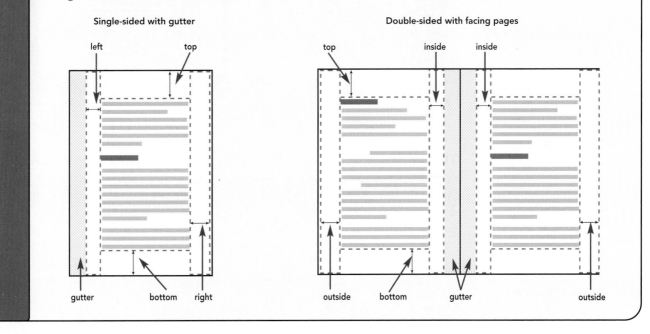

The default document setting for the left and right margins is 1 inch. You would like to see how the document would look if you decreased the size of the right and left margin widths. The Page Setup group is used to change settings associated with the layout of the entire page.

**1** ● **Open the Page Layout tab.**

● **Click** 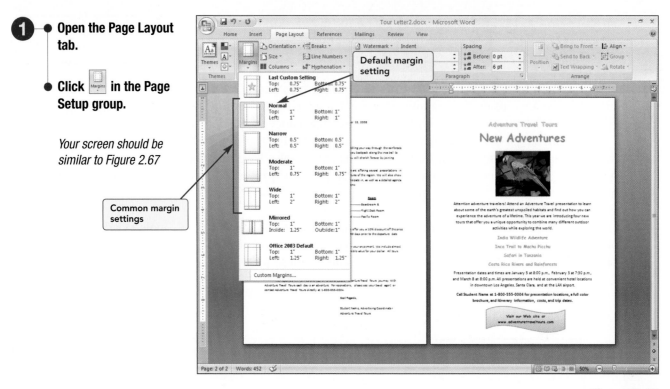 **in the Page Setup group.**

*Your screen should be similar to Figure 2.67*

Common margin settings

Figure 2.67

The Margins drop-down menu displays several common margin setting options for a single-sided document, including the default setting of Normal. The Mirrored option is used for documents that will be printed double-sided with facing pages, such as a book. Additionally, if you have used a custom margin setting, it also appears in the menu.

You decide to try the Narrow option first.

**2** ● **Choose Narrow.**

*Your screen should be similar to Figure 2.68*

Narrow margin setting applied to document

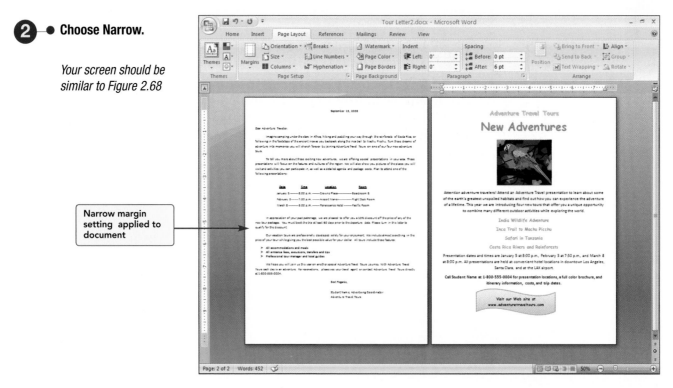

Figure 2.68

You do not like how this setting looks at all and will undo the change. Then you will create a custom setting to change this document to 0.8-inch side margins. Custom margin settings are specified using the Custom Margins option on the Margins drop-down menu. You also can double-click on the margin section of the ruler to access this feature.

**3** ● Click 🔄 Undo to cancel this change.

● Double-click the margin section of the ruler.

*Your screen should be similar to Figure 2.69*

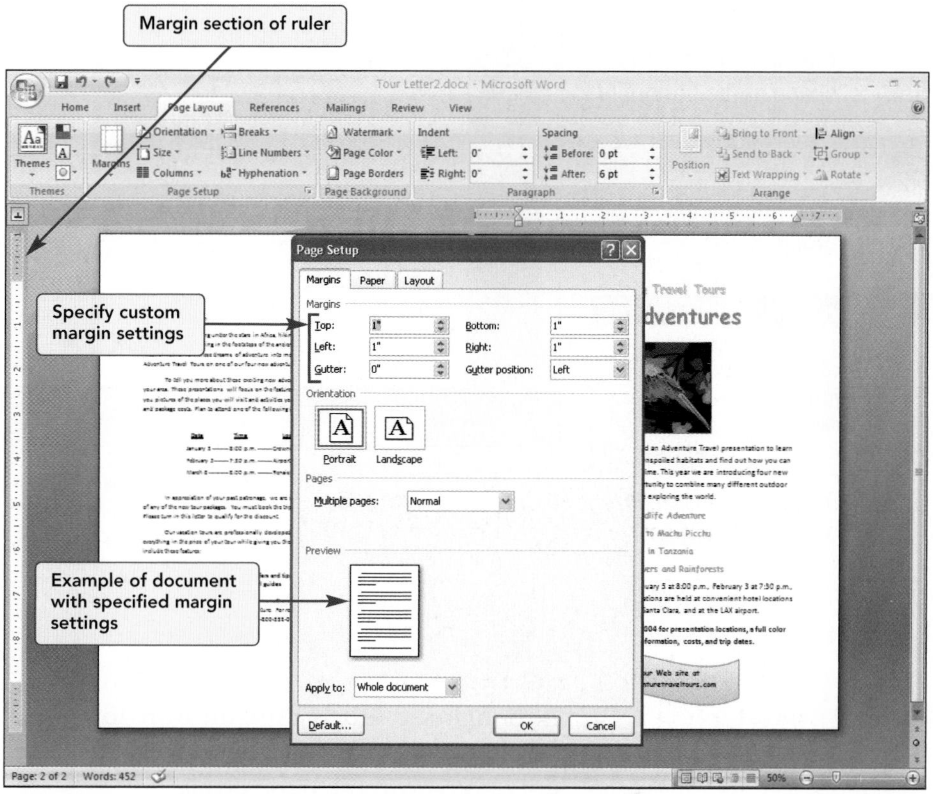

Margin section of ruler

Specify custom margin settings

Example of document with specified margin settings

**Figure 2.69**

The Margins tab of the Page Setup dialog box displays the default margin settings for a single-sided document. The Preview box shows how the current margin settings will appear on a page. New margin settings can be entered by typing the value in the text box, or by clicking the  and ▼ scroll buttons or pressing the ↑ or ↓ keys to increase or decrease the settings by tenths of an inch.

**4** • Using any of these methods, set the left and right margins to 0.8 inch.

• Click [ OK ].

• If necessary, readjust the placement of the shape at the bottom of the flyer.

• Save the document again.

**Additional Information**

You also can change the margins by dragging the left and right margin boundaries on the ruler.

*Your screen should be similar to Figure 2.70*

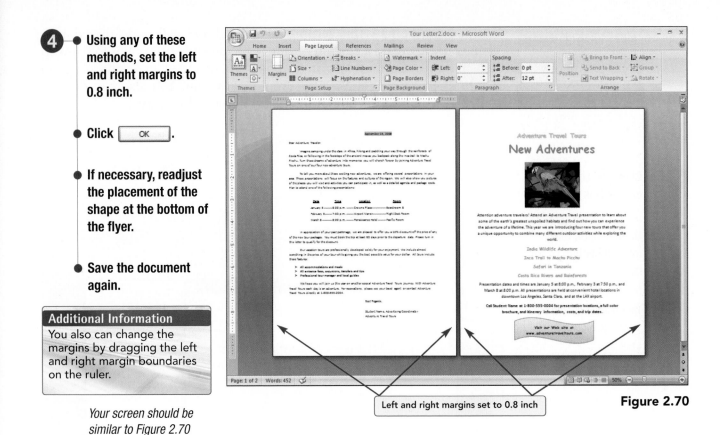

Left and right margins set to 0.8 inch

**Figure 2.70**

Although the text is difficult to read, you can easily see the layout of the pages and that the margin settings have been changed for both pages. You are happy with the new settings.

# Printing the Document

Now that the document has been edited and formatted the way you want, you will print a copy of the document using the default print settings.

**Note:** If you need to specify a different printer, you will need to use the Print command on the Office Button menu.

**1** • Click Office Button and choose Print/Quick Print.

The printed output should be similar to text shown in the Case Study at the beginning of the lab.

**2** ● Click ⊠ to close the Tour Letter2 document.

● Click ⊠ Close to close the wd02_Flyer2 document.

**Additional Information**

Using ⊠ Close both closes the file and exits the application. If you want to keep the application open, use the Close command in the 🔵 Office Button menu.

● If a question dialog box appears about modified styles, click [ No ].

● If a question dialog box appears about a large amount of text in the Clipboard, click [ No ].

If you were using your own computer, you would want to save the modified block style so that it would be available the next time you used the application.

# Focus on Careers

## EXPLORE YOUR CAREER OPTIONS

**Assistant Broadcast Producer**
Have you wondered who does the background research for a film or television broadcast? Or who is responsible for making sure a film production runs on schedule? Assistant producers are responsible for background research and the daily operations of a shooting schedule. They also may produce written materials for broadcast. These written materials are often compiled from multiple documents and sources. The typical salary range for an assistant broadcast producer is $27,000 to $38,000. Demand for those with relevant training and experience is expected to continue in this competitive job market.

**Thesaurus** (WD2.9)

Word's Thesaurus is a reference tool that provides synonyms, antonyms, and related words for a selected word or phrase.

**Move and Copy** (WD2.12)

Text and graphic selections can be moved or copied to new locations in a document or between documents, saving you time by not having to retype the same information.

**Page Break** (WD2.20)

A page break marks the point at which one page ends and another begins. Two types of page breaks can be used in a document: soft page breaks and hard page breaks.

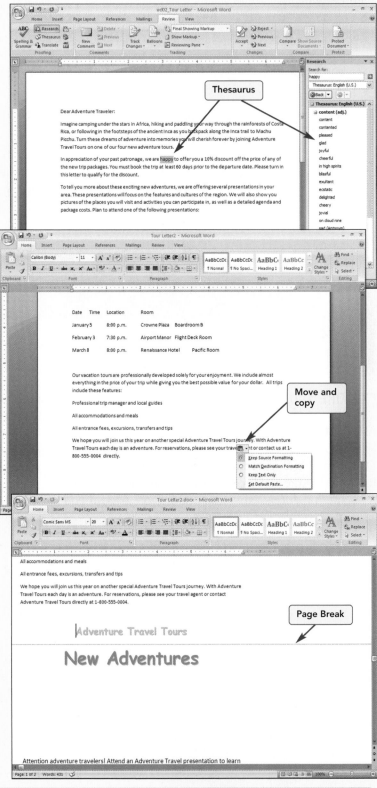

## Find and Replace (WD2.22)

To make editing easier, you can use the Find and Replace feature to find text in a document and replace it with other text as directed.

## Field (WD2.29)

A field is a placeholder that instructs Word to insert information into a document.

## Indents (WD2.32)

To help your reader find information quickly, you can indent paragraphs from the margins. Indenting paragraphs sets them off from the rest of the document.

## Line Spacing (WD2.41)

Adjusting the line spacing, or the vertical space between lines of text, helps set off areas of text from others and, when increased, makes it easier to read and edit text.

## Bulleted and Numbered Lists (WD2.48)

Whenever possible, add bullets or numbers before items in a list to organize information and make your writing clear and easy to read.

## Sort (WD2.52)

Word can quickly arrange or sort text, numbers, or data in lists or tables in alphabetical, numeric, or date order based on the first character in each paragraph.

## Page Margin (WD2.65)

The page margin is the blank space around the edge of the page. Standard single-sided documents have four margins: top, bottom, left, and right.

# Lab Review

LAB 2

## Revising and Refining a Document

## key terms

active window   WD2.17

antonym   WD2.9

building blocks   WD2.53

bulleted list   WD2.48

case sensitive   WD2.24

control   WD2.54

destination   WD2.12

drag and drop   WD2.15

field   WD2.29

field code   WD2.29

field result   WD2.29

Format Painter   WD2.47

gradient   WD2.59

hard page break   WD2.20

hyperlink   WD2.60

indent   WD2.32

leader character   WD2.38

line spacing   WD2.41

numbered list   WD2.48

Office Clipboard   WD2.12

outline numbered list   WD2.48

page break   WD2.20

page margin   WD2.65

soft page break   WD2.20

sort   WD2.52

source   WD2.12

synchronized   WD2.17

synonym   WD2.9

system Clipboard   WD2.12

tab stop   WD2.35

thesaurus   WD2.9

URL   WD2.60

## MCAS skills

The Microsoft Certified Applications Specialist (MCAS) certification program is designed to measure your proficiency in performing basic tasks using the Office 2007 applications. Getting certified demonstrates that you have the skills and provides a valuable industry credential for employment. See Reference 2 MCAS Certification Guide for a complete list of the skills that were covered in Lab 2.

# command summary

| Command | Shortcut | Action |
|---|---|---|
| **Home tab** | | |
| *Clipboard group* | | |
| ✂ Cut | Ctrl + X | Cuts selection to Clipboard |
| 📋 Copy | Ctrl + C | Copies selection to Clipboard |
| 📄 Paste | Ctrl + V | Pastes item from Clipboard |
| *Editing group* | | |
| 🔍 Find ▾ | Ctrl + F | Locates specified text |
| Replace | Ctrl + H | Locates and replaces specified text |
| *Font group* | | |
| U ▾ Underline | Ctrl + U | Underlines selected text with single line |
| *Paragraph group* | | |
| ☰ ▾ Bullets | | Creates a bulleted list |
| ☰ ▾ Numbering | | Creates a numbered list |
| ↕ Sort | | Rearranges information in a list in alphabetical order |
| Increase Indent | | Increases indent of paragraph to next tab stop |
| Line Spacing | | Changes spacing between lines of text |
| □/ Tabs... | | Specifies types and positions of tab stops |
| □/Indents and Spacing/ Special/First Line | Tab | Indents first line of paragraph from left margin |
| □/Indents and Spacing/ Line Spacing | Ctrl + # | Changes the spacing between lines of text |
| **Insert tab** | | |
| *Pages group* | | |
| Page Break | Ctrl + Enter | Inserts hard page break |
| *Illustrations group* | | |
| Shapes | | Inserts graphic shapes |
| *Text group* | | |
| Quick Parts ▾ | | Inserts Building Blocks |
| Date & Time | | Inserts current date or time, in selected format |

# Lab Review

## command summary

| Command | Shortcut | Action |
|---|---|---|
| **Page Layout tab** | | |
| *Page Setup group* | | |
| Margins | | Sets margin sizes |
| Breaks ▾ | | Inserts page and section breaks |
| **Review tab** | | |
| *Proofing group* | | |
| Spelling & Grammar | F7 | Starts Spelling and Grammar Checker |
| Thesaurus | ⇧Shift + F7 | Opens Thesaurus tool |
| **View tab** | | |
| *Window group* | | |
| Arrange All | | Arranges all open windows horizontally on the screen |
| View Side by Side | | Displays two document windows side by side to make it easy to compare content |

# Lab Exercises

## matching

Match the item on the left with the correct description on the right.

1. ![checkmark] _____      **a.** indents first line of paragraph

2. [Tab ⮂] _____      **b.** mouse procedure that moves or copies a selection to a new location

3. synonyms _____      **c.** placeholder that instructs Word to insert information into a document

4. [A↓Z] _____      **d.** automatically starts a new page when a previous page is filled with text

5. drag and drop _____      **e.** arranges selection in sorted order

6. field _____      **f.** inserts a hard page break

7. soft page break _____      **g.** words with similar meaning

8. [Ctrl] + [←Enter] _____      **h.** copies formatting to another place

9. leader character _____      **i.** vertical space between lines of text

10. line spacing _____      **j.** solid, dotted, or dashed lines between tab stops

## multiple choice

Circle the correct response to the questions below.

1. Word includes preformatted content, called _____, that gives you a head start in creating content such as page numbers, cover pages, headers and footers, and sidebars.
   **a.** drag and drop
   **b.** Format Painter
   **c.** building blocks
   **d.** AutoContent

2. A _____ marks the point at which one page ends and another begins.
   **a.** leader character
   **b.** selection point
   **c.** field code
   **d.** page break

3. The _____ is a reference tool that provides synonyms and antonyms.
   **a.** find and replace feature
   **b.** research
   **c.** thesaurus
   **d.** clipboard

4. The information that is displayed as a result of a field is called _____.
   a. a field code
   b. a field result
   c. a quick part
   d. a wildcard

5. The blank space around the edge of the page is called the _____.
   a. gutter
   b. indent
   c. margin
   d. white space

6. The field _____ contains the directions that identify the type of information to insert.
   a. results
   b. code
   c. placeholder
   d. format

7. To convey a sequence of events in a document, you should consider using a _____.
   a. bulleted list
   b. numbered list
   c. sorted list
   d. paragraph list

8. A _____ is a Web site address.
   a. URL
   b. RUL
   c. WSL
   d. ULR

9. The feature most useful for copying or moving short distances in a document is _____.
   a. drag and drop
   b. drop and drag
   c. move and place
   d. drag and place

10. _____ is a feature that applies the formats associated with a selection to another selection.
    a. Format Painter
    b. Find and Replace
    c. AutoFormat
    d. Format Designer

Circle the correct answer to the following questions.

1. The thesaurus identifies synonyms for common words.      True     False
2. Draft view does not display graphics.      True     False
3. Indents are used to set paragraphs off from the rest of the text.      True     False
4. The Find and Replace feature is used to locate misspelled words in a document.      True     False
5. A sorted list conveys a sequence of events.      True     False
6. A source is the location from which text is moved or copied.      True     False
7. Soft page breaks are automatically inserted whenever the text reaches the bottom margin.      True     False
8. The Clipboard is a permanent storage area.      True     False
9. The Quick Parts feature can be used to quickly insert text and graphics.      True     False
10. A hyperlink is a connection to a location in the current document, to another document, or to a Web site.      True     False

## fill-in

Complete the following statements by filling in the blanks with the correct terms.

1. Windows that are _____ scroll together.

2. A(n) _____ code instructs Word to insert the current date in the document using the selected format whenever the document is printed.

3. As you add or remove text from a page, Word automatically _____ the placement of the soft page break.

4. Double-sided documents with facing pages typically use _____ margins.

5. _____ are reuseable pieces of content that can be quickly inserted in a document.

6. In a _____ style letter, all parts are aligned with the left margin.

7. _____ and _____ organize information and make your writing clear and easy to read.

8. A _____ is a gradual progression of colors and shades.

9. Two types of page breaks that can be used in a document are _____ and _____.

10. When a selection is moved or copied, the selection is stored in the _____ Clipboard, a temporary Windows storage area in memory.

# Hands-On Exercises

**step-by-step**

## Expanding the Note-Taking Skills Handout ★

**1.** You are continuing to work on the handout to supplement your lecture on note-taking skills and tips. Although the content is nearly complete, there are several more tips you need to add to the document. You also want to rearrange the order of the tips. This handout is also going to be included in the freshman orientation information packet and needs to include formatting to make the document interesting and appealing to students. Your completed document will be similar to the one shown here.

**a.** Open the file wd02_Note Taking Tips. Spell-check the document.

**b.** Use the thesaurus to find a better word for "gist" in the first tip.

**c.** Open the document Note Taking Skills you created in Step-by-Step Exercise 4 in Lab 1. Display the document windows side by side. Copy the tips from the wd02_Note Taking Tips document to the end of the tips in the Note Taking Skills document. Close the wd02_Note Taking Tips document without saving your changes.

### Tips for Taking Better Classroom Notes

**Be Ready**

- Review your assigned reading and previous notes you've taken before class.
- Bring plenty of paper and a sharpened pencil, an erasable pen or a pen that won't skip or smudge.
- Write the class name, date and that day's topic at the top the page.

**Write Legibly**

- Print if your handwriting is poor. Use a pencil or erasable pen if you cross out material a lot so that your notes are easier to read.
- Take notes in one-liners rather than paragraph form.
- Skip a line between ideas to make it easier to find information when you're studying for a test.

**Use Abbreviations**

- Abbreviations let you write more quickly.
- To abbreviate, condense a word or phrase into initials, or use a symbol. For instance, use b/c for because; w/ for with; w/o for without; and govt for government.
- Always use the same abbreviations for the same words and phrases so you'll immediately know what they stand for.

**Use Wide Margins**

- Leave a wide margin on one side of your paper so you'll have space to write your own thoughts and call attention to key material.
- Draw arrows or stars beside important information like dates, names and events.
- If you miss getting a date, name, number or other fact, make a mark in the margin so you'll remember to come back to it.

**Fill in Gaps**

- Check with a classmate or your teacher after class to get any missing names, dates, facts or other information you could not write down.

**d.** Increase the size of the title to 24 points. Use Format Painter to change the format of the new headings to the same as the existing headings.

**e.** Move the "Use Abbreviations" tip below the "Write Legibly" tip. Move the "Check the Board" tip to below the "Mark Questionable Materials" tip.

**f.** Change the margins to Moderate. Change the space after paragraphs to 6 points for the entire document. Remove any blank lines between topics.

**g.** Break the tips under each topic heading into separate bulleted items using bullet styles of your choice. (A bulleted item may be more than one sentence if it contains an explanation or is a continuation of the same tip topic.)

h. Insert a hard page break before the Mark Questionable Materials topic.

i. Left-align your name and the date. Delete your name and replace it using the Author quick part. Replace the date with a date field using a format of your choice.

j. Add the shape "Curved Down Ribbon" from the Stars and Banners category to the bottom of the document.

k. Add the text **Good Notes = Better Grades** to the shape. Bold, center, and size the text to 18 pt. Size the shape to display the text on two lines.

l. Add a fill color to the shape and color to the text to complement the colors you used in the document. Center the shape at the bottom of the document.

m. Add document properties. Save the document as Note Taking Skills2 and print it.

---

**Mark Questionable Material**

- Jot down a "?" in the margin beside something you disagree with or do not think you recorded correctly.
- When appropriate, ask your teacher, classmate, or refer to your textbook, for clarification.

**Check the Board**

- ✓ When your teacher writes something on the board or projects it, that's a signal that the information is important. Copy everything down, and note that it was on the board.

**Listen for Cues**

- ❖ Don't try to write everything down.
- ❖ Listen for cues from your teacher about what is important. When you hear "The reasons why..." "Here is how..." or a change in tone of voice, that indicates something noteworthy is about to be said.
- ❖ Write down dates, names, definitions, and formulas, and why they are important.
- ❖ Write down the idea of any examples or stories your teacher gives when explaining a point or concept. These will help you remember the material.

**Keep Organized**

- ✓ Keep notes for the same class together, along with any handouts.

**Review and Highlight**

- ➤ Go over your notes after class or after school while the lecture is still fresh in your mind.
- ➤ Complete any partially recorded notes and clarify any unintelligible sections as quickly as possible.
- ➤ Add information that will help you comprehend the material. Use a highlighter or a different color of ink to highlight, underline or circle important words and phrases.

Student Name
September 15, 2008

# Water Conservation Article ★★

2. Each month, the town newsletter is included with the utility bill. This month the main article is about conserving water. You started the column a few days ago and need to expand the article by adding a few more suggestions. Then you need to edit and format the text and include a graphic to enhance the appearance of the article. Your completed article will be similar to that shown here.

a. Open the document wd02_Water Conservation. Spell and grammar-check the document.

b. Center the title. Change the font to Impact with a point size of 24. Add a color of your choice to the title.

c. Change the three category heads to bold with a type size of 14 pt. Center the heads. Use the same color as in the title for the heads.

d. Change the alignment of the introductory paragraph to justified.

e. Insert the picture wd02_Water Hose (from your data files) below the main title of the article.

f. Size the picture to be 2 inches wide (use the ruler as a guide). Center it below the title.

g. Save the document using the file name Water Conservation Column.

h. Open the document wd02_Conservation Tips. Find and replace all occurrences of "h2o" with "water."

**i.** Display the document windows side by side. Copy the tips from the wd02_Conservation Tips document to the appropriate categories in the wd02_Water Conservation Column document. Close the wd02_Conservation Tips document without saving your changes.

**j.** Save the document again.

**k.** Change the line spacing of the tips by decreasing the spacing after to 0 points.

**l.** Change the top and bottom margins to 0.75 inch. Change the right and left margins to 1 inch.

**m.** Apply three different bullet styles to the tips under the three categories. Indent the bulleted tips to the 0.5-inch position.

**n.** Use the thesaurus to find a better word for "biggest" in the first paragraph. Indent the first line of the first paragraph.

**o.** Two lines below the last group of tips, insert a shape that includes the text **Visit us for more water conservation tips at www.citywaterprogram.com**. Remove the hyperlink formatting. Apply formatting, such as color and bold, of your choice to this line. Fill the shape with a gradient color.

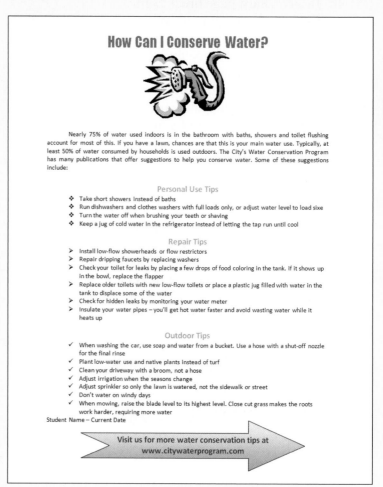

**p.** Add your full name using the Author quick part and the current date as a date field below the last line of tips.

**q.** Preview the document and, if necessary, reduce the size of the graphic to make the entire document fit on one page. Print the document.

**r.** Add document properties. Save and close the document.

## Promoting New Fitness Classes ★★

3. The Lifestyle Fitness Club has just started a new series of informal classes for the members and their families. You want to spread the word by creating a flyer for club members to pick up at the front desk. You have created a Word document with the basic information that you want to include in the flyer. Now you just need to make it look better. Your completed flyer will be similar to the one shown here.

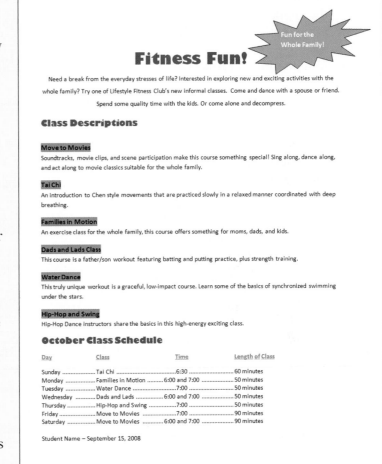

a. Open the file wd02_Fitness Fun.

b. Find each occurrence of "class" and replace it with "Class" where appropriate. Be sure to use the match case and whole words only options. Find and replace all occurrences of "mins" with "minutes."

c. Use the spelling and grammar checker to correct the identified errors.

d. Save the document as Fitness Fun Flyer.

e. Change the title font to Gill Sans Ultra Bold (or a font of your choice), 26 pt, and a color of your choice. Center the title.

f. Center the introductory paragraph and set line spacing to 1.5.

g. Use Format Painter to format the "Class Descriptions" heading the same as the title. Reduce the font size to 14 and left align it. Add space before the paragraph.

h. Use Format Painter to increase the font size to 12; add bold and a color highlight to the eight class titles.

i. Delete the class title, description, and scheduling information on the Beginning Ballroom Dance class because you do not have an instructor for this month.

j. Set the margins to Moderate.

k. Use drag and drop to move the Tai Chi class description below the Move to Movies description. Adjust the line spacing as needed between descriptions.

l. Create a tabbed table of the schedule. Add left tab marks at 1.5, 3, and 5 inches. Bold, add color, and underline the words only of the table heads: Day, Class, Time, and Length of Class. Move the tab marker from the 5-inch position to the 4.5-inch position for the entire table. Change the tab at the 3-inch position to a center tab stop at the 3.25-inch position. Add tab leaders of your choice between the columns of data. Add space after the heading line only of the tabbed table.

**m.** Above the table, add the heading **October Class Schedule**. Format it the same as the "Class Descriptions" heading. Insert a hard page break above the table heading.

**n.** Add the shape "Explosion 2" from the Stars and Banners section below the Line Dancing description at the bottom of page one. Add the text **Fun for the Whole Family!**. Bold and size the text to 12 pt. Add fill color and font color of your choice to the shape. Size and position the shape appropriately.

**o.** Delete the Line Dancing class title and description. Delete the hard page break. Move and size the shape to fit at the top right of the flyer title.

**p.** Add your name using the Author quick part and the current date (as a field) on the last line on the page.

**q.** Add document properties. Save and print the document.

## Orientation Meeting Schedule ★★★

**4.** The Animal Rescue Foundation is actively seeking volunteers to help with an upcoming conference. You are preparing the information that will appear on the Web site and the flyer that will be distributed to local businesses. Your completed document will be similar to the one shown here.

**a.** Open a new document and set the left and right page margins to 1.5 inch.

**b.** On the first line, center the title **ARF Needs You!**. Increase the font to 26 points and apply formats of your choice.

**c.** Several lines below the title, type the following paragraphs:

**The Animal Rescue Foundation needs volunteers to help with our upcoming conference.**

### ARF Needs You!!

The Animal Rescue Foundation needs volunteers to help with our upcoming conference.

**Registration and Hospitality**

We need help at registration throughout the conference, assembling packages several days prior to the conference, and with answering questions and giving directions at hospitality tables.

**Education: Session Moderators**

We need assistance in preparing rooms for presentations, assisting and introducing speakers, collecting evaluations sheets, assisting with poster session.

**Special Events**

We need help greeting, collecting tickets, loading buses and decorating.

**Volunteer Times Available**

| Day | Date | Time |
| --- | --- | --- |
| Monday | May 8 | 10:00 AM to 1:00 PM |
| Tuesday | May 9 | 7:00 PM to 9:00 PM |
| Saturday | May 13 | 10:00 AM to 7:00 PM |
| Sunday | May 14 | 9:00 AM to 4:00 PM |

If you are interested in serving in any of these areas, please contact: Student Name, Volunteer Coordinator at (800) 555-8023

**For more information visit us at**
www.arf.com

**Registration and Hospitality**

We need help at registration throughout the meeting, assembling packets several days prior to the meeting, and with answering questions and giving directions at hospitality tables.

**Education: Session Moderators**

We need help in preparing rooms for presentations, assisting and introducing speakers, collecting evaluation sheets, assisting with poster session.

**Special Events**

We need help greeting, collecting tickets, loading buses and decorating.

If you are interested in serving in any of these areas, please contact:

[Your Name], Volunteer Coordinator at (800) 555-8023

**d.** Spell-check the document. Use the thesaurus to find a better word for "help" in the Education: Session Moderators paragraph.

**e.** Find and replace all occurrences of "meeting" with "conference."

**f.** Save the document as Conference Volunteers.

**g.** Center the first line and increase the font size to 14. Add bold and color to the three headings. Indent the paragraphs below each heading 0.5 inch and set the line spacing to double.

**h.** Below the Special Events topic, enter the title **Volunteer Times Available**. Use the same formatting as the main title with a font size of 14 points.

**i.** Below this heading, you will create a table. Place center tab stops at 1, 2.5, and 4.25 inches on the ruler. Enter the word **Day** at the first tab stop, **Date** at the second tab stop, and **Time** at the third tab stop.

**j.** Press ⟨←Enter⟩, then clear the tab stops. Create a left tab at 0.75 and 2.25 and a right tab stop at 5. Enter the schedule information shown here into the table.

| Monday | May 8 | 10:00 AM to 1:00 PM |
|--------|-------|---------------------|
| Tuesday | May 9 | 7:00 PM to 9:00 PM |
| Saturday | May 13 | 10:00 AM to 7:00 PM |
| Sunday | May 14 | 9:00 AM to 4:00 PM |

**k.** Change the font size of the table headings to 12 points, bold, and the same color as the title. Add an underline style of your choice to the table headings. Bold the text in the remainder of the table. Change the line spacing of the entire table to single with no space after.

**l.** Create a shape of your choice and add the text **For more information visit us at www.arf.com** using a font size of 12 points and bold. Size the shape appropriately. Remove the hyperlink format from the URL. Add color to the URL. Add a fill color to the shape. Center the shape at the bottom of the page.

**m.** Add document properties. Save and print the document.

## Advertising Weekly Specials ★★★

5. Now that the Downtown Internet Cafe has had its grand re-opening celebration, the owner wants to continue to bring in new and repeat customers by offering weekly specials. You want to create a flyer describing the coffee varieties and specials for the week. Your completed flyer will be similar to the one shown here.

   a. Open a new document.

   b. Enter the title **Downtown Internet Cafe** on the first line. Change the font to Arial Rounded MT Bold. Add three blank lines.

   c. Enter **Italian Market Reserve** on the line followed by two blank lines.

   d. On line 7, place a left tab stop at 0.5 and center tabs at 3.25 and 5.75 inches.

   e. Enter the word **Coffee** at the first tab stop, **Description** at the second tab stop, and **Cost/Pound** at the third tab stop.

   f. On the next line, clear all the tab stops and enter the rest of the information for the table shown in the final document using left tabs at 0.5, 2, and 5.5.

| Original | Our Signature Coffee! With Old World charm | $10.49 |
| --- | --- | --- |
| Decaffeinated | All the original has to offer — decaffeinated natural. | $13.49 |
| Reduced Caffeine | All the original has to offer with half of the caffeine. | $13.49 |

   g. Add tab leaders of your choice between the data in the table. Remove the space after each line in the table.

   h. Center the first title line and change the font color to green with a font size of 28 pt.

   i. Center the second title line and change it to purple with a font size of 22 pt.

   j. Increase the font of the table headings to 14 pt. Add bold, color, and an underline style of your choice to the table headings.

   k. Save the document as Weekly Specials.

   l. Open the file wd02_Coffee Flyer. Display the document windows side by side. Copy the first two paragraphs and insert them above "Italian Market Reserve" in the new document.

   m. Spell-check the document. Use the thesaurus to find better words for "desire" and "giant" in the first paragraph.

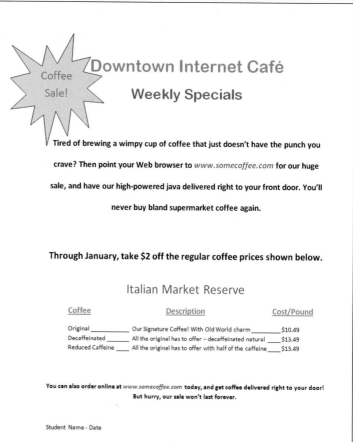

**n.** Use Find and Replace to replace all occurrences of "java" with "coffee" (except the one following "high-powered").

**o.** Center the words **Weekly Specials** below the title. Use the same font as the title, change the font size to 24 points, and select a color of your choice.

**p.** Make the paragraph that begins with "Tired" bold, centered, and 14 pt, and set the line spacing to double. Add blue color to the URL.

**q.** Increase the font size of the line above "Italian Market Reserve" to 16 pt. Center the text.

**r.** Copy the remaining paragraph from the wd02_Coffee Flyer document and insert it at the bottom of the new document. Include two blank lines between the table and the paragraph. Close the wd02_Coffee Flyer document.

**s.** Bold and center the final paragraph. Remove the hyperlink format from the URL. Format the URL as italic and blue.

**t.** Increase the top, left, and right margins to 1.5 inches.

**u.** Create the Explosion 1 shape from the Stars and Banners group. Enter and center the text **Coffee Sale!** in red, 22 pt font size within it. Add a fill color. Size the shape appropriately. Move the shape to the left of the pricing table.

**v.** Adjust the formatting of the document as needed to improve its appearance.

**w.** Add your name using the Author quick part and the current date (as a field) several lines below the final paragraph.

**x.** Add document properties. Save and print the document.

# Lab Exercises

## on your own

### Requesting a Reference ★

1. Your first year as a business major is going well and you are looking for a summer internship with a local advertising firm. You have an upcoming interview and want to come prepared with a letter of reference from your last position. Write a business letter directed to your old supervisor, Kevin Westfall, at your former position, R & A Publishing. Use the modified block letter style shown in the lab. Be sure to include the date, a salutation, two paragraphs, a closing, and your name as a signature. Spell-check the document, save the document as Reference Letter, and print it.

### Cell Phone Rates ★

2. MyRatePlan.com posts up-to-date rate information on cell phone rates and available minutes at each price break. The company wants you to create the following table of rates for quick reference. Create a tabbed table using the information shown below. Bold and underline the column heads. Add style 2 tab leaders to the table entries. Above the table, write a paragraph explaining the table contents.

|          | Cingular | NEXTEL      | Sprint      | T-Mobile    | Verizon Wireless |
|----------|----------|-------------|-------------|-------------|------------------|
| $39.99   | 450      | 300-400     | 300-400     | 600-1,000   | 450              |
| $49.99   |          |             |             | 1,000       |                  |
| $59.99   | 900      | 500-1,000   | 500-1,000   | 1,500       | 900              |
| $79.99   | 1,350    | 800-1,400   | 800-1,400   |             | 1,350            |
| $99.99   | 2,000    | 1,000-2,000 | 2,000-1,000 | 2,500       | 2,000            |

Include your name and the date below the table. Save the document as Cell Phone Rates and print the document.

### Yard Sale ★★

3. Create a flyer to advertise a yard sale you plan for Saturday morning. Include the following features on your flyer:

- Different fonts in different sizes, colors, and styles.
- Bulleted or numbered list.
- Indents.
- A shape with appropriate text.
- A graphic.
- A tabbed table with tab leaders.

Include your name as the contact information. Save the document as Yard Sale Flyer and print it.

## Wyoming Relocation ★★

4. You work for the Department of Tourism for the state of Wyoming. You have been asked to produce a relocation packet to aid people planning to move to the state. This packet includes information on state history, the weather, geography, major cities, population statistics, and so forth. Research information on the Web about Wyoming and create a one-page fact sheet of your findings. Your completed project should include an introductory paragraph on relocation, graphics, table with the average weather statistics, a bulleted list of attractions, and shapes. Include your name as the contact and save the file as Wyoming Facts. Print the file.

## Downloading Music ★★★

5. Your ethics class is studying the ethics of downloading free music from online sources. Your instructor has divided the class into groups and assigned each group a research project. Your group is to find out about court cases related to copyright infringement. Use the Web to research this topic and write a one-page report on your findings. Include a table of the data you found. Use other features demonstrated in this lab, including shapes, indents, bulleted lists, font colors, and so forth to make your report attractive and easy to read. Be sure to reference your sources on the Web for the data you located. Include your name and the current date below the report. Save the report as Ethics Report and print your report.

# Creating Reports and Tables

LAB **3**

## Objectives

After you have completed this lab, you will know how to:

**1** Create and modify an outline.

**2** Create a cover page.

**3** Apply and customize Document Themes.

**4** Apply and customize Quick Styles.

**5** Create and update a table of contents and table of figures.

**6** Navigate using hyperlink, Document Map, and thumbnails.

**7** Add citations and create a bibliography.

**8** Add footnotes, captions, and cross-references.

**9** Wrap text around graphics.

**10** Create and format a simple table.

**11** Create and format sections.

**12** Add headers, footers, and page numbers.

# Adventure Travel Tours

**A**dventure Travel Tours provides information on their tours in a variety of forms. Travel brochures, for instance, contain basic tour information in a promotional format and are designed to entice potential clients to sign up for a tour. More detailed regional information packets are given to people who have already signed up for a tour, so they can prepare for their vacation. These packets include facts about each region's climate, geography, and culture. Additional informational formats include pages on Adventure Travel's Web site and scheduled group presentations.

**P**art of your responsibility as advertising coordinator is to gather the information that Adventure Travel will publicize about each regional tour. Specifically, you have been asked to provide background information for two of the new tours: the Tanzania Safari and the Machu Picchu trail. Because this information is used in a variety of formats, your research needs to be easily adapted. You will therefore present your facts in the form of a general report on Tanzania and Peru.

**I**n this lab, you will learn to use many of the features of Office Word 2007 that make it easy to create an attractive and well-organized report. A portion of the completed report is shown here.

Adventure Travel Tours

# Tanzania and Peru

region to region, ranging from tropical to arctic. Its varied climate corresponds to the sharply contrasting geographical features of seafront, mountains, and rainforests.

### La Costa
Occupying the slender area along Peru's western coastline, La Costa, provides a division between the mountains and sea. Although some of this area is fertile, mostly it is extremely d and arid. This region's temperature averages approximately 68°F, and it receives almost 2 inc of rainfall annually. The Andes Mountains prevent greater annual precipitation coming from t east. Some areas in the south are considered drier than the Sahara. Conversely, there are a few areas in this region where mountain rivers meet the ocean that are green with life and do not gi the impression of being in a desert at all.

### La Selva
La Selva, a region of tropical rainforest, is the easternmost region in Peru. This region, with the eastern foot of the Andes Mountains, forms the Amazon Basin, into which numerous rivers flow The Amazon River begins at the meeting point of the two dominant rivers, the Ucayali and Marañón. La Selva is extremely wet, with some areas exceeding an annual precipitation of 137 inches. Its wettest season occurs from November to April. The weather here is humid and extremely hot.

### La Sierra
Inland and to the east is the mountainous region called La Sierra, encompassing Peru's share of the Andes mountain range. The southern portion of this region is prone to volcanic activity, and some volcanoes are active today. La Sierra is subject to a dry season from May to September, which is winter in that part of the world. T in some areas during the night. The weathe precipitation. The former Incan capital Cu the Incas. This region also contains Lake T

| Region | An |
| --- | --- |
| La Costa | |
| La Sierra | |
| La Selva | |

Table 1: Peru Climate

---
¹ Lake Titicaca is 12,507 feet above sea level.

## Table of Contents

American and European ancestry), 15 percent white, and 3 percent other (primarily Black and Asian). The official language is Spanish, and the predominant religion is Roman Catholic.

### Animal Life

Peru is home to many exotic animals, but is particularly known for its large population of birds. More than 1,700 species can be found, including parakeets, toucans, and Amazon parrots. Many extremely rare families of birds also live here. Each geographical region of Peru boasts its own distinct habitat, and some types of birds cannot else.

Figure 2: Amazon Parrots

The popular Manu National Park spanning over 4.5 mil unbroken Peruvian rain forest is alive with several species of monkeys, the oce boars, iguana, and the anaconda. It is also considered one of the best places in t the elusive jaguar. Both the squirrel monkey, named for its relatively small size monkey, which is quite loud vocally, can be spotted throughout the rainforests. many of the Amazon River basins and lakes. Though they are known to be vici common misconception that they are man-eaters; in fact, they will graciously s with human swimmers. Also found in the remote Yarapa and Amazon Rivers i pink dolphin, so named because of its striking pink hue.

### Table of Figures

**A cover page and table of contents listing can be created quickly using Word's built-in features.**

### Works Cited
Camerapix, comp. <u>Spectrum Guide to Tanzania</u>. Edison: Hunter, 1992.

Country Studies US. <u>Peru</u>. 2003-2005. 3 November 2006 <http://countrystudies.us/peru/23.htm>.

Wikipedia: The Free Encyclopedia. <u>Tanzania</u>. 5 October 2006. 3 November 2006 <http://en.wikipedia.org/wiki/Tanzania>.

**Tables, footnotes, cross-references, and headers and footers are many standard features that are quick and easy to include in a report.**

**Wrapping text around graphics, adding figure captions, and applying a document theme are among many features that can be used to enhance a report.**

**A bibliography can be quickly generated from cited sources.**

# Concept Preview

**The following concepts will be introduced in this lab:**

**1** **Quick Styles** Applying a quick style, a predefined set of formatting characteristics, allows you to quickly apply a whole group of formats to a selection in one simple step.

**2** **Document Theme** A document theme is a predefined set of formatting choices that can be applied to an entire document in one simple step.

**3** **Table of Contents** A table of contents is a listing of the topic headings that appear in a document and their associated page references.

**4** **Citations and Bibliography** Parenthetical source references, called citations, give credit for specific information included in the document. Complete information for citations is included in a bibliography at the end of the report.

**5** **Footnote and Endnote** Footnotes and endnotes are used in documented research papers to explain or comment on information in the text, or provide source references for text in the document.

**6** **Text Wrapping** You can control the appearance of text around a graphic object by specifying the text wrapping style.

**7** **Captions and Cross-References** A caption is a numbered label for a figure, table, picture, or graph. A cross-reference is a reference from one part of a document to related information in another part.

**8** **Table** A table is used to organize information into an easy-to-read format of horizontal rows and vertical columns.

**9** **Table of Figures** A table of figures is a list of the figures, tables, or equations used in a document and their associated page references.

**10** **Header and Footer** A header is a line or several lines of text in the top margin of each page. A footer is a line or several lines of text in the margin space at the bottom of every page.

**11** **Section** To format different parts of a document differently, you can divide a document into sections.

## Creating and Modifying an Outline

After several days of research, you have gathered many notes from various sources including books, magazines, and the Web. However, the notes are very disorganized and you are having some difficulty getting started writing the report. Often the best way to start is by creating an outline of the main topics.

Word 2007 allows you to create and view document content easily as an outline using Outline view. Outline view shows the hierarchy of topics in a document by displaying the different heading levels indented to represent their level in the document's structure, as shown in the example at right. The

- Tanzania
  - Culture
  - Geography
    - Climate
  - Animal Life
- Peru
  - Culture
    - Historical Culture
      - *Machu Picchu*
  - Geography and Climate
  - Animal Life

arrangement of headings in a hierarchy of importance quickly shows the relationship between topics. You can use Outline view to help you create a new document or to view and reorganize the topics in an existing document.

## Using Outline View

You will use Outline view to help you organize the main topics of the report.

**1** ● **Start Office Word 2007.**

● **Click** [≣] **Outline View in the status bar.**

● **If necessary, increase the zoom to 100%.**

**Another Method**

You also can use [Outline] in the Document Views group of the View tab.

*Your screen should be similar to Figure 3.1*

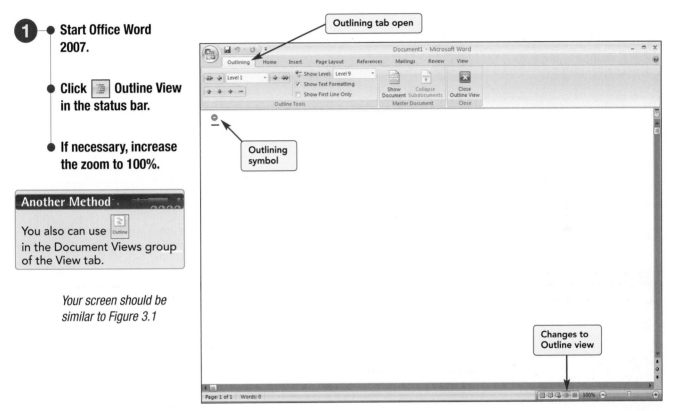

Figure 3.1

The Outlining tab containing buttons that make it easy to create and modify the outline is displayed. Notice the first line of the blank document displays the ⊖ outline symbol. This symbol indicates that the line does not contain subtopics. You will begin by entering the main topic headings for the report.

**2** ● **Type the following
headings, pressing
[←Enter] after each
except the last:**

**Tanzania**

**Climate**

**Geography**

**Animal Life**

**Peru**

**Culture**

**Historical Culture**

**Machu Picchu**

**Geography and
Climate**

**Animal Life (do not
press [←Enter])**

● **Correct any misspelled
words and use Ignore
All for any identified
proper names.**

*Your screen should be
similar to Figure 3.2*

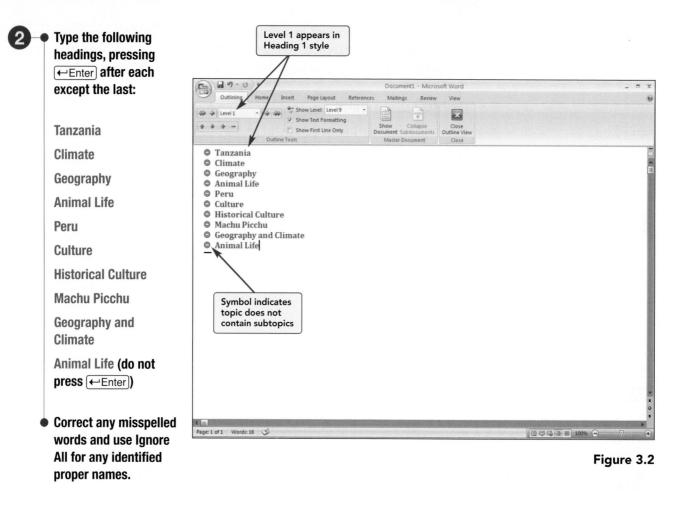

Figure 3.2

As you create a new document in Outline view, Word automatically
applies styles to the text as it is entered in the outline.

## Quick Styles

**1** Applying a **quick style**, a predefined set of formatting characteristics, allows you to quickly apply a whole group of formats to a selection in one simple step. Word includes 75 predefined quick styles. Each quick style is assigned a name. You also can create your own custom styles. Many styles are automatically applied when certain features, such as footnotes, are used. Others must be applied manually to selected text.

Styles can be applied to characters, paragraphs, tables, and lists as described below.

| Type of Style | Description |
|---|---|
| Character | Affects selected text within a paragraph, such as the font and size of text, and bold and italic formats. |
| Paragraph | Controls all aspects of a paragraph's appearance, such as text alignment, tab stops, and line spacing. It also can include character formatting. The default paragraph quick style is named Normal, which includes character settings of Calibri, 11 pt, and paragraph settings of left indent at 0, 1.15 line spacing, and left alignment. In addition, many paragraph styles are designed to affect specific text elements such as headings, captions, and footnotes. |
| Table | Provides a consistent look to borders, shading, alignment, and fonts in tables. |
| List | Applies similar alignment, numbering or bullet characters, and fonts to lists. |

**Having Trouble?**

If your document does not display the styles, click ☑ Show Text Formatting in the Outline Tools group to turn on this feature.

The outline levels are automatically formatted using **heading styles**. They are designed to identify different levels of headings in a document. Heading styles include combinations of fonts, type sizes, color, bold, italics, and spacing. The heading styles used here are those associated with the default document settings. The heading styles and the formats associated with each are shown in the table below:

| Heading Level | Appearance |
|---|---|
| Heading 1 | **Cambria, 14 pt, bold, left align, spacing 24 pt before, 0 pt after, blue** |
| Heading 2 | **Cambria, 13 pt, bold, left align, spacing 10 pt before, 0 pt after, blue** |
| Heading 3 | Cambria, 13 pt, left align, spacing 10 pt before, 0 pt after, blue |
| Heading 4 | *Cambria, 11 pt, bold italic, left align, spacing 10 pt before, 0 pt after, blue* |

The Outline Level button in the Outlining tab shows that the selected item is a Level 1 heading, which is automatically assigned a Heading 1 style. This style is the largest and most prominent. The Level 2 headings (subheadings) are assigned the Heading 2 style, and so on. Headings give the reader another visual cue about how information is organized in your document.

## Changing Outline Levels

Next, you need to arrange the headings by outline levels. As you rearrange the topic headings and subheadings, different heading styles are applied based upon the position or level of the topic within the outline hierarchy. Headings that are level 1 appear as the top level of the outline and appear in a Heading 1 style, level 2 headings appear indented below level 1 headings and appear in a Heading 2 style, and so on.

First you will make the Climate topic heading a subtopic below the main heading of Tanzania. The ◄ Promote and ► Demote buttons in the Outline Tools group are used to change outline levels one level at a time.

**Additional Information**

Clicking 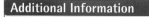 promotes the item directly to a Heading 1 level and ⇥ demotes the item to body text.

● **Click on the Climate topic.**

● **Click ► Demote in the Outline Tools group.**

*Your screen should be similar to Figure 3.3*

Level 2 indented one level

Symbol indicates topic includes subtopics

Level 2 appears in Heading 2 style

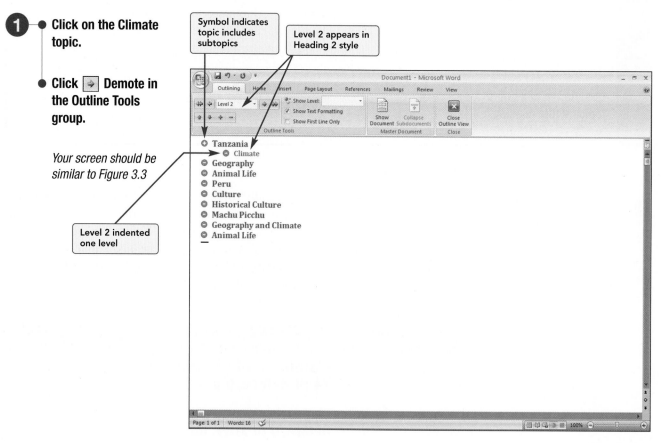

Figure 3.3

The Climate heading has changed to a Heading 2 style and the heading is indented one level to show it is subordinate to the heading above it. The Tanzania heading now displays an outline ⊕ symbol, which indicates the topic heading includes subtopics.

The outline symbols also can be used to select and move the heading to a new location or level within the document. Dragging the outline symbol to the right or left changes the level. To demote a heading to a lower level, drag the symbol to the right; to promote a heading to a higher level, drag the symbol to the left. As you drag the symbol, a vertical solid gray line appears at each outline level to show where the heading will be placed.

**2** ● **Drag the ⊖ symbol of the Geography heading to the right two levels (Level 3).**

● **Demote the remaining topics to the heading levels shown below.**

| | |
|---|---|
| Animal Life | Level 2 |
| Culture | Level 2 |
| Historical Culture | Level 3 |
| Machu Picchu | Level 4 |
| Geography and Climate | Level 2 |
| Animal Life | Level 2 |

*Your screen should be similar to Figure 3.4*

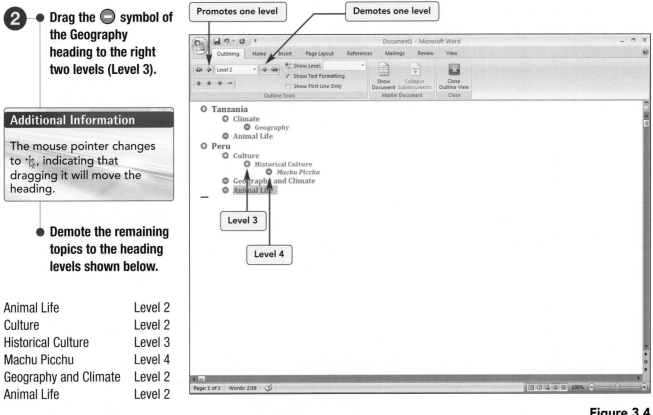

Figure 3.4

## Moving and Inserting Outline Topics

Next, you want to change the order of topics. To move a heading to a different location, drag the outline symbol up or down. As you drag, a horizontal line shows where the heading will be placed when you release the mouse button. You also realize you forgot to include a heading for Culture under Tanzania and will insert the new topic at the appropriate location in the outline.

**1** • Drag the Geography heading up above the Climate heading.

• Promote the Geography heading to a level 2.

• Demote the Climate heading to a level 3.

• Move to the beginning of the Geography heading.

• Press ⟨←Enter⟩ to insert a blank topic heading.

• Type Culture on the blank heading line.

*Your screen should be similar to Figure 3.5*

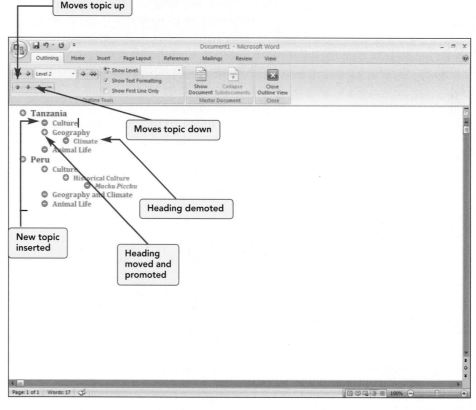

**Figure 3.5**

When you are satisfied with the organization, you can close Outline view to add detailed body text and graphics.

**2** • Click [Close Outline View] in the Close group.

• If necessary, set the zoom to 100%.

**Another Method**
You also could switch directly to another view to close Outline view.

*Your screen should be similar to Figure 3.6*

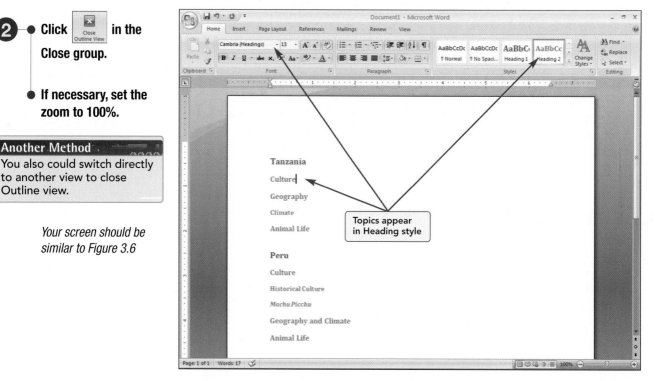

**Figure 3.6**

The topic headings appear left-aligned on the page in the heading style that was applied to the text as the outline was created. You will learn more about using Styles later in the lab.

## Collapsing and Expanding the Outline

You have continued to work on the outline and report organization. Then you entered much of the information for the report and saved it. You will open the document to see the information that has been added to the report.

**1** ● **Open the file**
wd03_Tour Research.

● **Switch to Outline view.**

● **Scroll the window to view the entire document.**

● **Return to the top of the document.**

*Your screen should be similar to Figure 3.7*

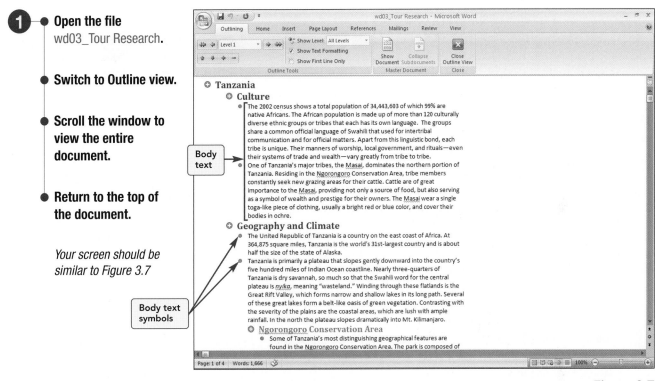

Figure 3.7

The document is displayed as an outline with the topic headings indented appropriately. The body text appears below the appropriate heading. Any text that has not been formatted in a heading style is considered body text and is identified in outline view by the small circles to the left of a paragraph.

In Outline view, you can display as much or as little of the document text as you want. To make it easier to view and reorganize the document's structure, you can "collapse" the document to show just the headings you want. Alternatively, you can "expand" the document to display part of the body text below each heading or the entire body text. You can then easily move the headings around until the order is logical, and the body text will follow the heading. The table below shows how you can collapse and expand the amount of text displayed in Outline view.

| To Collapse | Do This |
|---|---|
| Text below a specific heading level | Select the lowest heading you want to display from the `Show Level: Level 1` drop-down menu. |
| All subheadings and body text under a heading | Double-click ⊕ next to the heading. |
| Text under a heading, one level at a time | Click the heading text, and then click ⊟ Collapse. |
| All body text | Select the heading level you want to see from the `Show Level: Level 1` drop-down menu. |
| All body text except first line | Click `☐ Show First Line Only`. |

| To Expand | Do This |
|---|---|
| All headings and body text | Select Show All Levels from the `Show Level: Level 1` drop-down menu. |
| All collapsed subheadings and body text under a heading | Double-click ⊖ next to the heading. |
| Collapsed text under a heading, one level at a time | Click the heading text; then click ⊞ Expand. |

To change the amount of information displayed, you will collapse the display of the text under the Geography and Climate heading first. Then you will collapse everything below a level 3 heading so you can quickly check the report organization.

**1**
- Double-click ⊕ of the Tanzania Geography and Climate heading.

- Open the `Show Level:` drop-down list.

- Choose Level 3.

*Your screen should be similar to Figure 3.8*

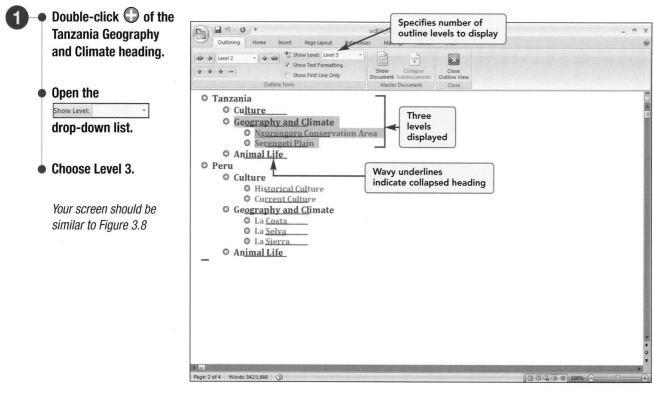

**Figure 3.8**

Now only the three heading levels are displayed. The wavy line below a heading means the heading includes hidden or collapsed headings or body text.

As you look at the organization of the report, you decide to move the discussion of culture to follow the Geography and Climate section. Moving headings in Outline view quickly selects and moves the entire topic, including subtopics and all body text.

**2** • Drag the Culture heading in the Tanzania section down to above the Animal Life heading in the same section.

• Drag the Culture heading in the Peru section down to above the Animal Life heading in the same section.

• Choose All Levels from the Show Level: Level 3 drop-down list.

• Scroll the report up to see the top of the Peru Culture section on page 3.

• Click in the document to deselect the text.

*Your screen should be similar to Figure 3.9*

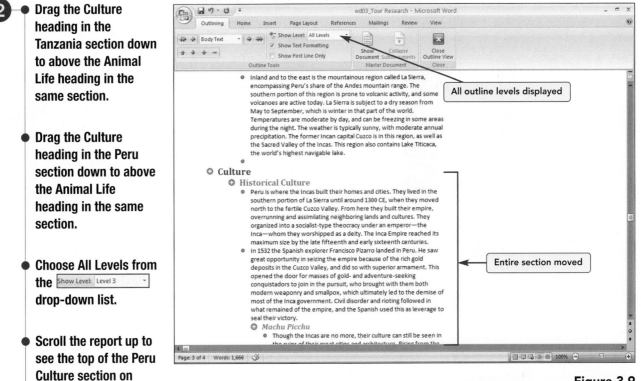

Figure 3.9

The subtopics and body text appear below the heading you moved. When you move or change the level of a heading that includes collapsed subordinate text, the collapsed text also is selected. Any changes you make to the heading, such as moving, copying, or deleting it, also affect the collapsed text.

## Saving to a New Folder

Next, you will save the outline and the research document with its changes in a folder that you will use to hold files related to the report. You can create a new folder at the same time you save a file.

**1** ● **Switch to Print Layout view.**

● **Click** 🏢 **Office Button and choose Save As.**

● **Change the Save In location to the appropriate location for your data files.**

● **Click** 📁 **Create New Folder.**

**Another Method**
The keyboard shortcut to create a new folder is
Alt + 4.

*Your screen should be similar to Figure 3.10*

**Additional Information**
See "Saving, Closing, and Opening Files" in Lab 1 for file-naming rules.

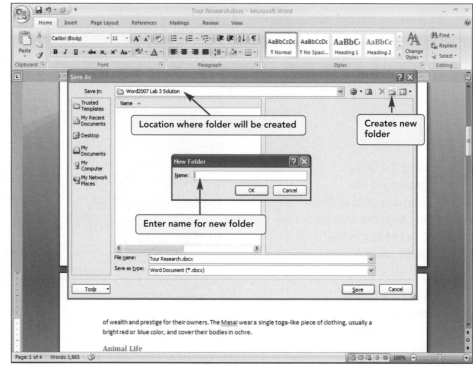

**Figure 3.10**

In the New Folder dialog box, you enter the folder name. The rules for naming folders are the same as for naming files, except they typically do not include an extension.

**2** ● **Type Report in the Name text box and click** [ OK ].

**Additional Information**
You can rename an existing folder by choosing Rename from the folder's shortcut menu and entering the new name.

● **Enter the file name Tour Research and click** [ Save ].

● **Switch to Document1 containing the outline document.**

**Having Trouble?**
Click the document name in the taskbar or use View/Switch Windows.

● **Save the outline to the Report folder with the file name Research Outline.**

● **Close the Research Outline document.**

The documents are saved in the newly created folder, Report.

# Hiding Spelling and Grammar Errors

As you have been working on the report, you have noticed that many spelling and grammar errors are identified. You want to scroll the document to take a quick look at the types of errors identified. You have noticed that scrolling a larger document in Print Layout view takes more time because the view displays the extra blank (white) space on the page and the space allocated for the headers and footers. You can hide the display of this white space to make it faster to move through the document.

**1** ● **Double-click on the blue page separator space between any pages.**

**Additional Information**
The mouse pointer appears as when you can hide the white space.

● **Scroll to see the bottom of page 1 and the top of page 2.**

**Additional Information**
The page number appears in a ScreenTip as you scroll by dragging the scroll box.

*Your screen should be similar to Figure 3.11*

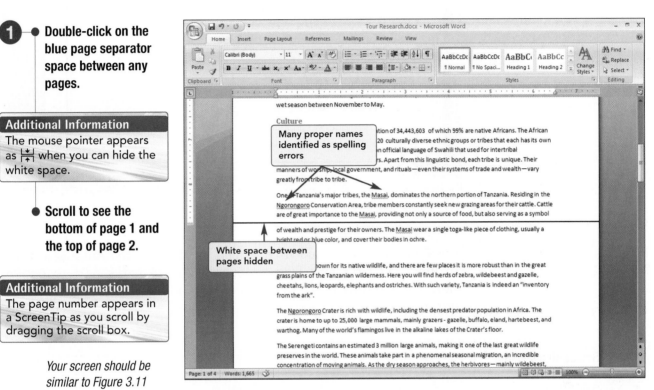

**Figure 3.11**

Any extra white space is eliminated, making scrolling much faster. As you scrolled the document, you noticed that most of the identified errors are for proper names and words that are not in the dictionary. While working on a document, you can turn off the display of these errors so that they are not distracting.

**2**
- Click 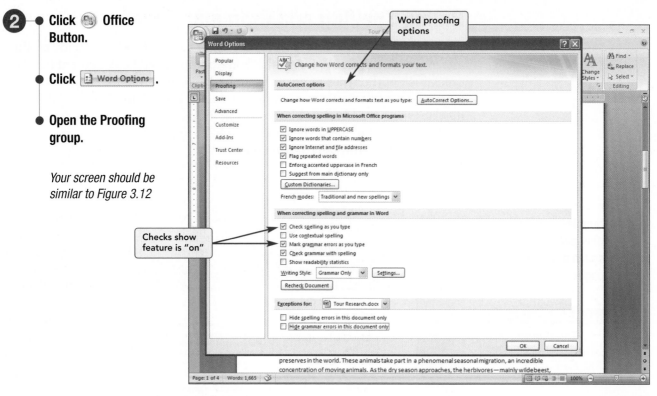 Office Button.
- Click Word Options .
- Open the Proofing group.

*Your screen should be similar to Figure 3.12*

Figure 3.12

The Proofing options are used to change the way the AutoCorrect and Spelling and Grammar features operate. Checkmarks next to options indicate the setting is on. You want to turn off the display of spelling and grammar errors.

**3**
- Select Hide spelling errors in this document only.
- Select Hide grammar errors in this document only.
- Click OK .
- Double-click on the page separator line to show the white space again.

**Additional Information**
The mouse pointer appears as ‡‡‡ when you can show white space.

*Your screen should be similar to Figure 3.13*

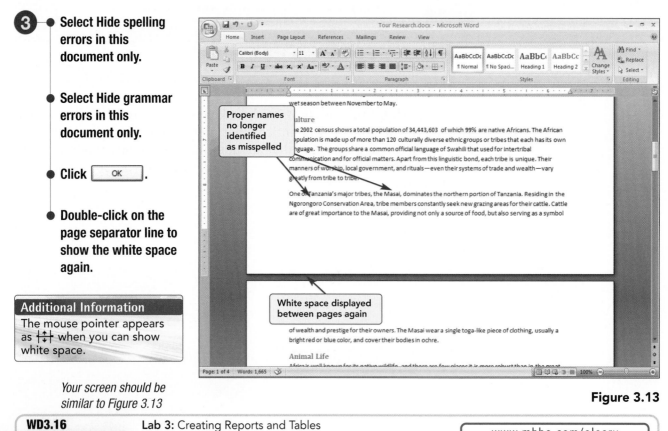

Figure 3.13

The red and green wavy lines are no longer displayed. You can still run spelling and grammar checking manually to check errors at any time. The extra blank space at the bottom of page 3 and the header and footer space are displayed again. Now that you know how to use this feature, you can turn it on and off whenever you want.

# Creating a Cover Page

Now that you have finished reorganizing the report, you want to add a title or cover page. Generally, this page includes information such as the report title, the name of the author, and the date.

When preparing research reports, two styles of report formatting are commonly used: MLA (Modern Language Association) and APA (American Psychological Association). Although they require the same basic information, they differ in how this information is presented. For example, MLA style does not include a separate title page, but APA style does. The report you will create in this lab will use many of the style requirements of the MLA. However, because this report is not a formal report to be presented at a conference or other academic proceeding, some liberties have been taken with the style to demonstrate Word 2007 features.

## Inserting and Modifying a Cover Page

Word 2007 includes many preformatted building blocks that help you quickly create professional-looking documents. The preformatted content includes cover pages, pull quotes, and headers and footers. They are fully formatted and provide spaces where you enter the title, date, and other information. You will use this feature to insert a cover page. Regardless of the location of the insertion point in a document, a cover page is always inserted at the beginning of the document.

① ● Open the Insert tab.

● Choose [Cover Page ▾] from the Pages group.

● Scroll the gallery and choose the Mod cover page design.

● Change the zoom to display two pages.

**Having Trouble?**
Use the Zoom slider or [Two Pages] on the View tab.

*Your screen should be similar to Figure 3.14*

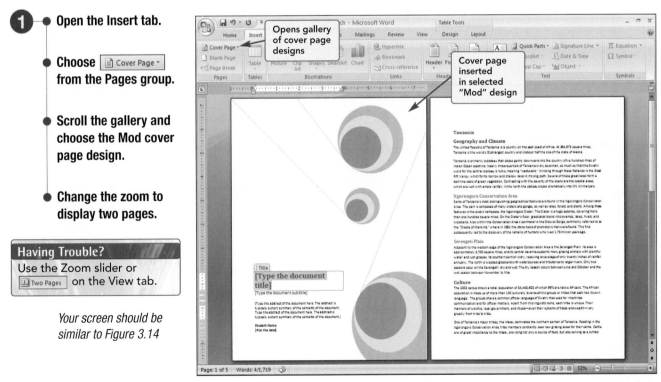

**Figure 3.14**

A new page is inserted at the beginning of the document with the selected cover page design. After looking at this design, you decide to change it to a more traditional cover page look.

**2** ● **Click** [Cover Page ▾].

● **Choose the Sideline design.**

*Your screen should be similar to Figure 3.15*

Cover page design updated to "Sideline" design

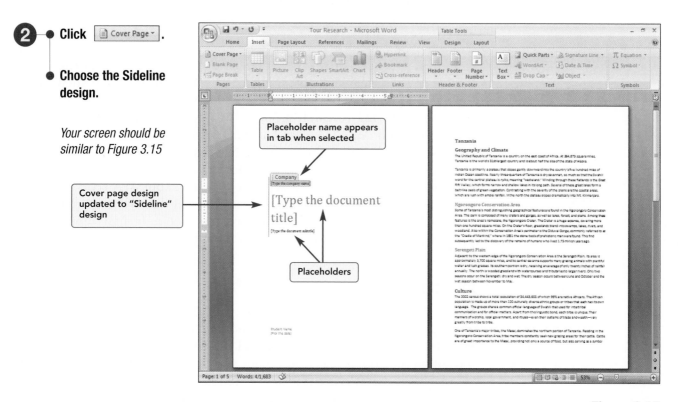

**Figure 3.15**

The new cover page design you selected replaces the first cover page you inserted. This design includes a blue vertical line to the left of the sample title information centered on the page. The title text is a larger font size and blue. Additionally, the design includes the author and date information in blue at the bottom of the page. In addition to the design elements, the cover page includes placeholders for the information you need to enter. A **placeholder** is a graphic element that is designed to contain specific types of information. In this case, placeholders identify the content that should be entered to complete the information for the cover page. If the company name and document title have already been entered in the document properties, the placeholders will automatically display this information.

**Additional Information**

To delete a cover page, choose Remove Current Cover Page from the  menu.

When you click on a placeholder, the placeholder name appears in a tab and the placeholder text is selected and ready to be replaced. You will replace the Company and Title placeholder text.

**3** **Increase the zoom to 80 percent and scroll the page so you can see both the report title and the author and date areas.**

**Click the Company placeholder and type Adventure Travel Tours.**

**Click the Title placeholder and type Tanzania and Peru.**

*Your screen should be similar to Figure 3.16*

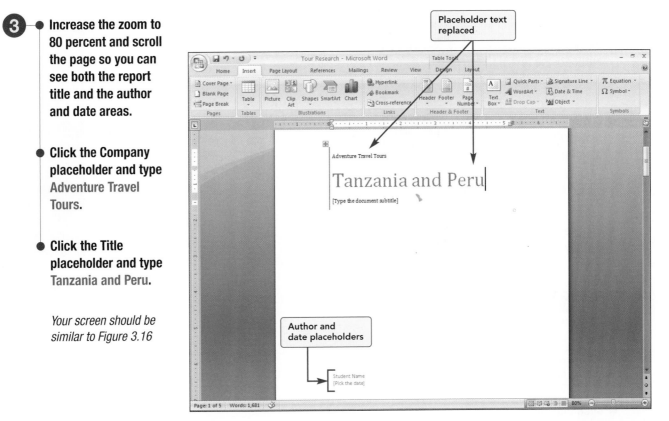

Figure 3.16

The placeholder text was replaced with the text you typed. Additionally, the company name and title information you entered have been automatically added to the document properties.

Finally, you will delete the Subtitle placeholder and add your name as author and the current date. Notice Student Name appears as the Author because this is the name that is stored in the document properties. Since the name is not placeholder text, you will need to select it before replacing it with your name. When you click on the date placeholder, you will use the date picker feature to quickly enter the current date from the pop-up calendar.

**4**

- Select the Subtitle placeholder and press Delete twice to delete the contents and then the placeholder.

- Click the Author placeholder, select the author name text, and enter your name.

- Click the Date placeholder and open the drop-down list to display the date-picker calendar.

- Choose Today to display the current date.

- Click outside the placeholder.

- Save the document.

*Your screen should be similar to Figure 3.17*

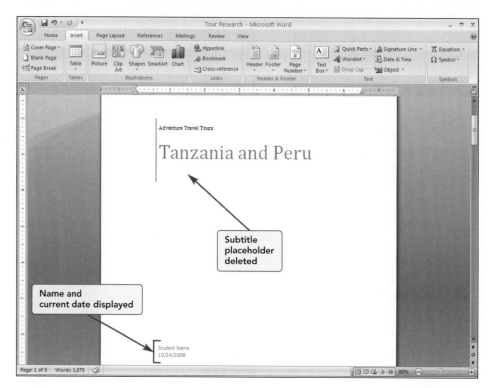

Figure 3.17

The cover page is now complete.

## Using Document Themes

Because color and design are important elements of documents, Word includes a collection of built-in document themes.

**2** A **document theme** is a predefined set of formatting choices that can be applied to an entire document in one simple step. Word includes 20 named built-in document themes. Each document theme includes three subsets of themes: colors, fonts, and effects. Each color theme consists of 12 colors that are applied to specific elements in a document. Each fonts theme includes different body and heading fonts. Each effects theme includes different lines and fill effects. You also can create your own custom themes by modifying an existing document theme and saving it as a custom theme. The default document (Normal.dotm) uses the Office theme.

Using themes gives your documents a professional and modern look. Because document themes are shared across 2007 Office applications, all your office documents can have the same uniform look.

## Applying a Theme

You decide to see how the report would look using a different document theme.

**1**
● **Change the zoom to display two pages.**

● **Open the Page Layout tab.**

● **Click** Themes **from the Themes group.**

*Your screen should be similar to Figure 3.18*

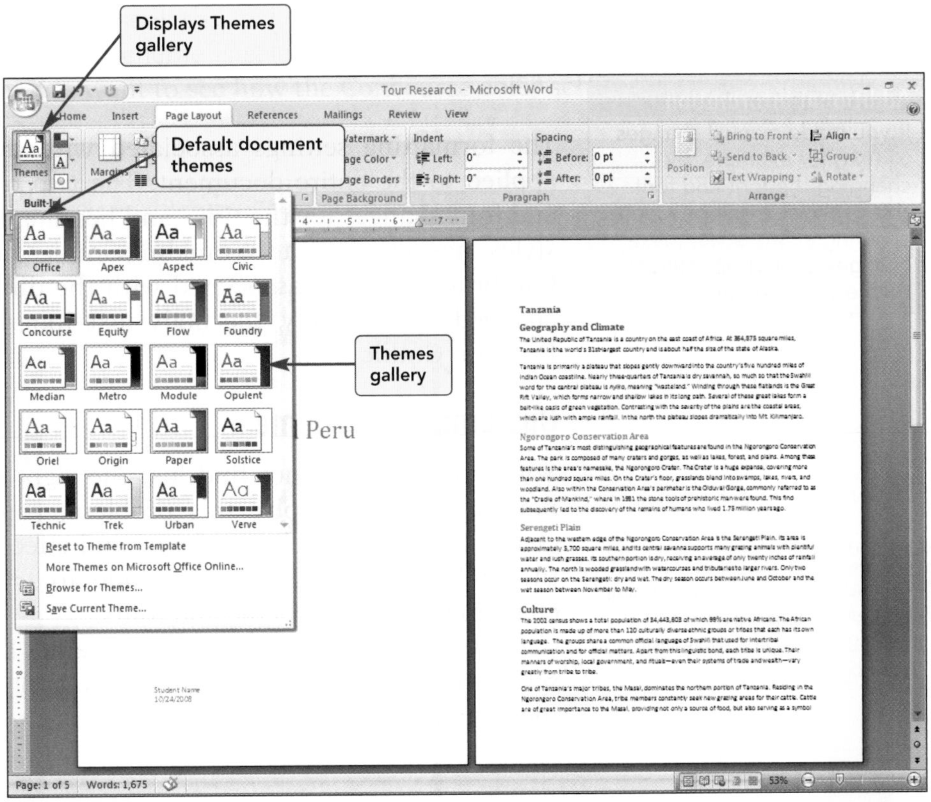

**Figure 3.18**

A gallery of 20 built-in named themes is displayed. A sample shows the color and font effects included in each theme. The Office theme is highlighted because it is the default theme and is the theme that is used in this document. Pointing to each theme will display a Live Preview of how it will appear in the document.

Next, you will change the theme fonts. Just like theme colors, you could change fonts by applying fonts from another theme to the selected theme. This time, however, you will specify your own font settings for the selected theme. Each theme contains a heading font and a body text font.

**3** ● Click [A] **Theme Fonts.**

**Additional Information**

The name of the heading and body text fonts for each theme appears below the Theme Fonts name in the Theme Fonts gallery.

● **Choose Create New Theme Fonts**

*Your screen should be similar to Figure 3.22*

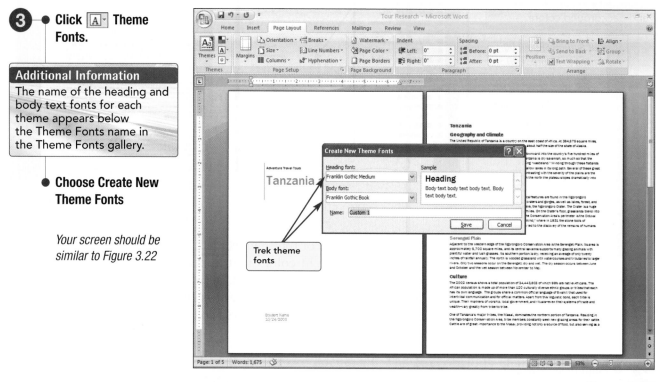

**Figure 3.22**

The fonts used in the current theme are displayed in the Heading and Body font text boxes. You will change the heading font to Constantia and the body font to Times New Roman.

**4** • From the Heading font drop-down list, select Constantia.

• From the Body font drop-down list, select Times New Roman.

• Replace the default name with Report Font.

• Click [ Save ].

• Click [A▾] Theme Fonts.

*Your screen should be similar to Figure 3.23*

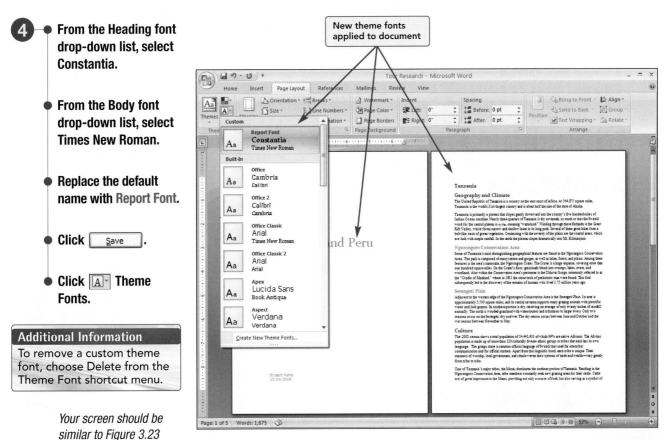

**Figure 3.23**

The name of the custom theme font appears at the top of the Theme Fonts gallery list and could be applied simply by selecting it from the list. As you add other features to the document, they will be formatted using the customized Trek theme colors and fonts.

## Saving a Custom Theme

After making all these changes to the Trek theme, you decide to save the changes as a custom theme. This will make it easy to reapply the same settings to another document in the future.

**1** • **Click**  .

• **Choose Save Current Theme.**

• **Enter Trek1 as the theme file name.**

• **Click** Save .

• **Click**  .

*Your screen should be similar to Figure 3.24*

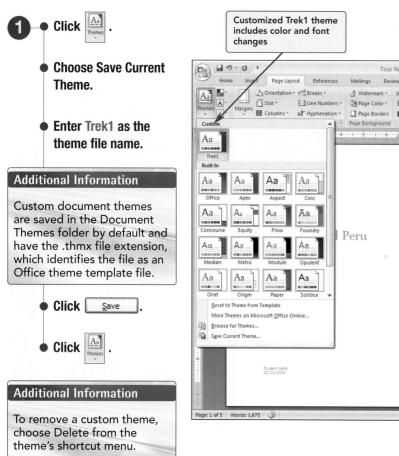
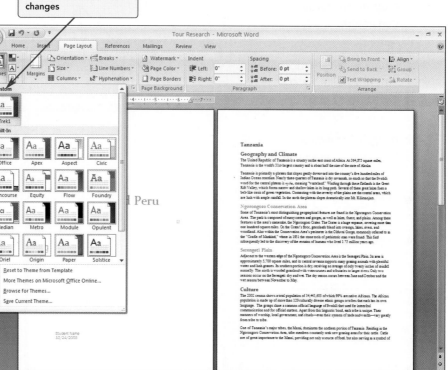

Customized Trek1 theme includes color and font changes

**Figure 3.24**

 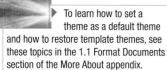
**MORE ABOUT**

▶ To learn how to set a theme as a default theme and how to restore template themes, see these topics in the 1.1 Format Documents section of the More About appendix.

The custom theme you created appears at the top of the Themes gallery. Now you can quickly reapply this entire theme in one step to another document, just like the built-in themes.

## Inserting a Blank Page

Next you will create a new page to contain a table of contents. You will enter a title for the page and then improve the appearance of the title by applying a style to the title. You want the new page to be inserted above the Tanzania topic heading. Blank pages are inserted above the location of the insertion point.

**1** ● Move to the blank line above the Tanzania heading at the top of page 2.

● Open the Insert tab and click ☐ Blank Page in the Pages group to create a blank page above it.

**Another Method**

You also could press Ctrl + ←Enter to insert a blank page.

*Your screen should be similar to Figure 3.25*

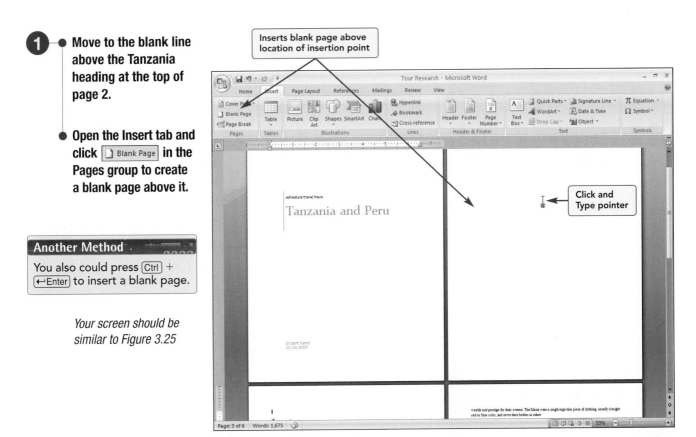

Figure 3.25

A blank page has been inserted in the document.

## Using Click and Type

Next you want to enter a title for the table of contents that you plan to display on this page. You will use the **Click and Type** feature to enter this information. This feature, available in Print Layout and Web Layout views, is used to quickly insert text, graphics, and other items in a blank area of a document, avoiding the need to enter blank lines. This feature also applies the paragraph formatting needed to position an item at the location you clicked.

Print Layout view includes formatting "zones" that control the formatting that will be applied. As you move the mouse pointer through the zones, the I-beam pointer displays an icon that indicates the formatting that will be applied when you double-click at that location. This is the Click and Type pointer. The pointer shapes and their associated formatting are described in the table below.

| Pointer shape | Formatting applied |
|---|---|
| I≡ | Align left |
| I̲ | Align center |
| ≡I | Align right |
| I≝ | Left indent |

To enable the Click and Type pointer, first click on a blank area; then, as you move the mouse pointer, the pointer shape indicates how the item will be formatted. Double-clicking on the location in the page moves the insertion point to that location and applies the formatting to the entry. You will enter the page title, Table of Contents, centered on the page.

**1** ● Click at the top of the new page to enable Click and Type.

● Increase the zoom to 100%.

● If necessary, display the ruler.

● Move the mouse pointer from left to right across the blank page and observe the change in the mouse pointer.

● Double-click on the center of the page at the 1-inch vertical ruler position while the mouse pointer is a ⌶.

● Type Table of Contents.

*Your screen should be similar to Figure 3.26*

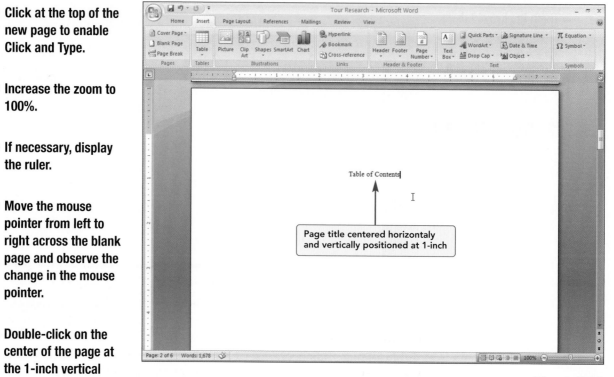

Page title centered horizontaly and vertically positioned at 1-inch

**Figure 3.26**

In one quick step, the insertion point moves to the location where you clicked and the center format was applied to the text you typed.

## Applying a Quick Style

Next, you will improve the appearance of the title by applying a quick style. As you learned when creating the outline, many styles are applied automatically to text. Others can be applied manually by selecting the quick style you want to use from the Styles gallery.

**1** ● **Open the Home tab.**

● **If necessary, move to anywhere in the line containing the Table of Contents title.**

● **Click** ☑ **More in the Styles group to open the Styles gallery.**

**Another Method**
You also can scroll the list of styles.

*Your screen should be similar to Figure 3.27*

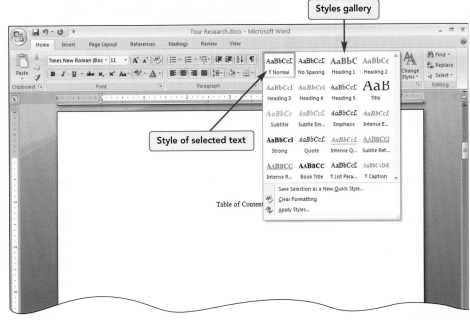

**Figure 3.27**

The Styles gallery appears with the current style of Normal for the selected text highlighted. Each quick style is named and displays a sample of the style above the name. The formatting of the different styles in the gallery reflects the new theme colors, fonts, and effects. When you point to a style, the document displays a Live Preview of how that style would appear if selected. If it is a paragraph style, the entire table of contents title will be affected. If it is a text style, only the word the insertion point is on will be affected.

**2** ● **Point to several quick styles to see how they would look.**

● **Choose Title.**

**Having Trouble?**
If you accidentally apply the wrong style, simply reselect the correct style.

*Your screen should be similar to Figure 3.28*

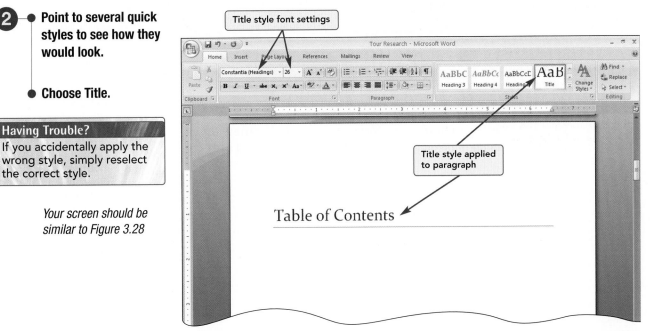

**Figure 3.28**

Notice that the entire title appears in the selected style. This is because the Title style is a paragraph style, affecting the entire paragraph at the insertion point. The Title style includes font settings of Constantia, 26 pt. in black. It also includes a blue line below the title that is part of the Trek theme effects.

## Creating a Custom Quick Style

Although the Title quick style looks good, you decide instead that you want the title to be the same color as the title on the cover page. To do this, you will modify the Title style and then save the modified design as a custom quick style so you can quickly apply the style in the future.

**1**

- **Right-click on the Table of Contents title and select Styles.**

- **Choose Save selection as a New Quick Style from the submenu.**

- **Click** Modify... **from the Create New Style from Formatting dialog box.**

   *Your screen should be similar to Figure 3.29*

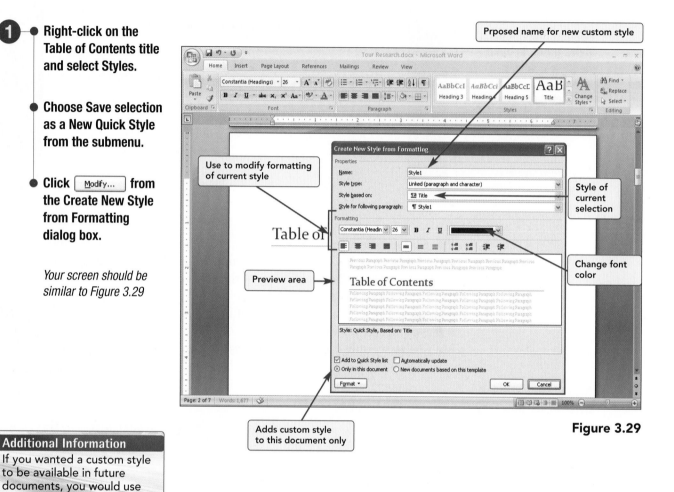

**Figure 3.29**

### Additional Information
If you wanted a custom style to be available in future documents, you would use the New documents based on this template option.

The Create New Style from Formatting dialog box displays the settings associated with the selected text. The only action you need to take is to change the font color and then give the custom style a descriptive name. The options to add the new style to the quick style list for this document only are appropriately selected. The preview area will show you how your selections will look.

**1**
● Open the Font Color drop-down menu and choose the Turquoise, Accent 1 theme color.

● In the Name text box, replace the default name with **TOC Title**.

● Click [ OK ].

*Your screen should be similar to Figure 3.30*

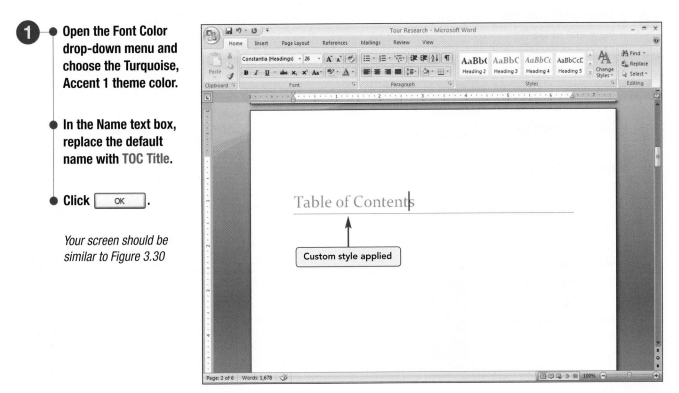

**Figure 3.30**

The new TOC Title style is applied to the selection and added to the gallery of quick styles. If you ever need to change a style back to the default document style, you can easily clear the style by moving to the text whose style you want removed and choosing Clear Formatting from the Style gallery or clicking [Aa] Clear Formatting in the Font group.

## Formatting Body Text

The last style change you want to make is to increase the font size of all body text to 12 points. You think this will make the report easier to read.

**1** ● **Select and format the body text of the first paragraph below the Tanzania heading to 12 points.**

● **Clear the selection.**

● **Right-click on the paragraph and select Styles from the context menu.**

● **Choose Update Normal to Match Selection.**

*Your screen should be similar to Figure 3.31*

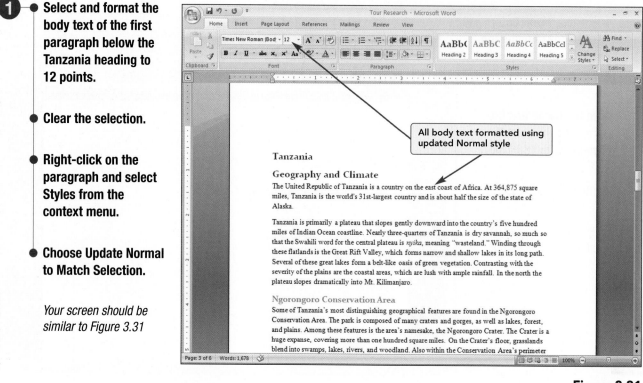

**Figure 3.31**

**MORE ABOUT**

To learn how to change all text formatted with one style to another style, see 2.1 Format Text and Paragraphs in the More About appendix.

All body text in the document that uses the Normal style has been immediately updated to the new font size of 12 points.

# Creating a Table of Contents

Now you are ready to create the table of contents.

---

## Concept 3

### Table of Contents

**3** A **table of contents** is a listing of the topic headings that appear in a document and their associated page references (see the sample below). It shows the reader at a glance the topics that are included in the document and makes it easier for the reader to locate information. Word can generate a table of contents automatically after you have applied heading styles to the document headings. To do this, Word first searches the document for headings. Then it formats and inserts the heading entry text into the table of contents. The level of the heading style determines the table of contents level.

The table of contents that is generated is a field that can be easily updated to reflect changes you may make to the document after the list is generated. Additionally, each entry in the table is a hyperlink to the heading in the document.

---

## Generating a Table of Contents

The report already includes heading styles to identify the different topics in the report. Now, all you need to do is select the style you want to use for the table of contents. You want the table of contents listing to be displayed several lines below the table of contents heading.

**Additional Information**

MLA and APA styles do not use a table of contents.

**1**
- Move to the blank line below the Table of Contents heading.

- Open the References tab.

- Click  in the Table of Contents group.

*Your screen should be similar to Figure 3.32*

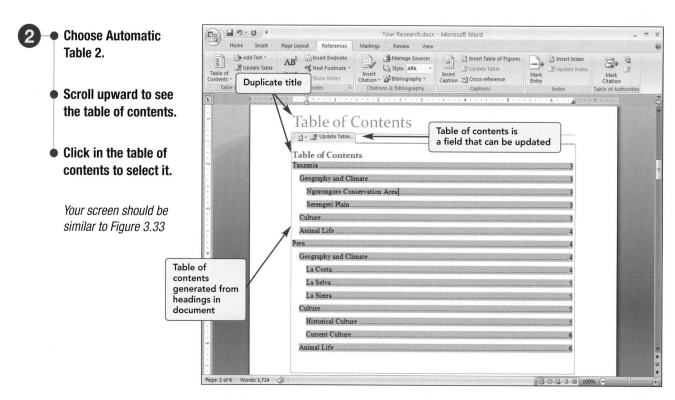

**Figure 3.32**

A gallery of three preformatted table of contents styles is displayed. The first two options automatically create a table of contents list using the heading 1–3 styles in the document. The main difference between these two options is that the title used in Automatic Table 1 is Contents and in Automatic Table 2 it is Table of Contents. The third option, Manual Table, creates a table of contents that you can fill out independent of the content in the document.

**2**
- Choose Automatic Table 2.

- Scroll upward to see the table of contents.

- Click in the table of contents to select it.

*Your screen should be similar to Figure 3.33*

**Figure 3.33**

Word searched for headings with the specified styles, sorted them by heading level, referenced their page numbers, and displayed the table of contents using the selected style in the document. The headings that were assigned a Heading 1 style are aligned with the left margin, and subordinate heading levels are indented as appropriate. The table of contents displays the page numbers flush with the right margin with a dotted-line tab leader between the heading entry and the page number. It includes all entries in the document that are formatted with Headings 1, 2, and 3.

The table of contents is a field that is highlighted and enclosed in a box when selected. The field tab provides quick access to the Table of Contents menu by clicking [image] and the [Update Table...] command button. Because it is a field, the table of contents can be easily updated to reflect changes you may make to the document after the list is generated.

### Modifying a Table of Contents

You want the table of contents to include topics formatted with the Heading 4 style also. Additionally, you want to remove the table of contents title that was automatically included with the listing. To do this, you need to modify the table of contents settings.

**1** ● **Click**  .

● **Choose Insert Table of Contents.**

*Your screen should be similar to Figure 3.34*

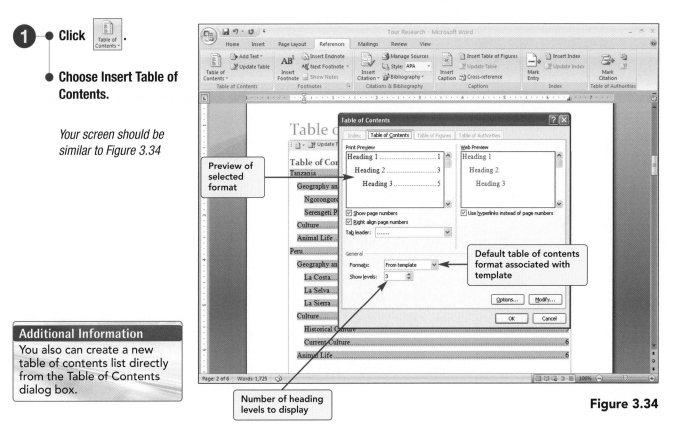

**Figure 3.34**

From the Table of Contents dialog box, you select the format (style) of the table and the number of levels to show. The default style is determined by the Normal template and the number of levels to show is set to three. The two Preview boxes display an example of how the selected format will look in a printed document or in a document when viewed in a Web browser. You will change the format to another and the level to four. You also will remove the duplicate table of contents title. The title is static text that can be removed without affecting the table of contents field.

**2** • Select Formal from the Formats list.

• Specify 4 in the Show Levels box.

• Click [ OK ].

• Click [ OK ] to replace the current contents list.

• Select and delete the table of contents title in the table of contents field.

*Your screen should be similar to Figure 3.35*

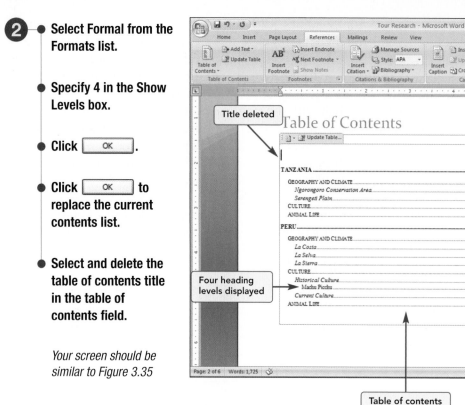

Title deleted

Each entry is a hyperlink

Four heading levels displayed

Table of contents in Formal style

**Figure 3.35**

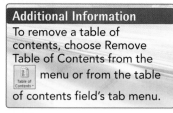

**Additional Information**

To remove a table of contents, choose Remove Table of Contents from the [ ] menu or from the table of contents field's tab menu.

The table is regenerated using the new style and the one level 4 heading for Machu Picchu is now displayed in the table of contents.

## Navigating a Document

In a large document, locating and moving to an area of text you want to view can take a lot of time. However, after headings have been applied to different areas of a document, there are several features that can make navigation easier. As a help when scrolling by dragging the scroll box, a ScreenTip identifies the topic heading in addition to the page number that will be displayed when you stop dragging the scroll box. If you have generated a table of contents, you can use the table of contents entries to quickly move to different areas. Even more convenient, however, is to use the Navigation window features to jump to a selected location.

## Using a Table of Contents Hyperlink

Not only does the table of contents display the location of topic headings in the report, but it also can be used to quickly move to these locations. This is because each entry in the table is a hyperlink to the heading in the document. A hyperlink, as you have learned, is a connection to a location in the current document, another document, or a Web site. To use a hyperlink in Word, hold down $\boxed{\text{Ctrl}}$ while clicking on the hyperlink.

**Additional Information**

Pointing to an entry in a table of contents displays a ScreenTip with directions on how to follow the hyperlink.

**1** — • **Hold down** $\boxed{\text{Ctrl}}$ **and click the Peru table of contents hyperlink.**

**Additional Information**

The mouse pointer shape changes to a 🖑 when holding down $\boxed{\text{Ctrl}}$ and pointing to a hyperlink.

*Your screen should be similar to Figure 3.36*

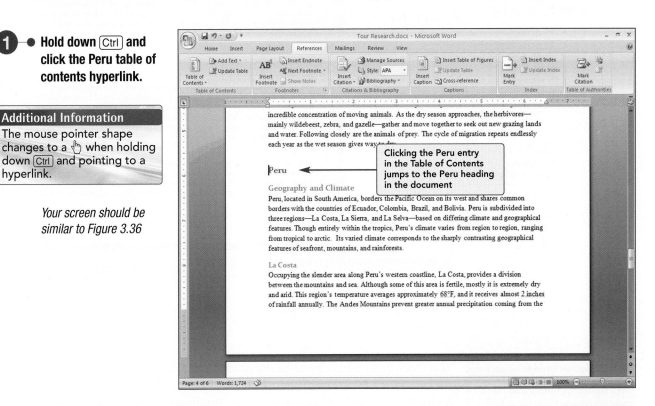

**Figure 3.36**

The insertion point jumps to the Peru heading in the document. Now, however, the table of contents is no longer visible. If you wanted to move to a different topic, you would need to return to the table of contents page and select another hyperlink.

## Using Document Map

Another way to quickly move to different locations in the document is to use the Document Map feature. **Document Map** displays in a separate pane called the **navigation window** a list of the items in a document that have been formatted using a heading style. It is used to quickly navigate through the document by clicking on a heading and keeps track of your location in it.

**1** ● **Open the View tab.**

● **Click** ☐ Document Map
**from the Show/Hide
group.**

*Your screen should be
similar to Figure 3.37*

Navigation window
displays Document Map

Turns on/off
Document Map

Document Map
displays all
headings
in document

Current location
in document is
highlighted

Indicates
subordinate
levels are displayed

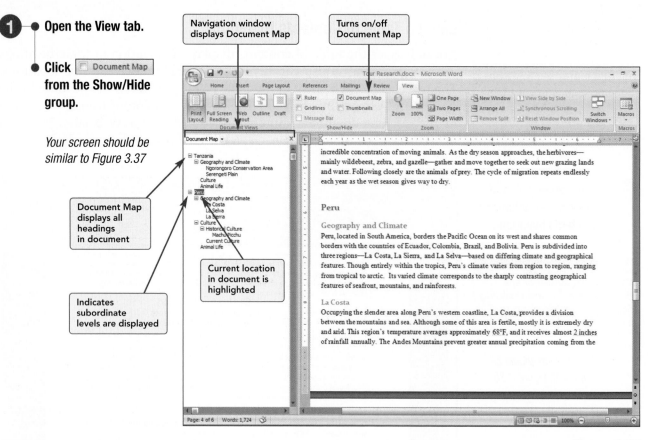

**Figure 3.37**

Additional Information
The navigation window pane
can be resized by dragging
the divider line between the
panes.

The Document Map opens in the navigation window and displays a list of all
the document headings. When your document does not contain any headings
formatted with heading styles, the program automatically searches the
document for paragraphs that look like headings (for example, short lines
with a larger font size) and displays them in the Document Map. If it cannot
find any such headings, the Document Map is blank.

Notice the ⊟ symbol to the left of many of the headings; this symbol
indicates that all subordinate headings are displayed. A ⊞ symbol would
indicate that subordinate headings are not displayed. The highlighted
heading shows your location in the document. Clicking on a heading in
the Document Map quickly jumps to that location in the document.

**2**

- Click on **Culture (under Peru)** in the Document Map.

- Click on **Tanzania.**

*Your screen should be similar to Figure 3.38*

Clicking heading in Document Map moves to that location in document

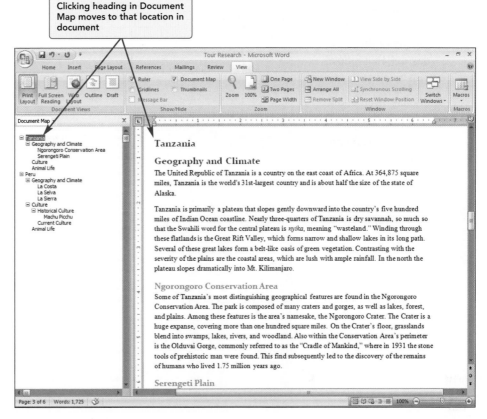

**Figure 3.38**

You quickly moved from one topic location in the document to another. When using the Document Map, the selected topic appears at the top of the window.

## Using Thumbnails

The navigation window also can display **thumbnails**, miniature images of each page in the document. Clicking on a thumbnail moves directly to that page.

**1** Open the Document Map ▾ drop-down button at the top of the navigation window.

● Choose Thumbnails.

● Scroll the navigation window and click on page 5.

**Another Method**
You also can click ☐ Thumbnails in the Show/Hide group.

*Your screen should be similar to Figure 3.39*

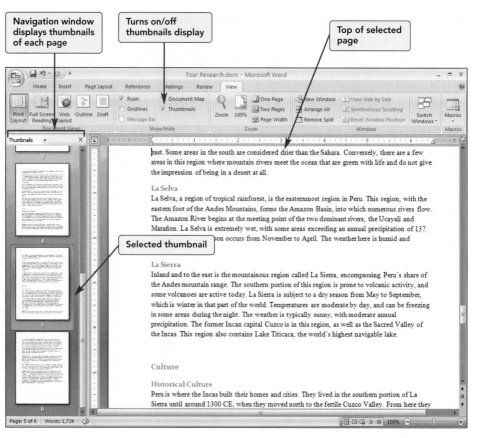

Navigation window displays thumbnails of each page

Turns on/off thumbnails display

Top of selected page

Selected thumbnail

**Figure 3.39**

The selected page is displayed in the document window and the selected thumbnail is highlighted.

The Document Map and Thumbnails features are available in all views. The navigation window remains open in the view you are using until you close the window or turn off the feature. It must be turned on and off in each view independently.

**Note:** If you are running short on time to complete this lab, this is an appropriate time to stop. Close the navigation window and save the document. When you begin again, open the saved document and the navigation window.

## Including Source References

Documented research papers typically provide credit for the sources of information that were used in developing the document. These sources are cited both within the text of the document and in a bibliography.

**4** Parenthetical source references, called **citations**, give credit for specific information included in the document. Complete source information for citations is included in a **bibliography** at the end of the report. Citations and bibliographies must be entered using the appropriate reference style, such as MLA or APA style. Word includes a feature that will automatically format citations and bibliographies according to different reference styles. This saves you the time it would take to learn the style from the documentation manuals, and of entering the citations and bibliographies using the correct format.

As you insert citations, Word asks for the bibliography information for each source. Once a source is created, it is stored in two places: a Master List and a Current List. The Master List is a database of all sources ever created. The Current List includes all of the sources that will be used in the current document. The purpose of the Master List is to save you from retyping and reentering information about sources that you commonly use. This is because you can select and copy sources in your Master List to add them to your Current List.

Word uses the information in the Current List to quickly generate a complete bibliographic list (similar to the sample shown here) of the information for each source according to the selected reference style.

**Works Cited**

Camerapix, comp. <u>Spectrum Guide to Tanzania.</u> Edison: Hunter, 1992.

Country Studies US. <u>Peru.</u> 2003-2005. 3 November 2006
<http://countrystudies.us/peru/23.htm>.

Wikipedia:The Free Encyclopedia. <u>Tanzania.</u> 5 October 2006. 3 November 2006
<http://en.wikipedia.org/wiki/Tanzania>.

Both citations and bibliography entries are inserted as fields in the document. This means that any changes you may make to the source information is automatically updated in both the citation and the bibliography.

## Selecting a Reference Style

You have been following the MLA reference style guidelines for this report and will specify the MLA reference style before you begin inserting citations. You can change the reference style at any point while working on your document and your citations and bibliography will be automatically updated to reflect the new style.

**Additional Information**

Changing reference styles allows you to repurpose documents to be submitted to a number of publications requiring different reference standards.

**1**
- **Open the References tab.**
- **Open the** [⧉ Style: APA ▾] **drop-down list in the Citations and Bibliography group.**
- **Choose MLA from the drop-down list.**

Now, as you enter citations and create a bibliography, they will be formatted using the MLA style guidelines.

## Creating Citations

Research papers using the MLA style require citations to include the author's last name and a page number or range within parentheses. The first citation that needs to be included in the document is to credit the source of the geography statistics about Tanzania. The source of this information was from the Wikipedia Web site. To create a citation, the bibliography information for the source is entered first.

**1**
- **Display the Document Map.**

- **Move to the end of the first paragraph (before the period) of the Tanzania Geography section.**

- **Click** [⧉ Insert Citation ▾] **in the Citations and Bibliography group.**

- **Choose Add New Source.**

*Your screen should be similar to Figure 3.40*

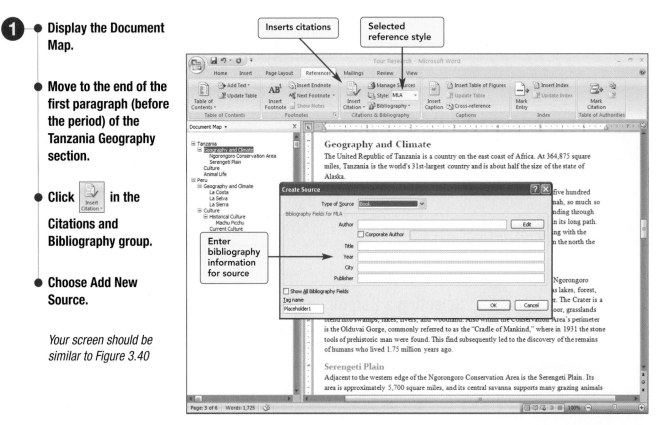

**Figure 3.40**

Inserts citations

Selected reference style

Enter bibliography information for source

In the Create Source dialog box, you first select the type of source, for example, a book, a journal article, or a Web site. Then you enter the bibliography information for the source in the appropriate text boxes for the selected source type.

**2** ● Choose Web site as the type of source.

● Enter the following in the appropriate locations to complete the bibliography information for this citation.

| Author | Wikipidea |
|---|---|
| Name of Web Page | Tanzania |
| Year | 2006 |
| Month | October |
| Day | 5 |
| Year Accessed | Enter the current year |
| Month Accessed | Enter the current month |
| Day Accessed | Enter the current day |
| URL | http://en.wikipedia.org/wiki/Tanzania |

● Click [ OK ].

*Your screen should be similar to Figure 3.41*

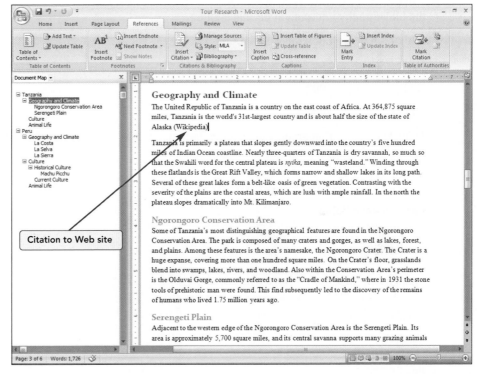

**Figure 3.41**

The citation is inserted at the location of the insertion point. It is a field that is linked to the source information. The source information is now stored in both the Master List and the Current List.

The next citation is also to the Wikipedia Web site. Once source information has been specified, it is easy to insert the citation again. This is because the Insert Citation drop-down menu displays a brief bibliographic entry for each source in the Current List. You will insert another citation for the same source in the report and then you will add a citation for the quote at the end of the first paragraph of the Tanzania Animal Life topic. This quote was found on page 252 of a book that was compiled by Camerapix Publishers International. Because this citation is to a quote, the page number must be included in the citation. You will enter the source information and then edit the citation to include the page.

**3** ● Using the Document Map, move to the end of the third sentence (before the period) in the first paragraph of the Tanzania Culture section.

● Click  and select the Wikipedia entry from the Citation list.

● Using the Document Map, move to the end of the first paragraph (before the period) of the Tanzania Animal Life section.

● Click [Insert Citation] and choose Add New Source.

● Choose Book as the type of source.

● Enter the following in the appropriate locations to complete the bibliography information for this citation.

| | |
|---|---|
| Author | Camerapix, comp. |
| Title | Spectrum Guide to Tanzania |
| Year | 1992 |
| City | Edison |
| Publisher | Camerapix Publishers International |

● Click [ OK ].

● Click on the citation and open the drop-down menu.

● Choose Edit Citation.

● Enter 252 as the page number.

● Click [ OK ].

*Your screen should be similar to Figure 3.42*

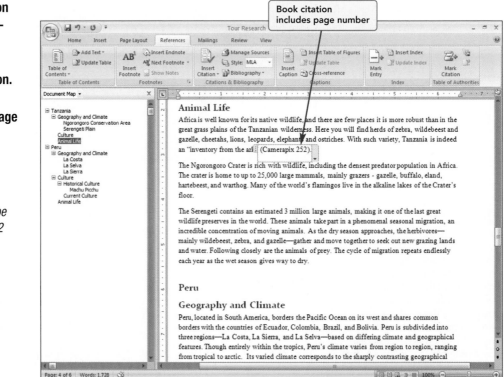

Book citation includes page number

**Figure 3.42**

The last citation you will complete for now is to credit the source of the geography statistics about Peru. The source of this information was from the Country Studies Web site. This Web site contains the online versions of books that were published by the Federal Research Division of the Library of Congress as part of the Country Studies/Area Handbook series.

**4** ● Using the Document Map, move to the end of the second sentence (before the period) in the first paragraph in the Peru Geography and Climate section.

● Insert a Web site citation using the following source information:

| | |
|---|---|
| **Corporate Author** | **Country Studies US** |
| **Name of Web Page** | **Peru** |
| **Year** | **2003-2005** |
| **Year Accessed** | **Enter the current year** |
| **Month Accessed** | **Enter the current month** |
| **Day Accessed** | **Enter the current day** |
| **URL** | **http://countrystudies.us/peru/23.htm** |

*Your screen should be similar to Figure 3.43*

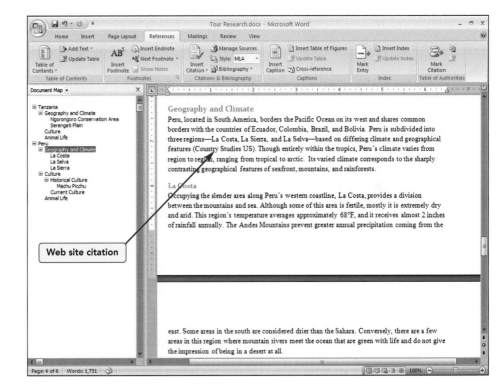

**Figure 3.43**

## Editing a Source

As you look back at the citations you just entered, you realize the author for the Wikipidea Web site should have been entered as a corporate author, not an individual author. Additionally, the Web site name is incomplete. You will quickly return to this citation using the GoTo feature and edit the source.

**1** ● Click 🔍 Find ▾ on the Home tab and open the Go To tab.

**Another Method**
You also can click on the page count indicator in the status bar to open the Go To dialog box.

● Select Field from the Go to What list.

● Click [ Previous ] three times to search backward through the document.

● Click [ Close ] when the Wikipidea citation is located.

● Choose Edit Source from the citation's drop-down list.

● Click Corporate Author to move the information in the Author text box to the Corporate Author text box.

● Type :The Free Encyclopedia following Wikipedia in the Author box.

● Click [ OK ].

● Click [ Yes ] to update both the Master and Current Lists.

*Your screen should be similar to Figure 3.44*

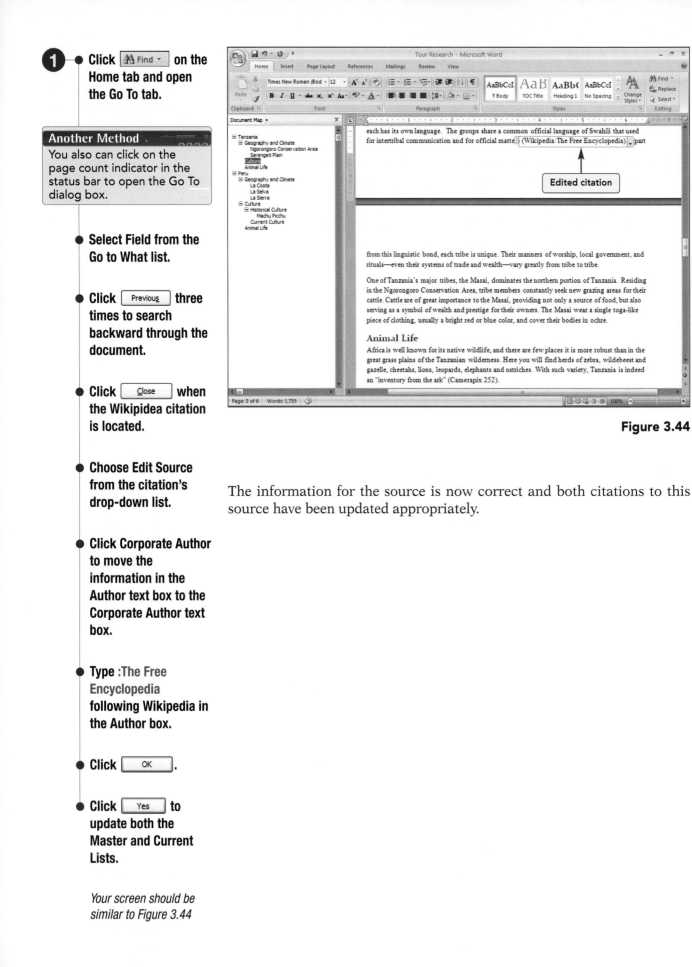

**Figure 3.44**

The information for the source is now correct and both citations to this source have been updated appropriately.

# Including Footnotes

You still have several reference notes you want to include in the report as footnotes to help clarify some information.

## Concept 5

### Footnote and Endnote

**5** Footnotes and endnotes are used in documented research papers to explain or comment on information in the text, or provide source references for text in the document. A **footnote** appears at the bottom of a page containing the material that is being referenced. An **endnote** appears at the end of a document. You can have both footnotes and endnotes in the same document.

Footnotes and endnotes consist of two parts, the **note reference mark** and the **note text**. The default note reference mark is a superscript number appearing in the document at the end of the material being referenced (for example, text). You also can use custom marks consisting of any nonnumeric character or combination of characters, such as an asterisk. The note text for a footnote appears at the bottom of the page on which the reference mark appears. The footnote text is separated from the document text by a horizontal line called the **note separator**. Endnote text appears as a listing at the end of the document.

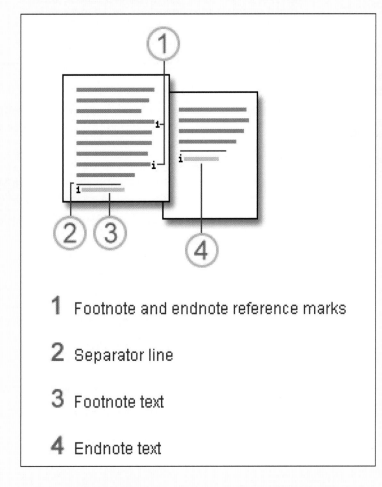

**1** Footnote and endnote reference marks

**2** Separator line

**3** Footnote text

**4** Endnote text

Note text can be of any length and formatted just as you would any other text. You also can customize the appearance of the note separators.

## Inserting Footnotes in Draft View

The first footnote reference you want to add is the height of Mt. Kilimanjaro. This note will follow the reference to the mountain at the end of the second paragraph in the Geography and Climate section for Tanzania. To identify the location of the footnote number in the document, you position the insertion point at the document location first. You want to create numbered footnotes, so the default settings are acceptable.

**1** ● Using the Document Map, move to the Tanzania Geography and Climate heading.

● Switch to Draft view.

● Move to the end of the second paragraph.

● Open the References tab.

● Click 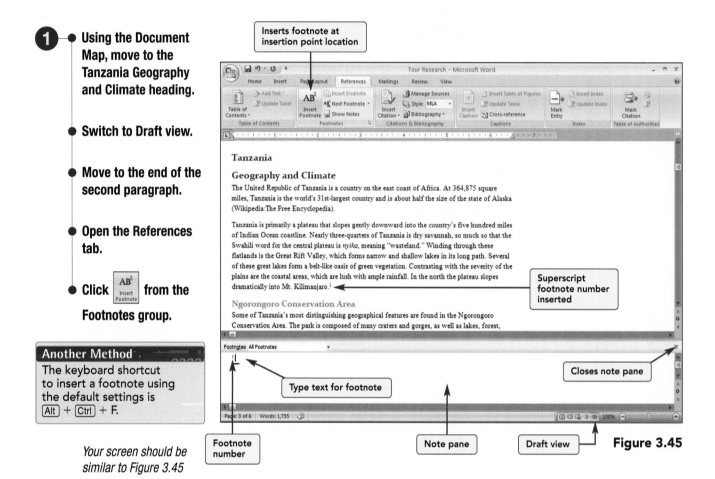 from the Footnotes group.

**Another Method**
The keyboard shortcut to insert a footnote using the default settings is Alt + Ctrl + F.

*Your screen should be similar to Figure 3.45*

**Figure 3.45**

The document window is now horizontally divided into upper and lower panes. The report is displayed in the upper pane. The footnote number, 1, appears as a superscript in the document where the insertion point was positioned when the footnote was created. The **note pane** displays the footnote number and the insertion point. This is where you enter the text for the footnote.

When you enter a footnote, you can insert, edit, and format footnotes just like any other text.

**2**

- **Type** Mt. Kilimanjaro is 19,340 feet high, making it the fourth tallest mountain in the world.

- **Click** ☒ **to close the note pane.**

- **Point to note reference mark 1 in the document.**

*Your screen should be similar to Figure 3.46*

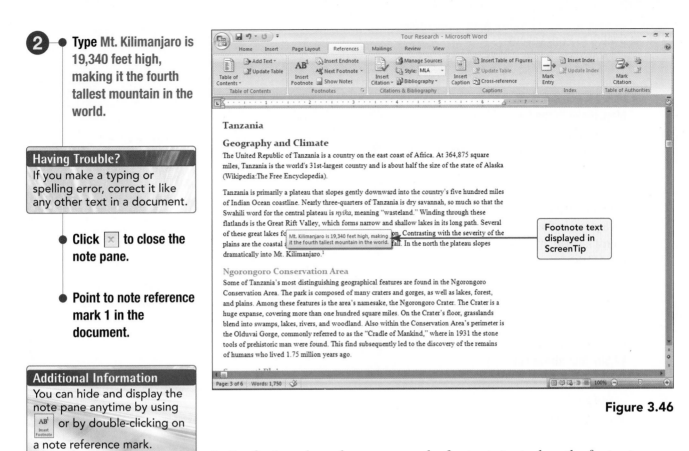

Figure 3.46

In Draft view, the only way to see the footnote text when the footnote pane is not open is in the reference mark's ScreenTip.

## Inserting Footnotes in Print Layout View

The second footnote you want to add is in the Geography and Climate section under Peru. You also can insert footnotes in Print Layout view. After using the command to insert a footnote, the footnote number appears in the footnote area at the bottom of the page, ready for you to enter the footnote text. You want to add a note about Lake Titicaca.

**1**
- **Switch to Print Layout view at 100% zoom.**

- **Using the Document Map, move to the La Sierra heading in the Peru Geography and Climate section.**

- **Click at the end of the paragraph in the La Sierra section after the word "lake."**

- **Click**  **.**

- **Type** Lake Titicaca is 12,507 feet above sea level.

*Your screen should be similar to Figure 3.47*

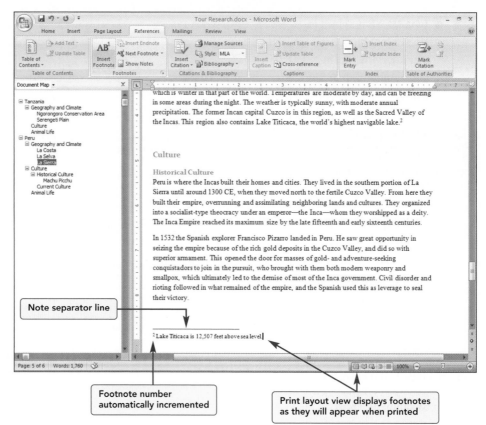

**Figure 3.47**

The footnote number 2 was automatically entered at the location of the insertion point in the text and the footnote text is displayed immediately above the bottom margin separated from the text by the note separator line. Footnotes are always displayed at the bottom of the page containing the footnote reference mark. Print Layout view displays footnotes as they will appear when the document is printed.

Now you realize that you forgot to enter a footnote earlier in the document, on page 2.

**2** ● Using the Document Map, move to the Ngorongoro Conservation Area heading.

● Move to after the period at the end of the first sentence of the first paragraph, following the word "Area."

● Insert the following footnote at this location: The Conservation Area is a national preserve spanning 3,196 square miles.

● Save the document.

*Your screen should be similar to Figure 3.48*

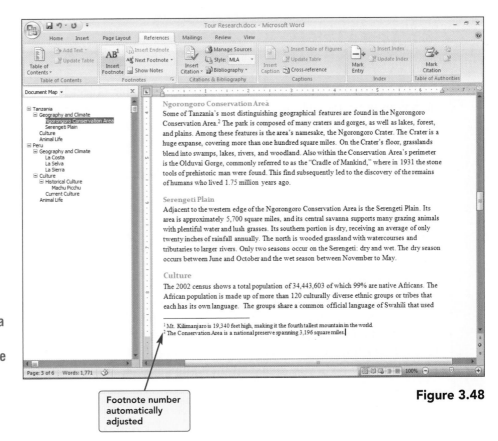

Footnote number automatically adjusted

**Figure 3.48**

Notice that this footnote is now number 2 in the document. Word automatically adjusted the footnote numbers when the new footnote was inserted.

You are finished entering footnotes for now. Footnotes can quickly be converted to endnotes and vice versa by right-clicking on the note you want to convert and choosing Convert from the context menu.

## Formatting Picture Layout

Next you want to add two pictures to the report and you want the text to wrap around the pictures. To do this, you change the text-wrapping layout for the picture.

# Concept 6

## Text Wrapping

**6** You can control the appearance of text around a graphic object by specifying the **text wrapping** style. The text in the paragraph may wrap around the object in many different ways as shown below.

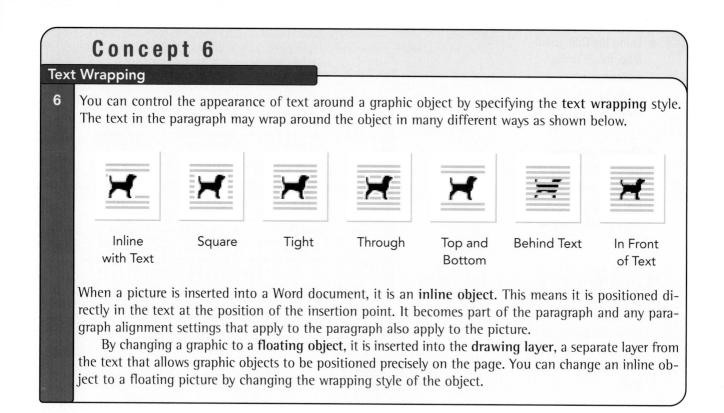

| Inline with Text | Square | Tight | Through | Top and Bottom | Behind Text | In Front of Text |

When a picture is inserted into a Word document, it is an **inline object**. This means it is positioned directly in the text at the position of the insertion point. It becomes part of the paragraph and any paragraph alignment settings that apply to the paragraph also apply to the picture.

By changing a graphic to a **floating object**, it is inserted into the **drawing layer**, a separate layer from the text that allows graphic objects to be positioned precisely on the page. You can change an inline object to a floating picture by changing the wrapping style of the object.

## Wrapping Text around Graphics

You will insert a picture of a giraffe next to the second paragraph on page 2.

**1**
- Use the Document Map to move to the Geography and Climate head under Tanzania.

- Close the Navigation window.

- Move to the beginning of the second paragraph.

- Insert the picture wd03_Giraffe from your data files.

- Reduce the size of the picture to approximately 2 by 2 inches.

**Additional Information**

Dragging the corner handle maintains the original proportions of the picture.

*Your screen should be similar to Figure 3.49*

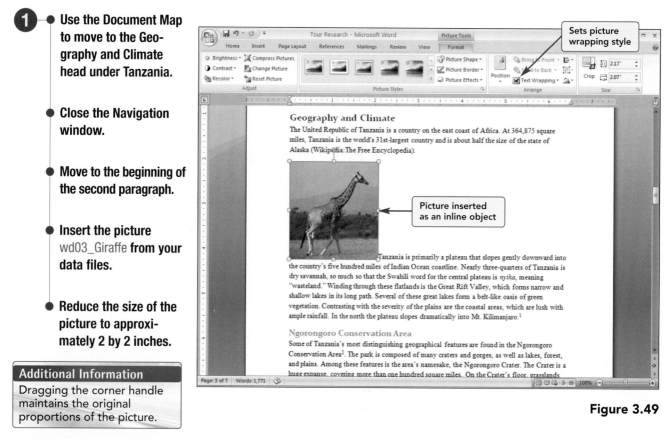

**Figure 3.49**

The picture has been inserted as an inline object and appears at the beginning of the paragraph like the first text characters of the paragraph. The text continues to the right of the picture. The Picture Tools Format tab is automatically displayed and is used to modify the selected picture object.

You want to change the wrapping style so that the text wraps around the picture. To do this, you will change the wrapping style to Square.

**2** ● Click [Text Wrapping ▾] from the Arrange group.

● Choose Square from the submenu.

● If necessary, resize and position the picture until the text wraps around it as in Figure 3.50.

*Your screen should be similar to Figure 3.50*

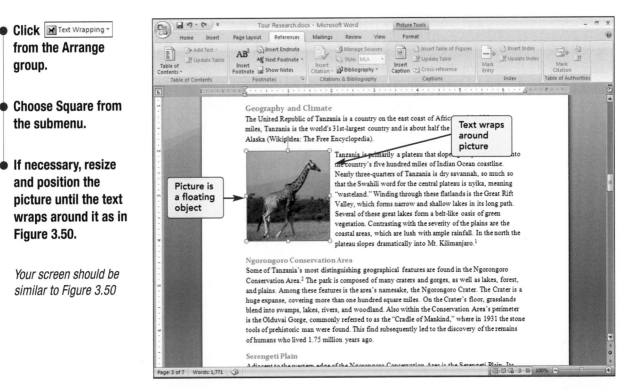

Figure 3.50

---

**Additional Information**

Sometimes a floating object is hidden behind another. If this happens, you can press [Tab ⇆] to cycle forward or [⇧ Shift] + [Tab ⇆] to cycle backward through the stacked objects.

---

The picture is changed to a floating object that can be placed anywhere in the document, including in front of or behind other objects including the text. Because the picture is even with the left margin, the text wraps to the right side of the object. If you moved the picture, because the wrapping style is Square, the text would wrap around the object on all sides.

Formatting Picture Layout      **WD3.53**

**Word 2007**

**3** ● Move the picture to the center of the page to see how the text wraps around it.

*Your screen should be similar to Figure 3.51*

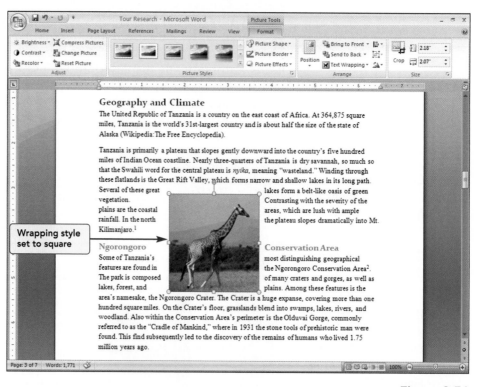

**Figure 3.51**

The text wraps on all sides of the object, depending on its location in the text. You will align this picture with the left margin again. Then you will add a second picture in the Peru Animal Life section.

**4** ● Move the picture back to the left margin and aligned with the top of the paragraph (see Figure 3.50).

● Move to the beginning of the first paragraph in the Peru Animal Life section.

● Insert the picture wd03_Parrots to the left of the first paragraph.

● Change the wrapping style to Square.

● Size and position the picture as in Figure 3.52.

● Save the document.

*Your screen should be similar to Figure 3.52*

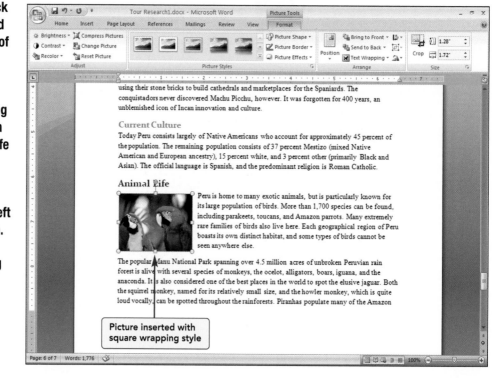

**Figure 3.52**

# Referencing Figures

After figures and other illustrative items have been added to a document, it is helpful to include figure references to identify the items. Figure references include captions and cross-references. If the reader is viewing the document online, the captions and cross-references become hyperlinks to allow the reader to jump around in the document.

## Concept 7

### Captions and Cross-References

**7** Using captions and cross-references in a document identifies items in a document and helps the reader locate information quickly. A **caption** is a numbered label for a figure, table, picture, or graph. Word can automatically add captions to graphic objects as they are inserted, or you can add them manually. The caption label can be changed to reflect the type of object to which it refers, such as a table, chart, or figure. In addition, Word automatically numbers graphic objects and adjusts the numbering when objects of the same type are added or deleted.

A **cross-reference** is a reference from one part of a document to related information in another part. Once you have captions, you also can include cross-references. For example, if you have a graph in one part of the document that you would like to refer to in another section, you can add a cross-reference that tells the reader what page the graph is on. A cross-reference also can be inserted as a hyperlink, allowing you to jump to another location in the same document or in another document.

## Adding a Figure Caption

Next, you want to add a caption below the picture of the giraffe.

**1** ● Select the Giraffe picture in the Tanzania section.

● Open the References tab.

● Click [Insert Caption].

*Your screen should be similar to Figure 3.53*

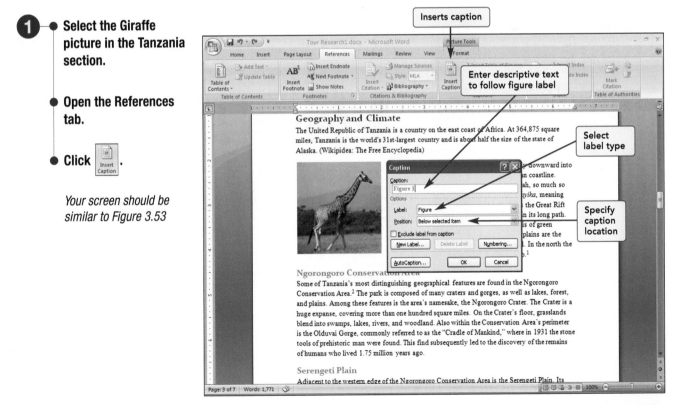

**Figure 3.53**

Referencing Figures **WD3.55**

**Word 2007**

The Caption options are described in the following table.

| Option | Description |
| --- | --- |
| Label | Select from one of three default captions: Table, Figure, or Equation. |
| Position | Specify the location of the caption, either above or below a selected item. When an item is selected, the Position option is available. |
| New Label | Create your own captions. |
| Numbering | Specify the numbering format and starting number for your caption. |
| AutoCaption | Turns on the automatic insertion of a caption (label and number only) when you insert selected items into your document. |

The default caption label is Figure 1. You will use this caption and add additional descriptive text. The default setting of "Below selected item" is also correct.

**2** ● In the Caption text box, following "Figure 1," type : Giraffe in Serengeti.

● Click [ OK ].

● If necessary, size and position the picture and caption as in Figure 3.54.

*Your screen should be similar to Figure 3.54*

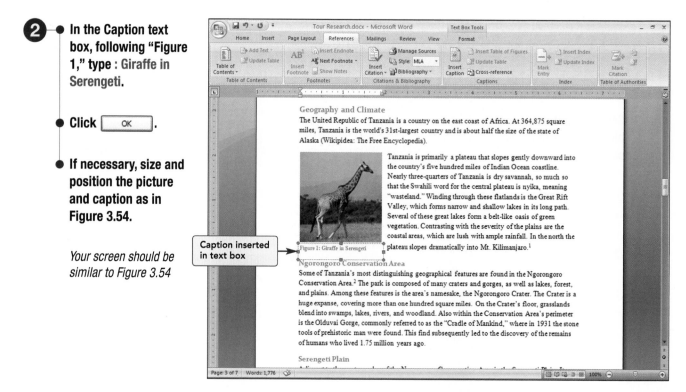

**Figure 3.54**

**Additional Information**

Only captions that are associated with floating graphic objects are in text boxes. Otherwise, they are text entries.

The caption label appears below the figure. It is formatted using the caption style associated with the selected theme. The figure number is a field that will update automatically as you add or delete captions in the document. The caption is contained in a **text box**, a container for text and other graphic objects that can be moved like any other object.

**Additional Information**

You will learn more about text boxes in later labs.

**3** ● In a similar manner, add a Figure 2: Amazon Parrots caption below the parrot picture.

● Size and position the picture and caption as in Figure 3.55.

*Your screen should be similar to Figure 3.55*

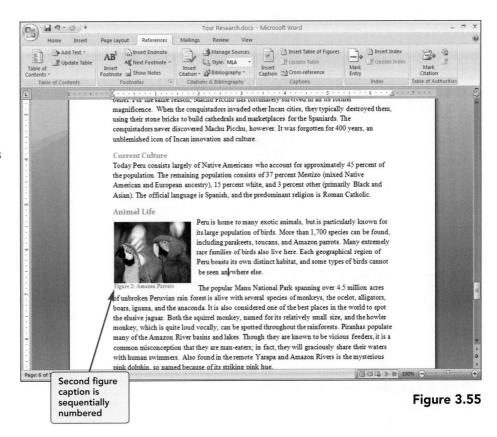

Second figure caption is sequentially numbered

**Figure 3.55**

## Adding a Cross-Reference

In the Animal Life section of the report, you discuss the animals found in the Serengeti. You want to include a cross-reference to the picture at this location. While doing this, you will **split** the document **window** into separate viewing areas so you can see the figure you will reference in one area and the text where you will enter the cross-reference in the other area.

**1**
- Open the View tab.

- Choose [Split] from the Window group.

- Drag the split bar to the position shown in Figure 3.56.

- Click to position the split at that location.

**Another Method**
You also can drag the split box located above the vertical scroll bar to create a split.

*Your screen should be similar to Figure 3.56*

**Additional Information**
You can display the document in different views in each pane. For example, you can display the document in Print Layout view in one pane and Draft view in the other.

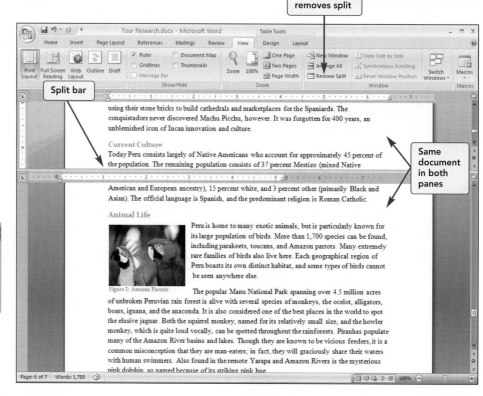

**Figure 3.56**

The document area is divided into two horizontal sections. Each section is displayed in a pane that can be scrolled and manipulated independently.

Next, you will scroll the document in the panes to display the areas you want to view. While using panes, the insertion point and the ruler are displayed in the active pane or the pane in which you are currently working.

**2**
- Scroll the upper pane to display the Figure 1 caption below the giraffe picture.

- Scroll the lower pane to display the third paragraph in the Tanzania Animal Life section (page 3, section 2).

*Your screen should be similar to Figure 3.57*

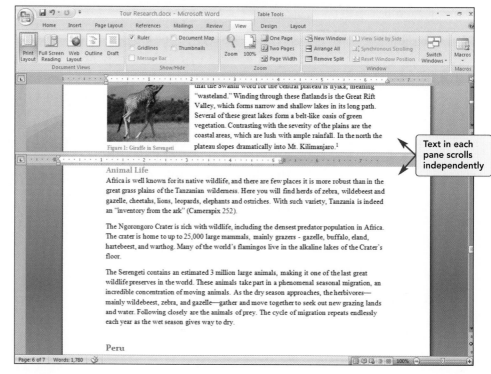

**Figure 3.57**

The text in each pane scrolls independently. Now you can conveniently see both areas of the document while you enter the cross-reference.

**3** • Move to after the word "water" (before the period) in the third paragraph in the Tanzania Animal Life section.

• Press Spacebar.

• Type (see and press Spacebar.

• Open the References tab.

• Click  from the Captions group.

*Your screen should be similar to Figure 3.58*

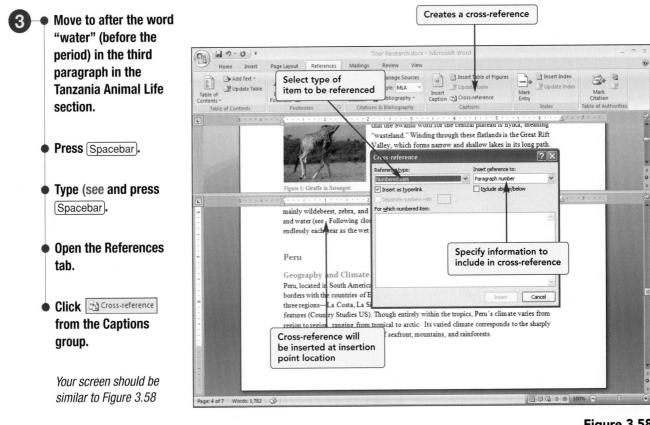

Figure 3.58

In the Cross-reference dialog box, you specify the type of item you are referencing and how you want the reference to appear. You want to reference the giraffe picture, and you want only the label "Figure 1" entered in the document. From the For Which Caption list box, you select the figure you want to reference from the list of all figure captions in the document. Notice that the Insert as Hyperlink option is selected by default. This option creates a hyperlink between the cross-reference and the caption. The default setting is appropriate.

**4** • From the Reference Type drop-down list box, select Figure.

• From the Insert Reference To drop-down list box, select Only label and number.

• Click [ Insert ▾ ]

• Click [ Close ].

• Type ).

• Click on the Figure 1 cross-reference.

*Your screen should be similar to Figure 3.59*

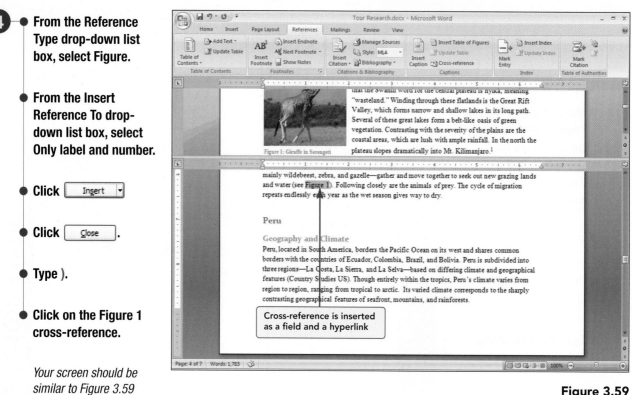

Cross-reference is inserted as a field and a hyperlink

**Figure 3.59**

The cross-reference to Figure 1 is entered into the document as a field. Therefore, if you insert another picture or item that is cross-referenced, the captions and cross-references will renumber automatically. If you edit, delete, or move cross-referenced items, you should manually update the cross-references using Update Field. When you are working on a long document with several figures, tables, and graphs, this feature is very helpful.

## Using a Cross-Reference Hyperlink

The cross-reference field is also a hyperlink and, just like a table of contents field, can be used to jump to the source it references.

**1** • Hold down `Ctrl` and click on the Figure 1 cross-reference.

*Your screen should be similar to Figure 3.60*

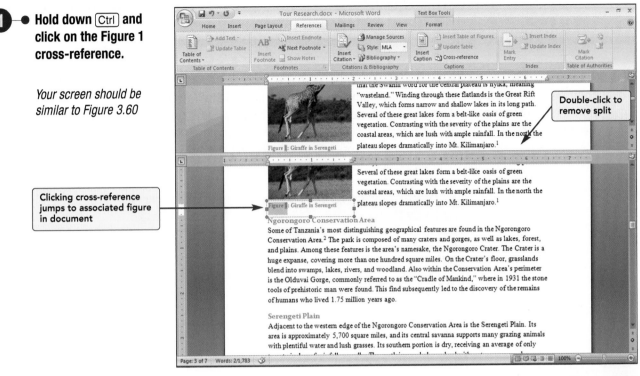

Clicking cross-reference jumps to associated figure in document

Double-click to remove split

**Figure 3.60**

The document in the lower pane jumped to the caption beneath the figure. You will clear the split and save the document next.

**2** • Double-click on the split bar (above the ruler) to remove the split.

• Save the document.

**Another Method**
You also can choose Remove Split from the Window group of the View tab or drag the split bar to the top of the document window.

The split is removed and the document window returns to a single pane. As you can see, splitting the document window is most useful for viewing different sections of the document at the same time and allows you to quickly switch between panes to access information in the different sections without having to repeatedly scroll to the areas.

## Creating a Simple Table

Next, you want to add a table comparing the rainfall and temperature data for the three regions of Peru.

8    A **table** is used to organize information into an easy-to-read format of horizontal rows and vertical columns. The insertion of a row and column creates a **cell** in which you can enter data or other information. Cells in a table are identified by a letter and number, called a **table reference**. Columns are identified from left to right beginning with the letter A, and rows are numbered from top to bottom beginning with the number 1. The table reference of the top-leftmost cell is A1 because it is in the first column (A) and first row (1) of the table. The second cell in column 2 is cell B2. The fourth cell in column 3 is C4.

| A | B | C | D | E |
|---|---|---|---|---|
| (A1) | Jan | Feb | Mar | Total |
| East | 7 (B2) | 7 | 5 | 19 |
| West | 6 | 4 | 7 | 17 |
| South | 8 | 7 (C4) | 9 | 24 |
| Total | 21 | 18 | 21 | 60 |

Tables are a very effective method for presenting information. The table layout organizes the information for readers and greatly reduces the number of words they have to read to interpret the data. Use tables whenever you can to make your documents easier to read.

The table you want to create will display columns for regions, rainfall, and temperature. The rows will display the data for each region. Your completed table will be similar to the one shown below.

| Region | Annual Rainfall (Inches) | Average Temperature (Fahrenheit) |
|---|---|---|
| La Costa | 2 | 68 |
| La Sierra | 35 | 54 |
| La Selva | 137 | 80 |

### Inserting a Table

Word includes several methods you can use to create tables. One method will quickly convert text that is arranged in tabular columns into a table. Another uses the Draw Table feature to create any type of table, but is most useful for creating complex tables that contain cells of different heights or a varying number of columns per row. Another method inserts a preformatted table containing sample data that you replace with your data.

The last method, which you will use, creates a simple table consisting of the same number of rows and columns by highlighting boxes in a grid to define the table size.

**1**

● Move to the blank line below the paragraph on La Sierra.

● Press ⏎Enter to insert another blank line.

● Open the Insert tab.

● Click [Table].

● Point to the boxes in the grid in the drop-down menu to highlight a 3-by-3 section.

**Additional Information**

The dimensions are reflected at the top of the grid and Live Preview shows you how it will look in the document.

● Click on the lower-right corner of the selection to insert it.

*Your screen should be similar to Figure 3.61*

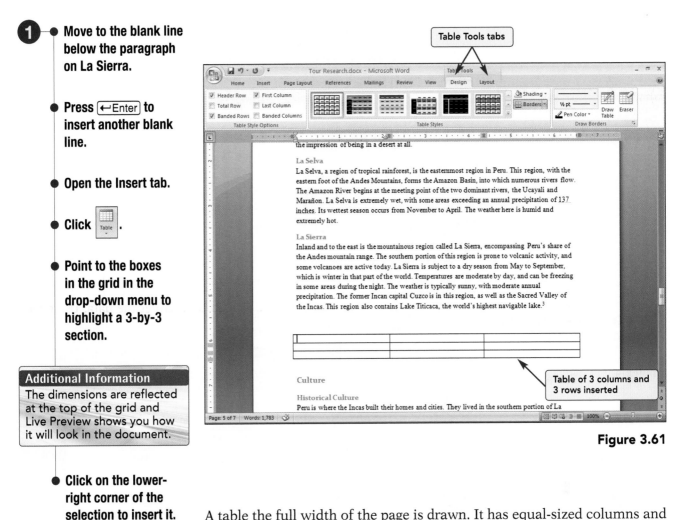

Figure 3.61

A table the full width of the page is drawn. It has equal-sized columns and is surrounded by a black borderline. The Table Tools tab is automatically open and includes a Design tab and a Layout tab that are used to work with the table.

## Entering Data in a Table

Now you are ready to enter information in the table. Each cell contains a single line space where you can enter data. You can move from one cell to another by using the arrow keys or by clicking on the cell. The insertion point appears in the cell that is selected. In addition, you can use the keys shown in the table below to move around a table.

| To Move to | Press |
|---|---|
| Next cell in row | [Tab ⇥] |
| Previous cell in row | [⇧ Shift] + [Tab ⇤] |
| First cell in row | [Alt] + [Home] |
| Last cell in row | [Alt] + [End] |
| First cell in column | [Alt] + [Page Up] |
| Last cell in column | [Alt] + [Page Down] |
| Previous row | [↑] |
| Next row | [↓] |

**Additional Information**
Pressing [Tab ⇥] when in the last cell of a row moves to the first cell of the next row.

The mouse pointer also may appear as a solid black arrow when pointing to the table. When it is a ↓, you can click to select the entire column. When it is ➔, you can click to select a cell. You will learn more about this feature shortly.

You will begin by entering the information for La Costa in cells A1 through C1. You can type in the cell as you would anywhere in a normal document.

**1**
- If necessary, click cell A1 to select it.

- Type La Costa.

- Press [Tab ⇥].

- In the same manner, type 2 in cell B1 and 68 in cell C1.

- Continue entering the information shown below, using [Tab ⇥] to move to the next cell.

| Cell | Entry |
|---|---|
| A2 | La Sierra |
| B2 | 35 |
| C2 | 54 |
| A3 | La Selva |
| B3 | 137 |
| C3 | 80 |

*Your screen should be similar to Figure 3.62*

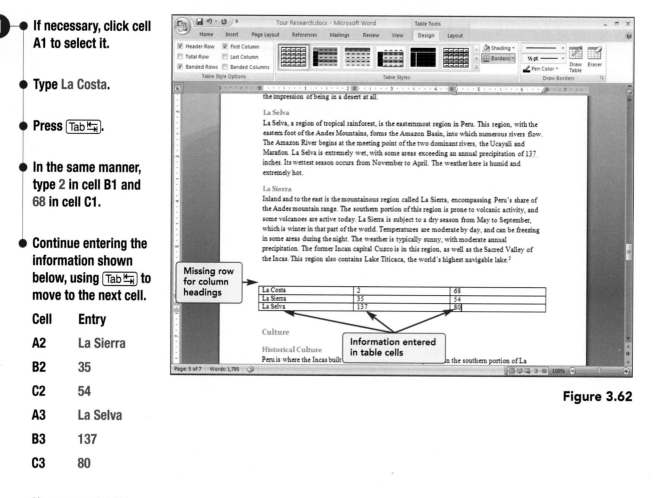

Figure 3.62

## Inserting a Row

After looking at the table, you realize you need to include a row above the data to display the descriptive column headings. To add a row, simply click in any cell above or below the location where you want to add the row and then use the appropriate command to insert a row. Once the row is inserted, you will enter the column headings in the cells.

**1** ● Move to any cell in row 1.

● Open the Table Tools Layout tab.

● Click [Insert Above] from the Rows & Columns group.

● In cell A1 type Region.

● In cell B1 type Annual Rainfall.

● Press ⏎Enter to insert a second line in the cell.

● Type (Inches).

● In cell C1 type Average Temperature on the first line and (Fahrenheit) on the second.

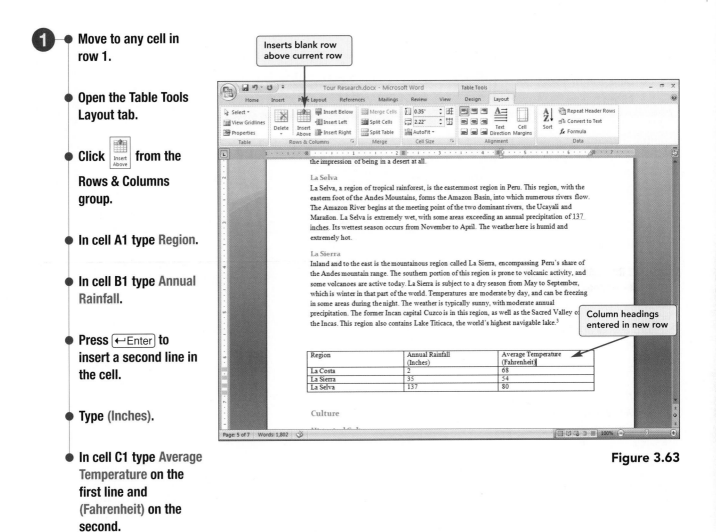

**Figure 3.63**

*Your screen should be similar to Figure 3.63*

## Sizing a Table

The table is much wider than it needs to be. To quickly reduce the overall table size, you can drag the resize handle □. This handle appears in the lower-right corner whenever the mouse pointer rests over the table. Once the table is smaller, you will select the entire table by clicking the ⊞ move handle and center it between the margins.

**1** • **Point to the table and drag the □ resize handle to decrease the width of the table to 5 inches (see Figure 3.64).**

**Additional Information**

The mouse pointer appears as ↖ when you point to the □ resize handle.

• **Click ⊞ to select the entire table.**

**Additional Information**

The mouse pointer appears as ✛ when you point to the ⊞ select handle.

• **Click ≣ Center on the Mini toolbar.**

**Another Method**

You also can drag the ⊞ move handle to move the table to any location or click ⊞ Center in the Table Properties dialog box.

*Your screen should be similar to Figure 3.64*

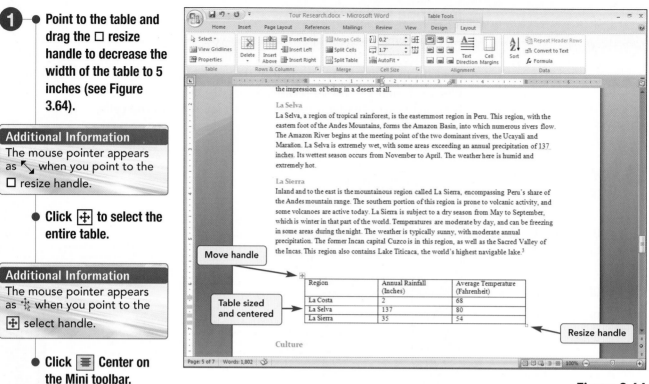

Figure 3.64

**Having Trouble?**

See Concept 9: Sort in Lab 2 to review this feature.

## Sorting a Table

Next you decide you want the three regions to appear in alphabetical order as they are presented in the report. To make this change quickly, you can **sort** the table. The process is similar to sorting a list.

You will use the default Sort settings that will sort by text and paragraphs in ascending order. Additionally, when sorting a table, the program assumes the first row of the table is a header row and uses the information in that row for you to select the column to sort on. The default is to sort on the first column. In this case, this is acceptable because you want to sort the table by Region.

**1**
• Click [A↓Z Sort] in the Data group of the Table Tools Layout tab.

• Click [ OK ] to accept all the default settings.

• Click in the table to clear the highlight.

*Your screen should be similar to Figure 3.65*

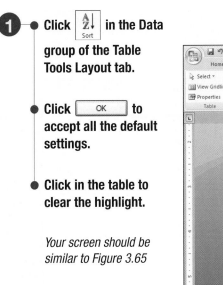

**Figure 3.65**

The three regions now appear in ascending sort order in the table.

## Formatting a Table

To enhance the appearance of the table, you can apply many different formats to the cells. This process is similar to adding formatting to a document, except that the formatting affects the selected cells only or the entire table.

The quickest way to apply formats to a table is to use a table style. This feature includes built-in combinations of formats that consist of different fill or background colors, patterns, borders, fonts, and alignment settings.

**1**
- **Open the Table Tools Design tab.**

- **Click ☰ More to open the table styles gallery.**

*Your screen should be similar to Figure 3.66*

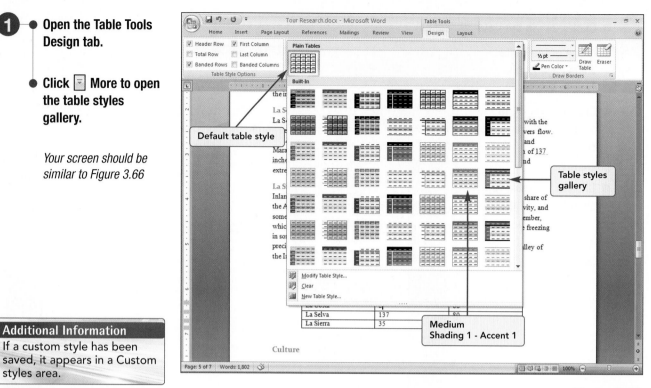

**Figure 3.66**

From the table styles gallery, you select the table design you want to use. There are 146 Built-in styles. As you point to the style, the style name appears in a ScreenTip and Live Preview shows how it will look.

**2**
- **Point to several styles and look at the Live Preview.**

- **Choose Medium Shading 1 - Accent 1 (4th row, 6th column).**

*Your screen should be similar to Figure 3.67*

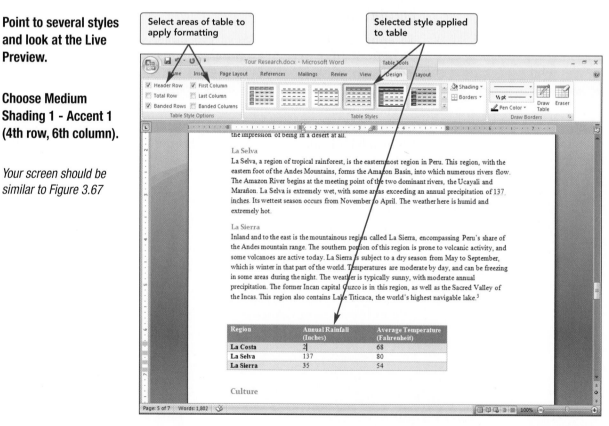

**Figure 3.67**

The table is reformatted to the new design. It includes a different color background for the heading row and banded shades of color for the table data. In addition, the row heading text is bold and the column heading text is white. Notice that the table is no longer centered; however, the table size was not changed. The table alignment was changed because the new design includes left alignment. Using a table style was much faster than applying these features individually.

Even after applying a table style, you may want to make additional changes. For example, the selected table style applies special formatting to the header row and first column. It also uses a banded row effect for the table data. If you do not want one or all of these features, you can turn them off using the quick styles options. You would like to see how the table would look without some of these features.

**3** ● Choose ☑ Header Row and ☑ First Column in the Table Style Options group to turn off these features.

● Click ☐ Last Column to turn on this feature.

*Your screen should be similar to Figure 3.68*

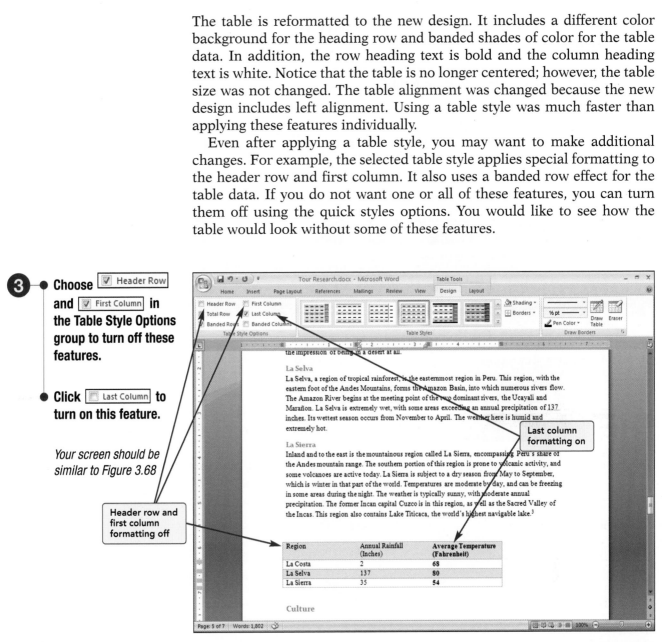

**Figure 3.68**

The dark blue color background was removed from the table header and the bold effect was removed from the row headings. Bold was added to the last column to emphasize the data. As you can see, the Table Style Options allow you to quickly emphasize different areas of the table. You prefer how the table looked before these changes and will restore these features.

**4** ● Choose ☐ Header Row and ☐ First Column to restore these settings.

● Click ☑ Last Column to turn off this feature.

However, there are a few changes you would like to make. As you continue to modify the table, many cells can be selected and changed at the same time. The table below describes the procedures to select information in a table.

| Area to Select | Procedure |
| --- | --- |
| Cell | Click the left edge of the cell when the pointer is ➚. |
| Row | Click to the left of the row when the pointer is ⤢. |
| Column | Click the top of the column when the pointer is ⬇. |
| Multiple cells, rows, or columns | Drag through the cells, rows, or columns when the pointer is ⬇, or select the first cell, row, or column and hold down ⇧Shift while clicking on another cell, row, or column. |
| Contents of next cell | Press Tab⇥. |
| Contents of previous cell | Press ⇧Shift + Tab⇥. |
| Entire table | Press Alt + 5 (on the numeric keypad with Num Lock off) or click ⊞. |

You want the entries in the header row (cells A1 through C1), and the table date in cells B2 through C4, to be centered in their cell spaces. You also want to increase the font size of the header text. Finally, you will add a caption below the table.

**5** ● Select cells A1 through C1 containing the table headings.

● Open the Table Tools Layout tab.

● Click ▣ Align Top Center from the Alignment group.

● In the same manner, center cells B2 through C4.

● Select the header row again.

● Click Ａ Grow in the Mini toolbar.

● Select the table and center it again.

● Add the caption Table 1: Climate below the table.

● Click outside the table to deselect it.

● Insert a blank line below the caption.

● Save the document.

**Figure 3.69**

*Your screen should be similar to Figure 3.69*

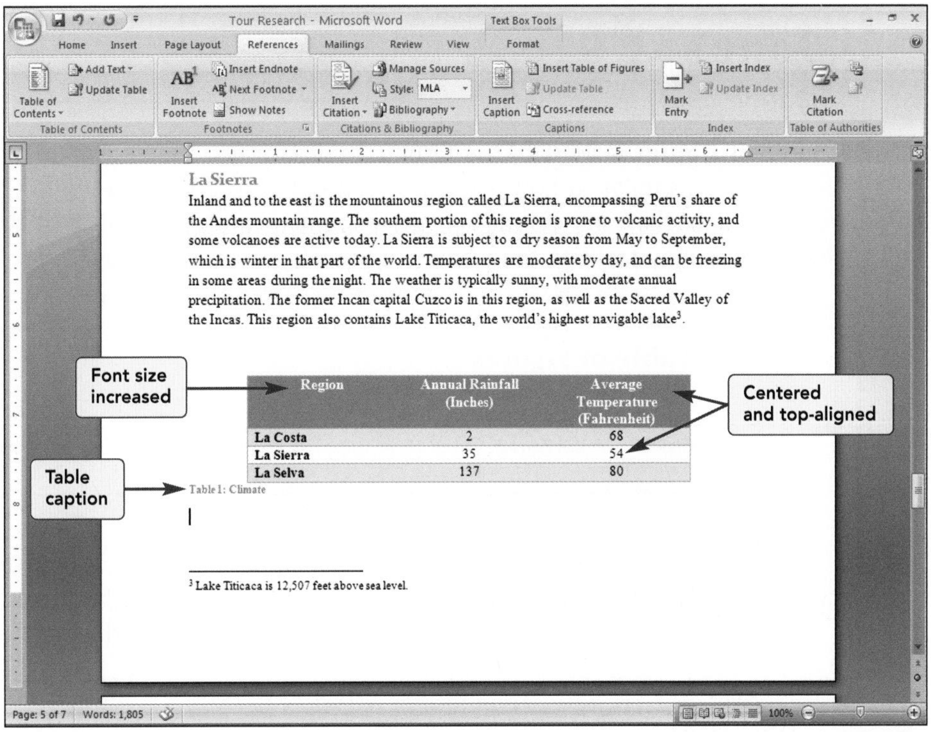

## Including a Table of Figures

The report is near completion and you want to add a table of figures to the report.

# Concept 9

## Table of Figures

**9** A **table of figures** is a list of the figures, tables, or equations used in a document and their associated page number, similar to how a table of contents lists topic headings. The table of figures is generated from captions that are included in the document and is a field that can be easily updated to reflect changes you may make to the document after the list is generated.

> ### Table of Figures
>

Additionally, each entry in the table is a separate field that is a hyperlink to the caption in the document. It can then be used to quickly locate specific figures or other items in the document.

The table of figures is typically placed at the end of a long document.

## Creating a Table of Figures

Because you have already added captions to several items in the report, creating a table of figures will be a simple process.

**1** ● Move to the end of the report.

● Enter the title Table of Figures and format it with a Heading 1 style.

● Press ←Enter to move to a blank line below the title.

● Open the References tab.

● Click 🗎 Insert Table of Figures in the Captions group.

*Your screen should be similar to Figure 3.70*

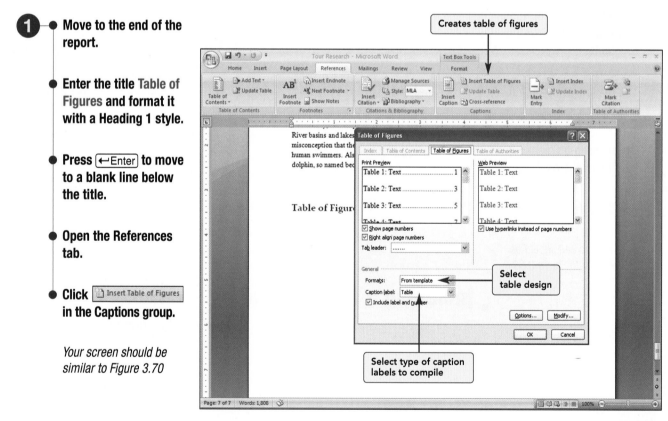

**Figure 3.70**

The Table of Figures dialog box options are very similar to those in the Table of Contents dialog box. The default options to show and right-align page numbers are appropriate as well as the use of the tab leaders. The Formats box is used to select a design for the table of figures. The default design is the design included in the Normal template and is displayed in the Preview boxes. In the Caption label box, you select the type of caption label you want to compile in the table of figures. The default is to display Table caption labels. You will change the Format to another style and the caption label to compile figures.

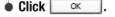
● **Select Distinctive from the Formats drop-down list.**

● **Choose Figure from the Caption label drop-down list.**

● **Click [ OK ].**

*Your screen should be similar to Figure 3.71*

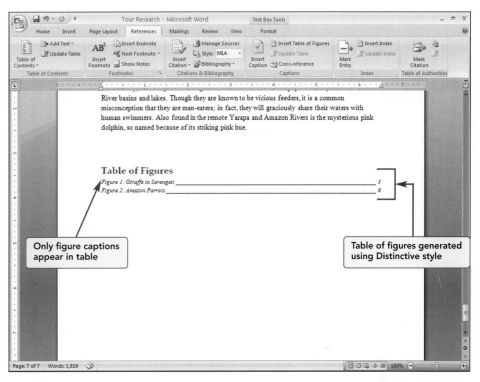

**Figure 3.71**

The program searched for all figure captions in the document and displays them in the table of figures in sorted order by number. The table appears formatted in the selected style.

## Modify a Table of Figures

You also want to include the table references in the table of figures. To do this, you could create a second table of figures to display the table references only. Alternatively, you can modify the table of figures to display all types of captions in a single table. You decide, since there are only three captions, to use one table. You also decide that you do not like how the Distinctive format looks and will use the default template formatting instead.

**1**
- Click [Insert Table of Figures] from the Captions group.

- Click [Options...].

- Choose Caption from the Style drop-down list.

- Click [OK].

- Change the Formats setting to From Template.

- Click [OK].

- Click [Yes] to replace the table of figures.

*Your screen should be similar to Figure 3.72*

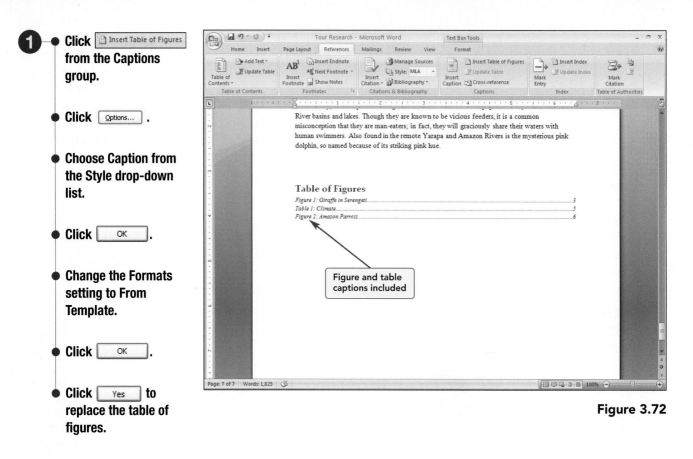

**Figure 3.72**

The table of figures now includes both table and figure captions using the default template style.

## Updating a Table of Figures

You have decided to change the table caption to Peru Climate to make it more descriptive of the table contents. Then you will update the table of figures to reflect this change.

**1** • Use the **Table 1: Climate** hyperlink in the table of figures to jump to that location in the document.

• Click in the caption before the word **Climate**, type **Peru**, and press [Spacebar].

• Click on the table of figures to select it and click [Update Table] in the Captions group.

• Choose Update entire table and click [OK].

**Another Method**
You also could press [F9] to update the table of figures or choose Update table from the table's context menu.

*Your screen should be similar to Figure 3.73*

**MORE ABOUT**
To learn about creating, modifying, and updating a table of authorities and an index, see 4.4 Insert and Format References and Captions in the More About appendix.

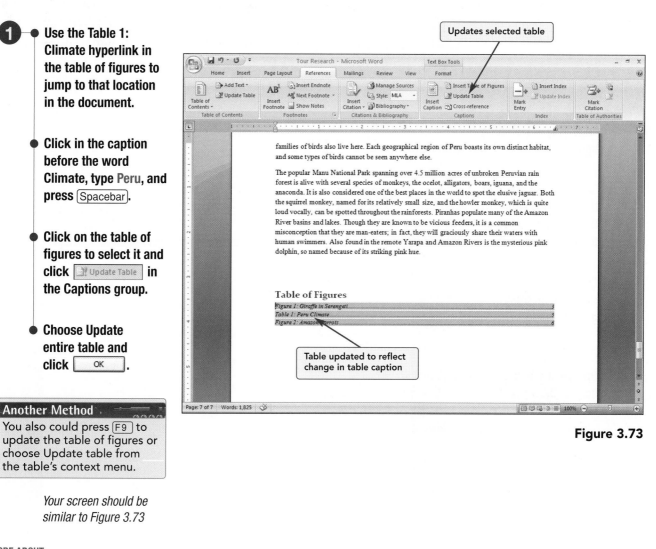

**Updates selected table**

**Table updated to reflect change in table caption**

**Figure 3.73**

The entry for the table is updated in the table of figures to reflect the change you made to the table caption.

# Creating a Bibliography

Finally, you are ready to create the bibliography for the report (see Concept 4). Word makes the process of creating a bibliography effortless by automatically generating the bibliography using the selected report style from the source information you entered when creating citations.

## Generating the Bibliography

**Additional Information**
Word can automatically generate a complete bibliography that lists all sources associated with the document or an abbreviated bibliography that lists only those sources that have been cited.

The requirements for formatting a bibliography vary depending on the report style used. You are using the MLA style for this report. This style requires that each work directly referenced in the paper be listed in alphabetical order by author's last name on a separate page with the title "Works Cited."

Because you have already specified the MLA reference style, when the Works Cited bibliography is generated, the entries will automatically appear using the selected reference style.

**1** ● Insert a new blank page after the table of figures.

● Click ⊞Bibliography ▾ in the Citations and Bibliography group of the References tab.

● Choose the Works Cited option from the gallery.

● If necessary, scroll to the top of the page to see the bibliography.

*Your screen should be similar to Figure 3.74*

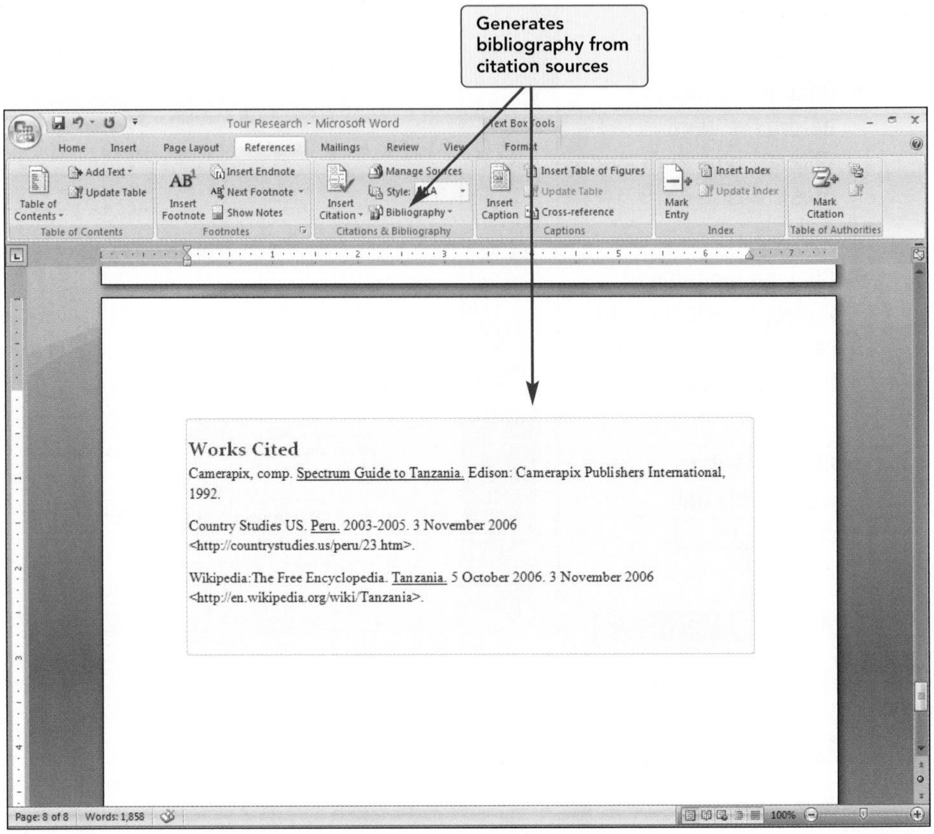

> Generates bibliography from citation sources

**Works Cited**

Camerapix, comp. Spectrum Guide to Tanzania. Edison: Camerapix Publishers International, 1992.

Country Studies US. Peru. 2003-2005. 3 November 2006 <http://countrystudies.us/peru/23.htm>.

Wikipedia:The Free Encyclopedia. Tanzania. 5 October 2006. 3 November 2006 <http://en.wikipedia.org/wiki/Tanzania>.

**Figure 3.74**

The Works Cited bibliography is formatted using the selected MLA documentation style. The page is labeled with a Works Cited heading and each citation source is listed in ascending alphabetical order.

## Updating a Bibliography

Now, as you look at the Works Cited list, you believe you entered the wrong publisher information for the Camerapix source. Even though the bibliography has been generated, it can easily be updated to reflect additions and modifications to the sources. This is because the bibliography is a field that is linked to the sources in the Current List. You will fix the source information and update the bibliography. Rather than return to the citation in the document for this source to edit it, you will use the Source Manager.

**1** • **Click** ⟦Manage Sources⟧ **in the Citations & Bibliography group.**

*Your screen should be similar to Figure 3.75*

Sources in Master List

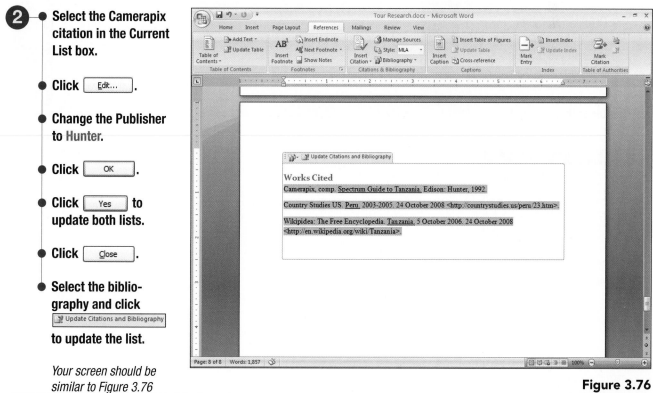

**Figure 3.75**

The Source Manager dialog box displays the three sources you entered in both the Master and Current List boxes. It is used to add, copy, delete, and edit sources. Notice that the items in the Current List are preceded with checkmarks. This indicates they have all been cited in the document. All items in the Current List will appear in the bibliography when it is generated. If a source appears in the Master List that you want to appear in the bibliography, you can select it and copy it to the Current List. You need to edit the Camerapix bibliography information.

**2** • **Select the Camerapix citation in the Current List box.**

• **Click** ⟦Edit...⟧.

• **Change the Publisher to Hunter.**

• **Click** ⟦OK⟧.

• **Click** ⟦Yes⟧ **to update both lists.**

• **Click** ⟦Close⟧.

• **Select the bibliography and click** ⟦Update Citations and Bibliography⟧ **to update the list.**

*Your screen should be similar to Figure 3.76*

**Figure 3.76**

The bibliography information for the Camerapix source is now correct and the Works Cited list has been appropriately updated.

## Modifying a Bibliography

Finally, you will modify the format of the Works Cited page to more closely meet the MLA requirements. The page title should be centered at the top of the page. The bibliography entries must be formatted as hanging indents—the first line is even with the left margin and subsequent lines of the same work are indented 0.5 inch. MLA formatting for the Works Cited page also requires that it should be double-spaced, as is the entire report.

First you will format the page title. In addition to centering the title at the top of the page, you decide to change the style of the title to the same as the table of contents title. Then you will change the paragraph formatting to a hanging indent.

**1** ● **Move to anywhere in the Works Cited title.**

● **Choose TOC Title from the Styles group of the Home tab.**

● **Click** 🗏 **Center.**

● **Select the three entries in the Works Cited list.**

● **Drag the hanging indent marker on the ruler to the 0.5-inch position.**

● **Clear the highlight.**

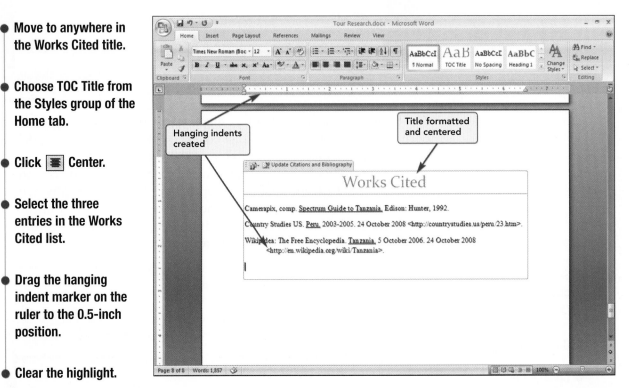

Hanging indents created

Title formatted and centered

Works Cited

Camerapix, comp. Spectrum Guide to Tanzania. Edison: Hunter, 1992.

Country Studies US. Peru. 2003-2005. 24 October 2008 <http://countrystudies.us/peru/23.htm>.

Wikipedia: The Free Encyclopedia. Tanzania. 5 October 2006. 24 October 2008 <http://en.wikipedia.org/wiki/Tanzania>.

**Figure 3.77**

**Another Method**

You also could choose Hanging from the Special drop-down list of the Paragraph dialog box or press Ctrl + T.

*Your screen should be similar to Figure 3.77*

Any entries that are longer than one line appear with a hanging indent.

# Creating Headers and Footers

Next you want to add information in a header and footer to the report.

## Concept 10

**Header and Footer**

**10** Headers and footers provide information that typically appears at the top and bottom of each page in a document and helps the reader locate information in a document. A **header** is a line or several lines of text in the top margin of each page. The header usually contains the title and the section of the document. A **footer** is a line or several lines of text in the margin space at the bottom of every page. The footer usually contains the page number and perhaps the date. Headers and footers also can contain graphics such as a company logo.

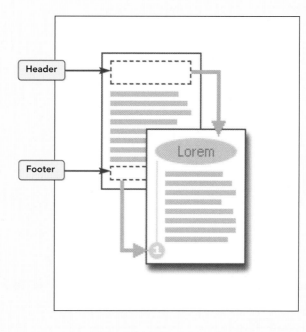

The same header and footer can be used throughout a document, or a different header and footer can be used in different sections of a document. For example, a unique header or footer can be used in one section and a different one in another section. You also can have a unique header or footer on the first page, or omitted entirely from the first page, or use a different header and footer on odd and even pages.

You want to add a header and footer to the entire document except for the first two pages.

## Creating Document Sections

Many format and layout settings, including headers and footers, when applied affect an entire document. To apply layout or formatting changes to a portion of a document, you need to create separate sections in the document by inserting section breaks

# Concept 11

## Section

**11** To format different parts of a document differently, you can divide a document into **sections**. Initially a document is one section. To separate it into different parts, you insert section breaks. The **section break** identifies the end of a section and stores the document format settings associated with that section of the document. Once a document is divided into sections, the following formats can be changed for individual sections: margins, paper size and orientation, paper source for a printer, page borders, vertical alignment, headers and footers, columns, page numbering, line numbering, and footnotes and endnotes.

The three types of section breaks, described below, control the location where the text following a section break begins.

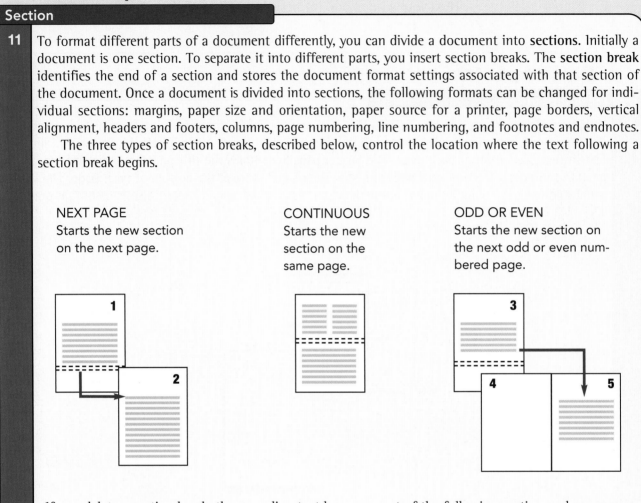

NEXT PAGE
Starts the new section on the next page.

CONTINUOUS
Starts the new section on the same page.

ODD OR EVEN
Starts the new section on the next odd or even numbered page.

If you delete a section break, the preceding text becomes part of the following section and assumes its section formatting.

Because you do not want headers and footers on the first two pages of the document, you need to divide the document into two sections. You will replace the hard page break that you inserted when creating the table of contents page with a Next Page section break.

**1** ● **Move to the table of contents page.**

● **Turn on display of paragraph marks.**

● **Select the hard page break line below the table of contents and press** Delete **to remove it.**

● **Open the Page Layout tab.**

● **Click** Breaks ▾ **from the Page Setup group.**

● **Choose Next Page from the Section Breaks category.**

● **If necessary, scroll to see the bottom of the table of contents list.**

*Your screen should be similar to Figure 3.78*

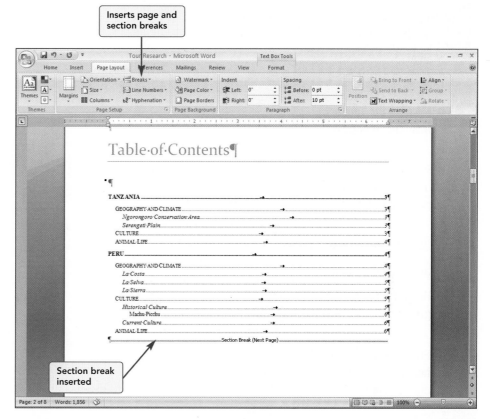

Figure 3.78

**MORE ABOUT**

▶ To learn how to delete a section break, see 2.3 Control Pagination in the More About appendix.

A double dotted line and the words "Section Break" identify the type of document break that was inserted. A section break, like a hard page break line, can be deleted.

You also decide to insert another section break at the beginning of the Peru topic. Again you want it to start on a new page.

**2** ● **Move to the Peru topic heading and insert a Next Page section break at that location.**

**Additional Information**

If you do not create a section break first, Word will automatically insert a section break for you if you change the formatting of selected text, such as inserting columns or centering selected text vertically on a page.

The report now contains two section breaks that divide the report into three sections that can each be formatted independently if needed.

## Using a Predesigned Header

Word includes many features that help you quickly create attractive headers and footers. Among these features are predesigned built-in header and footer designs that include placeholders to help you enter information. You will create a header for the report using this feature.

**1** ● Move to the Tanzania heading on page 3.

● Press $\boxed{\text{Ctrl}}$ + * to turn off the display of paragraph marks.

● Open the Insert tab and click 🗐 in the Header & Footer group.

● From the gallery of header designs, choose Sideline.

*Your screen should be similar to Figure 3.79*

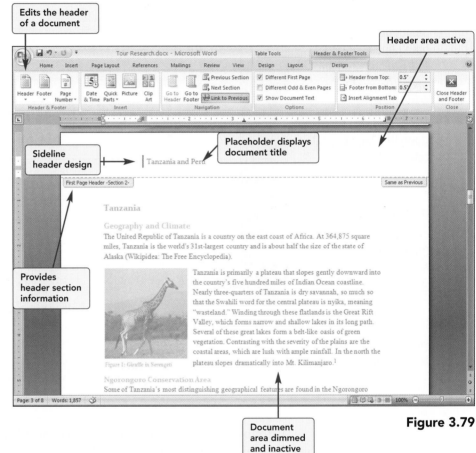

**Figure 3.79**

**MORE ABOUT**

You also can insert pre-designed headers using the Quick Parts Building Blocks Organizer. To learn how to do this, see 4.1 Structure Content Using Quick Parts in the More About appendix.

The document area dims and the header area, above the dashed line, is active. The Header and Footer Tools Design tab is automatically displayed. Its buttons are used to add items to the header and footer and to navigate between headers and footers.

The Sideline design includes a graphic bar like that used in the cover page and the report title placeholder that displays the title from the document properties in blue. Notice that in addition to the Header and Footer Tools tab, the Table Tools tab is displayed. This is because the design is contained in a table consisting of a single cell that is used to control the placement of items.

## Modifying Header Settings

Notice the tab on the left below the dashed line of the header. This tab identifies the section information for each page of the document. Each section has its own header areas that can be formatted differently.

**1** ● **Change the zoom to 39%.**

*Your screen should be similar to Figure 3.80*

Each section includes two types of headers

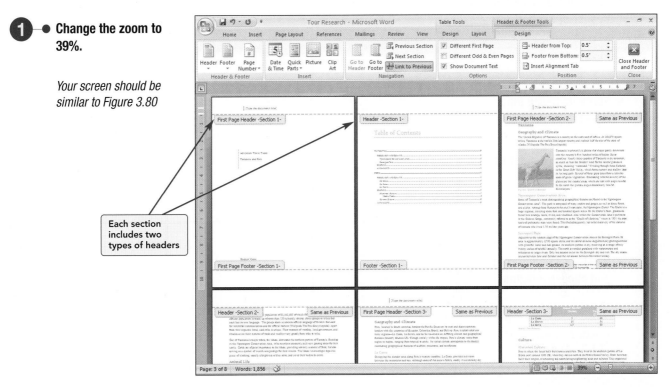

**Figure 3.80**

Now you can see that each section is made up of two types of headers: "First Page Headers" and running "Headers." Word automatically added first page headers because it detected that the document includes a cover page. This allows you to create a unique header for the first page. Notice the Sidelines design has been inserted only in the "First Page Header" headers and that the headers on the following pages of the same section are blank.

Since it is not necessary to have a separate First Page Header in sections 2 and 3, you will remove them and then insert the Sideline design again for the running headers in the two sections.

**2**

- Click [ Different First Page ] to turn off this feature for Section 2.

- Click [ Next Section ] to move to the First Page Header of Section 3.

- Click [ Different First Page ].

- Scroll up to see the top of the window.

- Click in the Header of the first page of section 2.

- Click [ Header ] in the Header & Footer group and choose Sideline.

*Your screen should be similar to Figure 3.81*

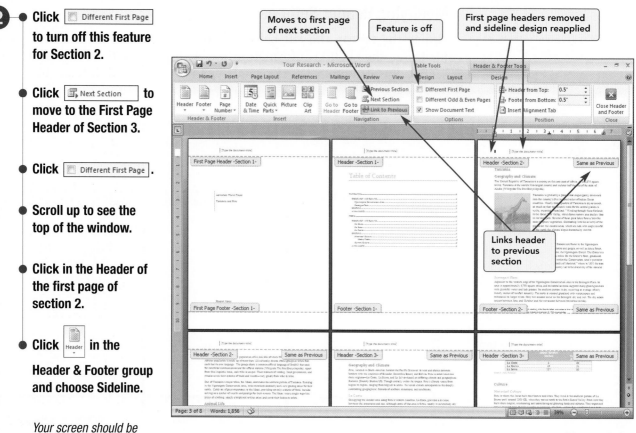

Moves to first page of next section

Feature is off

First page headers removed and sideline design reapplied

Links header to previous section

**Figure 3.81**

Now all headers in all sections of the document are formatted using this design. The same design was applied to all sections because the headers are initially linked even though the document is divided into sections. Notice the tab on the right displays "Same as Previous." When this setting is on, the header in the previous sections will have the same settings as the header in the section you are defining. Because you do not want the title or contents pages in section 1 to display information in the header, you will break the connection between sections 1 and 2 by turning off this option. Then you will remove the header from section 1.

**3** • Click [Link to Previous].

• Click [Previous Section]

• Click [Different First Page].

• Click [Header] and choose Remove Header.

*Your screen should be similar to Figure 3.82*

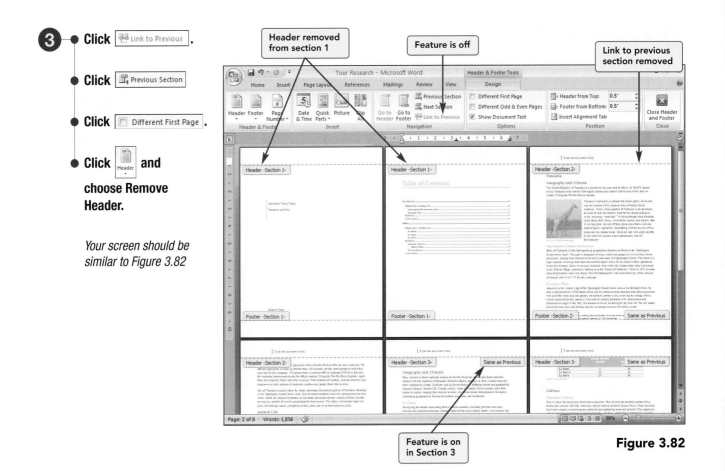

Figure 3.82

The header information is removed from Section 1. It is displayed in Section 3 because the Same as Previous option is on for that section. You can tell if the headers are linked because "Same as Previous" appears in a tab below the header area.

## Changing Header Content

Instead of the report title, you want to display the section title, Tanzania. To do this, you need to remove the title placeholder and type the section heading. You edit the content of a header as if it were a mini-document.

**1** ● Click ⬚ Next Section .

● Increase the zoom to 100%.

● Triple-click on the document title placeholder and press Delete to remove it.

● Type Tanzania.

*Your screen should be similar to Figure 3.83*

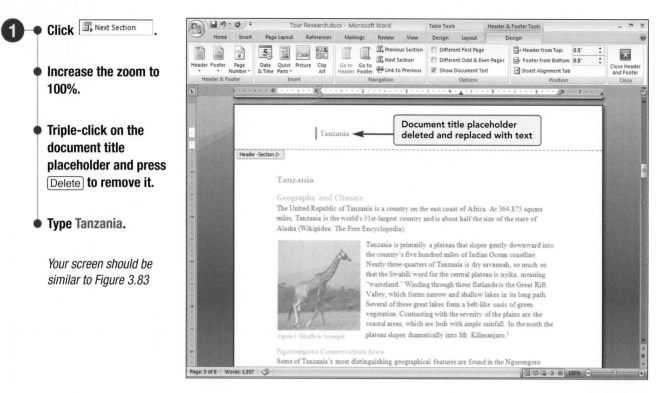

Figure 3.83

Next, you want to add your name right-aligned to the header. To quickly add this information, you will use a Quick Parts entry. Quick Parts insert built-in information automatically for you, such as document and user information.

**2** ● Click ⬚ Insert Alignment Tab .

● Choose Right and click OK .

● Click ⬚ in the Insert group.

● Select Document Property and choose Author.

*Your screen should be similar to Figure 3.84*

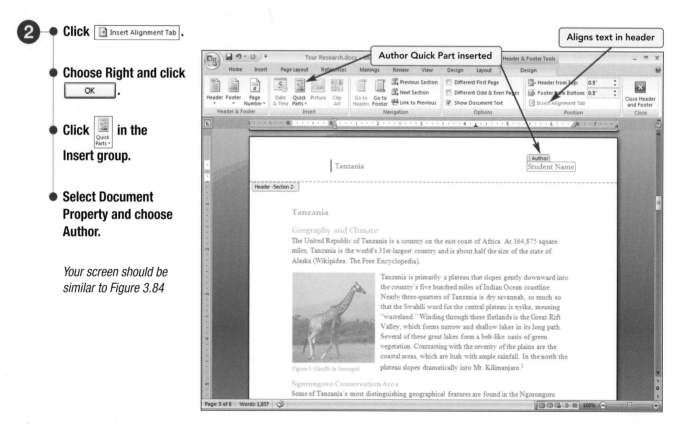

Figure 3.84

The Author placeholder is right-aligned in the header and displays your name because this information is stored in the document properties.

## Inserting and Modifying the Date

Finally, you will add an automatic date stamp to display the current date after your name in the header.

**1** • Press Tab, →, and Spacebar to move to the end of the Author placeholder and enter a space.

• Click [Date & Time] in the Insert group.

• If necessary, select Update Automatically to turn on this feature.

• Click [ OK ] to insert the date in the default format.

*Your screen should be similar to Figure 3.85*

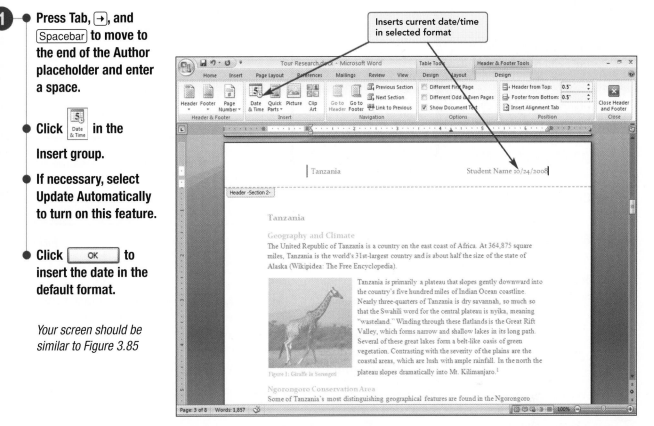

Inserts current date/time in selected format

**Figure 3.85**

The current date is inserted as a field and will update when the system date changes. Instead you decide to change the date to display the date the document was last saved using a Quick Parts entry.

**2** ● Select and delete the date placeholder.

● Click [Quick Parts] and choose Field.

● Choose Date and Time from the Categories list.

● Choose SaveDate from the Field Names list.

● Choose the M/d/yyyy h:mm am/pm date and time format (10/12/2008 11:09 AM).

● Click [ OK ].

● Reduce the zoom to 39%.

*Your screen should be similar to Figure 3.86*

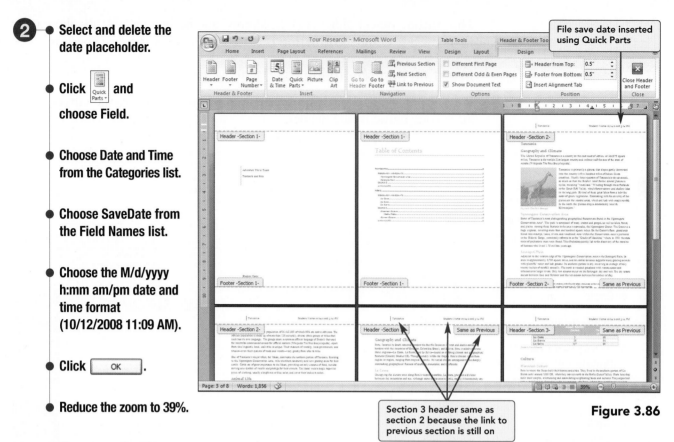

File save date inserted using Quick Parts

Section 3 header same as section 2 because the link to previous section is still on

**Figure 3.86**

The date and time reflect the date and time the file was last saved. It can be updated when you save the file again. Notice that the same header information is used in Section 3. You want to break the link between the Section 3 header and the Section 2 header so you can change the section title from Tanzania to Peru in the Section 3 header.

**3** ● Click on the Section 3 header and click [Link to Previous] to break the link.

● Select the text Tanzania and replace it with Peru.

● Scroll up to see the first six pages as in Figure 3.87.

*Your screen should be similar to Figure 3.87*

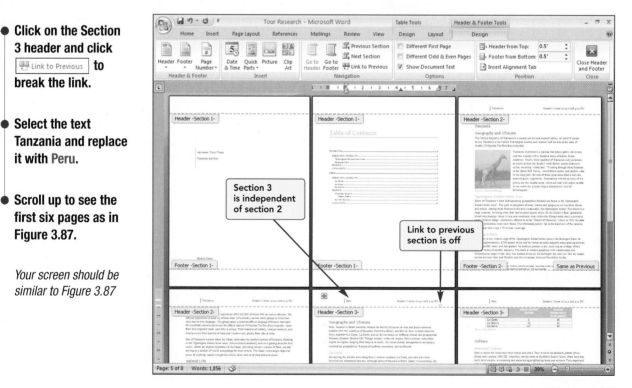

Section 3 is independent of section 2

Link to previous section is off

**Figure 3.87**

You can now see that the header for Sections 2 and 3 are formatted independently and that Section 1 does not display any header information.

## Inserting and Modifying Page Numbers

Next, you will add information to the footer. You want the footer to display the page number, file name, and date. Page numbers can be added to the top, bottom, or side margins of the page. Word includes many built-in page number designs that include formatting and graphic elements to help you quickly create attractive page numbers. You will add the number to the bottom of the page, which inserts it in the footer.

**MORE ABOUT**

You also can insert page numbers in the text of a document. To learn about this feature, see 1.2 Lay Out Document in the More About appendix.

**1** • Click 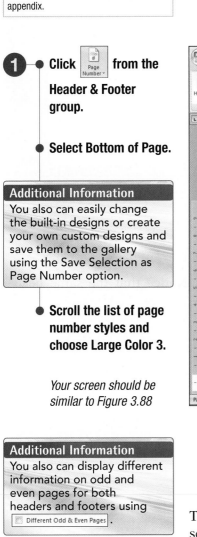 from the **Header & Footer** group.

• Select **Bottom of Page**.

**Additional Information**
You also can easily change the built-in designs or create your own custom designs and save them to the gallery using the Save Selection as Page Number option.

• Scroll the list of page number styles and choose **Large Color 3**.

*Your screen should be similar to Figure 3.88*

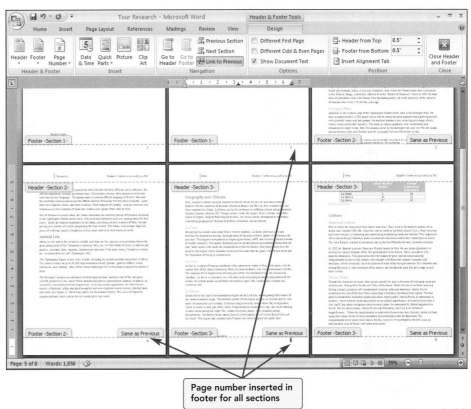

Page number inserted in footer for all sections

**Figure 3.88**

**Additional Information**
You also can display different information on odd and even pages for both headers and footers using Different Odd & Even Pages .

**Additional Information**
You also can change the format of page numbers from Arabic to Roman Numerals or letters and include chapter numbers.

The footer area is active and the page number appears right-aligned in the selected design in the footer of all sections. The number is a field that updates to reflect the document page. By default, when you insert sections, page numbering continues from the previous section. Because you do not want the title or contents pages in section 1 to display the footer information, you will break the connection between sections 1 and 2 by turning off this option. Then you will remove the footer from section 1 and begin page numbering with section 2.

**2** • Move to the section 2 footer.

• Click Link to Previous.

• Move to the footer of section 1.

• Click 📄 Footer and choose Remove Footer.

• Move to the footer of section 2.

• Click 📄 Page Number in the Header and Footer group.

• Choose Format Page Numbers.

• Choose Start At.

**Additional Information**
The default Start At setting begins numbering with 1.

• Click OK.

• Increase the zoom to 100%.

• Click in the footer area to clear the selection.

*Your screen should be similar to Figure 3.89*

**Additional Information**

You also can use 📄 Footer on the Insert tab or the Header & Footer Tools Design tab to insert a predesigned footer with placeholders for items such as the date and page number.

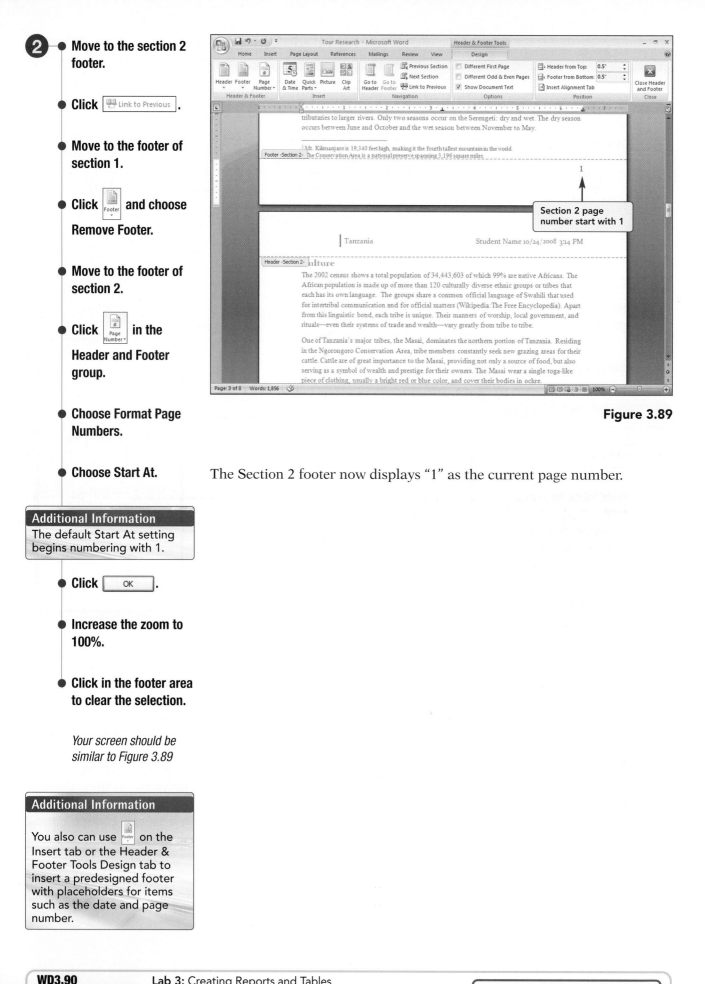

**Figure 3.89**

The Section 2 footer now displays "1" as the current page number.

## Adding the File Name Quick Parts

Next, you will add the file name centered in the footer. To quickly add the file information, you will use a Quick Parts entry. Then you will save the document and update the date field in the header.

**1** • Use the Click and Type pointer to insert a center tab in the Section 2 footer.

• Click [Quick Parts] and choose Field.

• Choose Document Information from the Categories list and choose FileName from the Field Names list.

• Click [ OK ].

• Save the report.

• Right-click on the date field in the header and choose Update Field from the context menu.

*Your screen should be similar to Figure 3.90*

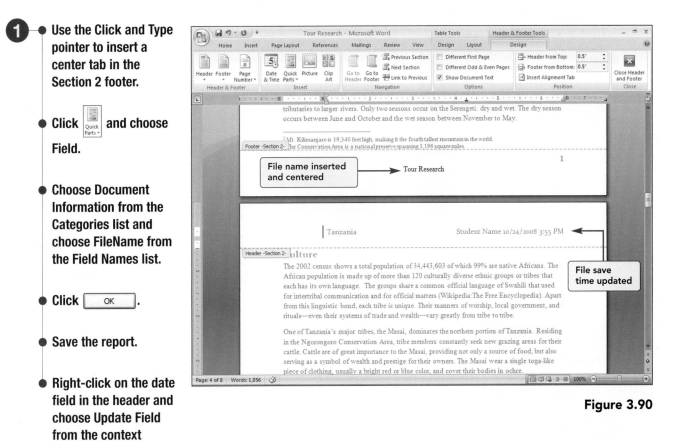

**Figure 3.90**

The date and time have updated to reflect the last time the file was saved. Likewise, because the file name is also a field, it can be updated if you change the file name to another. Notice the file name is in black font. This is because it was not entered using a design style and formats using the default font color setting.

**2** ● Select the file name and use the Mini toolbar to change the font color to the Turquoise, Accent 1 theme color.

● Click [Close Header and Footer].

**Another Method**
You also can double-click in the document area to make it active again.

*Your screen should be similar to Figure 3.91*

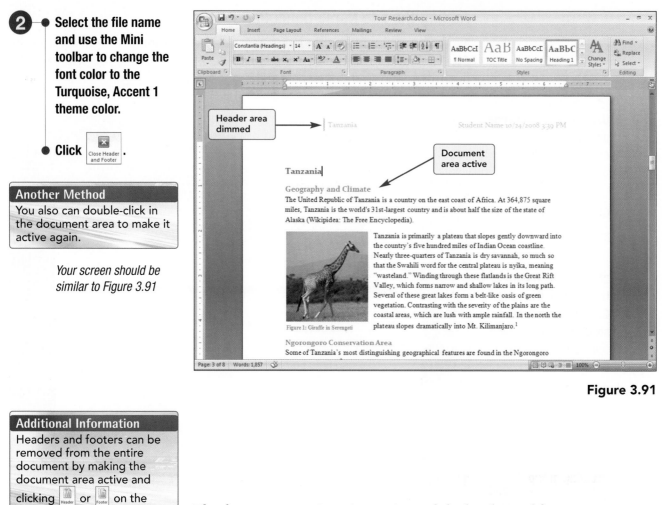

**Figure 3.91**

**Additional Information**
Headers and footers can be removed from the entire document by making the document area active and clicking [Header] or [Footer] on the Insert tab and choosing Remove Header or Remove Footer from the menu.

The document area is active again, and the header and footer text appears dimmed. The header and footer can only be seen in Print Layout view and when the document is printed.

## Redisplaying Spelling and Grammar Errors

Now you will turn on the display of spelling and grammar errors again and then spell and grammar check the document.

**1**

- If necessary, move to the top of page 1 of section 2.

- Choose 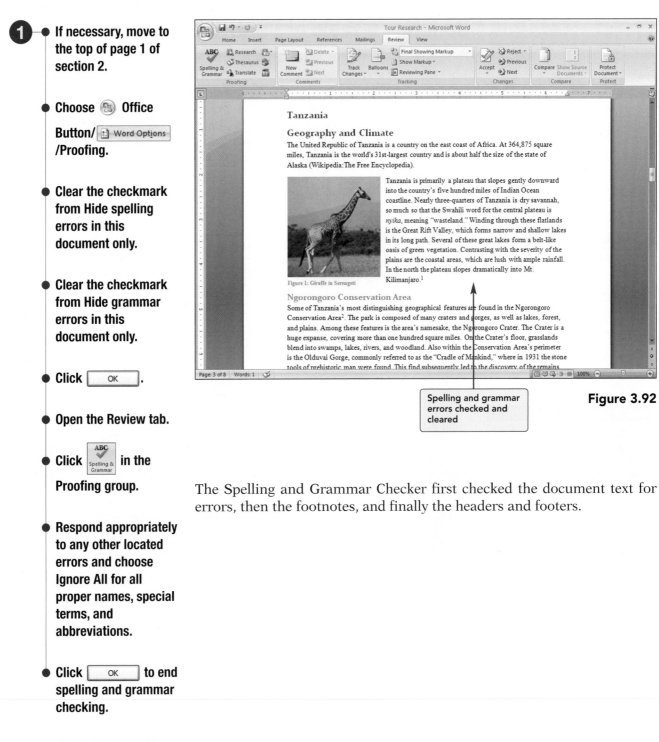 Office Button/ Word Options /Proofing.

- Clear the checkmark from Hide spelling errors in this document only.

- Clear the checkmark from Hide grammar errors in this document only.

- Click OK.

- Open the Review tab.

- Click Spelling & Grammar in the Proofing group.

- Respond appropriately to any other located errors and choose Ignore All for all proper names, special terms, and abbreviations.

- Click OK to end spelling and grammar checking.

*Your screen should be similar to Figure 3.92*

### Tanzania

#### Geography and Climate

The United Republic of Tanzania is a country on the east coast of Africa. At 364,875 square miles, Tanzania is the world's 31st-largest country and is about half the size of the state of Alaska (Wikipedia: The Free Encyclopedia).

Tanzania is primarily a plateau that slopes gently downward into the country's five hundred miles of Indian Ocean coastline. Nearly three-quarters of Tanzania is dry savannah, so much so that the Swahili word for the central plateau is *nyika*, meaning "wasteland." Winding through these flatlands is the Great Rift Valley, which forms narrow and shallow lakes in its long path. Several of these great lakes form a belt-like oasis of green vegetation. Contrasting with the severity of the plains are the coastal areas, which are lush with ample rainfall. In the north the plateau slopes dramatically into Mt. Kilimanjaro.[1]

Figure 1: Giraffe in Serengeti

#### Ngorongoro Conservation Area

Some of Tanzania's most distinguishing geographical features are found in the Ngorongoro Conservation Area[2]. The park is composed of many craters and gorges, as well as lakes, forest, and plains. Among these features is the area's namesake, the Ngorongoro Crater. The Crater is a huge expanse, covering more than one hundred square miles. On the Crater's floor, grasslands blend into swamps, lakes, rivers, and woodland. Also within the Conservation Area's perimeter is the Olduvai Gorge, commonly referred to as the "Cradle of Mankind," where in 1931 the stone tools of prehistoric man were found. This find subsequently led to the discovery of the remains

Page: 3 of 8    Words: 1

Spelling and grammar errors checked and cleared

**Figure 3.92**

The Spelling and Grammar Checker first checked the document text for errors, then the footnotes, and finally the headers and footers.

# Updating a Table of Contents

You have made many modifications to the report since generating the table of contents, so you want to update the listing. Because the table of contents is a field, if you add or remove headings, rearrange topics, or make other changes that affect the table of contents listing, you can quickly update the table of contents. In this case, you have added pictures, a table, a bibliography, and a table of figures that have affected the paging and content of the document. You will update the table of contents to ensure that the page references are accurate and that any new content is included.

**1** ● Move to the table of contents page.

● Click anywhere on the table of contents area.

● Click [Update Table] in the field tab.

### Another Method

You also can use [Update Table] on the References tab, or choose Update Field from the table of contents context menu, or press F9 to quickly update a table of contents field.

● Choose Update entire table.

● Click [ OK ].

*Your screen should be similar to Figure 3.93*

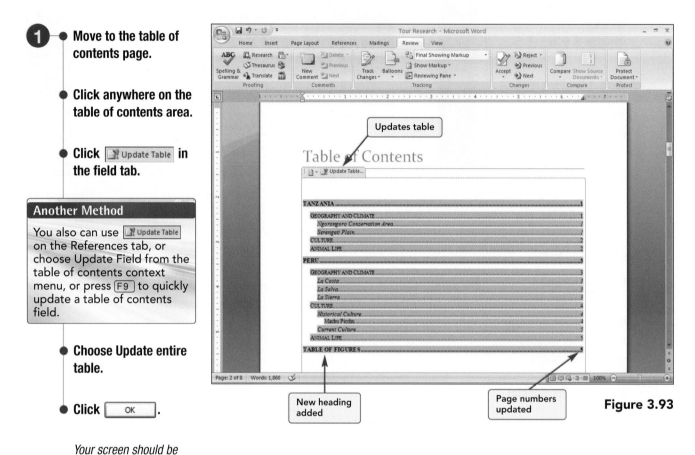

Figure 3.93

The page numbers referenced by each table-of-contents hyperlink have been updated as needed and the Table of Figures heading has been added to the list. However, the Works Cited page is not included. This is because the Works Cited page title is formatted using the TOC Title style, not a heading style. You will add the Works Cited page to the table of contents listing by marking the individual entry.

- Move to the Works Cited page title.

- Click 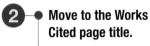 Add Text ▾ in the Table of Contents group of the References tab.

- Select Level 1 as the level for the heading.

- Click 🗐 Update Table in the Table of Contents group.

- Choose Update entire table.

- Click ⬚ OK ⬚.

- Display the table of contents page.

*Your screen should be similar to Figure 3.94*

**MORE ABOUT**

To learn how to update a table of contents with selected text, see 1.3 Make Documents and Content Easier to Find in the More About appendix

**Figure 3.94**

The listing now includes a hyperlink to the Works Cited page.

# Printing Selected Pages

You are now ready to print the report.

**1**
- Click 🖫 Save.

- Choose 🏢 Office Button/Print/Print Preview.

- Reduce the zoom to display all eight pages.

*Your screen should be similar to Figure 3.95*

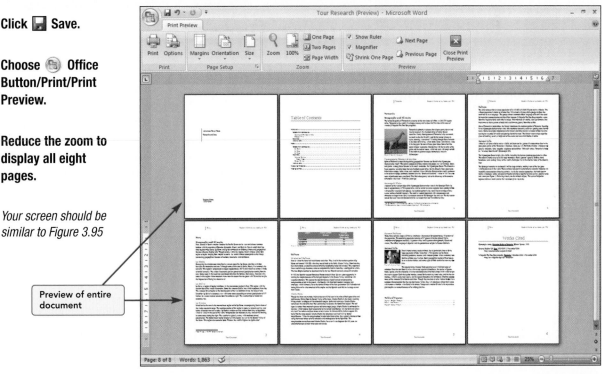

**Figure 3.95**

You would like to print only the first and second pages in section one, and the sixth, seventh, and eighth pages in section three of the document. To do this, you use the Print dialog box to select the pages you want to print. When printing pages in different sections, the page number and section number (p#s#) must be identified in the page range.

**2**
- Click [Print].
- If necessary, select the appropriate printer for your computer system.
- Type **p1s1, p2s1, p2s3-p4s3** in the Pages text box.
- Click [OK].
- Return the zoom to Whole Page.
- Click [Close Print Preview].
- Exit Word.

Your printed output should be similar to that shown in the Case Study at the beginning of the lab.

# Focus on Careers

## EXPLORE YOUR CAREER OPTIONS

Market Research Analyst

Have you ever wondered who investigates the market for new products? Ever thought about the people who put together phone surveys? Market research analysts are responsible for determining the potential sales for a new product or service. They conduct surveys and compile statistics for clients or their employer. These reports usually include report features like a table of contents, cross-references, headers and footers, and footnotes for references. Market research analysts may hold positions as faculty at a university, work for large organizations, or hold governmental positions. The salary range for an entry-level market research analyst position is $39,300 to $49,400 and demand is high in a strong economy.

# Concept Summary

## LAB 3

## Creating Reports and Tables

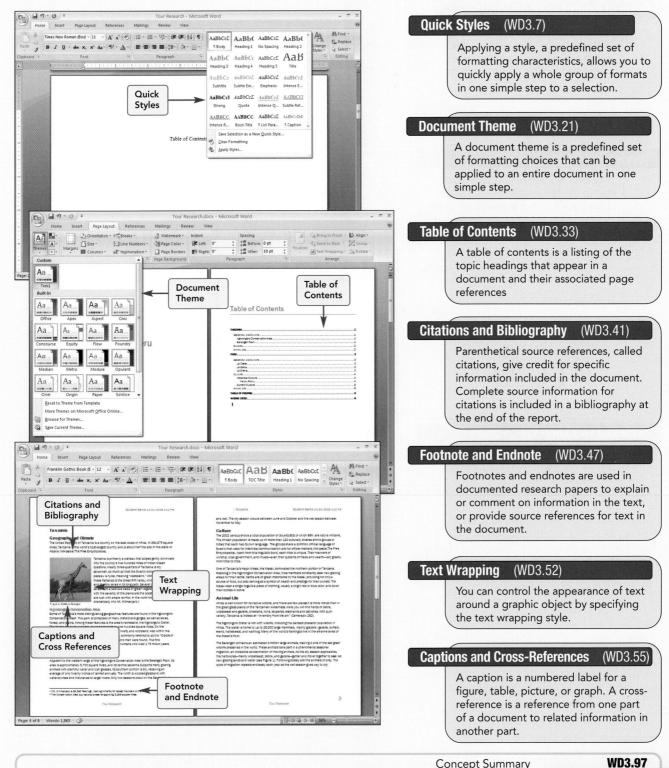

### Quick Styles  (WD3.7)

Applying a style, a predefined set of formatting characteristics, allows you to quickly apply a whole group of formats in one simple step to a selection.

### Document Theme  (WD3.21)

A document theme is a predefined set of formatting choices that can be applied to an entire document in one simple step.

### Table of Contents  (WD3.33)

A table of contents is a listing of the topic headings that appear in a document and their associated page references

### Citations and Bibliography  (WD3.41)

Parenthetical source references, called citations, give credit for specific information included in the document. Complete source information for citations is included in a bibliography at the end of the report.

### Footnote and Endnote  (WD3.47)

Footnotes and endnotes are used in documented research papers to explain or comment on information in the text, or provide source references for text in the document.

### Text Wrapping  (WD3.52)

You can control the appearance of text around a graphic object by specifying the text wrapping style.

### Captions and Cross-References  (WD3.55)

A caption is a numbered label for a figure, table, picture, or graph. A cross-reference is a reference from one part of a document to related information in another part.

## Table  (WD3.62)

A table is used to organize information into an easy-to-read format of horizontal rows and vertical columns.

## Table of Figures  (WD3.72)

A table of figures is a list of the figures, tables, or equations used in a document and their associated page number.

## Header and Footer  (WD3.79)

A header is a line or several lines of text in the top margin of each page. A footer is a line or several lines of text in the margin space at the bottom of every page.

## Section  (WD3.80)

To format different parts of a document differently, you can divide a document into sections.

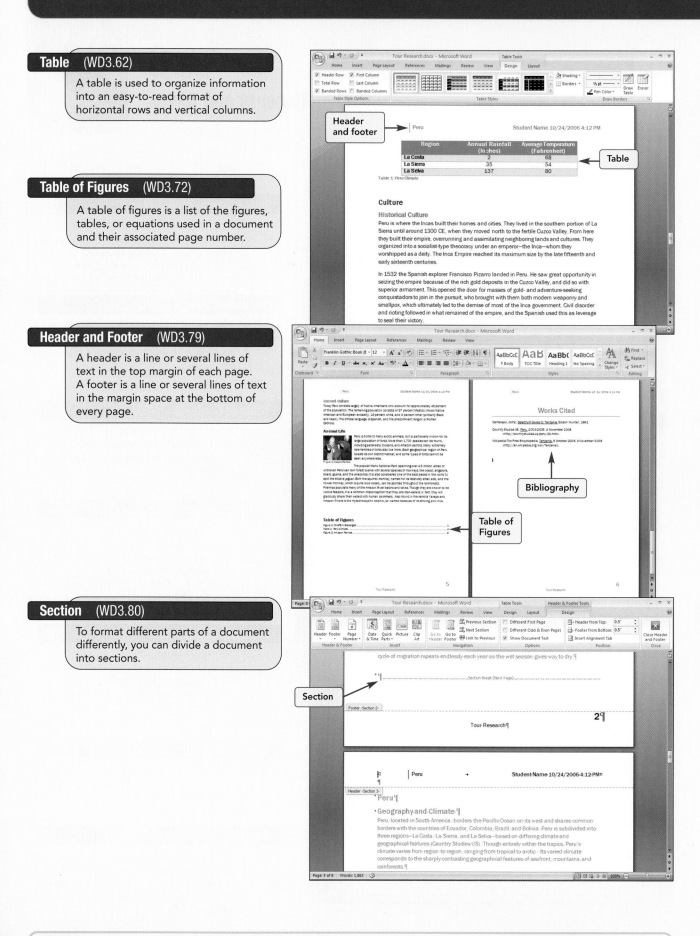

# Lab Review

LAB 3
## Creating Reports and Tables

## key terms

bibliography   WD3.41

caption   WD3.55

cell   WD3.62

citations   WD3.41

Click and Type   WD3.27

cross-reference   WD3.55

Document Map   WD3.37

document theme   WD3.21

drawing layer   WD3.52

endnote   WD3.47

floating object   WD3.52

footer   WD3.79

footnote   WD3.47

header   WD3.79

heading style   WD3.7

inline object   WD3.52

navigation window   WD3.37

note pane   WD3.48

note reference mark   WD3.47

note separator   WD3.47

note text   WD3.47

placeholder   WD3.18

quick style   WD3.7

section   WD3.80

section break   WD3.80

sort   WD3.66

split window   WD3.57

table   WD3.62

table of contents   WD3.33

table of figures   WD3.72

table reference   WD3.62

text box   WD3.57

text wrapping   WD3.52

thumbnails   WD3.39

## MCAS skills

The Microsoft Certified Applications Specialist (MCAS) certification program is designed to measure your proficiency in performing basic tasks using the Office 2007 applications. Getting certified demonstrates that you have the skills and provides a valuable industry credential for employment. See Reference 2 MCAS Certification Guide for a complete list of the skills that were covered in Lab 3.

# Lab Review

## command summary

| Button/Command | Shortcut | Action |
|---|---|---|
| **Office Button Menu** | | |
| Print/Print Preview | | Displays document as it will appear when printed |
| Word Options /Proofing | | Changes settings associated with Spelling and Grammar checking |
| Word Options /Advanced/Mark formatting inconsistencies | | Checks for formatting inconsistencies |
| **Home tab** | | |
| *Font group* | | |
| A˙ Grow Font | | Increases selected font size by increments |
| *Paragraph group* | | |
| Sort | | Rearranges items in a selection into ascending alphabetical/numerical order |
| *Styles group* | | |
| More | | Opens Quick Styles gallery |
| **Insert tab** | | |
| *Pages group* | | |
| Cover Page | | Inserts a preformatted cover page |
| Blank Page | | Inserts a blank page |
| *Tables group* | | |
| Table | | Inserts table at insertion point |
| *Header and Footer group* | | |
| Header | | Inserts predesigned header style |
| Footer | | Inserts predesigned footer style |
| **Page Layout tab** | | |
| *Themes group* | | |
| Themes | | Applies selected theme to document |
| | | Changes colors for current theme |
| A | | Changes fonts for current theme |

# command summary

| Button/Command | Shortcut | Action |
|---|---|---|
| **Page Setup group** | | |
| Breaks ▾ | | Inserts page and section breaks |
| **Arrange group** | | |
| Text Wrapping ▾ | | Controls how text wraps around a selected object |
| **References tab** | | |
| *Table of Contents group* | | |
| Table of Contents ▾ | | Generates a table of contents |
| Add Text ▾ | | Adds selected text as an entry in table of contents |
| Update Table | F9 | Updates the table of contents field |
| *Footnotes group* | | |
| Insert Footnote | Alt + Ctrl + F | Inserts footnote reference at insertion point |
| *Citations & Bibliography group* | | |
| Insert Citation ▾ | | Creates a citation for a reference source |
| Manage Sources | | Displays list of all sources cited |
| Style: MLA ▾ | | Sets the style of citations |
| Bibliography ▾ | | Creates a bibliography list of sources cited |
| *Captions group* | | |
| Insert Caption | | Adds a figure caption |
| Cross-reference | | Creates figure cross-references |
| **View tab** | | |
| *Document Views group* | | |
| Outline | | Changes to Outlining view |
| *Show/Hide group* | | |
| Document Map | | Displays or hides Document Map in navigation pane |
| Thumbnails | | Displays or hides thumbnails in navigation pane |

# Lab Review

## command summary

| Button/Command | Shortcut | Action |
|---|---|---|
| **Window group** | | |
| ▦ Split | | Divides a document into two horizontal sections |
| **Picture Tools Format tab** | | |
| *Arrange group* | | |
| ▦ Text Wrapping ▾ | | Specifies how text will wrap around picture |
| **Table Tools Design tab** | | |
| *Table Style Options group* | | |
| ☑ Header Row | | Turns on/off formats for header row |
| ☑ First Column | | Turns on/off formats for first column |
| ☐ Last Column | | Turns on/off formats for last column |
| *Table Styles group* | | |
| ▾ More | | Opens Table Styles gallery |
| **Table Tools Layout tab** | | |
| *Rows & Columns group* | | |
| ▦ Insert Above | | Inserts a new row in table above selected row |
| *Alignment group* | | |
| ▦ Align top center | | Aligns text at top center of cell space |
| **Header & Footer Tools Design tab** | | |
| *Header & Footer Group* | | |
| ▦ Page Number ▾ | | Inserts page number in header or footer |
| *Insert group* | | |
| ▦ Date & Time | | Inserts current date or time in header or footer |
| ▦ Quick Parts ▾ /Document Property | | Inserts selected document property into header or footer |
| ▦ Quick Parts ▾ /Field | | Inserts selected field Quick Part |

# command summary

| Button/Command | Shortcut | Action |
|---|---|---|
| **Navigation group** | | |
| Go to Footer | | Switches to footer area |
| Next Section | | Navigates to next section |
| Previous Section | | Navigates to previous section |
| Link to Previous | | Turns on/off link to header or footer in previous section |
| **Option group** | | |
| Different First Page | | Specify a unique header and footer for the first page |
| **Position group** | | |
| Insert Alignment Tab | | Inserts a tab stop to align content in header/footer |
| **Close group** | | |
| Close Header and Footer | | Closes header/footer area |
| **Outlining tab** | | |
| **Outline Tools group** | | |
| Promote to Heading 1 | | Promotes selected item to Heading 1 level |
| Promote | Alt + ⇧Shift + ← | Promotes selected item one level |
| Level 1 ▾ Outline Level | | Choose outline level for selected item |
| Demote | Alt + ⇧Shift + → | Demotes selected item one level |
| Demote to body text | | Demotes selected item to body text |
| Move Up | Alt + ⇧Shift + ↑ | Moves selected item up |
| Move Down | Alt + ⇧Shift + ↓ | Moves selected item down |
| Expand | Alt + ⇧Shift + + | Expand the selected item |
| Collapse | Alt + ⇧Shift + − | Collapse the selected item |
| Level 9 ▾ Show Level | | Choose levels to display in outline |
| ✓ Show Text Formatting | | Show the outline as formatted text |
| Show First Line Only | | Shows only the first line of each item |
| Close Outline View | | Closes Outline view and displays last used view |

# Lab Exercises

## matching

Match the item on the left with the correct description on the right.

1. citation _____    **a.** combination of fonts, type sizes, bold, and italics used to identify different topic levels in a document

2. heading style _____    **b.** inserts built-in pieces of information automatically

3. cross-reference _____    **c.** graphic positioned directly in the text

4. tight wrap _____    **d.** a predefined set of formatting choices

5. Document Map _____    **e.** letter and number used to identify table cells

6. section break _____    **f.** uses headings to navigate through the document

7. inline image _____    **g.** text closely follows contours around a graphic

8. Quick Parts _____    **h.** reference from one part of the document to another part

9. document theme _____    **i.** instructs Word to end one set of format settings and begin another

10. table reference _____    **j.** parenthetical source reference

## multiple choice

Circle the correct response to the questions below.

1. A _____ allows you to see two parts of the same document at the same time.
   - **a.** divided window
   - **b.** split window
   - **c.** sectioned window
   - **d.** note pane

2. _____ are lines of text at the top and bottom of a page outside the margin lines.
   - **a.** Characters and paragraphs
   - **b.** Headers and footers
   - **c.** Tables and text wrappers
   - **d.** Styles and sections

3. A(n) _____ displays information in horizontal rows and vertical columns.
   - **a.** Document Map
   - **b.** cell reference
   - **c.** object
   - **d.** table

4. A _____ is inserted automatically when a new page is created in a document.
   a. hard page break
   b. section break
   c. soft page break
   d. page division

5. _____ shows the hierarchy of topics in a document.
   a. Full Screen Reading view
   b. Outline view
   c. Print Layout view
   d. Multiple page view

6. You can control how text appears around a graphic with _____ styles.
   a. sorting
   b. text wrapping
   c. section
   d. caption

7. A(n) _____ is a predesigned set of formats that can be applied to an entire document.
   a. AutoFormat
   b. document theme
   c. style
   d. Quick Part

8. A _____ is a reference from one part of a document to related information in another part of the same document.
   a. citation
   b. caption
   c. heading
   d. cross-reference

9. _____ inserts items in a blank area of a document, avoiding the need to press ⏎Enter.
   a. Type and Point
   b. Click and Type
   c. Point and Type
   d. Type and Click

10. A _____ is a line of text that describes the object that appears above it.
    a. citation
    b. cross-reference
    c. caption
    d. footnote

## true/false

Circle the correct answer to the following questions.

| | | |
|---|---|---|
| 1. Character styles are a combination of any character formats and paragraph formats that affect all text in a paragraph. | True | False |
| 2. Word automatically applies styles to the text in an outline as it is entered. | True | False |

| | | | |
|---|---|---|---|
| 3. | Footnotes must be manually renumbered as you move text around in a document. | True | False |
| 4. | The navigation window displays the headings in your document. | True | False |
| 5. | A document theme is applied to selected characters and paragraphs. | True | False |
| 6. | A section break identifies the end of a section and stores the document format settings. | True | False |
| 7. | A table of contents hyperlink is used to jump directly to a specific location in a document. | True | False |
| 8. | A style is a combination of character formats. | True | False |
| 9. | A table of contents and a cross-reference are fields. | True | False |
| 10. | Thumbnails are small pictures of each page of a document. | True | False |

## fill-in

Complete the following statements by filling in the blanks with the correct terms.

1. A _____ identifies the content to be entered in a cover page.

2. A(n) _____ is a set of formats that is assigned a name and can be quickly applied to a document.

3. The _____ for a footnote appears at the bottom of the page on which the reference mark appears.

4. By changing a graphic to a(n) _____, it is inserted into the drawing layer.

5. The intersection of a row and a column creates a(n) _____.

6. A _____ is a small picture of each page of the document.

7. A(n) _____ is a line or several lines of text at the top of each page in a document.

8. A(n) _____ is used to organize information into horizontal rows and vertical columns.

9. Specifying _____ controls how text appears around a graphic object.

10. The _____ is used to move by headings or pages in a document.

# Hands-On Exercises

## Creating and Modifying an Outline ★

1. You are just starting work on a research report on Internet Spam. To help organize your thoughts, you decide to create an outline of the main topics to be included. Your completed outline will be similar to the one shown here.

   **a.** Open a new blank document. Switch to Outline view.

   **b.** The topics you want to discuss are shown below. Enter these topics at the outline level indicated, pressing [←Enter] at the end of each.

   **Why Am I Getting All This Spam? (Level 1)**

   **Summary (Level 2)**

   **Introduction (Level 2)**

   **Major Findings (Level 2)**

   **Methodology (Level 2)**

   **Experimental Anti-Spam Measures (Level 3)**

   **Removal from public accessibility (Level 4)**

   **Posting in "human-readable" form (Level 4)**

   **Posting in HTML-obscured form (Level 4)**

   **Posting in unreadable form (Level 4)**

   **Changing personal preferences on a Web site (Level 4)**

   **Tips for Avoiding Spam (Level 3)**

   **Disguise e-mail addresses (Level 4)**

   **Use multiple e-mail addresses (Level 4)**

   **Use long e-mail addresses (Level 4)**

   **Use a filter (Level 4)**

   **Results (Level 2)**

   **Addresses Posted on the Public Web (Level 3)**

   **Public Postings to USENET Newsgroups (Level 3)**

   **Consumer Preferences (Level 3)**

   **Web Discussions (Level 3)**

   **Domain Name Registration (Level 3)**

   **Conclusions (Level 2)**

   **Appendix 1 (Level 2)**

   **Appendix 2 (Level 2)**

   | Student Name | ~ 1 ~ | October 30, 2008 |
   |---|---|---|

   **Why am I getting all this Spam?**
   Summary
   Introduction
   **Major Findings**
   **Methodology**
   Tips for Avoiding Spam
   *Disguise e-mail addresses*
   *Use multiple e-mail addresses*
   *Use a filter*
   *Use long e-mail addresses*
   Experimental Anti-Spam Measures
   *Removal from public accessibility*
   *Posting in "human-readable" form*
   *Posting in HTML-obscured form*
   *Changing personal preferences on a Web site*
   Results
   Addresses posted on the Public Web
   Public Postings to USENET Newsgroups
   Consumer Preferences
   Web Discussions
   Domain Name Registration
   Mail Server Attacks
   **Conclusions**
   **Appendix 1**
   **Appendix 2**

   **c.** Correct any spelling errors.

   **d.** Move the "Experimental Anti-Spam Measures" topic and all subtopics to below the "Tips for Avoiding Spam" topic. In the "Tips for Avoiding Spam" topic, move "Use long e-mail addresses" to below "Use a filter."

**e.** Change the level of the "Conclusions", "Appendix 1", and "Appendix 2" topics to level 1.

**f.** Add a new level 3 topic, **Mail Server Attacks**, as the last subtopic under "Results."

**g.** Delete the "Posting in unreadable form" topic under "Experimental Anti-Spam Measures."

**h.** Switch to Print Layout view. Remove the space after paragraphs. Change the theme to Aspect.

**i.** Insert the Blank (Three Columns) built-in header. Use the Author quick part to add your name in the left placeholder. Insert the page number in the middle placeholder using the Current Position page number option and the Tildes design. Enter the current date in the right placeholder using the month xx, xxxx format.

**j.** Save the outline as Spam Outline in a new folder named Research.

**k.** Print the outline. Close the file.

## Creating a Table ★

**2.** You work for the Animal Rescue Foundation and are putting together a list of contact information. You would like to display the information in a table. Your completed document will be similar to the one shown here.

**a.** Open a new document and use Click and Type to enter the title **Animal Rescue Foundation** left-aligned at the top of the document on the first line and **Telephone Contacts** on the second line. Apply the Title style to the first line and the Subtitle style to the second line.

**b.** Enter the following introductory paragraph left-aligned below the title.

**This listing of direct-dial telephone numbers will make it easy for you to contact the ARS department you need. If you are unsure of your party's extension, please dial the main number, (555) 545-0900. You will be greeted by an automated attendant, which will provide you with several options for locating the party with whom you wish to speak.**

### Animal Rescue Foundation

*Telephone Contacts*

This listing of direct-dial telephone numbers will make it easy for you to contact the ARS department you need. If you are unsure of your party's extension, please dial the main number, (555) 545-0900. You will be greeted by an automated attendant, which will provide you with several options for locating the party with whom you wish to speak. *

| Department | Contact | Telephone Number |
|---|---|---|
| Behavior Helpline | Samantha Wilson | 555-545-8532 |
| Education Department | Jon Willey | 555-545-4722 |
| Job Hotline | Gavin Smith | 555-545-8533 |
| Membership & Giving | Mike Miller | 555-545-4332 |
| Pet Adoption | Wendy Jones | 555-545-0958 |
| Therapeutic Programs | Samantha Wilson | 555-545-8532 |
| Volunteer Services | James Thomas | 555-545-5873 |

_____

* If you need operator assistance, simply press "0" at any time.

**c.** Several lines below the paragraph, insert a simple table with 3 columns and 7 rows. Enter the following information into the table:

| | | |
|---|---|---|
| **Pet Adoption** | **Wendy Jones** | **555-545-0958** |
| **Behavior Helpline** | **Samantha Wilson** | **555-545-8532** |
| **Education Department** | **Jon Willey** | **555-545-4722** |
| **Therapeutic Programs** | **Samantha Wilson** | **555-545-8532** |

| | | |
|---|---|---|
| **Volunteer Services** | **James Thomas** | **555-545-5873** |
| **Job Hotline** | **Gavin Smith** | **555-545-8533** |
| **Membership & Giving** | **Mike Miller** | **555-545-4332** |

**d.** Insert a new row above the first entry and enter the following headings:

| | | |
|---|---|---|
| **Department** | **Contact** | **Telephone Number** |

**e.** Change the sort order of the table so that it is sorted by department in ascending order.

**f.** Select a document theme and then apply a table style of your choice to the table.

**g.** Reduce the size the table to just small enough to display the data in each row on a single line. Center the table.

**h.** Insert the footnote **If you need operator assistance, simply press "0" at any time.** using the * symbol instead of a number. Place the reference mark at the end of the introductory paragraph.

**i.** Add a footer to the document using the Motion design. Use the Author quick part to display your name left-aligned in the footer.

**j.** Save the document as ARS Department Contacts.

**k.** Print the document.

## Creating an Informational Sheet ★★

**3.** You are the manager of Elaina's Cameragraphics, a small camera repair and retail shop. You have fielded many different questions about digital cameras lately and have decided to compile these questions into an informational sheet. Your completed informational sheet will answer your customer's most frequently asked questions about digital technology to help them make an informed choice when buying a new camera. Your completed document will be similar to the one shown here.

**a.** Open the file wd03_Digital Cameras.

**b.** Apply the Title style to the main title.

**c.** Use the Document Map to locate the headings in the document and apply Level 1 headings to them.

**d.** Create a bulleted list in the Advantages of Digital Cameras section. Change the hanging indent to the 2.25 position and add a left tab at the 0.5 position. Use Format Painter to add bold and underlines to the beginning of each sentence, before the semicolon. Do the same for the Disadvantages of Digital Cameras section.

**e.** Select a document theme of your choice.

**f.** Use the following information to create a simple table below the paragraph on Pixels & Resolution.

| Number of Pixels | Print Size |
|---|---|
| Less than 1 megapixel | Good for e-mail |
| 1 megapixel | 4 × 6-inch prints |
| 2 megapixels | 5 × 7-inch prints |
| 3 megapixels | 8 × 10-inch prints |
| 4 megapixels | 11 × 14-inch prints |
| 5 megapixels | 16 × 20-inch prints |

**g.** Remove the space after paragraphs in the table. Apply a table style of your choice. Turn off the first column style effect. Center-align all the text in the table. Increase the font size of the column headings to 16 points. Size the table to the contents and center the table.

**h.** Insert the wd03_Camera image to the left side of the main title.

**i.** Insert the wd03_Computer image in front of the Storage & Software paragraph. Use the tight wrapping style and position the graphic to the left of the paragraph. Add the following caption below the graphic: **Figure 1: Manipulate images on a computer**.

**j.** Insert a hard page break above the Pixels & Resolution section.

**k.** Insert the Stacks style footer and enter the name of the store followed by the phone number **(555) 977-1650**.

**l.** Insert the Conservative style header. Replace the document title with your name using the Quick Parts feature. Enter the current date.

**m.** Make any adjustments to make the information sheet layout look like the one pictured.

**n.** Save the document as Digital Cameras. Print the document.

## Creating a Brochure ★ ★ ★

**4.** Your next project as marketing coordinator at Adventure Travel Tours is to create a brochure promoting three new adventures. You have already started working on the brochure and have added most of the text content. Because this brochure is for clients, you want it to be both factual and attractive. To do this, you plan to enhance the appearance of the document by adding some finishing formatting touches. Additionally, you want to include a table of contents on the second page of the document, several pictures, and a table of tour dates. Your completed brochure will be similar to that shown here.

**a.** Open the file wd03_ATT Brochure.

**b.** Create a cover page using the Pinstripes design. Enter the title **Three New Adventures** and subtitle **Kayaking the Blue Waters of Mexico, Hiking the Great Eastern Trail, Alaska Scenic Rail Tour**. Select the current date. Add your name as the Author and **Adventure Travel Tours** as the Company Name.

**c.** Create a custom document theme that includes custom colors and fonts for the brochure. Add a coordinating color to the title and subtitle on the cover page.

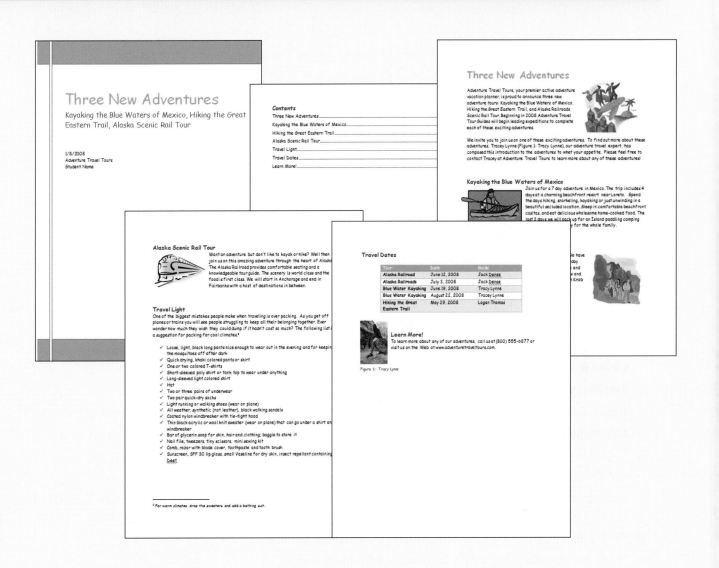

**d.** Create a custom heading style for the first topic heading line. Apply Heading 1 styles to the following five topic headings.

**e.** Insert a new page as page 2 and insert a Contents listing.

**f.** In this step, you will be inserting several graphics. For each of these, size the graphic appropriately. Wrap the text around the picture using a text wrapping style of your choice.

- Insert the graphic wd03_ATT to the right of the first paragraph.

- Insert the graphic wd03_Kayaking to the left of the first paragraph of the "Kayaking the Blue Waters of Mexico" section.

- Insert the graphic wd03_Hiking to the right of the first paragraph of the "Hiking the Great Eastern Trail" section.

- Insert the graphic wd03_Train to the left of the paragraph in the "Alaska Railroads Scenic Rail Tours" section.

- Insert wd03_Tracey to the left of the last paragraph in the last section of the report.

**g.** Add the caption **Tracy Lynne** below her photograph.

**h.** In the second paragraph of the "Three New Adventures" section, after the word "Lynne," add a cross-reference, with the figure number and caption, for the photo of Tracey. Use the split window feature to add the cross-reference.

**i.** Add a bullet style of your choice to the packing list items.

**j.** At the end of the first sentence in the section "Hiking the Great Eastern Trail," add the following text as a footnote: **The Appalachian Trail is 2,155 miles long.**

**k.** At the end of the first paragraph in the "Travel Light" section, add the following text as a footnote: **For warm climates drop the sweaters and add a bathing suit.**

**l.** Add a new section titled **Travel Dates** before the "Learn More!" section. Apply a Heading 1 style to the section heading. Insert a hard page break above this section.

**m.** Enter the following information in a table:

| Tour | Date | Guide |
|------|------|-------|
| Hiking the Great Eastern Trail | May 29, 2008 | Logan Thomas |
| Alaska Railroad | June 12, 2008 | Jack Denae |
| Blue Water Kayaking | June 19, 2008 | Tracey Lynne |
| Alaska Railroads | July 3, 2008 | Jack Denae |
| Blue Water Kayaking | August 22, 2008 | Tracey Lynne |

**n.** Size the table appropriately. Apply formatting of your choice to the new table. Sort the table in ascending sort order by tour. Center the table.

**o.** Change the heading for the Alaska railroad tour to **Alaska Scenic Rails Tour**. Insert a hard page break above this section.

**p.** Update the table of contents and adjust formatting as needed.

**q.** Add a header that includes a right-aligned page number.

**r.** Save the document as ATT Brochure. Print the report.

## Writing a Report ★★★

**5.** As a senior trainer at Lifestyle Fitness Club, you are responsible for researching new fitness trends and sharing your findings with other trainers and clients. You have written a Beginner's Guide to Yoga for this purpose. Pages two and three contain the body of your report. You still need to add several pictures, footnotes, and citations to the report. Your completed report will be similar to that shown here.

**a.** Open the file wd03_Yoga Guide.

**b.** Turn off the display of spelling and grammar errors.

**c.** Create a cover page using a design of your choice. Include the report title, **Beginner's Guide to Yoga** and your name as the author. Remove any other placeholders.

**d.** Apply a Heading 1 style to the five topic headings.

**e.** Create a table of contents on a separate page after the cover page.

**f.** Insert the graphic wd03_Yoga Pose to the right of the second paragraph in the "What is Yoga" section as shown in the example. Size the graphic appropriately and use the square text wrapping style. Include the figure caption **Yoga emphasizes breathing and meditation** below the graphic.

**g.** Insert the graphic wd03_History to the left of the first two paragraphs in the "History of Yoga" section as shown in the example. Size the graphic appropriately and use the square text wrapping style. Include the figure caption **Yoga's roots lie in ancient India** below the graphic.

**h.** Apply a document theme of your choice for the report.

**i.** In the "History of Yoga" section, move to the end of the second sentence in the first paragraph after the word "poses" and add the following text as a footnote:

**Ancient ceramics found in the caves of Mojendro-Daro and Harappa depict recognizable yoga positions.**

**j.** In the "Ashtanga (Power Yoga)" description, move to the end of the second sentence after the word "style" and add the following text as a footnote:

**Vinyasa is a flow or sequence of poses.**

**k.** Display the six types of yoga in alphabetical order.

**l.** Enter citations in the text at the locations specified below using the information in the following four reference sources:

| Location | Source |
|----------|--------|
| End of second sentence, first paragraph | Sparrowe |
| End of third paragraph | Wilber |
| Fifth paragraph, end of third sentence | Iyengar |
| End of second paragraph | Phillips |

| Type | Author | Title | Year | City | Publisher |
|------|--------|-------|------|------|-----------|
| Book | Linda Sparrow | Yoga | 2002 | New York | Hugh Lautner Levin Associates |
| Book | B. K. S. Iyengar | Yoga: The Path to Holistic Health | 2001 | Los Angeles | DK Publishing |
| Book | Kathy Phillips | The Spirit of Yoga | 2002 | Los Angeles | Barrons Educational Series |
| Book | Ken Wilber | The Yoga Tradition: History, Religion, Philosophy and Practice Unabridged | 2001 | Philadelphia | Hohm Printers |

**m.** At the end of the document, create a table of figures and a Works Cited bibliography. Add a title above the table of figures formatted using the Heading 1 style.

**n.** Update the table of contents and adjust any formatting as necessary.

**o.** Use the Alphabet footer design and use the document quick part to add the company name, **Lifestyle Fitness Club**. Do not display the footer on the cover page.

**p.** Redisplay spelling and grammar errors. Check the document for errors and fix any located errors appropriately.

**q.** Save the document as Yoga Guide in a new folder named Yoga. Print the report.

## on your own

### Designing a Flyer ★

1. The Sports Company is introducing a new line of kayaking and equipment. It is holding a weekend promotional event to familiarize the community with paddling equipment. You have already started designing a flyer to advertise the event, but it still needs additional work.

- Open the file wd03_Kayaking Flyer.

- Create the following table of data below the " . . . boat giveaway!" paragraph. Use an appropriate table style.

| TIME | EVENT |
|------|-------|
| 12:00 p.m. | Freestyle Whitewater Panel Discussion |
| 1:15 p.m. | Kids Canoe Relay Race |

| 1:30 p.m. | Becky Andersen & Brad Ludden Autographed Boats Charity Auction |
| 2:30 p.m. | Drawing for Extrasport Joust Personal Flotation Device |
| 3:00 p.m. | Team Dagger Autograph Session |
| 5:00 p.m. | Free BBQ dinner |

- Insert the picture wd03_Kayacking from your data files to the right of the text "Meet Team Dagger." Size and position the graphic appropriately.
- Add a caption below the image.
- Add formatting and styles of your choice to the document.
- Make any editing changes you feel are appropriate.
- Enter your name and the date centered in the footer.
- Save the document as Kayaking Flyer.
- Print the document.

## Creating a Report from an Outline ★★

2. You are working on the Downtown Internet Café Web site and want to include information about the characteristics of the different coffee beans. You have created an outline that includes the main characteristics of coffee beans, with examples of different beans that emphasize these characteristics. Expand on the outline by researching the topics in the outline on the Web. Include the following features in your report:

- Open the file wd03_Coffee Outline.
- Create a cover page and table of contents.
- Select a Document theme.
- The body of the report should include at least three footnotes and two cross-referenced images.
- Include three citations. Generate a bibliography of your sources.
- Add page numbers to the report, excluding the title page.
- Include your name, file name, and the date in the footer.
- Save the report as Coffee Report in a new folder. Preview and print the title page, the first page, and the works cited page.

## Preparing for a Job Search ★★

3. You are graduating next June and plan to begin your job search early. To prepare for getting a job, locate three sources of information on how to conduct a job search. Use your school's career services department, the library, newspapers, magazine articles, and the Web as possible sources. Begin by creating an outline of the topics you will include in the report. Using the outline, write a brief report about your findings. Include the following features in your report:

- A cover page that displays the report title, your name, and the current date.
- A table of contents page.
- The body of the paper should include at least two levels of headings.
- A minimum of three citations and three footnotes.
- A header that includes your name and page numbers on the top-right corner of every page (excluding the title page).
- At least one picture with a caption and cross-reference.

- A table that compares the jobs you are interested in and a table caption.
- A table of figures that has a formatted title that will appear in the table of contents.
- A bibliography of your reference sources. Format the bibliography appropriately.
- Include a page title and format it to appear in the table of contents.

Save the report as Job Search in a new folder. Print the document.

## Writing a Research Paper ★★★

4. Create a brief research report (or use a paper you have written in the past) on a topic of interest to you. The paper must include the following features:

- A cover page that displays the report title, your name, and the current date.
- A table of contents.
- At least two levels of headings and a minimum of three footnotes and three citations.
- At least one picture with a caption and cross-reference.
- A table of information with a caption.
- A table of figures.
- A bibliography page of your reference sources.
- A header and/or footer that displays the page numbers, file name, and date. Do not include this information on the cover page or table of contents page.

Save the document as Research in a new folder. Print the cover page, table of contents page, and the last page of the report.

## Researching Virus Hoaxes ★★★

5. There are a lot of real computer viruses that can wreak havoc with your computer. This makes virus hoaxes even more annoying, as they may lead some users to ignore all virus warning messages, leaving them vulnerable to a genuine, destructive virus.

Use the Web as a resource to learn more about virus hoaxes. Write a brief report defining virus hoaxes. Describe three hoaxes, how they are perpetuated, and the effect they could have if the receiver believes the hoax. The report must include the following features:

- A cover page that displays the report title, your name, and the current date.
- A table of contents.
- The body of the paper should include at least two levels of headings and a minimum of two footnotes and three citations.
- At least one picture with a caption and cross-reference.
- A table of information with a caption.
- A table of figures.
- A bibliography page of your reference sources.
- The page numbers, file name, and date in a header and/or footer. Do not include this information on the cover page or table of contents page.

Save the document as Computer Viruses. Print the document.

# Working Together 1: Word 2007 and Your Web Browser

## Case Study

## Adventure Travel Tours

The Adventure Travel Tours Web site is used to promote its products and broaden its audience of customers. In addition to the obvious marketing and sales potential, it provides an avenue for interaction between the company and the customer to improve customer service. The company also uses the Web site to provide articles of interest to customers. The articles, which include topics such as travel background information and descriptions, changes on a monthly basis as an added incentive for readers to return to the site.

You want to use the flyer you developed to promote the new tours and presentations on the Web site. To do this, you will use Word 2007's Web-editing features that help you create a Web page quickly and easily. While using the Web-editing features, you will be working with Word and with a Web browser application. This capability of all 2007 Microsoft Office applications to work together and with other applications makes it easy to share and exchange information between applications. Your completed Web pages are shown here.

**Note:** The Working Together tutorial is designed to show how two applications work together and to present a basic introduction to creating Web pages.

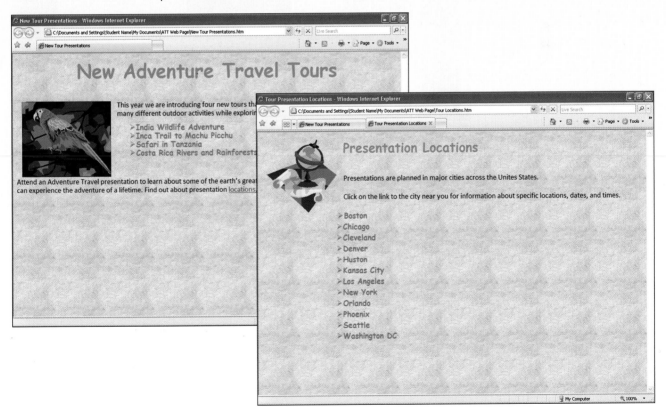

# Saving a Word Document as a Web Page

You want to create a Web page to be used on the company's Web site. A **Web page** is a document that can be used on the World Wide Web (WWW). The Web page you will create will provide information about the tour presentations. Word offers two ways to create or **author** Web pages. One way is to start with a blank Web page and enter text and graphics much as you would a normal document. Another is to quickly convert an existing Word document to a Web page.

Because the tour flyer has already been created as a Word document and contains much of the information you want to use on the Web page, you will convert it to a Web page document. You made a couple of changes to the flyer, giving it a title that is more appropriate for the Web page and removing the banner. You will use the modified version of the flyer as the basis for the Web page.

**1** • **Start Word 2007.**

• **Open the file**
wdwt_Presentations
**from the appropriate
location.**

*Your screen should be
similar to Figure 1*

Revised flyer

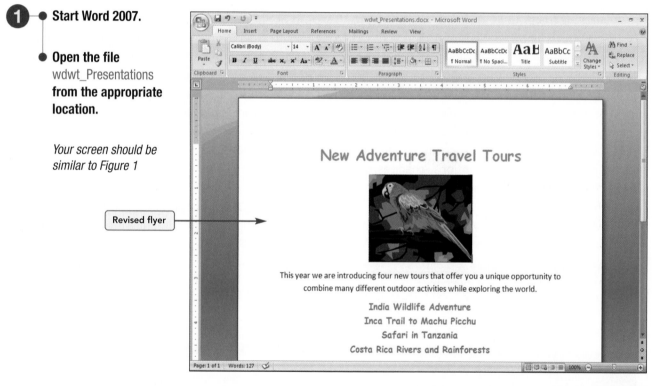

**Figure 1**

Word converts a document to a Web page by adding HTML coding to the document. **HTML (HyperText Markup Language)** is a programming language used to create Web pages. HTML commands control the display of information on a page, such as font colors and size, and the way an item will be processed. HTML also allows users to click on hyperlinks and

# Making Text Changes

Next, you want to change the layout of the Web page so that more information is displayed in the window when the page is viewed in the browser. To do this, you will delete any unnecessary text and change the paragraph alignment to left-aligned.

**1** ● Delete the last two paragraphs.

● Left-align all the text below the picture.

● Add bullets preceding the list of four tours.

● Increase the font size of the title to 36 points.

● Clear the highlight.

*Your screen should be similar to Figure 4*

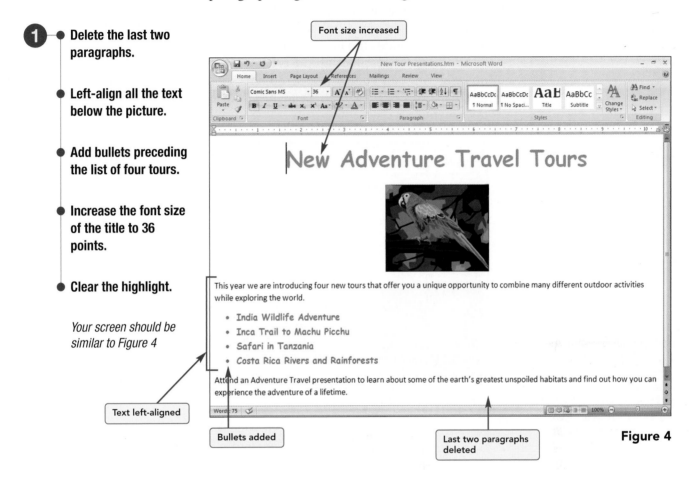

**Font size increased**

New Adventure Travel Tours

This year we are introducing four new tours that offer you a unique opportunity to combine many different outdoor activities while exploring the world.

- India Wildlife Adventure
- Inca Trail to Machu Picchu
- Safari in Tanzania
- Costa Rica Rivers and Rainforests

Attend an Adventure Travel presentation to learn about some of the earth's greatest unspoiled habitats and find out how you can experience the adventure of a lifetime.

**Text left-aligned**

**Bullets added**

**Last two paragraphs deleted**

**Figure 4**

Now, all the information is visible within the window.

# Changing the Picture Layout

**Additional Information**

When graphic files are added to a Web page, they are copied to the same folder location as the Web page. The graphic files must always reside in the same location as the HTML document file in which they are used.

Next, you want to move the picture to the left edge of the window and wrap the text to the right around it. Unlike a normal Word document, a Web page document does not have pictures and other graphic elements embedded in it. In an HTML file, each graphic object is stored as a separate file that is accessed and loaded by the browser when the page is loaded. Word creates a link to the object's file in the HTML file. The link is a **tag** that includes the location and file name of the graphic file.

Additionally, graphics are inserted into a Web page document as inline objects. You can change the wrapping style and move, size, and format graphic objects in a Web page just like embedded objects in a Word document.

**1** ● Click on the picture to select it.

● Drag the picture to the "T" in "This" at the beginning of the first paragraph.

● From the Picture Tools Format tab, click ⬚ Text Wrapping ▾ and select Square.

*Your screen should be similar to Figure 5*

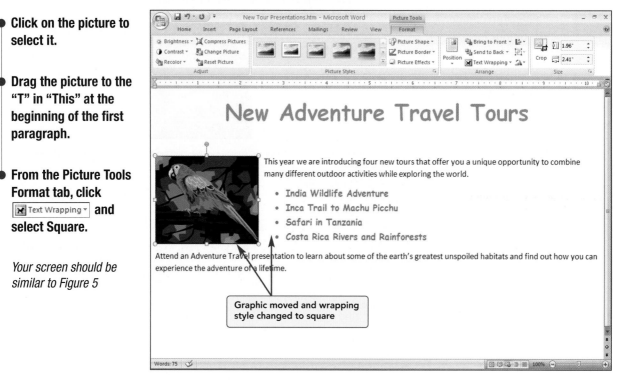

**Figure 5**

Next, you will make a few other adjustments to improve the appearance.

# Applying Page Color

Because color and design are important elements of Web pages, you can add a background color to the Web page. You think a light blue may look good.

**1**
- Deselect the graphic.
- Open the Page Layout tab.
- Click [Page Color ▾] in the Page Background group.
- Point to several different shades of blue to see how they look in Live Preview.

**Additional Information**

The gallery of colors associated with the default Office theme is displayed.

*Your screen should be similar to Figure 6*

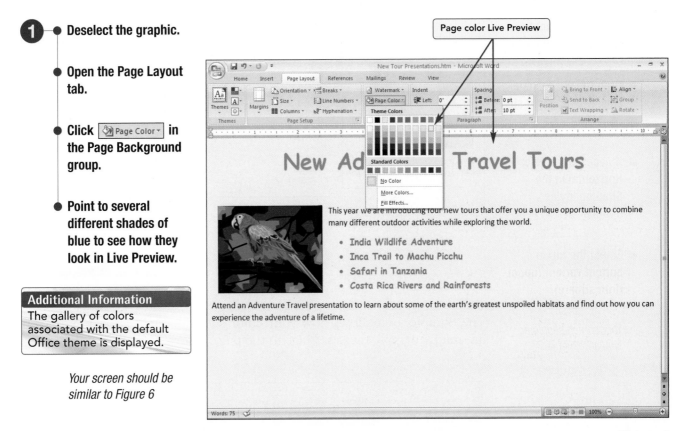

**Figure 6**

You do not really like how any of these colors look and decide to try a fill effect instead. Fill effects include gradient color, texture, patterns, or pictures. These effects should be used in moderation—you want them to enhance, not detract from, the content. You will try a blue gradient effect first.

**2** ● **Choose Fill Effects.**

● **Choose One color.**

● **From the Color1 drop-down list, select Blue, Accent 1, Lighter 40%**

● **Drag the shade slider closer to the Light side (see Figure 7).**

● **If necessary, select Horizontal in the Shading styles options.**

● **Select the top to bottom variant (upper-right square).**

*Your screen should be similar to Figure 7*

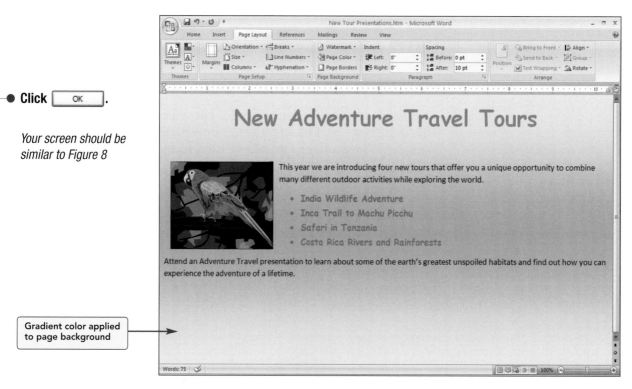

**Figure 7**

The Sample area shows how your color selections will appear. Now you are ready to apply these settings to the page.

**3** ● **Click** [ OK ].

*Your screen should be similar to Figure 8*

**Figure 8**

Although adding gradient color shading looks nice, you still are not satisfied. You will try a texture instead.

**4** ● Click 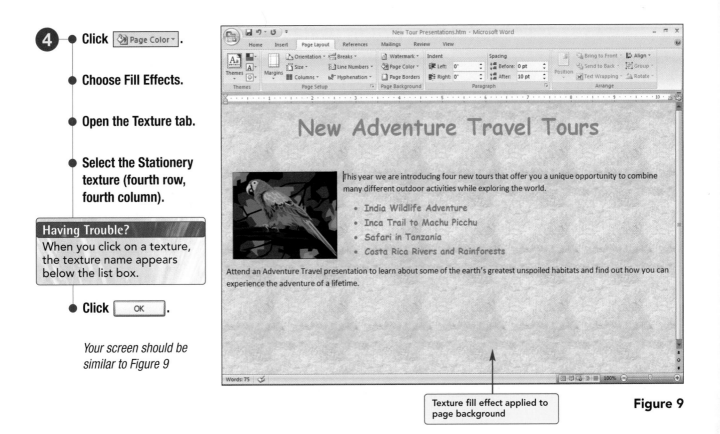 Page Color ▼ .

● Choose Fill Effects.

● Open the Texture tab.

● Select the Stationery texture (fourth row, fourth column).

**Having Trouble?**
When you click on a texture, the texture name appears below the list box.

● Click OK .

*Your screen should be similar to Figure 9*

Texture fill effect applied to page background

**Figure 9**

You like the more natural effect of this background.

# Changing Bullet Styles

The last enhancement you want to make is to change the bullet style.

**1** ● Select the four
bulleted items.

● Open the Home tab.

● Open the 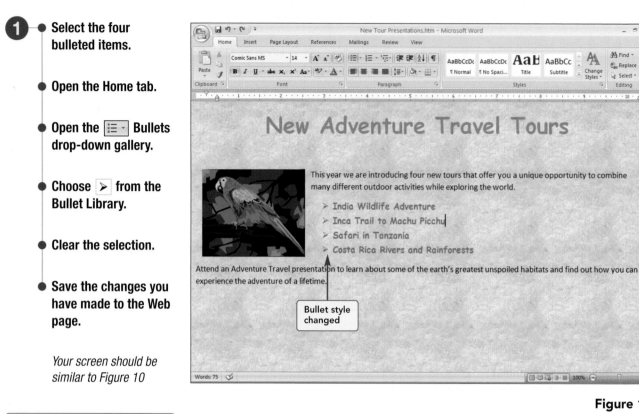 Bullets
drop-down gallery.

● Choose ➢ from the
Bullet Library.

● Clear the selection.

● Save the changes you
have made to the Web
page.

*Your screen should be
similar to Figure 10*

**Figure 10**

# Creating a Hyperlink

Next, you want to create another Web page that will contain a list of presentation locations. You will then add a hyperlink to this information from the New Tour Presentations page. As you have learned, a hyperlink provides a quick way to jump to other documents, objects, or Web pages. Hyperlinks are the real power of the WWW. You can jump to sites on your own system and network as well as to sites on the Internet and WWW.

The list of tour locations has already been entered as a Word document and saved as a file.

**1** ● Open the file
wdwt_Locations.

● Save the document as a Web page to the ATT Web Page folder with the file name Tour Locations and a page title of Tour Presentation Locations.

● Apply the same bullet style to this page.

● Apply the Stationery texture background page color.

● Save the page again.

*Your screen should be similar to Figure 11*

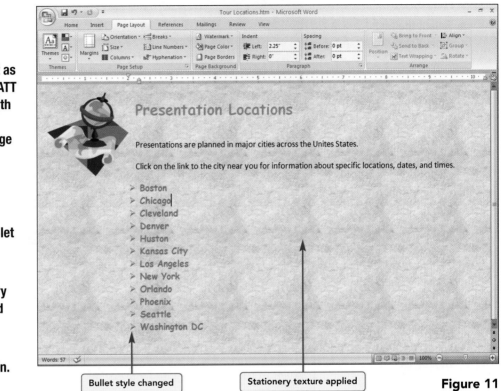

**Figure 11**

Now you are ready to create the hyperlink from the New Tour Presentations page to the Tour Locations page.

**2** ● **Switch to the New Tour Presentations window.**

● **Add the following text to the end of the last paragraph:** Find out about presentation locations, dates, and times.

● **Select the text "locations, dates, and times."**

● **Open the Insert tab.**

● **Select**  Hyperlink **from the Links group.**

*Your screen should be similar to Figure 12*

Create hyperlink

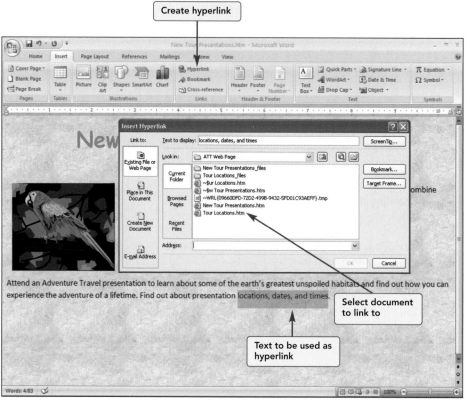

Select document to link to

Text to be used as hyperlink

**Figure 12**

From the Insert Hyperlink dialog box, you need to specify the name of the document you want the link to connect to.

**3** ● **Select** Tour Locations.htm **from the file list.**

● **Click** OK .

● **Save the document.**

*Your screen should be similar to Figure 13*

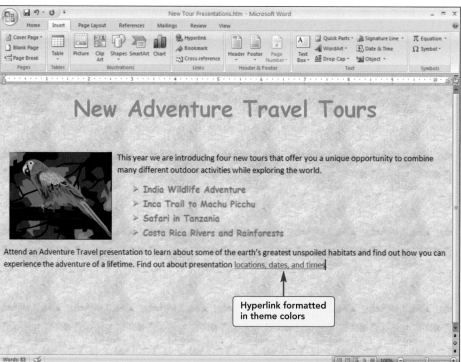

New Adventure Travel Tours

This year we are introducing four new tours that offer you a unique opportunity to combine many different outdoor activities while exploring the world.

➢ India Wildlife Adventure
➢ Inca Trail to Machu Picchu
➢ Safari in Tanzania
➢ Costa Rica Rivers and Rainforests

Attend an Adventure Travel presentation to learn about some of the earth's greatest unspoiled habitats and find out how you can experience the adventure of a lifetime. Find out about presentation locations, dates, and times.

Hyperlink formatted in theme colors

**Figure 13**

The selected text appears as a hyperlink in the design colors specified by the theme.

Next, you will use the hyperlink to display the Presentation Locations document.

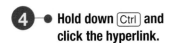

**4 Hold down Ctrl and click the hyperlink.**

*Your screen should be similar to Figure 14*

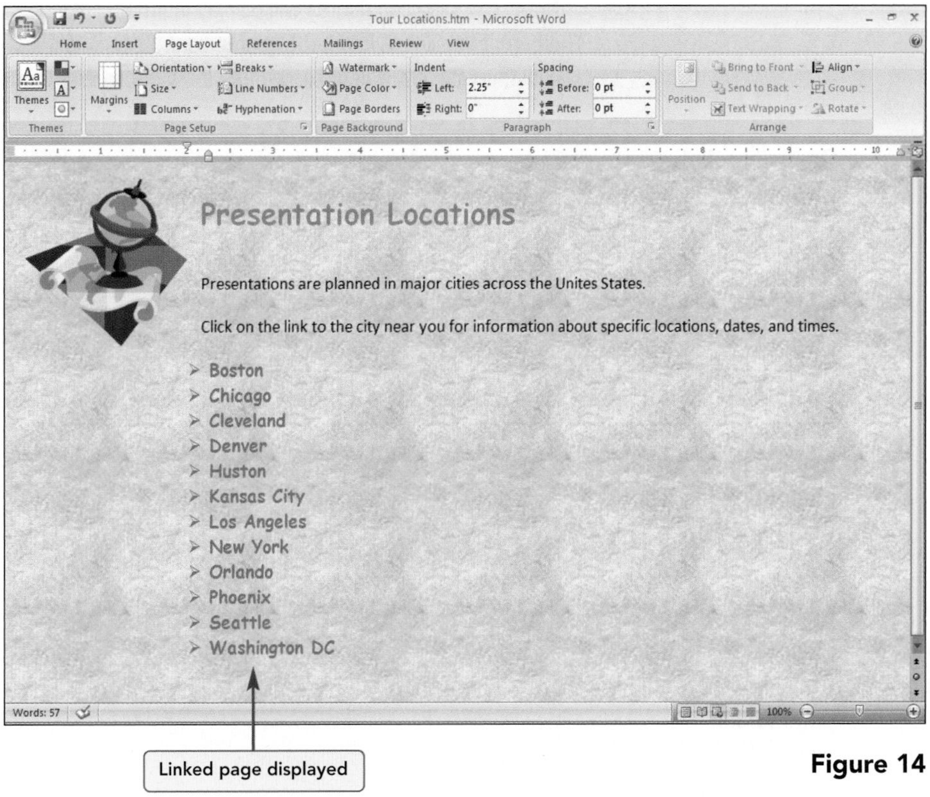

Tour Locations.htm - Microsoft Word
Home
Insert
Page Layout
References
Mailings
Review
View
Presentation Locations
Presentations are planned in major cities across the Unites States.
Click on the link to the city near you for information about specific locations, dates, and times.
Boston
Chicago
Cleveland
Denver
Huston
Kansas City
Los Angeles
New York
Orlando
Phoenix
Seattle
Washington DC
Words: 57
Linked page displayed


**Figure 14**

Because the Locations document is already open in a window, clicking the hyperlink simply switches to the open Word window and displays the page. You plan to add hyperlinks from each location to information about specific location dates and times at a later time.

# Previewing the Page

To see how your Web page will actually look when displayed by your browser, you can preview it.

**Note:** The following figures will display Internet Explorer 7, If you are using a different browser or a different version of Internet Explorer, your screens will look different. Additionally, you will need to substitute the equivalent procedures for your browser in the following steps.

**1** ● **Open your Web browser.**

● **If necessary, maximize the browser window.**

● **Open the Location drop-down menu and change to the location containing the ATT Web Page folder.**

● **Choose** New Tour Presentations.htm **from the ATT Web page folder.**

*Your screen should be similar to Figure 15*

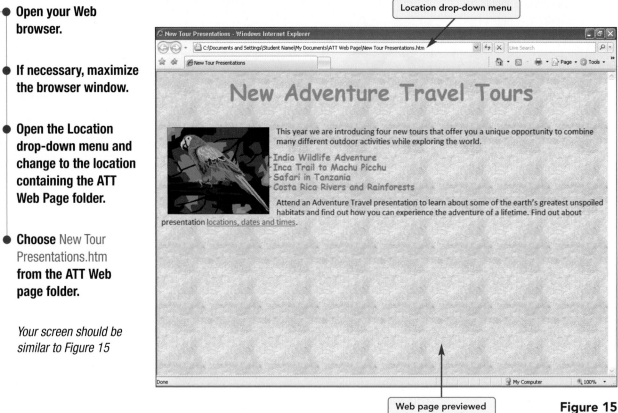

Figure 15

The Web page you created is displayed in the browser window. Sometimes the browser may display a page slightly differently from the way it appears in Web Page view. In this case, the bulleted list overlaps the picture and the last paragraph wraps to the side of the picture. To stop this from happening, you will insert a special text wrapping break that is used in Web pages to separate text around objects.

**2**

- Switch to the New Tour Presentation document in the Word 2007 application window.

- Select the bulleted list of tours and drag the left indent marker to the 3.25-inch position on the ruler.

- Move to the beginning of the last paragraph, before the word Attend.

- Click `Breaks ▾` in the Page Setup group of the Page Layout tab.

- Choose Text Wrapping.

- Save the document.

- Turn on the display of formatting marks.

*Your screen should be similar to Figure 16*

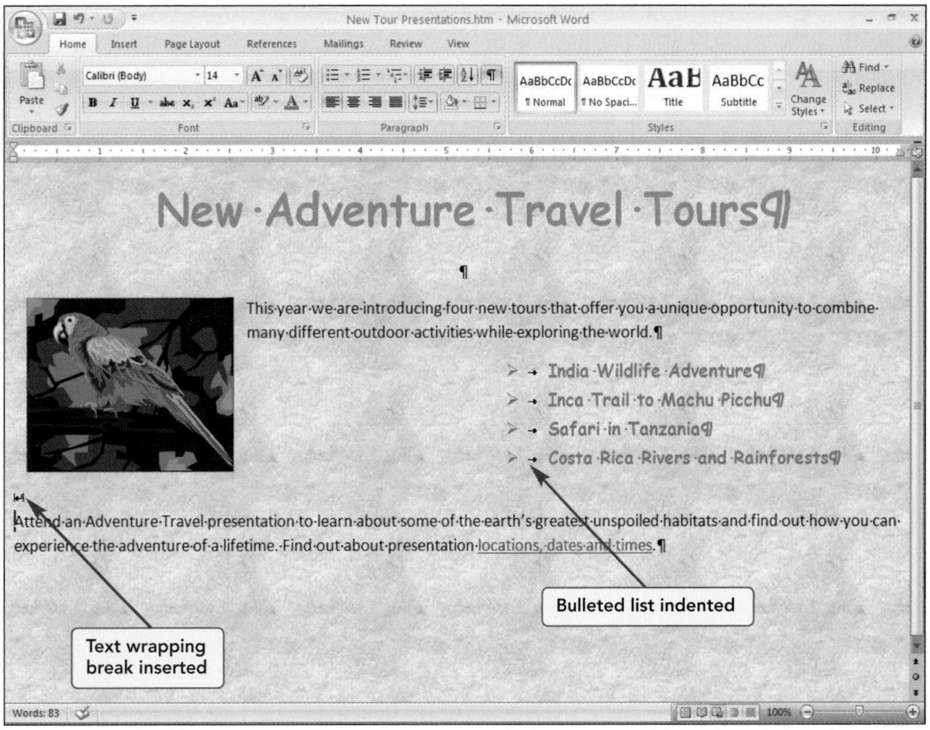

**Figure 16**

Although the bulleted list does not display as you want it in the Word document, the list wll indent appropriately when viewed in the browser. The text wrapping break that was inserted before the paragraph stopped the text following the break from wrapping around the object. The text wrapping break character |↵| is not visible unless you display formatting marks.

**3** ● Switch to the browser window and click the Refresh button to see the revised version of the Web page.

**Additional Information**
In Internet Explorer 7, the Refresh button is ↻.

*Your screen should be similar to Figure 17*

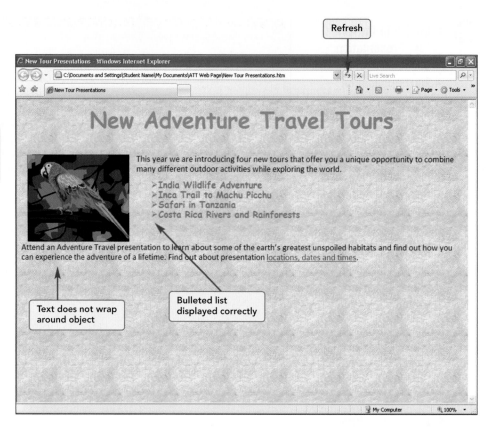

Refresh

Text does not wrap around object

Bulleted list displayed correctly

**Figure 17**

Inserting the text wrapping break stopped the text in the last paragraph from wrapping around the object. Next, you will use the hyperlink to open the Presentation Locations Web page in the browser.

**4** ● **Click on the hyperlink.**

● **If necessary, open the Tour Presentation Locations tab.**

*Your screen should be similar to Figure 18*

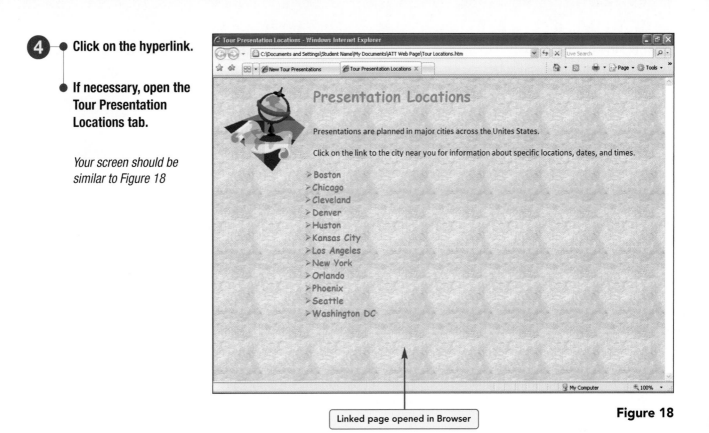

Linked page opened in Browser

**Figure 18**

This page looks fine and does not need any additional formatting.

**5** ● **Click ☒ in the title bar to exit the browser program.**

● **Close both documents and exit Word 2007.**

## Making a Web Page Public

Now that you have created Web pages, you need to make them available on the Internet for others to see them. The steps that you take to make your pages public depend on how you want to share them. There are two main avenues: on your local network or intranet for limited access by people within an organization or on the Internet for access by anyone using the WWW. To make pages available to other people on your network, save your Web pages and related files, such as pictures, to a network location. To make your Web pages available on the WWW, you need to install Web server software on your computer or to locate an Internet service provider that allocates space for Web pages.

# Lab Review

## key terms

| | | |
|---|---|---|
| **author** WDWT1.2 | **HTML (HyperText Markup Language)** WDWT1.2 | **tag** WDWT1.6 |
| **browser** WDWT1.3 | | **Web page** WDWT1.2 |

## MCAS skills

The Microsoft Certified Applications Specialist (MCAS) certification program is designed to measure your proficiency in performing basic tasks using the Office 2007 applications. Getting certified demonstrates that you have the skills and provides a valuable industry credential for employment. See Reference 2 MCAS Certification Guide for a complete list of the skills that were covered in this lab.

## command summary

| Command | Shortcut | Action |
|---|---|---|
| **Office Button** | | |
| Save/Save as Type/Web Page | | Saves file as a Web page document |
| **Insert tab** | | |
| *Links group* | | |
| Hyperlink | Ctrl + K | Inserts hyperlink |
| **Page Layout tab** | | |
| *Page Setup group* | | |
| Breaks ▾ /Text Wrapping | | Stops text from wrapping around objects in a Web page |
| *Page Background group* | | |
| Page Color ▾ | | Adds selected color to page background |
| Page Color ▾ /Fill Effects | | Adds selected color effect to page background |

# Lab Exercises

## step-by-step

### Adding a New Web Page ★

1. You want to continue working on the Web pages about the new tour presentations for the Adventure Travel Web site. Your next step is to create links from each location on the Presentation Locations Web page to information about each location's presentation date and times. Your completed Web page for the Los Angeles area should be similar to the one shown here.

   a. In Word, open the Web page file Tour Locations you created in this lab.

   b. Open the document wdwt_LosAngeles. Save the document as a Web page to the ATT Web Page folder with the file name LosAngeles and a page title of **Los Angeles Presentation Information**.

   c. Change the page color to a gradient fill effect of your choice. Change the first title line to the Title style and the second title line to a Heading 1 style. Change the title lines to a color of your choice.

   d. Increase the font size of the table to 12 points. Add color to the table headings. Enhance the Web page with any features you feel are appropriate.

   e. Two lines below the table, add the text **Contact [your name] at (909) 555-1212 for more information.** Apply the Emphasis style to this line and increase the font size to 14 points.

   f. On the Tour Locations page, create a link from the Los Angeles text to the Los Angeles page. Test the link.

   g. Resave both Web pages and preview them in your browser. Print the Los Angeles Web page.

   h. Exit the browser and Word.

## Converting a Flyer to a Web Page ★★

**2.** The Westbrook Parks and Recreation Department has asked you to modify the Celebrate Bikes article you created and convert it into a Web page to add to the Web site. Your completed Web page should be similar to the one shown here.

**a.** Open the file Bike Event you created in Step-by-Step Exercise 2 in Lab 1.

**b.** Convert the article to a Web page and save it as Celebrate Bicycling in a new folder. Include an appropriate page title.

**c.** Apply a page background color effect of your choice.

**d.** Change the text wrapping style of the graphic to square. Move the graphic to the left of the title. Left-align the title and increase the size of the title to 36 points. Size and position the graphic appropriately.

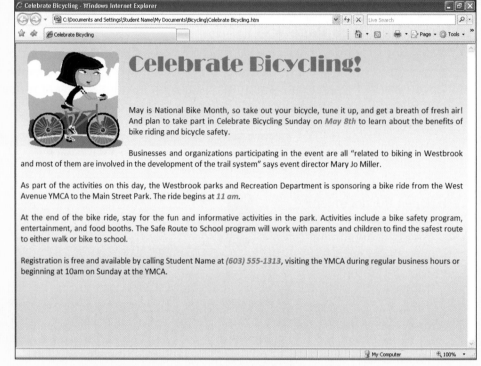

**e.** Delete your name and the date from the document. Add **[Your name] at** before the phone number in the last line.

**f.** Save the Web page. Preview the page in your browser. Adjust the layout as needed. Close your browser. Resave the Web page.

**g.** Print the Web page.

## Advertising on the Web ★★★

3. You would like to advertise the grand re-opening of the Internet Café on the Web. You plan to use the information in the advertisement flyer you created as the basis for the Web pages. Your completed Web pages should be similar to those shown here.

Grand Re-Opening Announcement - Windows Internet Explorer

C:\Documents and Settings\Student Name\My Documents\DownTown Internet Café\Cafe Flyer.htm

Live Search

Grand Re-Opening Announcement          Page ▾ Tools ▾

**Grand Re-Opening Celebration**

# Downtown Internet Café

Your Newly Remodeled Neighborhood Coffee Shop

Stop on by and enjoy an excellent dark Italian Roast coffee, premium loose teas, blended drinks and quality light fare of sandwiches, pitas and salads.

Starting Friday, September 1st and continuing all week through Sunday, September 10th we will take 15% off all cappuccino and blended drinks. Plus take $2.00 off any sandwich order.

So enjoy a drink and use our FREE WIFI to get online with the fastest connection in the neighborhood!

2314 Telegraph Avenue

Café Hours: Sunday – Thursday 8:00a.m. to 9:00p.m. Friday and Saturday 8:00a.m. to 12:00a.m.

Student Name-Date

Your Neighborhood - Windows Internet Explorer

C:\Documents and Settings\Student Name\My Documents\DownTown Internet Café\Cafe Locations.htm

Live Search

Your Neighborhood          Page ▾ Tools ▾

## Café Locations

❖ 251 N ILLINOIS ST # 223 INDIANAPOLIS, IN 46204-1927

❖ 4112 LINCOLN WAY E MISHAWAKA, IN 46544-4022

❖ 210 N GREEN RIVER RD EVANSVILLE, IN 47715-2405

❖ 1597 W GLEN PARK AVE GRIFFITH, IN 46319-3703

❖ 112 E MAIN ST MADISON, IN 47250-3459

❖ 65 N GRANT ST BLOOMINGTON, IN 47408-4026

Done          My Computer          100%

**a.** Open the file Grand Re-Opening you created in Step-by-Step Exercise 3 in Lab 1. Convert the document to a Web page, add a title of **Grand Re-Opening Announcement**, and save it as Café Flyer in a new folder.

**b.** Delete the graphic. Insert the image wdwt_Coffee. Change the picture text wrapping style to square. Move the picture to the left of the three title lines, as shown above, and size it appropriately. Left-align the three title lines.

**c.** Save the changes.

**d.** Open the file wdwt_Café Locations. Save the document as a Web page to your Web Page folder with the file name Café Locations and a page title of **Your Neighborhood**.

**e.** Create a link from the text **Your Newly Remodeled Neighborhood Coffee Shop** in the Café Flyer page to the Locations page. Test the link.

**f.** Enhance the pages with any features you feel are appropriate.

**g.** Resave the Web pages and preview them in your browser.

**h.** Print the pages.

# 2007 Word Brief Command Summary

| Command | Shortcut | Action |
|---|---|---|
| 🪟 **Office Button** | | **Opens File menu** |
| New | Ctrl + N | Opens new document |
| Open | Ctrl + O | Opens existing document file |
| Save | Ctrl + S, 💾 | Saves document using same file name |
| Save As | F12 | Saves document using a new file name, type, and/or location |
| Save as/Save As type/ Web Page | | Saves file as a Web page document |
| Print | Ctrl + P | Specify print settings before printing document |
| Print/Print Preview | | Displays document as it will appear when printed |
| Print/Quick Print | | Prints document using default printer settings |
| Prepare/Properties | | Opens Document Information Panel |
| Close | Ctrl + F4 | Closes document |
| Word Options/Proofing | | Changes settings associated with Spelling and Grammar checking |
| Word Options/Advanced/ Mark formatting inconsistencies | | Checks for formatting inconsistencies |
| ✕ Exit Word | Alt + F4, ✕ | Closes the Word application |
| **Quick Access Toolbar** | | |
| 💾 Save | | Saves document using same file name |
| ↺ Undo | Ctrl + Z | Restores last editing change |
| ↻ Redo | Ctrl + Y | Restores last Undo or repeats last command or action |
| **Home tab** | | |
| *Clipboard Group* | | |
| ✂ Cut | Ctrl + X | Cuts selection to Clipboard |
| 📋 Copy | Ctrl + C | Copies selection to Clipboard |
| 📋 Paste | Ctrl + V | Pastes item from Clipboard |
| 🖌 Format Painter | | Copies format to selection |

| Command | Shortcut | Action |
| --- | --- | --- |
| **Font Group** | | |
| Calibri (Body) Font | | Changes typeface |
| 11 Size | | Changes font size |
| A˄ Grow Font | | Increases font size |
| Clear Formatting | | Clears all formatting from selected text, leaving plain text |
| **B** Bold | Ctrl + B | Makes selected text bold |
| *I* Italic | Ctrl + I | Applies italic effect to selected text |
| U Underline | Ctrl + U | Adds underline below selected text |
| Aa˅ Change Case | | Changes case of selected text |
| Text Highlight Color | | Applies highlight color to selection |
| A˅ Font Color | | Changes selected text to selected color |
| **Paragraph group** | | |
| Bullets | | Creates a bulleted list |
| Numbering | | Creates a numbered list |
| Indents and Spacing | | Indents paragraph from left margin |
| Sort | | Rearranges items in a selection into ascending alphabetical/numerical order |
| ¶ Show/Hide | Ctrl + → + * | Displays or hides formatting marks |
| Align Text Left | Ctrl + L | Aligns text to left margin |
| Center | Ctrl + E | Centers text between left and right margins |
| Align Text Right | Ctrl + R | Aligns text to right margin |
| Justify | Ctrl + J | Aligns text equally between left and right margins |
| Line Spacing | Ctrl + # | Changes amount of white space between lines |
| **Styles Group** | | |
| More | | Opens Quick Styles gallery |
| **Editing Group** | | |
| Find ▾ | Ctrl + F | Locates specified text |
| Replace | Ctrl + H | Locates and replaces specified text |

## Insert tab

| Command | Shortcut | Action |
| --- | --- | --- |
| **Pages group** | | |
| Cover Page ▾ | | Inserts a preformatted cover page |
| Blank Page | | Inserts a blank page |
| Page Break | Ctrl + ↵Enter | Inserts a hard page break |
| **Tables group** | | |
| Table | | Inserts a table |

| Command | Shortcut | Action |
|---|---|---|
| **Illustrations group** | | |
| [Picture] | | Inserts a picture from file |
| [Clip Art] | | Inserts clip art, drawings, movies, sound |
| [Shapes] | | Inserts ready-made shapes |
| **Links group** | | |
| [Hyperlink] | Ctrl + K | Inserts hyperlink |
| **Header and Footer group** | | |
| [Header] | | Inserts predesigned header style |
| [Footer] | | Inserts predesigned footer style |
| [Page Number] | | Inserts page number in document |
| **Text group** | | |
| [Quick Parts] | | Inserts reusable pieces of content |
| [Date & Time] | | Inserts current date or time, maintained by computer system, in selected format |

## Page Layout tab

| Command | Shortcut | Action |
|---|---|---|
| **Themes group** | | |
| [Themes] | | Applies selected theme to document |
| [Colors] | | Changes colors for current theme |
| [Fonts] | | Changes fonts for current theme |
| **Page Setup group** | | |
| [Margins] | | Sets document or section margin sizes |
| [Breaks] | Ctrl + E | Inserts page and section breaks |
| [Breaks]/Text Wrapping | | Stops text from wrapping around objects on Web page |
| **Page Background group** | | |
| [Watermark] | | Inserts ghosted text behind page content |
| [Page Color] | | Adds selected color to page background |
| [Page Color]/Fill Effects | | Adds selected color effect to page background |
| [Page Borders] | | Adds a border around page |
| **Arrange group** | | |
| [Text Wrapping] | | Controls how text wraps around a selected object |

| Command | Shortcut | Action |
|---|---|---|
| **References tab** | | |
| *Table of Contents group* | | |
| Table of Contents ▾ | | Generates a table of contents |
| ⊟ Add Text ▾ | | Adds selected text as an entry in table of contents |
| ⊟ Update Table | F9 | Updates the table of contents field |
| *Footnotes group* | | |
| AB¹ Insert Footnote | Alt + Ctrl + F | Inserts footnote reference at insertion point |
| *Citations & Bibliography group* | | |
| Insert Citation ▾ | | Creates a citation for a reference source |
| Manage Sources | | Displays list of all sources cited |
| Style: MLA ▾ | | Sets the style of citation to use in document |
| Bibliography ▾ | | Creates a bibliography list of sources cited in document |
| *Captions group* | | |
| Insert Caption | | Adds a figure caption |
| Cross-reference | | Creates figure cross-references |
| **Review tab** | | |
| *Proofing group* | | |
| ABC Spelling & Grammar | F7 | Starts Spelling and Grammar Checker |
| Thesaurus | ⇧Shift + F7 | Starts Thesaurus tool |
| **View tab** | | |
| *Document Views group* | | |
| Print Layout | | Shows how text and objects will appear on printed page |
| Full Screen Reading | | Displays document only, without application features |
| Web Layout | | Shows document as it will appear when viewed in a Web browser |
| Outline | | Shows structure of document |
| Draft | | Shows text formatting and simple layout of page |
| *Show/Hide group* | | |
| ☑ Ruler | | Displays/hides horizontal ruler bar |
| ☐ Document Map | | Displays or hides Document Map window |
| ☐ Thumbnails | | Displays or hides Thumbnails window |

| Command | Shortcut | Action |
|---|---|---|
| *Zoom group* | | |
| Zoom | | Opens the Zoom dialog box |
| 100% | | Zooms document to 100% of normal size |
| One Page | | Zooms document so an entire page fits in window |
| Page Width | | Zooms document so width of page matches width of window |
| *Window group* | | |
| Arrange All | | Arranges all open windows horizontally on screen |
| Split | | Divides a document into two horizontal sections |
| View Side by Side | | Displays two document windows side by side to make it easy to compare content |
| Synchronous Scrolling | | Turns on/off synchronized scrolling |
| Switch Windows | | Switches between open document windows |

## Picture Tools Format tab

| | | |
|---|---|---|
| Text Wrapping | | Specifies how text will wrap around picture |

## Table Tools Design tab

| Command | Shortcut | Action |
|---|---|---|
| *Table Styles group* | | |
| More | | Opens gallery of predesigned table formats |
| *Table Style Options group* | | |
| Header Row | | Turns on/off formats for header row |
| First Column | | Turns on/off formats for first column |
| Last Column | | Turns on/off formats for last column |

## Table Tools Layout tab

| Command | Shortcut | Action |
|---|---|---|
| *Rows & Columns group* | | |
| Insert Above | | Inserts a new row in table above selected row |
| *Alignment group* | | |
| Align Top Center | | Aligns text at top center of cell space |

## Header & Footer Tools Design tab

| Command | Shortcut | Action |
|---|---|---|
| *Header & Footer Group* | | |
| Page Number | | Inserts page number in header, footer, or document |
| *Insert group* | | |
| Date & Time | | Inserts current date or time in header or footer |
| Quick Parts /Document Property | | Inserts selected document property |

| Command | Shortcut | Action |
|---|---|---|
| [Quick Parts] /Field | | Inserts selected Quick Part |
| **Navigation group** | | |
| [Go to Footer] | | Switches to footer area |
| [Previous Section] | | Navigates to previous section's header/footer |
| [Next Section] | | Navigates to next section's header/footer |
| [Link to Previous] | | Turns on/off link to header or footer in previous section |
| **Options group** | | |
| [ ] Different First Page | | Specify a unique header and footer for the first page |
| **Position group** | | |
| [ ] Insert Alignment Tab | | Inserts a tab stop to align content in header/footer |
| **Close group** | | |
| [Close Header and Footer] | | Closes header/footer area |

## Outlining tab

| Command | Shortcut | Action |
|---|---|---|
| **Outline Tools group** | | |
| Promote to Heading 1 | | Promotes selected item to Heading 1 level |
| Promote | Alt + ⇧Shift + ← | Promotes selected item one level |
| Level 1 ▾ Outline Level | | Choose outline level for selected item |
| Demote | Alt + ⇧Shift + → | Demotes selected item one level |
| Demote to body text | | Demotes selected item to body text |
| Move Up | Alt + ⇧Shift + ↑ | Moves selected item up in outline |
| Move Down | Alt + ⇧Shift + ↓ | Moves selected item down in outline |
| Expand | Alt + ⇧Shift + + | Expand selected item |
| Collapse | Alt + ⇧Shift + − | Collapse selected item |
| Level 9 ▾ Show Level | | Shows only specified outline levels |
| ☑ Show Text Formatting | | Show outline as formatted text |
| ☐ Show First Line Only | | Show only first line of each item |
| **Close group** | | |
| [Close Outline View] | | Closes outline view and displays last used view |

# Glossary of Key Terms

**active window**    The window containing the insertion point and that will be affected by any changes you make.

**alignment**    How text is positioned on a line between the margins or indents. There are four types of paragraph alignment: left, centered, right, and justified.

**antonym**    A word with the opposite meaning.

**author**    The process of creating a Web page.

**AutoCorrect**    A feature that makes basic assumptions about the text you are typing and automatically corrects the entry.

**bibliography**    A listing of source references that appears at the end of the document.

**browser**    A program that connects you to remote computers and displays the Web pages you request.

**building blocks**    Document fragments that include text and formatting and that can be easily inserted into a document.

**bulleted list**    Displays items that logically fall out from a paragraph into a list, with items preceded by bullets.

**caption**    A title or explanation for a table, picture, or graph.

**case sensitive**    The capability to distinguish between uppercase and lowercase characters.

**cell**    The intersection of a column and row where data are entered in a table.

**character formatting**    Formatting features such as bold and color that affect the selected characters only.

**citations**    Parenthetical source references that give credit for specific information included in a document.

**Click and Type**    A feature available in Print Layout and Web Layout views that is used to quickly insert text, graphics, and other items in a blank area of a document, avoiding the need to enter blank lines.

**clip art**    Professionally drawn graphics.

**control**    A graphic element that is a container for information or objects.

**cross-reference**    A reference in one part of a document related to information in another part.

**cursor**    The blinking vertical bar that shows you where the next character you type will appear. Also called the insertion point.

**custom dictionary**    A dictionary of terms you have entered that are not in the main dictionary of the spelling checker.

**default**    The initial Word document settings that can be changed to customize documents.

**destination**    The location to which text is moved or copied.

**Document Map**    A feature that displays the headings in the document in the navigation window.

**document properties**    Details about a document that describe or identify it and are saved with the document content.

**document theme**    A predefined set of formatting choices that can be applied to an entire document in one simple step.

**document window**    The area of the application window that displays the contents of the open document.

**drag and drop**    A mouse procedure that moves or copies a selection to a new location.

**drawing layer**    The layer above or below the text layer where floating objects are inserted.

**drawing object**    A simple object consisting of shapes such as lines and boxes.

**edit**    The process of changing and correcting existing text in a document.

**embedded object** An object such as a picture graphic that becomes part of the Word document and that can be opened and edited using the program in which it was created.

**end-of-file marker** The horizontal line that marks the end of a file.

**endnote** A reference note displayed at the end of the document.

**field** A placeholder that instructs Word to insert information in a document.

**field code** The code containing the instructions about the type of information to insert in a field.

**field result** The results displayed in a field according to the instructions in the field code.

**floating object** A graphic object that is inserted into the drawing layer and can be positioned anywhere on the page.

**font** A set of characters with a specific design. Also called a typeface.

**font size** The height and width of a character, commonly measured in points.

**footer** The line or several lines of text at the bottom of every page just below the bottom margin line.

**footnote** A reference note displayed at the bottom of the page on which the reference occurs.

**format** To enhance the appearance of the document to make it more readable or attractive.

**Format Painter** The feature that applies formats associated with the current selection to new selections.

**gradient** A gradual progression of colors and shades, usually from one color to another, or from one shade to another of the same color.

**grammar checker** The feature that advises you of incorrect grammar as you create and edit a document, and proposes possible corrections.

**graphic** A nontext element in a document.

**hard page break** A manually inserted page break that instructs Word to begin a new page regardless of the amount of text on the previous page.

**header** The line or several lines of text at the top of each page just above the top margin line.

**heading style** A style that is designed to identify different levels of headings in a document.

**HTML (HyperText Markup Language)** The programming language used to create Web pages.

**hyperlink** A connection to locations in the current document, other documents, or Web pages. Clicking a hyperlink jumps to the specified location.

**indent** To set in a paragraph from the margins. There are four types of indents: left, right, first line, and hanging.

**inline object** An object that is inserted directly in the text at the position of the insertion point, becoming part of the paragraph.

**Insert mode** Method of text entry in which new characters are inserted into existing text, which moves to the right to make space for the new characters; the text on the line is reformatted as necessary.

**insertion point** The blinking vertical bar that shows you where the next character you type will appear on the line. Also called the cursor.

**leader characters** Solid, dotted, or dashed lines that fill the blank space between tab stops.

**line spacing** The vertical space between lines of text.

**Live Preview** A feature that allows you to preview in your document the results of applying formatting changes as you select different format options.

**main dictionary** The dictionary of terms that comes with Word 2007.

**navigation window** A separate window that displays the Document Map and thumbnails.

**note pane** Lower portion of the window that displays footnotes.

**note reference mark** A superscript number or character appearing in the document at the end of the material being referenced.

**note separator** The horizontal line separating footnote text from the main document text.

**note text** The text in a footnote.

**numbered list** Displays items that convey a sequence of events in a particular order, with items preceded by numbers or letters.

**object** An item that can be sized, moved, and manipulated.

**Office Clipboard** A temporary Windows storage area in memory.

**outline numbered list** Displays items in multiple outline levels that show a hierarchical structure of the items in the list.

**page break** Marks the point at which one page ends and another begins.

**page margin**   The blank space around the edge of the page.

**paragraph formatting**   Formatting features such as alignment, indentation, and line spacing that affect an entire paragraph.

**picture**   An illustration such as a scanned photograph.

**placeholder**   A graphic element that is designed to contain specific types of information.

**quick styles**   A gallery of predefined sets of formatting characteristics that allows you to quickly apply a whole group of formats in one simple step to a selection.

**ruler**   The ruler located below the Formatting toolbar that shows the line length in inches.

**sans serif font**   A font such as Arial or Helvetica that does not have a flair at the base of each letter.

**section**   A division into which a document can be divided that can be formatted separately from the rest of the document.

**section break**   Marks the point at which one section ends and another begins.

**selection rectangle**   The rectangular outline around an object that indicates it is selected.

**serif font**   A font such as Times New Roman that has a flair at the base of each letter.

**sizing handles**   Black squares around a selected object that can be used to size the object.

**soft page break**   A page break automatically inserted by Word to start a new page when the previous page has been filled with text or graphics.

**soft space**   A space between words automatically entered by Word to justify text on a line.

**sort**   To arrange alphabetically or numerically in ascending or descending order.

**source**   The location from which text is moved or copied.

**source program**   The program in which an object was created.

**spelling checker**   The feature that advises you of misspelled words as you create and edit a document, and proposes possible corrections.

**split window**   A division of the document window into two horizontal sections making it easier to view different parts of a document.

**synchronized**   Documents in multiple open windows that move together when you scroll the window.

**synonym**   A word with a similar meaning.

**system Clipboard**   Where a selection that has been cut or copied is stored.

**tab stop**   A marked location on the horizontal ruler that indicates how far to indent text when the [Tab⇆] key is pressed.

**table**   Displays information in horizontal rows and vertical columns.

**table of contents**   A listing of topic headings and associated page numbers in a document.

**table of figures**   A listing of figures and associated page numbers in a document.

**table reference**   The letter and number (for example, A1) that identify a cell in a table.

**tag**   Embedded codes that supply information about a Web page's structure, appearance, and contents.

**template**   A document that includes predefined settings and content that is used as the basis for a new document.

**text box**   A container for text and other graphic objects.

**text wrapping**   Controls how text appears around a graphic.

**thesaurus**   Word feature that provides synonyms and antonyms for words.

**thumbnail**   A miniature representation of a picture or object.

**TrueType**   A font that is automatically installed when you install Windows.

**typeface**   A set of characters with a specific design. Also called a font.

**URL**   The address that indicates the location of a document on the World Wide Web. URL stands for Uniform Resource Locator.

**watermark**   Text or pictures that appear behind document text.

**Web page**   A document that can be used on the World Wide Web and viewed in a browser.

**word wrap**   A feature that automatically determines where to end a line and wrap text to the next line based on the margin settings.

# Appendix

## 1. CREATING AND CUSTOMIZING DOCUMENTS

### 1.1 CREATE AND FORMAT DOCUMENTS

**SET THEMES AS DEFAULT**

Whenever you start Microsoft Office Word 2007, the Normal.dotm template opens. It includes default settings such as margins, page size, and theme that determine the basic look of a document. You can change the settings in the Normal.dotm template so that whenever a new document is opened, the settings you specified are used in all new documents you create. To change the default theme from the Office theme to another, follow these steps:

- Click 🔘 Office Button.
- Choose Open.

Do one of the following:
In Microsoft Windows Vista:

- Choose Templates, and then double-click the Normal.dotm file to open it.

In Microsoft Windows XP or Microsoft Windows Server 2003:

- Click Templates next to File name.
- Double-click Normal.dotm to open it.

The default document template file is opened and Normal.dotm appears in the Word title bar. This file can be modified like any other file. Next, to change the theme associated with the default document template,

- Open the Page Layout tab.
- Click [Themes] and select a built-in theme of your choice or create your own custom theme.

If you wanted, you also could make changes to the fonts, margins, spacing, and other settings. Once you are done and the file contains the settings you want the Normal.dotm to include, you save the changes you have made to the template.

- Click 🔘 Office Button and choose Save.
- Save the document as Normal.dotm to replace the contents of the template file with the new settings you specified.

Next time you open a new blank document, the new settings you specified will be the default document settings.

**RESTORE TEMPLATE THEMES**

Many times after applying a different theme or customizing a theme, you may decide you want to restore the default document theme. Use the following steps to restore the theme associated with the template you are using:

- Open the Page Layout tab.
- Click [Themes] and choose Reset to Theme from Template in the Themes menu.

The theme associated with the template file you are using is reapplied to the entire document.

> **Having Trouble?**
>
> If no templates are listed in the Open dialog box, open the Files of type list box, and then choose All Word Templates.

## CHANGE THEME COLORS

Each theme has a color scheme that consists of a set of 12 theme colors that are applied to different elements of the theme. To customize a theme, you can apply a different built-in color scheme to your selected theme or customize the theme's color scheme by changing the colors associated with the different elements. The new color scheme can then be saved as a Custom Theme Color and can then be quickly applied to other themes. Follow these steps to change theme colors:

- Open the Page Layout tab.
- Click [Aa Themes] and choose a theme of your choice.
- Click [▪▾] Theme Colors.
- Choose Create New Theme Colors.

The Theme Colors dialog box identifies the colors associated with the different elements. The Sample box shows where the selected colors are used in a document. Theme colors contain four text and background colors, six accent colors, and two hyperlink colors.

- Click the button of the theme color element that you want to change.
- Choose the color that you want to use.
- In the same manner, select and change colors for all of the theme color elements that you want to change.

The Sample box reflects the new colors you selected so you can see the effect of the changes that you make. Once you are satisfied with your selections, you save the color scheme.

- In the Name text box, type a name that will identify the color scheme.
- Click [ Save ].

**Additional Information**

To return all theme color elements to their original theme colors, you can click Reset before you click Save.

The custom theme color name appears at the top of the Theme Colors menu so you can quickly select and apply it to other themes.

## CHANGE THEME EFFECTS

Each theme includes a set of lines and fill effects. Although you cannot create your own set of theme effects, you can apply a different built-in theme effect from another theme to your own document theme. To do this, follow these steps:

- Open the Page Layout tab.
- Click [◯▾] Theme Effects in the Themes group.

The lines and fill effects that are used for each set of theme effects appear in the graphic that is displayed next to the theme effects name.

- Select the effect that you want to use.

The effects for the current theme have been changed to the selected theme effects.

## 1.2 LAY OUT DOCUMENTS

### ADD PAGE NUMBERS

In addition to adding page numbers in headers and footers, you can insert page numbers within the text of the document. To do this, follow these steps:

- Move to the location in the text where you want the number to appear.
- Click Quick Parts ▾ in the Text group of the Insert tab.
- Choose Field.
- Choose the Numbering category.
- Select Page from the field list.
- Select a format of your choice.
- Click OK.

The number of the current page is inserted in the document at the location of the insertion point. It is a field that can be updated if the page number changes.

## 1.3 MAKE DOCUMENTS AND CONTENT EASIER TO FIND

### ADD TEXT TO TABLE OF CONTENTS

You also can add static text (not a field) to a table of contents. For example, in the table of contents you created in Lab 3, you might want to add the continents above each country. To insert text in a table of contents, follow these steps:

- Click in the table of contents to select it.
- Move the insertion point to the location where you want to enter text.
- If you want the text on a new line, press ⏎Enter to insert a new line.
- Type the text you want to include.

Because the text you entered is static, if you regenerate the table of contents list, the text is lost and would need to be entered again. If you simply update the page numbers of the table of contents, the text remains.

### MARK AN ENTRY FOR INDEXING

An index is a list of the terms and topics that are discussed in a document, along with the pages that they appear on. An index generally appears at the end of the document and makes it easy for readers to locate information in the document.

To create an index, you first mark the index entries by providing the name of the main entry and the cross-reference in your document. Then you select an index design and build the index.

To identify the text you want to appear in the index, you select the text and mark it as an index entry. Word then adds a special XE (Index Entry) field that includes the marked main entry and any cross-reference information that you choose to include.

You can create an index entry for an individual word, phrase, or symbol; a selection; or a cross-reference that refers to another entry.

To mark existing words or phrases as index entries:

- Select the text.
- Click Mark Entry in the Index group of the References tab.
- Click Mark.

To enter your own text as an index entry:

- Click where you want to insert the index entry.
- Click [Mark Entry] in the Index group of the References tab.
- Type or edit the text in the Main entry box.
- Click [Mark].

To mark entries that span a range of pages:

- Select the range of text that you want the index entry to refer to.
- Click [Bookmark] in the Links group of the Insert tab.
- In the Bookmark name box, type a name and then click [Add].
- In the document, click at the end of the text that you marked with a bookmark.
- Click [Mark Entry] in the Index group of the References tab.
- In the Main entry box, type the index entry for the marked text.
- Under Options, choose Page range.
- In the Bookmark box, type or select the bookmark name that you typed.
- Click [Mark].
- Click [Close] to end marking entries.

If you want, you can customize the entry by creating a subentry, a third-level entry, or a cross-reference to another entry. You also can format the page numbers that will appear in the index using bold or italic.

### CREATE THE INDEX

After you mark all the index entries, you choose an index design and build the finished index. Word collects the index entries, sorts them alphabetically, references their page numbers, finds and removes duplicate entries from the same page, and displays the index in the document.

- Click where you want to add the index.
- Click [Insert Index] in the Index group of the References tab.
- Select a design in the Formats box or click [Modify...] to design a custom index layout by modifying a built-in design.
- Select any other index options that you want, such a number of columns and page number alignment.
- Click [OK] to complete the command.

### MODIFY AND UPDATE THE INDEX

An index, like a table of contents, is a field that can easily be updated if you add, edit, format, or delete index entries after the index is generated.

To edit or format an existing index entry:

- Locate and click on the index entry in the text (each index entry is enclosed in a special XE (Index Entry) field).
- Change the text inside the quotation marks or apply formatting.

To delete an index entry

- Select the entire index entry field, including the braces ({}), and then press [Delete].

After modifying the index entries, you update the index.

- Click the index and press F9 or click [Update Index] in the Index group on the References tab.

The index is updated using the same index design settings. If you want to both change the design and update the index, you can regenerate the entire index again.

- Click the index and click [Insert Index] in the Index group of the References tab.
- Select a design in the Formats box or click [Modify...] to design a custom index layout by modifying a built-in design.
- Select any other index options that you want, such as number of columns and page number alignment.
- Click [OK] twice to complete the command and replace the existing index.

## 1.4 PERSONALIZE OFFICE WORD 2007

### CUSTOMIZE AUTOCORRECT OPTIONS

Word includes many default program settings that you can change to personalize how Word works for you. The AutoCorrect settings make corrections to text automatically as you type. To change these settings:

- Click [Office Button] Office Button and click [Word Options].
- Choose the Proofing group.
- Click [AutoCorrect Options...].
- On the AutoCorrect tab, select or clear any of the following check boxes:
  Correct TWo INitial CApitals
  Capitalize first letter of sentences
  Capitalize first letter of table cells
  Capitalize names of days
  Correct accidental use of cAPS LOCK key
  Replace text as you type
  Automatically use suggestions from the spelling checker
- Click [OK].

The changes you make to the AutoCorrect settings will remain in effect until you change them again.

### CUSTOMIZE THE QUICK ACCESS TOOLBAR

The Quick Access Toolbar includes three buttons initially: Save, Undo, and Redo. You can customize the Quick Access Toolbar to personalize it for your own use by adding and removing any commands that you want. The first method you can use to do this is to select the commands from a list.

- Click [Office Button] Office Button and click [Word Options].
- Open the Customize group.
- Open the Choose commands from drop-down list and choose the command category that you want.
- In the list of commands in the selected category, click the command that you want to add to the Quick Access Toolbar and then click [Add >>].
- Alternatively, to remove commands from the Quick Access Toolbar, select the command that you want to remove from the Quick Access Toolbar list and click [Remove].
- After you finish adding/removing any commands that you want, click [OK].

You also can add a command to the Quick Access Toolbar directly from commands that are displayed on the Ribbon. Only commands can be added to the Quick Access Toolbar. The contents of most lists, such as indent and spacing values and individual styles, which also appear on the Ribbon, cannot be added to the Quick Access Toolbar.

- On the Ribbon, click the appropriate tab or group to display the command that you want to add to the Quick Access Toolbar.
- Right-click the command and then choose Add to Quick Access Toolbar from the shortcut menu.

### SET THE DEFAULT SAVE LOCATION

Word includes many default program settings that you can change to personalize how Word works for you. Among these settings are the default document format (.docx), the time interval to perform automatic backup for recovery, and locations to save files and recovered files. The default location to save a file is in the current user's My Document folder. To change the default location to save a file:

- Click Office Button and click Word Options.
- Open the Save group.
- Click Browse... next to the Default Save Location text box.
- Find the location where you want your files saved and click OK.
- Click OK to complete the change.

### PERSONALIZE USER NAME AND INITIALS

Word includes many default program settings that you can change to personalize how Word works for you. You can personalize your copy by adding your user name and initials to the program settings so that this information is automatically recorded in a file's document properties.

- Click Office Button and click Word Options.
- Open the Popular group.
- Enter your name in the User Name text box.
- Enter your initials in the Initials text box.
- Click OK to complete the change.

## 2. FORMATTING CONTENT

### 2.1 FORMAT TEXT AND PARAGRAPHS

### CHANGE ALL TEXT FORMATTED WITH ONE STYLE TO ANOTHER STYLE

Sometimes, you may have applied a Quick Style such as a heading to many areas in a document and then you decide to change the style to another for all those entries. To quickly change all text that is formatted in one style to another throughout the document, follow these steps:

- Select the text that is formatted using the Quick Style you want to change.
- Right-click on the selection and choose Styles/Select text with similar formatting.
- Choose another Quick Style.

All text that is formatted in the original quick style is updated to the newly selected style.

## SECTION BREAKS

Section breaks, like hard page breaks, can easily be removed. When deleting section breaks, however, all formatting that was associated with that section before the break is removed and the text assumes the formatting of the following section.

- Switch to Draft view or display paragraph marks in Print Layout view so that you can see the double-dotted-line section break line.
- Select the section break that you want to delete.
- Press [Delete].

# 4. ORGANIZING CONTENT

## *4.1 STRUCTURE CONTENT USING QUICK PARTS*

### INSERT, EDIT, AND SORT BUILDING BLOCKS

As you learned, building blocks are predesigned pieces of content, such as cover pages, that give you a head start in creating many common types of content. A feature, called the Building Block Organizer, allows you to view, organize, edit properties of, and insert building block elements.

- Click where you want to insert a building block in the document.
- Click [Quick Parts ▾] in the Text group of the Insert tab.
- Choose Building Blocks Organizer.
- If you know the name, gallery, or category of the building block you want to use or modify, click the column header button to sort the building blocks by the information in the column.
- Select the building block you want to use. (A preview and description of the selected item are displayed.)
- To edit the properties of the selected item, click [Edit Properties...] and make any changes to the properties, such as the category or description of the building block.
- Click [OK] and click [Yes] to update the existing building block with the property changes you made.
- Click [Insert] to insert the building block in the document.

### SAVE COMPANY CONTACT INFORMATION AS BUILDING BLOCKS

In Lab 2, you created a building block for a closing. In a similar manner, you could create a building block to save company contact information. To do this, follow these steps:

- Enter the text for the company contact information as you want it to appear when inserted in the document.
- Select the text.
- Click [Quick Parts ▾] in the Text group of the Insert tab.
- Choose Save Selection to Quick Part Gallery.
- Enter a name and other information that is needed to identify and use the building block in the Create New Building Blocks dialog box and click [OK].

## MODIFY AND SAVE BUILDING BLOCKS

You also can modify an existing building block and use the same name. For example, you may have created a building block for the company contact information but have forgotten to include the telephone number. To do this, follow these steps:

- Insert the existing building block in the document.
- Edit the building block as needed.
- Select the text to include in the building block.
- Click [ Quick Parts ▾ ] in the Text group of the Insert tab.
- Choose Save Selection to Quick Part Gallery.
- Enter the same name to identify the building block in the Create New Building Blocks dialog box and click [ OK ].
- Click [ Yes ] to redefine the existing building block.

## INSERT HEADERS FROM QUICK PARTS AND EDIT DOCUMENT TITLES

Another way you can add information in a header or footer is to use the Quick Parts Organizer and select the header or footer building block you want to use. To do this, follow these steps:

- Click [ Quick Parts ▾ ] in the Text group of the Insert tab.
- Choose Building Blocks Organizer.
- Double-click the Gallery heading to sort the building blocks by gallery.
- Select the header building block you want to use. (A preview and description of the selected item are displayed.)
- Click [ Insert ].

The selected header building block is inserted in the document and the header area is active, ready for you to complete or modify the placeholder information.

### 4.4 INSERT AND FORMAT REFERENCES AND CAPTIONS

## CREATE, MODIFY, AND UPDATE A TABLE OF AUTHORITIES

A table of authorities is a list of the references in a legal document, such as to cases, statutes, and rules, along with the numbers of the pages the references appear on. The process of creating a table of authorities is similar to creating a bibliography.

First, you identify the citations by marking them. As you mark citations, you specify the category you want the citation to appear in, such as cases or statutes. You also can change or add categories of citations. To do this, follow these steps:

- Select the legal citation text that has already been entered in the document.
- Click [Mark Citation icon] in the Table of Authorities group of the References tab.
- Select the category for the citation and click [ Mark ]. Use [ Mark All ] to locate and mark identical citations in the document.
- Click [ Close ] when you are finished.
- Continue to mark all citations in the document in the same manner.

Next, you build the table of authorities. When you build a table of authorities, Word searches for the marked citations, organizes them by category, references their page numbers, and displays the table of authorities in the document. To do this, follow these steps:

- Move to the location in the document where you want the table of authorities inserted.
- Click [icon] Insert Table of Authorities in the Table of Authorities group of the References tab.

- Select All from the Categories list if you want to display citations in all categories, or select only the category you want generated.
- Select a design from the Format list or click [ Modify... ] to design a custom format by modifying the built-in template design.
- Select any other options for the table of authorities that you want to use, such a tab leaders.
- Click [ OK ].

The table of authorities is generated. Citations appear listed in the categories that they were assigned along with the page number the citation is on. The table of authorities is a field that can be updated, just like updating a table of figures. To do this, follow these steps:

- Click the table of authorities and press [F9] or click [icon] Update Table of Authorities in the Table of Authorities group on the References tab.

The table of authorities is updated using the same format settings. If you want to both change the format and update the table, you can regenerate the entire table of authorities again.

- Click the table of authorities and click [icon] Insert Table of Authorities in the Table of Authorities group of the References tab.
- Select the category and format and any other options that you want.
- Click [ OK ] to complete the command and click [ Yes ] to replace the existing table of authorities.

## 6. SHARING AND SECURING CONTENT

### 6.1 PREPARE DOCUMENTS FOR SHARING

#### SAVE TO APPROPRIATE FORMATS

Word 2007 uses a new file format based on the Office Open XML format (XML is short for Extensible Markup Language). This new format makes your documents safer by separating files that contain scripts or macros to make it easier to identify and block unwanted code or macros that could be dangerous to your computer. It also makes file sizes smaller and makes files less susceptible to damage. The file extensions shown in the table below are used to identify the different types of Word document files.

| FILE EXTENSION | DESCRIPTION |
| --- | --- |
| .docx | Word 2007 document without macros or code |
| .dotx | Word 2007 template without macros or code |
| .docm | Word 2007 document that could contain macros or code |
| .xps | Word 2007 shared document (see note below) |
| .doc | Word 95–2003 document |

**Note:** XPS file format is a fixed-layout electronic file format that preserves document formatting and ensures that when the file is viewed online or printed, it retains exactly the format that you intended. It also makes it difficult to change the data in the file. To save as an XPS file format, you must have installed the free add-in.

There are several ways to save a Word document as any of these types:
- Click ⊞ Office Button and choose Save As.
- Choose Word Document or Other Formats to open the Save As dialog box.
- Open the Save as Type drop-down list and select the file type.
- Specify a name for the file and location to save it.
- Click [ Save ].

  OR

- Click ⊞ Office Button and choose Save As.
- Select Word Document, Word Template, or Word 97-2003 Document. (The default file type in the Save as Type drop-down list will reflect the file type of your selection. You could still change it to any other type.)
- Specify a name for the file and location to save it.
- Click [ Save ].

If you open a file in Word 2007 that was created in an earlier version, the automatic option in the Save As dialog box is to save it as the previous version type (.doc).

### USE THE COMPATIBILITY CHECKER

In Word 2007, you can open files created in previous versions of Word, from Word 95 to Word 2003. You also can create a file in Word 2007 format and then save it as the previous version (.doc). If any 2007 features are not compatible with the previous version, the Compatibility Checker tells you so and any new features will not work. The Compatibility Checker runs automatically; however, you can run it manually if you want to find out what features in a document you are creating will be incompatible. The Compatibility Checker identifies those features that are incompatible and the number of occurrences in the document.

Follow these steps to run the Compatibility Checker:
- Click ⊞ Office Button and choose Prepare.
- Choose Run Compatibility Checker.
- Click [ OK ] after looking at the features that were identified and the number of occurrences.

## Data File List

| Use | Create |
| --- | --- |
| **Lab 1** | |
| wd01_Flyer1.docx | |
| wd01_Lions.wmf | Flyer.docx |
| wd01_Parrot.wmf | Flyer1.docx |
| **Step-by-Step** | |
| 1. | Web Site Memo.docx |
| 2. wd01_Child on Bike.wmf | Bike Event.docx |
| 3. wd01_Coffee.wmf | Grand Re-Opening.docx |
| 4. wd01_Note Taking Skills.docx | Note Taking Skills.docx |
| 5. wd01_History of Ice Cream.docx | Ice Cream History.docx |
|    wd01_Ice Cream.wmf | |
| **On Your Own** | |
| 1. | Mexico Adventure.docx |
| 2. | Pool Rules.docx |
| 3. | Astronomy Basics.docx |
| 4. | Volunteer Opportunities.docx |
| 5. | Career Report.docx |
| **Lab 2** | |
| wd02_Tour Letter.docx | Tour Letter2 |
| wd02_Flyer2.docx | |
| **Step-by-Step** | |
| 1. wd02_Note Taking Tips.docx | Note Taking Skills2.docx |
|    Note Taking Skills.docx (Lab 1) | |
| 2. wd02_Water Conservation.docx | Water Conservation Column.docx |
|    wd02_Conservation Tips.docx | |
|    wd02_Water Hose | |
| 3. wd02_Fitness Fun.docx | Fitness Fun Flyer.docx |
| 4. | Conference Volunteers.docx |
| 5. wd02_Coffee Flyer.docx | Weekly Specials.docx |

| Use | Create |
|---|---|
| **On Your Own** | |
| 1. | Reference Letter.docx |
| 2. | Cell Phone Rates.docx |
| 3. | Yard Sale Flyer.docx |
| 4. | Wyoming Facts.docx |
| 5. | Ethics Report.docx |
| **Lab 3** | |
| wd03_Tour Research.docx | Research Outline.docx |
| wd03_Giraffe.wmf | Tour Research.docx |
| wd03_Parrots.wmf | |
| **Step-by-Step** | |
| 1. | Spam Outline.docx |
| 2. | ARS Department Contacts.docx |
| 3. wd03_Digital Cameras.docx | Digital Cameras.docx |
|    wd03_Camera.wmf | |
|    wd03_Computer.wmf | |
| 4. wd03_ATT Brochure.docx | ATT Brochure.docx |
|    wd03_ATT.wmf | |
|    wd03_Hiking.wmf | |
|    wd03_Kayaking.wmf | |
|    wd03_Tracey.wmf | |
|    wd03_Train.wmf | |
| 5. wd03_Yoga Guide.docx | Yoga Guide.docx |
|    wd03_History.wmf | |
|    wd03_Yoga Pose.wmf | |
| **On Your Own** | |
| 1. wd03_Kayaking flyer.docx | Kayaking Flyer.docx |
|    wd03_Kayaking.wmf | |
| 2. wd03_Coffee Outline.docx | Coffee Report.docx |
| 3. | Job Search.docx |
| 4. | Research.docx |
| 5. | Computer Viruses.docx |
| **Working Together 1** | |
| wdwt_Presentations.docx | New Tour Presentations.html |
| wdwt_Locations.docx | Tour Locations.html |
| **Step-by-Step** | |
| 1. wdwt_LosAngeles.docx | LosAngeles.html |
|    Tour Locations (Lab WT1) | |
| 2. Bike Event.docx (Lab 1) | Celebrate Bicycling.html |
| 3. Grand Re-Opening.docx (Lab 1) | Café Locations.html |
| | Cafe Flyer.html |
|    wdwt_Coffee.wmf | |
|    wdwt_Café Locations.docx | |

# Reference 2

## Microsoft Office Word 2007

The Microsoft Certified Applications Specialist (MCAS) certification program is designed to measure your proficiency in performing basic tasks using the Office 2007 applications. Getting certified demonstrates that you have the skills and provides a valuable industry credential for employment.

After completing the labs in the Microsoft Office Word 2007 Brief edition, you have learned the following MCAS skills:

| Description | Lab |
|---|---|
| **1. Creating and Customizing Documents** | |
| 1.1 Create and Format documents | |
| Work with templates | Lab 1 |
| Apply Quick Styles to documents | Lab 3 |
| Format documents by using themes | Lab 3, More About |
| Customize themes | Lab 3, More About |
| Format document backgrounds | Lab 1 |
| Insert blank pages or cover pages | Lab 3 |
| 1.2 Lay Out Documents | |
| Format Pages | Labs 1, 2, More About |
| Create and modify headers and footers | Lab 3 |
| 1.3 Make Documents and Content Easier to Find | |
| Create, modify, and update tables of contents | Lab 3, More About |
| Create, modify, and update indexes | More About |
| Modify document properties | Lab 1 |
| Insert document navigation tools | Lab 3, Working Together 1 |
| 1.4 Personalize Office Word 2007 | |
| Customize Word options | Lab 1 |

| Description | Lab |
|---|---|
| **2. Formatting Content** | |
| 2.1 Format text and paragraphs | |
| Apply styles | Labs 2, 3, More About |
| Create and modify styles | Lab 3 |
| Format characters | Labs 1, 2 |
| Format paragraphs | Labs 1, 2 |
| Set and clear tabs | Lab 2 |
| 2.2 Manipulate text | |
| Cut, copy, and paste text | Lab 2 |
| Find and replace text | Lab 2 |
| 2.3 Control pagination | |
| Insert and delete page breaks | Labs 2, 3 |
| Create and modify sections | Lab 3 |
| **3. Working with Visual Content** | |
| 3.1 Insert illustrations | |
| Insert pictures from files and clip art | Labs 1, 3 |
| Insert shapes | Lab 2 |
| 3.2 Format illustrations | |
| Format text wrapping | Lab 3, Working Together 1 |
| Format by sizing | Lab 1 |
| Add text to SmartArt graphics and shapes | Lab 2 |
| **4. Organizing Content** | |
| 4.1 Structure content by using Quick Parts | |
| Insert building blocks in documents | Lab 3, More About |
| Save frequently used data as building blocks | Lab 3, More About |
| Insert formatted headers and footers from Quick Parts | Lab 3, More About |
| Insert fields from Quick Parts | Lab 3 |
| 4.2 Use tables and lists to organize content | |
| Create tables and lists | Labs 2, 3 |
| Sort content | Labs 2, 3 |
| Modify list formats | Lab 2 |
| 4.3 Modify tables | |
| Apply Quick Styles to tables | Lab 3 |
| Modify table properties and options | Lab 3 |
| Merge and split table cells | Lab 3 |

Reference 2: Microsoft Certified Applications Specialist (MCAS)

www.mhhe.com/oleary

| Description | Lab |
|---|---|
| 4.4 Insert and format references and captions | |
| Create and modify sources | Lab 3 |
| Insert citations and captions | Lab 3 |
| Insert and modify bibliographies | Lab 3 |
| Select reference styles | Lab 3 |
| Create, modify, and update tables of figures | Lab 3 |
| Create, modify, and update tables of authorities | More About |
| **5. Reviewing Documents** | |
| 5.1 Navigate documents | |
| Move quickly using the Find and Go To commands | Labs 2, 3 |
| Change window views | Labs 1, 2, 3 |
| **6. Sharing and Securing Content** | |
| 6.1 Prepare documents for sharing | |
| Save to appropriate formats | Lab 1, Working Together 1 |
| Identify document features not supported by previous versions | More About |

# Index